Library & Information Department
Arundel House, 13-15 Arundel Street
London WC2R 3DX
tel +44 (0)20 7395 9122 *e-mail* library@iiss.org

This book is to be returned on or before the last date below.
Renewals (max. 2) may be made by telephone and e-mail.

International Terrorism Post-9/11

This edited volume brings together both Western and non-Western approaches to counter-terrorism in the post-9/11 era.

This multi-cultural study of counter-terrorism strategies identifies common lessons from failed and successful attempts to counter the terrorist threat and provides guidelines for an effective counter-terrorism strategy. The book explores the changing dynamics of terrorism from a range of perspectives – from the global threat posed by home-grown terrorism in North Africa and the larger security dimensions in the Middle East, to the various strategies employed by Western and non-Western societies in their efforts to develop effective counter-terrorism strategies. Core themes in the book include the divergent dynamics of the phenomena categorized under the 'terrorism' label, and the domestic, national and regional variants of international terrorism. As such, the book offers in-depth analysis of the relationship between the local and the global, both in the root causes of, and responses to, terrorism since 9/11.

This book will be of much interest to students of terrorism and political violence, security studies and IR.

Asaf Siniver is Lecturer in International Security in the Department of Political Science and International Studies at the University of Birmingham, United Kingdom.

Contemporary terrorism studies

Religion and Political Violence
Sacred protest in the modern world
Jennifer L. Jefferis

International Terrorism Post-9/11
Comparative dynamics and responses
Edited by Asaf Siniver

International Terrorism Post-9/11

Comparative dynamics and responses

Edited by Asaf Siniver

Routledge
Taylor & Francis Group

LONDON AND NEW YORK

First published 2010
by Routledge
2 Park Square, Milton Park, Abingdon, Oxon OX14 4RN

Simultaneously published in the USA and Canada
by Routledge
270 Madison Avenue, New York, NY 10016

Routledge is an imprint of the Taylor & Francis Group, an informa business

© 2010 Selection and editorial matter, Asaf Siniver; individual chapters, the contributors

Typeset in Times by Wearset Ltd, Boldon, Tyne and Wear
Printed and bound in Great Britain by TJI Digital, Padstow, Cornwall

British Library Cataloguing in Publication Data
A catalogue record for this book is available from the British Library

Library of Congress Cataloging-in-Publication Data
A catalog record has been requested for this book

ISBN10: 0-415-55230-3 (hbk)
ISBN10: 0-203-85200-1 (ebk)

ISBN13: 978-0-415-55230-1 (hbk)
ISBN13: 978-0-203-85200-2 (ebk)

Contents

Contributors

David Barnard-Wills is a Research Fellow in the Department of Informatics and Sensors at Cranfield University. He has previously been a Research Fellow in Political Science and International Studies at the University of Birmingham, and the Parliamentary Office of Science and Technology. He holds a PhD in Politics from the University of Nottingham. His research includes surveillance, the politics of information technology, terrorism and international security.

Oz Hassan is a Research Fellow in the Department of Politics and International Studies at the University of Warwick. He is currently working on the European Union funded FP7 program EU-GRASP, having formally completed his PhD on America's Freedom Agenda for the Middle East and North Africa. He has also recently finished a British Research Council Fellowship in the John W. Kluge Center, at the United States Library of Congress, Washington, DC.

David Hastings Dunn is Reader in International Politics in the Department of Political Science and International Studies at the University of Birmingham. His main research interests are US foreign and security policy, Security Studies, European security and diplomacy.

Steve Hewitt is Senior Lecturer in American and Canadian Studies at the University of Birmingham. He has written a number of books and articles related to security and intelligence, both in the past and present, including *The British War on Terror: Terrorism and Counter-Terrorism on the Home Front since 9/11*. His next book will be *Snitch! A History of the Modern Intelligence Informer*.

Jack Holland is Lecturer in International Relations at the University of Leeds where he teaches 'US foreign policy'. His doctoral thesis, completed at the University of Warwick, analyzes American, British and Australian foreign policy discourse in the War on Terror. He was recently a British Research Council Fellow at the Library of Congress, where he conducted the research for this volume and wrote on '9/11' in the journal *International Political Sociology*. His wider research interests cover critical approaches to international relations, security and terrorism.

George Joffé was Deputy Director and Director of Studies at the Royal Institute of International Affairs (Chatham House) between 1997 and 2000. He is now visiting professor at Kings College, London University, and is attached to the Centre of International Studies in Cambridge University. He teaches on undergraduate and postgraduate courses in both universities. As well as being an Associate Fellow of the Middle East & North Africa Programme at the Royal United Services Institute, he is also a member of the Instituto de Estudos Estratégicos e Internacionais in Lisbon where he manages the EuroMeSCo network of strategic studies institutes in Europe and the Mediterranean basin on behalf of the European Union, as part of the Euro-Mediterranean Partnership. His research interests include transnational risk in the Mediterranean, legal systems and migrant communities and Euro-American relations.

Clive Jones is Professor of Middle East Studies and International Politics and Head of School in the School of Politics and International Studies (POLIS), University of Leeds, UK. His books include *Britain and the Yemen Civil War* (2004), *Soviet Jewish Aliyah 1989–92* (1996, with Emma Murphy), *Israel: Challenges to Democracy, Identity and the State* (2002), and co-editor with Ami Pedahzur, *The al-Aqsa Intifada: Between Terrorism and Civil War* (2005). His latest volume is *Israel and the Hizb'allah: An Asymmetric Conflict in Comparative Perspective*.

Matt McDonald is Associate Professor in International Security at the University of Warwick. His research interests are in the area of critical theoretical approaches to security and their application to environmental change, Australian foreign and security policy, Asia-Pacific security dynamics and the War on Terror. He has published on these themes in a range of journals, including *European Journal of International Relations* and *Review of International Studies*, and is co-editor (with Anthony Burke) of *Critical Security in the Asia-Pacific* (Manchester University Press, 2007). He is currently completing a book on the relationship between security and environmental change.

Major General Graham Messervy-Whiting has been Deputy Director of University of Birmingham's Centre for Studies in Security and Diplomacy since 2003 and a member of the Judiciary's Tribunal Service since 2005. Appointments during his Armed Forces career include: Deputy Secretary of the UK Chiefs of Staff Committee; Briefing Officer for General John Galvin, NATO's Supreme Allied Commander Europe during the ending of the Cold War; Military Adviser to Lord Owen, European Union Co-Chairman of the International Conference on the Former Yugoslavia; UK's Director Defence Commitments for Asia-Pacific, Latin America and the Caribbean; Director of the Western European Union's Planning Cell; and Assistant Director Operations at GCHQ. In March 2000, he was selected by Javier Solana and promoted to Major General to assist him to develop a security and defense capability for the European Union. He is a Fellow of the Royal United Services Institute.

Cerwyn Moore is Lecturer in International Relations in the Department of Political Science and International Studies (POLSIS) at the University of Birmingham. His work focuses on interpretive IR theory (hermeneutics, continental philosophy, aesthetics and global politics), studies of political violence, terrorism (suicide attacks) and war, particularly related to Chechnya, and more generally, post-Soviet security. He has published widely on these themes in *Global Society, Europe–Asia Studies, British Journal of Politics and International Relations, Studies in Conflict and Terrorism, Alternatives* and the *Journal of Communist Studies and Transition Politics*. He has also published (with Stephen Chan) two four-volume sets of IR readers, *Theories of International Relations Theory* (London: Sage, 2006) and *Approaches to International Relations* (London: Sage, 2009), and a co-edited collection (with Chris Farrands) entitled *International Relations and Philosophy: Interpretive Dialogues* (London: Routledge, 2010).

Gerd Nonneman is Professor of Middle East Politics and International Relations at Exeter University, where he also holds the Al-Qasimi Chair in Arab Gulf Studies. He is Associate Fellow of the Middle East Programme at Chatham House (Royal Institute of International Affairs). He served as Executive Director of the British Society for Middle Eastern Studies (BRISMES), 1998–2002. Aside from his academic work, he has written for the Economist Intelligence Unit and acted as a consultant to a range of companies, national governments and international official institutions including the Foreign & Commonwealth Office and the European Commission, to European governments, and to various NGOs, as well as the national and international media. Among his recent publications are: *Saudi Arabia in the Balance: Political Economy, Society, Foreign Affairs* (with Paul Aarts) (New York: New York University Press, 2006); and *Analyzing Middle East Foreign Policies, and the Relationship with Europe* (London and New York: Routledge, 2005).

Sir Francis Richards was, after brief service in the Army terminated by injury, for 37 years a member of the British Diplomatic Service. He served twice in Moscow, latterly as Minister in the early 1990s, was Britain's first High Commissioner to Namibia between 1990 and 1992, and served also in India and at arms-control talks in Vienna. From 1998 to 2003 he was Director of Government Communications Headquarters (GCHQ). On his retirement from GCHQ he became Governor and Commander in Chief of Gibraltar between 2003 and 2006. He has, since 2006, been Director of the Centre for Studies in Security and Diplomacy and an Honorary Professor at the University of Birmingham, and holds a number of other appointments in the private and voluntary sectors.

Asaf Siniver is Lecturer in International Security in the Department of Political Science and International Studies at the University of Birmingham. His research interests include contemporary US foreign policy, conflict management and resolution, and Middle East politics. His work has appeared in several journals, including *Review of International Studies* and *Political Studies*, and he is the author of *Nixon, Kissinger and US Foreign Policy: The Machinery of Crisis* (New York: Cambridge University Press, 2008). He is also the co-editor of the journal *Civil Wars*, and currently works on a study of international mediation and a biography of Abba Eban.

Ted Svensson is completing his PhD in the Department of Politics and International Studies at the University of Warwick, United Kingdom. His research interests lie in the broad area of identity politics, and his thesis focuses on the moment of partition/independence of Pakistan and India and its impact on the formation of the post-colonial state. Ted has recently published the article 'Frontiers of Blame: India's "War on Terror"' in *Critical Studies on Terrorism*.

Andrew T.H. Tan is Associate Professor and Convenor for International Studies at the University of New South Wales, Australia. He is also supported by the university's Strategic Priority Fund to do research on defense and security issues. He was previously Senior Lecturer in Defence Studies, King's College London, and taught at the Joint Services Command and Staff College, UK. Educated in Singapore, Cambridge and Sydney (where he obtained his PhD), his advice on security issues is sought by governments, armed forces, universities and research institutes. He has published ten books (with another two forthcoming) and over 30 internationally refereed journal articles and book chapters. His recent sole-authored and edited books include: *Security Perspectives of the Malay Archipelago* (Cheltenham: Edward Elgar, 2004), *A Political and Economic Dictionary of South-East Asia* (London: Europa, 2004), *The Politics of Terrorism* (London: Routledge, 2006), *A Handbook of Terrorism and Insurgency in Southeast Asia* (Cheltenham: Edward Elgar, 2007), *The Politics of Maritime Power* (London: Routledge, 2007), *The Global Arms Trade* (London: Routledge, 2009) and *US Strategy Against Global Terrorism Since 9/11* (New York: Palgrave Macmillan, 2009).

Acknowledgments

This book would not have been possible without the enthusiasm and dedication of Khadija Benlabbah, my former graduate student in the Department of Political Science and International Studies at the University of Birmingham. Thanks to her unremitting nudging and cajoling, several of the contributors to this book were invited by Mr Mohamed Yassine Mansouri, Director of Morocco's Intelligence Agency (DGED), to Rabat in October 2008 to speak about international terrorism and counter-terrorism post-9/11. We are all extremely grateful for the hospitality and generosity of our hosts, and wish to thank them for the opportunity to discuss these timely issues with a very welcoming and engaging audience. The book is the direct result of this very productive experience, and I would like to thank all the contributors for their cooperation and enthusiasm for this project at its various phases.

My thanks are also extended to Rebecca Brennan and Andrew Humphrys at Routledge for their continued support and patience, and to the anonymous reviewers for their helpful and insightful comments at the early stages of this project.

Asaf Siniver
University of Birmingham

Abbreviations

AIS	Armée Islamique du Salut
ALP	Australian Labor Party
ANZAC	Australian and New Zealand Army Corps
ANZUS	Australia, New Zealand, United States Security Treaty
APEC	Asia-Pacific Economic Cooperation
AQ	al-Qaeda
ARF	ASEAN Regional Forum
ASEAN	Association of Southeast Asian Nations
ASG	Abu Sayaff Group
BJP	Bharatiya Janata Party
CFSP	Common Foreign and Security Policy
CI	Counter-Intelligence
CIA	Central Intelligence Agency
CIS	Commonwealth of Independent States
CT	Counter-terrorism
DFAT	Australian Department of Foreign Affairs and Trade
DI	Darul Islam
ESDP	European Security and Defence Policy
EUROPOL	European Police Office
FBI	Federal Bureau of Investigation
FCO	Foreign and Commonwealth Office
FIS	Front Islamique du Salut
FLN	Front de Libération Nationale
FSB	Federal Security Service
GAM	Gerakan Aceh Merdeka
GCHQ	Government Communications Headquarters
GIA	Groupes Islamiques Armés
GSPC	Groupe Salafiste du Predication et du Combat
GSS	General Security Service
HUMINT	Human Intelligence
IDF	Israel Defense Forces
IED	Improvised Explosive Device
IMINT	Imagery Intelligence

JHA	Justice and Home Affairs
JI	Jemaah Islamiah
JTAC	Joint Terrorism Analysis Centre
KMM	Kampulan Militan Malaysia
MENA	Middle East and North Africa
MEPI	Middle East Peace Initative
MILF	Moro Islamic Liberation Front
MMI	Majelis Mujiheddin of Indonesia
MoD	Ministry of Defence
MPS	Metropolitan Police Service
MVD	Ministry of Internal Affairs
NATO	North Atlantic Treaty Organization
NGO	Non-Governmental Organization
OSCT	Office of Security and Counter Terrorism
OSINT	Open Source Intelligence
PLO	Palestine Liberation Organization
POTA	Prevention of Terrorism Act
RAF	Royal Air Force
ReCAAP	Regional Cooperation Agreement on Combating Piracy and Armed Robbery Against Ships in Asia
SEARCCT	Southeast Asian Regional Center for Counter-Terrorism
SIGINT	Signals Intelligence
SIS	Secret Intelligence Service
SIV	Single Intelligence Vote
TIPS	Terrorism Information and Prevention System
UAPA	Unlawful Activities Prevention Act
UNSC	United Nations Security Council
WMD	Weapons of Mass Destruction

1   Introduction

Asaf Siniver

Since the terrorist attacks on the World Trade Center and the Pentagon on 11 September 2001, governments across the world have found themselves confronted by the dual challenge of adapting to a new security environment while almost simultaneously trying to propagate an adequate response to this seemingly new wave of terrorism. The fast flow of actions and reactions since the 9/11 attacks have left policy-makers little time for close introspection or long-term planning and evaluation of their chosen counter-terrorism (CT) strategies. This invariably resulted in a plethora of approaches, diverse in scope and objectives, many of them with little coherence and coordination of and between themselves.

This book attempts to identify some of the most important dynamics and responses to international terrorism post-9/11 by looking at how various governments around the world have reacted to the changing security environment. Existing studies of counter-terrorism tend to be overly reliant on single case studies, particularly that of the American-led 'global war on terror', while neglecting other important regions and countries which have either been affected by the events of 9/11, or have proclaimed to be victims of the 'new' wave of international terrorism in that period.[1] This book presents a multi-cultural study of approaches to CT, ranging from the Bush administration's 'Grand Strategy' and affiliated responses from Britain and the European Union, to the case studies of Middle Eastern and North African regimes, Israel, Russia, India, Australia and South East Asia. In an attempt to identify common lessons from failed and successful attempts to counter the terrorist threat post-9/11, the conceptual framework of this book consists of the following comparative themes, which are visited in varying degrees in subsequent chapters:

1   How have the security/terrorist threats been conceptualized by various governments and with what justification?
2   What was the nature of the CT strategies subsequently developed?
3   How successful have these strategies been in countering the terrorist threat, and how can this be measured?

Importantly, the chapters in this edited volume are concerned with cause and effect. A key theme that cuts across the case studies is that the way in which the security/terrorist threat has been conceptualized by governments in the post-9/11 environment was instrumental to the development of subsequent CT strategies. This seemingly causal relationship between the nature of the threat and the designated mechanisms to fight it is not as palpable as it may seem at first glance. It is interesting to note that, almost regardless of their geopolitical environment, the type of regime or the degree of political cohesion, Western as well as non-Western states have used similar rhetoric to justify their responses to the changing security discourse. Thus several North African regimes, as well as the governments of Israel, Australia, India and Russia have all seemed keen to jump on the Bush rhetoric bandwagon and framed their local experiences with terrorism as their 'own 9/11', and accordingly their CT responses have been rhetorically (though not necessarily substantively) justified as an integral part of the 'global war on terror'. Even Britain has moved considerably from its traditional criminal-law framework to align itself in accordance with the American model. Moreover, whereas these governments (the United States included) were quick to put in place the modus operandi to fight terrorism, none of them has shown a great deal of introspection as far as understanding the root causes of these security threats. Instead they pointed to international events or fundamentalist ideologies as the prime catalysts for this rise in security threats, dismissing in the process any responsibility for their own actions and behaviors. In this regard, South East Asia stands out as a case where a more holistic and pluralistic approach to CT has been developed, thus offering more than narrow security and military responses. This exception reinforces the instrumentality of how threat is conceptualized in the first place as determinant of consequent CT policies.

Another central theme to the chapters in this book is the largely absent attempt by governments to conceptualize a coherent and practical model by which to evaluate the efficacy of relevant CT methods. Indeed this is a much visited point in contemporary studies of counter-terrorism.[2] We therefore see that regardless of regime types and the nature of localized threats, states rarely stop to think about what 'success' or 'victory' mean in the context of combating terrorism. As Martha Crenshaw notes,[3] success here cannot mean the total eradication of a terrorist organization, but instead it must be understood in terms of balancing forces and creating conditions that are more favorable to the public sphere (such as reducing public anxiety and providing effective security measures). Subsequently, successful CT methods must incorporate better cooperation between states and regional and global agencies, better intelligence-gathering and analysis, and more discriminate use of force. Ultimately governments must satisfy the demands of their publics for increased safety while not losing state legitimacy and accountability in the process.

One evident conclusion that emerges from the case studies in this book is that the war fighting model has proven largely ill-fitted to address effectively the complex and dynamic challenges of terrorism since the events of 9/11. By the same token, it seems that a narrowly defined law-enforcement model is inadequate, on its own, to achieve 'victory' or 'success' in this context. It may well be argued that it will take decades to solve these problems, just as it took decades to create them, though fighting terrorism in these lengthy timeframes is as problematic and as contentious as some of the ad-hoc methods currently on display.

In order to provide the necessary contextualization of the aforementioned themes, Gerd Nonneman introduces in his chapter a useful discussion of the concepts of 'political violence' and, more specifically, 'terrorism'. The state of dissensus between observers, students and policy-makers with regard to a definition of terrorism is well documented.[4] However, without a clear conceptualization of what one means when referring to these symbolically and value-laden notions, we risk misjudging the threat itself and subsequently our reaction to it – a particularly dangerous practice in the political context of the Middle East, a region long-associated with variants of political extremism and terrorism. Nonneman provides a useful working definition of terrorism for this book: 'the act or threat of violent targeting of non-combatant populations and/or institutions, often but not always in arbitrary fashion, in order to create fear and/or to damage the institutions that are being challenged.' Importantly, terrorism is understood here as a tactic, rather than an ideology, and accordingly there are many different 'terrorisms', with various causes for the adoption of such a tactic by groups, as well as state actors. It will therefore be erroneous to speak of al-Qaeda as a 'terrorist organization', but rather an extremist group that adopts such tactics as identified in the aforementioned definition.

Nonneman then moves to dispel some popular myths in the literature on terrorism, chief amongst them is the assertion that religiously and ideologically-driven terrorists are 'irrational' and hold uncompromising beliefs which preclude any scope for compromise or negotiations. Similarly, he questions the widely held assertion that religious terrorism is quantitatively and qualitatively different from other 'terrorisms', as propagated by Hoffman, Rapoport and others.[5] Indeed, whereas some were quick to conclude in the aftermath of the 9/11 attacks that this 'new' wave of terrorism is characterized by religious fervor, hierarchical organization, the fusion of ends and means (destruction and violence as ends in themselves), and greater lethality, upon scrutinizing some basic methodological and epistemological practice, it is fairly evident that the only 'new' thing about the current terrorist threat is our attention to some hitherto neglected aspects of the global security environment. In other words, rather than explaining terrorism through the prism of linear historical changes, we ought to explain the presence or absence of certain factors by the idiosyncrasies of particular conflicts and regions, and as Nonneman demonstrates in his survey of Middle Eastern and North African regimes, this is the first crucial step toward an effective combating of terrorist threats.

This point is reinforced in George Joffé's chapter, dealing with the North African experience of extremism in the past two decades. Here Joffé shows how security threats presented regimes with new opportunities for reasserting control through increased securitization of the political discourse, both domestically and in their foreign relations. Rather than looking inwards to understand the root causes of these security threats, North African governments have tended to dismiss these threats to their own legitimacy as irrational and driven by international events, particularly in the aftermath of 9/11. As Joffé explains, the problem with this response is that it both trivializes the violence to which the Maghreb states have been subjected, and normativizes it into a discourse parallel to the dominant Western view of transnational violence during this decade. In other words, there is little governmental effort here to understand the root causes of the phenomenon, or indeed to conceptualize 'terrorism' within the unique North African experience. One of the direct consequences of this reorientation of the terrorism discourse is the way in which North African regimes have successfully redefined their relationships with the United States and Europe, from that of 'petitioners of attention' to important partners, at least in the realm of security, despite the very different causes and contexts of the terrorist threat in North Africa to those experienced by the United States.

The literature on the Bush administration's global war on terror is immense, and as David Dunn and Oz Hassan point out in their chapter, the strategy that unfolded in the aftermath of 9/11 remains central to ongoing debates about America's role in the world. It would be erroneous, however, to conceptualize the War on Terror as a homogenous project. Instead, Dunn and Hassan chart a dynamic process that has evolved over time into three distinct strategies, each in response to different perceptions of threat as propagated by the Bush administration. Accordingly the War on Terror is conceptualized here as counter-terrorism, pre-emption and pre-eminence, and a 'Freedom Agenda'; each of these strands adding another layer to existing strategies, rather than replacing them altogether. However, while this accumulative approach was the result of the administration's responses to unfolding external events as well as internal policy processes, these strategies have proved to be largely contradictory of each other and of themselves. This is hardly surprising given that these strategies were rooted, respectively, in divergent doctrines such as *realpolitik*, pre-emption and pre-eminence, and democratic imperialism. Rhetorically as well as substantively, Dunn and Hassan argue, these evolved as responses to three questions asked by President Bush himself shortly after the 9/11 attacks, namely, 'Who is the enemy?'; 'Why do they hate us?'; and 'How can we win this war?'

Importantly, the legacy left to the Obama administration is a confused one, inevitably resulting in a dual policy of change and continuity, rather than a complete shift away from the practices of the Bush administration on each of the three strands of the War on Terror. In following the articulation and execution of American foreign policy in the aftermath of the attacks, it is evident that elements of the first (counter-terrorism) and third (Freedom Agenda) bore most resonance, and still continue to set the tone in the Obama administration. The second strand (pre-emption and pre-eminence), however, has proven to be much more difficult for the Obama administration to defend, resulting in the inevitable acceptance of the limitations on American power.

It is well documented that these embedded inconsistencies in America's War on Terror were severely compounded by inadequate intelligence.[6] Despite (and, to a large extent, because of) its unrivaled technological reach, the Bush administration did not enjoy high-quality intelligence from human sources inside Iraq and Afghanistan. The situation was so acute that at the time of the invasion of Iraq there were fewer than five CIA officers operating within the country.[7] Almost in an act of desperation, one way in which the administration sought to redress this imbalance in intelligence quality was by dramatically expanding an existing, though somewhat faltering, program designed to recruit informers. However, as Steve Hewitt shows in his chapter, this system proved just as controversial and costly as other programs that emanated out of the White House in this period as part of the global War on Terror strategy.

Perhaps most pertinently, Hewitt's analysis shows us that the Rewards for Justice Program, while paying tens of millions of dollars to informers since its foundation in 1984, has faced little scrutiny, particularly with regard to its effectiveness as a method of combating terrorism. Still, this relatively under-studied program has important lessons about a plethora of issues concerned with the limitations of Human Intelligence (HUMINT) capabilities of American intelligence agencies both well before and after 9/11. Moreover, it confirms existing perceptions of the flawed apparatus of the War on Terror across a range of issues, such as the American challenge to the sovereignty of other countries through gradual hegemonic encroachment (as represented by Dunn and Hassan as the second, 'pre-eminence', strand of the grand strategy). The haphazard Rewards for Justice Program also demonstrates an acute failure to adequately understand what motivates terrorists. Despite the failure to recruit high-profile informers who operated within the core of al-Qaeda, the administration continued to pour millions of dollars into this initiative, without a pause for introspection. Somewhat surprisingly, it appears that the administration failed to appreciate the limitations of material incentives in 'turning' ideologically driven individuals who were willing to give their lives for a cause they had devoutly pursued for much of their adult lives. This approach, based on a criminal model that treats potential informers as corrupt and driven by monetary gains, could not be more inappropriate in its application to al-Qaeda. Ultimately, the story of this program sheds a new light on the evolution of American counter-terrorism from one conceptualized within a criminal-law framework, to the more complex strategy which has emerged in the aftermath of 9/11, not least with regard to the challenge of measuring the success of such counter-terrorism efforts.

The subsequent two chapters provide fascinating insiders' accounts of the organizational and institutional responses of the European Union and Britain to the events of 9/11. Much like the American case, any verdict on the success of these new mechanisms is premature and tentative at best. With regard to the British strategy, however, both chapters conclude that Britain, shocked by the 7 July 2005 bombings of the London transport system, has traveled some way from its traditional criminal-law framework to fight terrorism to one more closely aligned with the security/militarized approach adopted by the United States.

In the first of the two chapters, Major General Graham Messervy-Whiting charts the development of CT approaches by the British armed forces and the EU, and their manifestation in the post-9/11 environment. As Chief of Staff of the EU Military Staff between 2000 and 2003, and with a long and distinguished career in the British Armed Forces, he draws on his personal experience to deliver an incisive analysis of current trends. Although over a dozen attacks may well have been successfully disrupted since 2001, it is nevertheless premature to draw comprehensive conclusions regarding the success of Britain's 'four Ps' CT strategy (Pursue, Prevent, Protect, Prepare); with particular regard to the 'Prevent' strand (preventing future attacks), the likely impact can only be measured in the longer term.

Most importantly, Messervy-Whiting identifies a pressing need for closer cooperation across relevant departments, agencies and the armed forces, to implement a truly comprehensive CT approach. This challenge is mirrored in the European Union's response to the current security environment. The EU's Counter-Terrorism Strategy is firmly placed within the overall framework of freedom, justice and security, and with close links to the European Security and Defence Policy (ESDP) and the Common Foreign and Security Policy (CFSP). Nevertheless, and despite the development of EU metrics and action plans in this area, the EU still falls short of managing a closely coordinated mechanism to handle major terrorist incidents, and perhaps most importantly, it lacks a coherent strategy to counter radicalization and recruitment into extremist organizations.

Sir Francis Richards' chapter examines the dramatic overhaul of the British intelligence community in the aftermath of 9/11. As Head of the British Government Communication Headquarters (GCHQ) between 1998 and 2003, Sir Francis played a central role in formulating the response of the UK intelligence community to the events of 9/11 and its subsequent development. In his chapter he first looks at the state of the intelligence agencies immediately before 9/11, and at how far they were already focused on international terrorism as a priority target. Importantly, he locates Britain's extremist threat within the global environment, while pointing to those features that make this country a prime target for such attacks. In considering how these threats have shaped the new organizational and cultural environment within the intelligence community, he suggests that the most important lesson learnt was the need to share information between the various intelligence agencies. Turning to evaluate the long-term success of such changes and the price attached to it, he concludes in similar fashion to the previous chapter that, while the changes undertaken by the intelligence community as a result of 9/11 have been very significant and largely effective (especially with regard to inter-agency cooperation), it may well take a generation before a decisive verdict of the success of the British strategy can be delivered.

The subsequent four chapters demonstrate the way in which various governments across the world, while confronting very different security threats and operating in divergent geopolitical environments, were quick to use the 9/11 attacks and the subsequent US-led War on Terror as catalysts for their own counter-terrorist strategies, either ongoing or freshly developed. In each case, the driving force behind these strategies, seemingly in tandem with the Bush administration's Grand Strategy (at least as far as rationale and objectives were concerned), were isolated terrorist attacks which had claimed the lives of many innocent people. One by one, the governments of Israel, Russia, India and Australia had claimed these terrorist attacks to represent their 'own 9/11', using language and images remarkably similar to those used by the Bush administration in the aftermath of 9/11. Taken together, these four chapters speak volumes about the pitfalls of such practices, which not only fail to address the peculiar causes and manifestations of these localized threats, but also fall short of delivering longer-term and more holistic approaches to counter-terrorism.

In the first of these chapters, Clive Jones charts the emergence of a conception (*conceptzia*) among policy-makers in Israel that the struggle against Palestinian groups must be viewed as part of the global fight against Islamist terrorism. The catalyst for the emergence of this *conceptzia* was the suicide bombing at the Park Hotel in Netanya in March 2002, killing scores of civilians. Taken as the 'last straw' in a succession of suicide attacks inside Israel in a short period of time, what followed was a counter-terrorism strategy that included targeted assassinations, mass detentions without trial and long-term curfews. Far from considering the application of criminal justice or legal frameworks, Israel consciously adopted a war-fighting model as its preferred means of countering terrorism. As Jones points out, this perception was certainly reinforced by the very public use of F-16 fighter jets, anti-tank attack helicopters and heavy armor to fight Palestinian militant groups in the West Bank and the Gaza Strip.

However, one of the consequences of Israel viewing the Palestinian threat as existential was the dismissal (though not silencing) of opposing and dissenting voices concerned with human rights violations. This was particularly evident with regard to the debate over Israel's assassination of military and political leaders of militant Palestinian groups. While many concluded that this policy has proved to be effective in forcing Hamas toward a unilaterally declared ceasefire in 2004, critics were quick to point to the collateral damage incurred in these attacks, which often claimed the lives of many innocent bystanders.

Israel's defiance in the face of criticism of its policies was undoubtedly bolstered by the almost unprecedented support it has received from the Bush administration. Adopting its own war-fighting model to counter al-Qaeda globally, Washington was sympathetic to the Israeli position and acquiesced in the depiction of groups like Hamas and Islamic Jihad as cut from the same cloth as al-Qaeda, harboring similar extremist and uncompromising ideologies.

Like Israel, Russia too used the events of 9/11 to construct a particular narrative in their localized struggle against Chechen rebels, which resonated well with the rhetoric used by the Bush administration to justify the global response to 9/11. Here, too, the strategy formulated by the Kremlin was heavily based on a war-fighting model and the increased securitization of both the discourse and the physical practices of security. Invariably, this has resulted in serious concerns over Russian violations and abuse of human rights.

It is important, as Cerwyn Moore and David Barnard-Wills show in their chapter, to contextualize the Russian experience and place it within the appropriate historical narrative. In particular, the cultural, political and social transformation that followed the breakdown of the Soviet Union at the end of the Cold War directly impacted on Russian counter-terrorism measures as they have evolved in the post-9/11 period. The authors identify a three-pronged strategy to Russian counter-insurgency in the context of the Chechen conflict, namely the linking of the Russian 'counter-terrorist' activity with the wider narrative of the War on Terror; the labeling of insurgents as terrorists, bandits and criminals; and finally the silencing of opposition voices, often by coercive and violent measures. Much like Israel's fight against armed Palestinian groups (though far more severe in its heavy handed treatment of opposition voices and media censorship), Russia has used these strategies to delegitimize Chechen activity while legitimizing Russian counter-terrorism operations.

For India, two traumatic events – the attack on the parliament in December 2001 and the November 2008 Mumbai attacks – were the crucial catalysts for the re-conceptualization of threat and its required response. As Ted Svensson points out, 'terrorism' in the Indian context thus became synonymous with the borderless and ever-present threat posed by global groups such as al-Qaeda, signaling a dramatic shift from historical portrays of terrorism as invariably related to localized conflicts in the Punjab and Kashmir. Thus the Indian experience is another case in point where the initiation of the War on Terror by the United States was used as a template for other countries to redefine their own insecurity by closely entwining it with a Western discourse which synonymized terrorist activities with Islamist extremism and religious fundamentalism.

The 2001 and 2008 attacks were quickly depicted as 'India's own 9/11' – not merely to project sympathy with the American people, but more to validate India's claim to be a victim of the same global terrorist threat. Accordingly the 'terrorist' in the Indian context was always foreign (and never Hindu), and any evidence to the contrary was effortlessly explained by links to foreign groups or illegal immigration. The Indian case therefore reinforces some of the abovementioned themes, including the transformation of the local and regional into the global, the absolving of the Indian state from any accountability in its fight against terrorism and, finally, the more subtle forms of violence whereby certain sections of Indian society have been ousted as potential terrorists or, at the very least, not loyal to the Indian state.

In a similar fashion to the India case, Jack Holland and Matt McDonald demonstrate the extent to which the identity discourse and the image of the other have played a significant part in Australia's decision to align with the United States and join the global War on Terror and, more broadly, in conceptualizing Australian national interests and security in the post-9/11 environment. Crucially, as the authors point out, the global War on Terror campaign created a context in which Australia was able to pursue a more robust, militaristic approach to regional relations, as illustrated by the 2003 intervention in the Solomon Islands. This approach to regional interventionism was underpinned by a conception of Australian identity that viewed the region's cultural and ethnic divergence as a potential source of threat. At the heart of this conception was Prime Minister John Howard's view of Australia as a Western nation with historical links to the Anglosphere (most acutely shaped by the experience of fighting together in two world wars). This traditionalist cultural identity thus enabled the Australian government to pursue a narrow foreign policy in the aftermath of 9/11, which for some reflected deeper, racist images of 'white Australia'. Here, too, as illustrated in the previous three chapters, critics of the government's policies were successfully branded as unpatriotic and 'un-Australian'.

While historically the Howard government's regional outlook was at odds with previous governments' attempts to portray Australia as an integral and multicultural society of the Asian region, it is unsurprising to find that the Australian government's supposition that the 9/11 attacks ushered in a 'new' era was certainly not shared by Australia's neighbors.

As Andrew Tan notes in the concluding chapter, the terrorist challenge in Southeast Asia predates the events of 9/11, and as such a more historically nuanced framework is needed to understand the responses of governments in Southeast Asia to the events of 9/11. Consequently, there are significant differences in the perceptions underlying these regional responses, compared to those of the United States (and Australia). In a marked shift from the predominantly Western discourse on terrorism and threat post-9/11, Tan suggests that because the challenge of terrorism in this strategic region is complex and historical, Southeast Asian governments have preferred to adopt more holistic and comprehensive counter-terrorism strategies, in contrast to the war-fighting models and hard security measures hitherto favored by the Bush administration and various other governments around the world, as conceptualized in the global War on Terror.

As Tan points out, the prevailing (Western) assumption that all Muslim rebel groups are linked to al-Qaeda and its fundamentalist ideology is overly simplistic and historically misguided. The widespread skepticism in the region to the notion of a 'new' terrorism is therefore not surprising. The roots of some terrorist groups in the region date back to the 1950s, while Muslim alienation and rebellion has been a long-standing security challenge to the region's governments, preceding by decades the events of 9/11 and the controversial US-led response that ensued. The persistence and severity of these regional groups is therefore attributed to the failure of state legitimacy following decolonization, rather than the heavy-handed American response to the events of 9/11. For these reasons (and with varying degrees of competence), the regional response and strategy against terrorism has differed from American prescriptions, emphasizing instead political negotiations, economic development and social measures. This is not to say, however, that these measures have proved to be more successful, at least in the short term, than the militarized approaches – though crucially, they had enjoyed a wider public support and significantly contributed to the legitimization of governmental action in these areas.

Ultimately, the dilemma faced by each government in its struggle against political extremism and terrorism more specifically is how to delineate the fine lines between the initiation of an effective response to the threat, on the one hand, and the legitimization of its policies in the public sphere on the other.

However, as the contributors to this edited volume have demonstrated, any counter-terrorism strategy, regardless of its effectiveness, comes with a price, be it the erosion of state legitimacy and governmental accountability or the increased securitization of the political discourse and the physical environment. In any case, there are no silver bullets for this particular predicament. Some solace can be found in the fact that, while some extremist groups inflict enormous harm and disrupt the daily lives of innocent people, they rarely realize their ultimate objectives. As Max Abrahams concluded in his study of terrorist groups, terrorism is not an effective coercive strategy.[8] Moreover, Richard Aldrich suggests that the prevailing assumption that terrorism is the defining feature of the security environment is fundamentally flawed.[9] Climate change, energy shortages and pandemics are some of the by-products of our globalized world that impact on significantly more people, and in more profound and long-term ways, than terrorists could ever hope to achieve.

Notes

1 See, for example, T. Badey, 'US Counter-Terrorism: Change in Approach, Continuity in Policy', *Contemporary Security Policy*, 27:2 (2006), pp. 308–324; D. Byman, 'US Counter-Terrorism Options: A Taxonomy', *Survival*, 49:3 (2007), pp. 121–150; A.Z. Huq, 'Imagining Counterterrorism's Future', *World Policy Journal*, 25:4 (2008/9), pp. 31–39; H. Frisch, 'Motivation or Capabilities? Israeli Counterterrorism Against Palestinian Suicide Bombings and Violence', *The Journal of Strategic Studies*, 29:5 (2006), pp. 843–869; A. Guelke, 'The Northern Ireland Peace Process and the War Against Terrorism: Conflicting Conceptions?', *Government and Opposition*, 42:3 (2007), pp. 272–291.
2 C. Lum, L.W. Kennedy and A.J. Sherley, 'The Effectiveness of Counter-Terrorism Strategies', *Campbell Systematic Reviews*, 2 (2006); M.R. Haberfeld, J.F. King and C.A. Lieberman, *Terrorism Within Comparative International Context: The Counter-Terrorism Response and Preparedness* (New York: Springer, 2009); B. Clark, 'Effective Counter-Terrorism: Sound Foreign Policy, Intelligence Gathering, Policing, Social Engineering and Necessary Use of Source', in R. Imre, T.B. Mooney and B. Clark (eds.), *Responding to Terrorism: Political, Philosophical and Legal Perspectives* (Aldershot: Ashgate, 2008), pp. 191–219; CRS Report for Congress, 'Combating Terrorism: The Challenges of Measuring Effectiveness' (12 March 2007), www.fas.org/sgp/crs/terror/RL33160.pdf.
3 M. Crenshaw, 'Analyzing the Effectiveness of Counterterrorism in Democracies', paper presented at the ISA 50th Annual Convention, New York, 15–18 February 2009.
4 See for example C. Carr, '"Terrorism": Why the Definition Must be Broad', *World Policy Journal*, 24:1 (2007), pp. 47–50; M. Crenshaw (ed.), *Terrorism in Context* (University Park: Pennsylvania State University Press, 1995); B. Hoffman, *Inside Terrorism* (New York: Columbia University Press, 2006); A.P. Schmidt and A.I. Jongman, *Political Terrorism* (Amsterdam: Transaction Books, 1988).
5 Hoffman, *Inside Terrorism*; D. Rapoport, 'The Four Waves of Modern Terrorism', in D. Rapoport (ed.), *Terrorism: Critical Concepts in Political Science* (New York: Routledge, 2006), pp. 3–30.
6 See, for example, M. Goodman, '9/11: The Failure of Strategic Intelligence', *Intelligence and National Security*, 18:4 (2003), pp. 59–71; D.M. Gormley, 'The Limits of Intelligence: Iraq's Lessons', *Survival*, 46:3 (2004), pp. 7–28; P. Pillar, 'Intelligence, Policy, and the War in Iraq', *Foreign Affairs*, 85:2 (2006), pp. 15–27; 'Ex-CIA Official

Faults Use of Data on Iraq', *The Washington Post*, 10 February 2006; 'The Record on Curveball: Declassified Documents and Key Participants Show the Importance of Phony Intelligence in the Origins of the Iraq War', *National Security Archive* (Georgetown University), Electronic Briefing Book No. 234, www.gwu.edu/~nsarchiv/NSAEBB/NSAEBB234/index.htm.

7 'With CIA Push, Movement to War Accelerated', *Washington Post*, 19 April 2004.
8 M. Abrahams, 'Why Terrorism Does Not Work', *International Security*, 31:2 (2006), pp. 42–78.
9 R. Aldrich, 'Setting Priorities in a World of Changing Threats', in S. Tsang (ed.), *Intelligence and Human Rights in the Era of Global Terrorism* (Westport, CT: Praeger, 2007), pp. 158–170.

2 'Terrorism' and political violence in the Middle East and North Africa

Drivers and limitations

Gerd Nonneman

Dealing usefully with the questions of political violence and of terrorism in particular requires us to disentangle what it is one is talking about – both in terms of definitions, and in terms of the different aspects of these phenomena. Without this, one tumbles into a morass of confusion both conceptually and, more to the point, in terms of identifying real-world dynamics and workable policy responses. For a start, there are, obviously, two sides to these concepts: on the one hand, there are the challenges and threats (acts) one might be concerned about – including those of a 'terrorist' variety; on the other there is that which is threatened. The latter may include physical safety, the economy and economic security, or regime survival. Clearly, not all people will feel similarly threatened by a particular challenge. Or, to put it a different way, one person's threat may be another's irrelevance or opportunity – although an arbitrary threat of physical harm is likely to unite most. Even there, though, it is important to keep in mind that calculation of likelihood of harm may influence how particular 'threats' are responded to: in a broader climate of physical threat from a variety of sides, ranging from individuals to groups to governments, not every action or threat classified formally as 'terrorist' will necessarily attract the same level of opprobrium amongst all.

What is needed here, then, is first an attempt at definition; second, to stress the diverse nature and drivers of the phenomenon; and third, some attention for the wider context within which political violence and terror tactics may occur – before moving on to particular examples of groups that have been labeled terrorist, and of their evolution. This need is present for any discussion of terrorism, but perhaps particularly so in a chapter focusing on the case of the Middle East and 'Islam', so thoroughly associated in the public and many a policy-maker's mind with supposedly peculiarly religious and irrational extremism and terrorism.

Terrorism: definitions

The first thing to stress is that terrorism is not an '-ism' at all: it is not an ideology, but a tactic. It can be used by states as well as by individuals and groups, for any number of ideological or other reasons. In essence, it is *the act or threat of violent targeting of non-combatant populations and/or institutions, often but not always in arbitrary fashion, in order to create fear and/or to damage the institutions that are being challenged.* The aims include (1) destabilizing the system that is the ultimate target; (2) removing a perceived state or communal threat to a group's or population's security and interests; (3) demonstrating the movement's strength; (4) forcing policy change; (5) extracting financial gain. Only in a few cases does the violence of terror tactics become an aim in its own right, incorporated in the mythology and self-image of the movement. In most cases, a tactic is all it is, either as just one part of a tool-box, to be picked up or discarded as befits the circumstances, or as the most important tool in that box if other means are deemed to be beyond reach or ineffective. Again, this goes for the use of terror tactics by states as much as that by non-state movements.

Inherent in the above is that there may be as many 'terrorisms', or drivers for the adoption of the tactic, as there are radical movements or violence-prone states. Underlying causes can range from fear of destruction by a much stronger opponent, to any variety of religious, nationalist or other ideological drivers, or struggles for freedom by groups perceiving themselves to be the weaker party. When it comes to states' use of the tactic, it can also of course simply aim for suppression of dissent and opposition.

Crucially, moreover, one needs to distinguish clearly between the drivers for those making up the leaders and core of such movements, and, on the other hand, the motivations for those who end up joining, supporting or tolerating it, including those who may carry out actual acts of violence decided by others. Again, something similar can be said for forms of state terrorism.

The fact that there is no internationally agreed definition is more a reflection of the fact that so many groups and states use the tactic for a variety of purposes, and of the varied aims, fears, interests and biases of those applying the label, than of any inherent problem of defining the tactic. The plurality of definitions has been much commented on and added to – including by Whittaker, Hoffmann and Martin, as well as in a book by Schmid and Jongman dedicated to the question, and recently in a high-profile article by Fettweis.[1]

Perhaps the best published definition of 'terrorism' is that by Gurr, who defines it as 'the use of unexpected violence to intimidate or coerce people in the pursuit of political or social objectives'.[2] Gurr's definition may serve as shorthand for my own. Hoffman defines terrorism as 'the deliberate creation and exploitation of fear through violence or the threat of violence in the pursuit of change'[3] – which also chimes with my observations above, except that he in effect, wrongly, excludes states using terrorist acts domestically to avoid change. Fettweis, in attempting to dismiss the unnecessary plethora of definitions, compounds the mistake by breezily stating – in a mere footnote – that 'terrorism is simply violence against civilians by non-state actors for political purposes'.[4] Others have similarly exempted state actors (presumably only state actors on 'the right side') and others they see as 'legitimate', with Laqueur, for instance, including 'the illegitimate use of force' in his definition, in line, naturally, with most governments – begging the question of who is to define this illegitimacy. If definitions are to be any use in understanding actual dynamics – and thus in achieving workable policy measures – they need to steer clear of ideological bias and of privileging the view from particular actors or normative systems. Definitional clarity does not, of course, negate moral or political judgments about various kinds of violence – but the judgment should not be part of defining the phenomenon if one is after analytical effectiveness rather than political benefit.

It is in this sense, as well as in advancing wider understanding, that the emerging field of 'critical terrorism studies', however faddish some may find its label, has been making a significant contribution, pointing out not only the fallacy of associating terrorism with non-state actors alone, but highlighting the complexity of the phenomena coming under the terrorist label, and countering, with evidence, the 'essentializing' that remains all-too-prevalent in both analysis and policy debate.[5] Part of the solution to this must be thorough familiarity with individual case studies of actors, movements and their wider environment – a point well made by Dalacoura with regard to the usefulness of cross-fertilization between area studies and terrorism studies in the case of the Middle East.[6]

We also need to be clear that attacks on armed forces or paramilitary forces cannot strictly be defined as terrorism but are simply a different form of warfare – even though they may be inspired by the same drivers referred to under the four categories above, and even if the authorities whose forces are being so targeted will often wish to attach the 'terrorist' label to such attacks and their perpetrators.

For the practical purposes of this chapter, however, the types of terror tactics we are concerned with are those employed by non-state actors against non-combatant civilian populations and institutions – what has been called 'terrorism from below', or 'dissident terrorism'.[7] Nothing stops such actions or groups, of course, from being supported by outside state actors. Nor does the focus here on non-state actors mean that their use of the tactic is necessarily more reprehensible or has a greater impact than when states have recourse to it. Indeed, under the definition offered above, the number of victims of state terrorism has vastly outstripped those of dissident terrorism. This is all the more relevant since non-state groups often react or refer to precisely what they perceive as terror tactics used by state authorities – a perception in which wider sections of the public may share.

Within this practical sub-group definition of 'dissident' terrorism, it is possible to distinguish four broad categories[8] (recognizing that there may be blurring of boundaries and movement across):

- *Revolutionary/ideological* – aiming to replace the existing order by a clearly defined new order. One can also identify what has been termed a 'sub-revolutionary'[9] variety – aiming at bringing change but not at overthrowing the system altogether. The ideology in question can be religious or secular. At the extreme end of the religious variant is the 'millenarian' type that in practice may lean close to the next category.

- *Nihilist/Anarchist* – aiming to destroy the existing order without any clear blueprint for what should replace it, but on the basis that any alternative can only be better.
- *Nationalist* – aiming to liberate a people or territory from what is seen as occupation or control by others, either by removing foreign powers or by achieving separate independence.
- *Criminal* – aiming to create or maintain an environment conducive to the interests of organized crime.

In the Middle East and North Africa (MENA) region as much as anywhere, groups using terror tactics often incorporate features of more than one of these, or, while starting in one, develop or attract elements of another. Thus, Hamas in Palestine and Hezbollah in Lebanon combine predominant nationalist features with ideological and decreasingly important revolutionary ones; al-Qaeda has religious-revolutionary overtones but is anything but clear in proposed alternative models and might in some senses be viewed as nihilistic; terror tactics in Iraq since 2003 have brought together nationalist, ideological-revolutionary and sub-revolutionary strands (both secular and religious), while also drawing in or enabling the criminal variety.

In the process, targets too can range from the institutions and representatives of state (or occupation) authority, to population groups associated with them or identified as threats or obstacles to the achievement of the interests of the in-group. Any or all of these types can operate at the local, national, cross-border and regional levels, as well as at the international level.

A quite different typology cutting across the above would be one that distinguishes between those groups and individuals, whatever their other characteristics, that adopt terrorist tactics as part of a rationally calculated strategy with defined, achievable ends; and, on the other, the 'millenarian' or nihilist type pursuing non-negotiable ends driven by absolutist ideological frameworks. Or, put more simply, 'strategic' and 'redemptive', to borrow Max Abrahms' labels.[10]

Fettweis has made a forceful case for simplifying the multifarious typologies into a mere two types (disregarding the criminal and state varieties altogether): ideological and nationalist.[11] He argues that this is needed if accumulation of knowledge is to occur, and links his binary division directly to the dynamics of terrorist groups and phenomena, and the search for effective policy responses. In so doing, he rightly dismisses the oft-adopted distinction between religious and other ideological terrorisms. Yet his stark 'binarism' ignores the variation in fundamental dynamics within the broad 'ideological' category, and hence inevitably (however confidently) draws quite the wrong policy conclusions.

The trouble is that, while debunking the 'religious' category, he replicates three mistakes that characterize many mainstream commentaries. The first is that all 'ideological' groups using terror tactics are deemed essentially similar. They emphatically are not. The differences lie not only in their ostensible aims and backgrounds, but equally in the types of drivers that motivate them and their membership, and in the extent to which they are liable to evolve and adopt relatively pragmatic positions.

Indeed, the second error (shared by many) is precisely the mistaken assessment that ideologically (and especially religiously) driven terrorist groups are, in essence, 'irrational' and not amenable to engagement either by negotiation or by addressing the environmental factors they might have grievances about, because they have 'unlimited ends' and thus 'inspire similarly unlimited means'.[12] A minority of these groups fit this description, or at least their core leaderships do – until, eventually, even some of them change. But ideological convictions and motivations are not necessarily an obstacle to pragmatic assessment of political possibility, and over time, to adaptation. Indeed, a majority of ideologically motivated groups and individuals – whether religious or secular – have proved just as changeable and adaptable as any others. The case of the Muslim Brotherhood is but one, if possibly the most telling, example.[13] But some of the most violent groups and ideologues from the Middle East provide plenty of corroboration as well – some of which will be reviewed below.[14]

Given the plethora of evidence to the contrary, it seems extraordinary, then, that such prominent scholars as Hoffmann can still jump to essentializing conclusions about movements such as Hamas supposedly acting from uncompromising religious motives – and hence in essence being beyond reason. Indeed, he makes the blanket assertion that religious terrorism is different in its methods and level of destructiveness from the secular sort.[15]

The broader focus on irrationality, too – whether driven by religion, ideology, or psychopathologies – as an explanation for terrorism, has been proved wanting. Indeed, it has been shown to be no explanation at all in perhaps the most striking of terror tactics – that of suicide attacks. A review of psychological studies of suicide attackers leads University of Michigan psychologist Scott Atran to conclude that suicide attackers have no appreciable psychological pathologies and are as educated and economically well-off as individuals from the surrounding population ... 'why non-pathological individuals volunteer to become suicide attackers depends on the situational factors which are largely sociological in nature.'[16] Robert Pape's landmark study adds to this, showing that there is a clear strategic logic to most suicide attacks: 'terrorists have learned that it pays.'[17]

The third common error replicated by Fettweis in assessing motivations of 'terrorist' groups and therefore the most likely viable policy responses, is the failure to distinguish between the leadership and core on the one hand, and, on the other, the members and wider support base.

While it is clear that in the 'strategic' (whether nationalist or other) types of groups using terror tactics, political strategies and addressing the wider grievances they might have provides a possibly viable policy avenue, this is also true for the wider actual or potential support base (or base of non-resistance), that more radical and 'irreconcilable' groups rely on. In other words, the wider context (and possible associated socio-economic, political or foreign policy measures) can be – indeed, are likely to be – part of the explanatory puzzle and part of the solution, regardless of whether they were a direct motivation for the most hard-line ideological leaders.

Tackling violent radicalism and 'terrorism'

In addressing violent radicalism and terrorism, then, it is necessary both to keep in mind the wider context, which will influence the extent to which utopian radicals may attract the necessary support for the movement to achieve 'critical mass', *and* to make clear the distinctions (a) between different types of movements, and (b) between leadership and core, wider membership, and broader support base.

As regards the first distinction, the types of movements and types of aims and means range all the way from the most radical and millenarian variety, such as Aum Shinrikyo in Japan and arguably al-Qaeda, to much more restrained groups such as Hamas, who have, in essence, a practical, rational goal – in this case of national liberation and socio-cultural authenticity.

For some, terror tactics are simply a pragmatic means of attack and 'theatre'. For others it may become part and parcel of the movement's charisma and mythology, sacralizing violence in some cases, and becoming part of an internal rite of passage and demonstration of status in others.[18] But those latter, more integrally violent, examples represent a minority among movements that have used terror tactics, and even in the case of those movements the true integration of that violence in their nature is, on the whole, limited to the core – not really extending sustainably to the wider membership or supporters. These are important distinctions to make, especially when assessing how and in what circumstances such movements and their supporters may evolve: something that is of critical importance when considering how best to tackle them.

In a nutshell:

- political or ideological activism does not equate to radicalism (but may include it);
- radicalism does not equal violence (but may include it);
- violence does not equal terrorism (but may include it);
- the use of terror tactics does not, in the vast majority of cases, equal mindless and irreversible attachment to such tactics (although for the core of the most extreme millenarian groups, it may).

Most movements associated with political violence and terror tactics, then, are amenable to evolution. Clearly the small, extreme, millenarian sort (Aum Shinrikyo, the core of al-Qaeda and like-minded actors) needs identifying, isolating and eliminating as a force. All others, though, require a more nuanced approach, given the more nuanced dynamics at work in and around them. It is true that many groups using terror tactics feature extremist positions (arguably not all, though, just as one can dispute whether states that have used terror tactics in the past were necessarily 'extremist' – think of the bombing of Dresden or the destruction of Hiroshima and Nagasaki; the Syrian regime's destruction of the city of Hama in 1982, killing anywhere between 10,000 and 20,000 people in an attempt to quash Muslim Brotherhood opposition; or, indeed, of collective punishment meted out by an otherwise democratic state such as Israel). It is also true that among the more extreme groups the core of the movement tends to adhere to utopian views of their cause. But that does not by any means indicate that the broader membership, the wider support base or the social environment that tolerates it share such utopianism or extremism at any depth.

Apart from such distinctions, the key point is that both cores and wider memberships and support bases can evolve and change, fluctuating over time and according to place, in accordance with shifting circumstances and changing leaderships. It is true that such changes can be more prevalent outside the core; but, in the core, too, change occurs and builds on the diversity of views and approaches that are usually present, even amongst the key leaders and ideologues.

The evidence, not least from the Middle East and North Africa, and indeed the wider Muslim world, is precisely:

1   that radical Islamist (or other) movements and organizations, including those adopting terror tactics, do evolve;
2   that the extent of support or tolerance they attract is related in large part to the wider environment, rather than to any inherent features of culture or the populations in question;
3   that, in addition, the role of leadership is very important in explaining shifts toward radicalization or de-radicalization (but such changes in leadership positions are themselves related in part to the changing environment); and
4   that any policies which aim to address *only* the security aspects of the phenomenon while ignoring or exacerbating the elements in the wider environment that influence it can at best be irrelevant, at worst dramatically counter-productive.

That environment includes the economic situation, broader state policies, the extent to which 'hearts and minds' are addressed as a priority, and regional and foreign policies – the latter linking in, of course, to the actions of external actors, either locally or globally: communications technology has seen to it that no government can hope to isolate its population from such external environments.

Quite apart from the impact that events and perceptions in the global environment (be it in Palestine, Iraq or Afghanistan) have on the local radicalization or de-radicalization dynamics, transnational 'terrorist' networks and transnational imitation and inspiration have also come to represent a significant phenomenon – although not one that is wholly new: while currently aided by communications technology and the 'draw' of Afghanistan and Iraq, it became prominent in the 1960s.

The relevance and threat of radical and violent movements aiming at governments or groups within the state or beyond, whether through terrorist tactics or otherwise, can only be viewed in the wider context referred to above. By the same token, policies that attempt to address radical violent movements (including those using terror tactics) can only be effective by combining security approaches with an eye on the context: the former without the latter will be irrelevant at best, and counterproductive at worst. Indeed, this is precisely the lesson of counterinsurgency experience around the world over many decades – as distilled by, among others, General Petraeus' new US Counter-Insurgency manual, and David Kilcullen.[19] It also very much underpins the principles adopted by the US's General McChrystal in Afghanistan, since his appointment as the top military officer in that theatre by President Obama in 2009.

Ultimately, such groups and individuals (excluding the purely criminal variety) are attacking an order – social, political or both – that they see as illegitimate, usually in order to replace it with something else, however vague and inchoate that 'something else' may be. They are therefore not merely attacking the individuals, structures and symbols of that order but will, or will attempt to, link in to wider societal questioning of the legitimacy of the established order – whether that questioning is shared widely or limited to certain sectors.

The wider context in the MENA region

In the MENA region, the system or order that is being attacked is that of current regimes, and in some cases the order that tolerates or fosters those of a persuasion seen as incompatible with, or threatening to, the attacker's own values or community. 'Regime' and 'order' are in fact often seen as connected, as is the role of external actors – who can become a target in their own right. Support for or tolerance of the actions of such radical, violent or 'terrorist' actors, therefore, often draws on disparate complaints and grievances, without there necessarily being any intellectual, ideological or social coherence amongst such supporters. Even so, that is little consolation for the 'systems' and external actors that find themselves targeted, and it does add up to, and stems from, questions over the legitimacy of the existing order.

External targets

There is no question but that the Palestine issue – viewed as a combination of colonial-settler occupation and the usurpation of Muslim and Palestinian rights – has been a central motivating issue for Islamist and nationalist activists, including those adopting violence. They intertwine with and affect domestic radical activism too, but make immediate external targets of Israel and Western interests – particularly the USA – within the region and outside. The invasion of Iraq had a related, exacerbating effect for such Western targets. In this context, the perception of Western actions elsewhere as anti-Muslim became part of a generalized feedback effect. In turn, this affected extremism both within the MENA region and outside it, with a link being formalized in the global 'franchise' of al-Qaeda. That link, however, was never all-encompassing: while local–global connections grew, and while the motifs of Palestine, Iraq and Western anti-Muslim 'imperialism' became common currency across the region – feeding radicalization everywhere – the immediate focus for most activism remained domestic and regional.[20]

Legitimacy and regime sustainability

Most political systems in the MENA region remain authoritarian/autocratic to a greater or lesser extent. While autocracy can in any case survive for a very long time through coercion, long-term sustainability depends also on a varying mix of other factors, not least including some measure of legitimacy: even authoritarian regimes will pay attention to the need to shore up their legitimacy – attempting to undercut the ideological ground that opposition, and especially radical opposition, can stand on.

The main factors that influence a regime's political sustainability can perhaps usefully be summed up under eight points – the first relating to the external environment, the remaining seven to the domestic scene:

1   *The external environment*, both in terms of the actions of particular actors and in terms of the wider environment of international political and economic norms and politically salient events – along with and aided by global communications. This external environment offers both resources and problems for domestic legitimacy.
2   *The nature of the state and the history and level of state formation.*
3   *The level and basis of regime legitimacy.* The actual or potential sources or types of legitimacy in the region (or indeed elsewhere) are (a) traditional, (b) personal/charisma, (c) ideological, (d) performance and (e) institutional.
4   *The resources–demands ratio.*
5   *The level of 'modernization'.*
6   *Social structure (presence and nature of a working class; middle class; civil society; kinship-based structures).*
7   *Regime policy choices.*
8   *Regime type* – for instance, the difference between (post-)populist republics and neo-traditional monarchies.

In today's MENA region, taking one's cue from the eighth factor, one can arguably talk about 'the monarchies v. the rest' – with the monarchies on the whole coming out better than the republics, although there are significant differences within the monarchical category, across the above seven internal factors.

Almost all MENA states, outside the Gulf, Algeria and Libya, have a serious problem when it comes to the resources–demands ratio. Clearly the GCC states are in a league of their own. Many MENA states suffer from a history and level of state formation that leaves them less than automatically and unquestionably accepted as legitimate both inside and outside their often recent borders.[21] Exceptions would include Morocco, Egypt, and in some ways the monarchies of the Gulf.[22] This indirectly also affects the legitimacy puzzle for the regimes.

There are significant legitimacy issues for most systems in the region. Traditional legitimacy is limited to those systems or dynasties that have long-established pedigrees, to the extent that that legitimacy has not been squandered in other ways. Such regimes would include those in Morocco and the Gulf monarchies, and, stretching its traditional links beyond its current territory, the Hashemite monarchy of Jordan. Very few leaders can boast significant personal or charismatic legitimacy since the deaths of Nasser, Hafiz al-Asad and King Hussein. Exceptions are King Abdullah of Saudi Arabia, Sultan Qaboos of Oman, some of the senior royals in the other Gulf monarchies, and to some extent King Mohammed VI of Morocco. In the republics, there are really no leaders with personal charismatic legitimacy left. Similarly, since the 1970s, there is little by way of ideological legitimacy left for the republican regimes. By contrast, some of the monarchies benefit from a different kind of 'ideological' legitimacy, i.e. of a traditional and/or religious variety, albeit by no means unchallenged. As to performance legitimacy – which includes performance both in terms of domestic 'delivery' of economic well-being and of foreign policy – again this is seriously limited, including in wealthy states such as Libya or Algeria, and all the more so in states such as Egypt and, these days, Syria. There are significant issues in this regard also in many of the Gulf monarchies – especially Bahrain and Saudi Arabia, although, not surprisingly, less so in extremely wealthy Qatar and the UAE. Finally, there is, given the very recent creation of the state apparatuses and systems of norms in most of these states, very little by way of institutional legitimacy – also because authoritarian regimes have, additionally, purposely limited the development of independent legal and civil service institutions. A partial exception is Egypt, with its centuries-long history of central state rule and its well-established civil service.

Everywhere, modernization and economic, educational and technological change have changed popular perceptions, access to information, social organization and expectations – thus putting greater potential pressures on regimes while at least potentially empowering populations. Yet, alongside this it should be noted, first, that modernization on its own is never a determinant factor; second, that regimes have options for 'subverting' those effects; and third, that 'modernization' has by no means proved a unilinear or uniform, all-encompassing process: indeed, if anything, the so-called 'mosaic model' of societal evolution seems more appropriate.[23]

A working class has of course arisen in most MENA countries – even if there has been a significant safety valve in emigration – whether to Europe or the Gulf. By contrast, in the GCC monarchies, with the exception of Bahrain, the working class has essentially been foreign, imported – making for quite different political dynamics and adding strength to the system as a whole. Different types of middle class have emerged, albeit often linked to the state or even created by it – as opposed to the independent sort of middle class and bourgeoisie typifying earlier developments in the West. Indeed, the argument has been that the 'rentier' nature of the economy and the polity in the region (based on the wealth created through extraction of oil and gas) has meant that there has not been any independent middle class at all.[24] By the same token, wider civil society (defined as independent of the state) has generally been thought to have been stymied both by this rent effect and by authoritarian controls.

Nevertheless, there are instances of more vibrant civil-society activity emerging, and of sections of the middle class in some countries flexing their muscles –

even in the very states at the basis of the 'rentier' idea, namely, the Gulf oil monarchies.[25] In the latter, though, such activity and emerging middle-class independence does not translate into revolutionary/violent activity: the other factors here discussed see to that, and most among these groups have too much to lose from chaos or a complete overturning of the system to risk such upsets.

The factor of regime policy is particularly important. It is not just that regimes do of course have the option, in most countries, to coerce acceptance (albeit far less so in Yemen, or indeed Iraq). It is that there are choices to be made in terms of addressing popular concerns, opting for forms of co-optation and/or adaptation as opposed to sheer coercion, implementing 'hearts and minds' campaigns, smoothing over regional or sectarian differences, etc.

Thus far, it would seem that the most successful systems overall have been the monarchies. They have also been the ones to appear most willing to contemplate some measure of adaptation – not having, in the first place, attempted the fundamental ideological rupture with the past that typified the early strategies of the ideological republics. The reasons follow in part from the factors discussed already in this chapter. The willingness to adapt, which helps the overall balance of legitimacy and thus sustainability, may also be related to the fact that these regimes, already starting from a better basis (in the GCC much enhanced because of the positive resources–demands ratio, and in the small Gulf states because of their very smallness), have the additional benefit of being monarchies: a system where the monarch can be presented as 'above the fray' and is not dependent on any particular ideological, economic or political program – in contrast to the one-party systems prevalent in the republics, basing their original claim to power on a grand ideological scheme.[26]

Everywhere, the border-transcending effects and influences of regional crises and 'Arab issues', of the behavior of external powers and Israel, and of the global networks and campaigns of radical groups, play a role. Yet while the performance of the regimes on these questions is scrutinized and matters, the effects in terms of broader stability will only become threatening (and are only likely to create a significant popular base or tolerance for radical – including violent – movements), when there are significant problems in terms of most other factors as well.

There is no natural continuum between 'opposition' and even 'radicalism' on the one hand, and 'terrorism' on the other. Indeed, being in opposition to, and harshly critical of, the governments of the day has not – either in the MENA region or elsewhere – meant a predisposition for violence, let alone terror tactics. Even so, those who do opt for, or are recruited to, such tactics nevertheless are likely to be inspired by similar grievances and/or find their ranks swelled and their room to operate enlarged by the existence of the wider legitimacy issues discussed above. While often essentially local, they may also be inspired or helped in resources, in personnel, or politically, by regional or global groups and networks. Essentially 'global' extremist franchises like al-Qaeda will find more fertile ground locally, the more inadequate the existing system's legitimacy is.

Yet the following review of particular cases from across the MENA region shows that, while all this is true, so is the pattern that sees striking diversity within, and at times quite dramatic evolution of, radical movements that at one point or another adopted terrorism. It also illustrates that the social 'traction' of the most violent groups and the appeal of violence as a tactic tends to wither among otherwise sympathetic local populations after a limited period, when the violence starts hitting these populations or their interests significantly. Alongside targeted security and inducement policies, government action to shore up their own legitimacy can also play a major role in sapping the force and room to act of the most violent radical groups.

Evolving 'terrorist' Islamist movements in the MENA region

Algeria

Algeria presents a changing mix of 'reconcilable' and 'irreconcilables' – the balance driven in large part by government policies and performance. One never need have had the extreme violence if the elections of 1991 had not been annulled, the FIS not outlawed, and its leadership not locked up – and if the successive governments had performed better in terms of economic delivery, as opposed to the general perception of ineptitude and corruption that prevailed. Algeria's problem, apart from a continuing lack of government effectiveness, is its difficult terrain, ethno-political schisms and its long history of political violence, almost ingrained in the country's political culture since French colonial days. One also cannot pass over the Algerian case without referring to the domestic use of terror tactics by the regime itself, tactics pursued while it was simultaneously labeling the main opposition group, the FIS (let alone the more radical offshoots such as GIA, 'Armed Islamic Group'), as terrorists – a tactic that of course has parallels in many other regional states – perhaps most strikingly in Tunisia where Racheed Ghannouchi's non-violent and, by other standards, rather mainstream movement al-Nahda has similarly been portrayed as a terrorist threat.[27]

Algeria's regime has been relatively successful in containing the most violent aspects of the threat – whatever one thinks of its methods; as elsewhere, quite apart from repression, it was the excesses of the more extreme Islamist groups such as the GIA themselves, that turned much of the population against them. In 1997, the armed wing of the FIS declared the end of its armed campaign. Parts of other, more extreme groups (GIA, the *Salafist Group for Preaching and Combat* (GSPC), and its further splinter, *al-Qa'ida in the Islamic Countries of al-Maghreb*) also followed suit – but in a process where those organizations underwent 'splintering and factionalization in all directions, whether toward radicalization, de-radicalization, or even along apolitical paths'.[28] The GSPC's erstwhile leader, Hassan Hattab, already argued in 2005 that many in the organization wanted to lay down their arms if their demands were addressed, and in early 2009 urged its members to do so. Late that year some of the GSPC leadership did indeed start a process of ideological discussion intended to legitimize an end to the use of arms.[29]

Iraq

The Iraqi case features a mix of mutually antagonistic groups (with attached criminal gangs) – mainly evolving toward pragmatic reconcilability, as long as there is an outlook of all getting some stake in the newly emerging Iraqi polity and economy: al-Qaeda's own overreaching, the striking policy shift under General Petraeus (along with the Surge), and the (excruciatingly slow) evolving Iraqi political negotiations, are critical to this evolution – along with the economic reconstruction that this has allowed. A majority of Shia and Sunni oppositionists have decided it was worth trying to achieve their ends by non-violent means, and in particular the insurgents of the Sunni heartlands turned against al-Qaeda and its like once resentment of the latter's extreme methods and the apparent availability of alternative opportunities combined. Questions remain, of course, over how tenable such advances will prove in the hands of an Iraqi government that remains partly sectarian in attitude, and in the absence of a satisfactory conclusion of the key constitutional and economic sovereignty debates. However, what is clear is both that, al-Qaeda apart (and even to an extent there), violence including 'terror' was an instrumental tactic; that activists and leaders were liable to shifting positions, including moving away from violent tactics; and that the extent to which the 'irreconcilables' (many of them non-Iraqi) were able to get social traction was much reduced when they themselves overreached and others perceived other opportunities for addressing their interests and grievances. By the same token, the case of Iraq also shows that violent radicalization does not come out of a socio-political vacuum: religion as such, or indeed psychological factors, cannot be the explanation unless tied into the socio-economic, political and international context within which such factors begin to take effect.[30]

Hezbollah in Lebanon

Classified by the US and in some European registers as a terrorist organization, Hezbollah is a case study of the problem of 'essentializing' by local interested parties and outside powers. Hezbollah grew from a particular political situation, where local relative deprivation of the Shia was combined with state inadequacy, foreign invasion and the interests of a key outside player – Iran. Religious–ideological themes were available for use, and used to good effect. It is also unquestionably true that Hezbollah has been involved in acts of violence and linked to instances of straightforwardly terrorist tactics – although not now for more than a decade (if one does not count the military operations against Israel). Yet, essentially, Hezbollah remains a nationalist and social–communitarian movement with religious overtones, originally created by the Iranian Revolutionary Guards but rooted in local realities and grievances, and supported but by no means controlled by Iran. It has evolved toward a political and non-totalitarian vision that accepts that the establishment of an Islamic state in Lebanon is not realistic. It takes part in the national political process and has a stake in it. That is not to say that it has evolved from one clearly defined type to another – but it undoubtedly features a number of different strands within it, amenable to real-world calculations and adaptation, not least to the preferences of its fluctuating support base and potential voters. Hezbollah, for one thing, and whatever the other aspects of its evolving, multifarious incarnations, has entered the competitive political game in the wider political system of Lebanon, and in practice if not in theory has shown a willingness to engage in pragmatic politics.[31]

Hamas in Palestine

Similarly (but without the foreign – Iranian – impetus and initial resources), Hamas is an essentially nationalist movement that grew from a social and cultural movement with religious agendas. It always contained different strands and its support base and voting constituency was for the most part less radical and less committed to the ostensible ideological principles than the radical wing of the leadership. Here is one example of a 'radical' movement whose internal diversity and pragmatic strands were unnecessarily stymied by wrongheaded policies on the part of both Israel and much of the international community. It is a textbook case of the origin and evolution of a radical Islamist movement from a particular socio-political set of circumstances; of a movement using, on occasion, terror tactics, but where different views within the leadership are reflected and magnified among the wider and shifting support base, and where both at the core and among supporters, ideological and practical–political adaptation continues to happen; and of a movement and a support base, above all, amenable to engagement.[32] As Gunning has observed, their trajectory is in some ways reminiscent of that of left-wing radicals in Europe. Most of the latter – and certainly their support base – migrated out of violent and revolutionary tactics when they had a chance of becoming part of the electoral process. In part this was an effect of the influence of the electorate – always less extreme than the party leaders. In part it also reflected their gradual acquisition of a stake in the system. The ceasefires Hamas observed in 2002 and after reflected a public opinion that was some 80 percent in favor of such a ceasefire; but the short life of these ceasefires arguably reflected the fact that, in the late 1990s and early 2000s, the party still engaged primarily with student and activist audiences. By the mid-2000s, the time of the next phase of cease-fire politics (this time more durable), it was no accident that Hamas was competing for the wider electorate, leading indeed to its participation in the elections of 2006.[33]

This dynamic has continued, featuring both setbacks for the pragmatists within Hamas – as Israeli blockade and international isolation followed their electoral victory – and their continued relevance. Indeed, among the persistence of the different strands, it seems clear that it is the pragmatic, 'political' strand that ulti-mately has the best prospects – provided they are given a chance to prove to the rest of the movement and their constituency that such a strategy brings results.

Fath al-Islam and the events at Nahr al-Bared (Lebanon)

There is no question but that the most extreme and violent of the armed men who ended up moving to the Nahr al-Bared Palestinian refugee camp in northern Lebanon in 2007 were for the most part non-Lebanese, although there is no evid-ence whatsoever that they were sponsored by either the Saudi or the Lebanese gov-ernment, as has been claimed. They were moving there in support of radical Sunni-jihadi tendencies and after having in effect been squeezed out of Iraq. Yet the internal weaknesses of the Lebanese state, alongside the recruiting theme of the Palestinian cause, provided an enabling environment for the organization's emer-gence from 2006. Government forces took a long time to try to isolate these fighters while trying to avoid excessive casualties among the rest of the camp residents; they also lacked adequate equipment, including among the air force. One of the most striking aspects of the conflict, though, emerged in its aftermath, when some of the Lebanese members of Fath al-Islam who had been killed were refused burial by their kin: a telling rejection by their own society of the means they had used. This parallels the finding that one of the reasons for their failure was that they did not receive the level of support from local salafi forces they had been expecting.[34]

Al-Gamaʿa al-Islamiya (the Islamic Group, Egypt)

The Gamaʿa emerged in the 1970s in a radical divergence from the Muslim Brotherhood's political pragmatist strategy, opting for violence as a key part of their strategy. Following a harsh crackdown on Islamist militancy in the early 1980s following the assassination of Sadat, it consolidated and built its networks and armed wing – including by sending members for training to Afghanistan in the late 1980s. What Ashour has called the 'confrontation phase' followed from 1989 to 2007 – involving 'an insurgency-based in Upper Egypt, a rise in the use of terror tactics,... assassinations, [and] bombings'.[35] Yet, from 1997, a de-radicalization process commenced, initiated by some key leaders, and following four stages, from searching for consensus among the leadership, to 'ideological legitimization' of the new approach, to 'convincing the middle-ranking leader-ship, the grassroots and the sympathizers', and finally addressing the Egyptian, Muslim and international audiences.[36] The case of the Gamaʿa illustrates once again the key features noted in the first part of this chapter: emergence in a spe-cific context, divergence within the core leadership, divergence between core, membership and support base; the possibility of evolution (including de-radicalization) at all levels including the core; and the impact of a variety of factors on such evolution – including the role of leadership 'agency', interaction with those of other persuasions and with the wider public, and, in some cases, the role of repression – but only if carefully applied and targeted without attempting to eradicate the whole leadership, and while holding out selective inducements.[37]

'Al-Qaeda in the Arabian Peninsula' (QAP) and Saudi Arabia

The example of 'Al-Qaeda in the Arabian Peninsula' in Saudi Arabia is perhaps the clearest possible case of the main argument I am making in this chapter: (1) a small extremist–millenarian core leadership, aided by a group of *déracinés* returnees from Afghanistan, achieves some initial successes in a campaign of violence by drawing on public resentment of domestic corruption and the regime's apparent association with Western powers, in light of regional military conflagrations and domestic socio-economic problems; (2) the government initially lacks the requisite counter-insurgency expertise and techniques; but (3) the violence starts to hit local and Muslim populations; (4) the government combines increasingly effective methods of intelligence and control with equally effective approaches of using local customs and tribal/kinship networks to co-opt actual or possible members and sympathizers and to tie clan and other kinship pressures on the erstwhile jihadists into their own hearts-and-minds campaign; it also brings authoritative Islamic scholars to bear in undermining the extremists' message and in re-integrating radicals; (5) QAP loses local traction and finds its room for maneuver and tolerance drastically curtailed.

Part of the explanation is that QAP launched its campaign of violence against the Saudi state too early without being fully prepared. But both the perceived need to do so and the effects this then had on its subsequent ability to prosper illustrate the limitations of its tactics and wider appeal in a context of appropriate government policy.[38]

The Saudi government was able largely to delegitimize both the ideology and tactics of QAP, and was helped by prominent government critics with religious authority and credibility in Islamist circles, such as Sheikh Salman Al-Awda, publicly turning against QAP.[39] The strategy also included the much-noted reintegration program of former jihadists, combining religious discussion with a variety of activities and extensive help for them and their families. While there has been some recidivism, the great majority of the some 300 men passing through the program have steered clear of active support for violent activity thereafter.[40] As for wider society, credible independent polling data in late 2007 showed close to 90 percent of the population positively agreeing with the government's anti-terror campaign.[41]

That does not mean the threat has vanished: in 2009 the porous border with Yemen became a particular concern as QAP figures based there increasingly tried to infiltrate the Kingdom, on one occasion launching an unsuccessful if spectacular suicide-bombing attempt on the life of Prince Muhammad bin Nayef, the deputy Minister of Interior and the person in charge of Saudi Arabia's whole counter-terrorism operation.[42] Yet, while a major attack cannot be ruled out, a return to the dark days of 2003–2004, when QAP violence was at its height, is unlikely.

QAP in Yemen

Al-Qaeda's presence in Yemen dates back to the early 1990s, when bin Laden associates returned from Afghanistan. The bombing of the USS *Cole* in Aden in October 2000 was one high-profile instance of a series of attacks on foreign (and some government) targets, and several Yemenis were part of the 9/11 attack. Following the routing of the Taliban in Afghanistan that followed, several Al-Qaeda figures – Yemeni, Saudi and other – moved to Yemen – in some cases after a period of arrest in Iran, Saudi Arabia or US internment camps at Guantanamo. Yet a combination of a security crackdown – several leading figures being locked up – and a modest deradicalization program kept the domestic threat contained. Indeed, until 2006, al-Qaeda in Yemen appeared not to consider the government in Sanaa as a priority target, while by the same token, Saleh's regime seemed ambivalent about tackling the jihadi tendency head-on as long as it was not itself threatened. Yet several factors came together to change this equation. Western, and in particular US, pressure on the government was gradually ratcheted up; Sanaa's economic problems multiplied and its need for aid increased; with the effective defeat of the jihadist campaigns in Iraq and Saudi Arabia, there was an influx of jihadists into Yemen (including Said al-Shihri, a Saudi who had passed through the Saudi deradicalization program); and, critically, in February 2006 there was a major prison break of 23 leading jihadi activists – several previously released from Guantanamo and including Osama bin Laden's former secretary in Afghanistan, Nasir al-Wahayshi. Yemen's deradicalization program also seems to have been less effective than the Saudi version – probably because of both a lack of resources and the difficulty of replicating the Saudi use of kinship networks when it came to the non-Yemenis who had come in.

From this point on, Al-Qaeda gradually reconstituted itself in Yemen; in 2008 a spate of attacks showed a new phase had begun, and in January 2009 the merger was announced of the Saudi and Yemeni operations under the QAP name, with al-Wahayshi and Al-Shihri as its the number 1 and number 2 figures. The attempt on Muhammad bin Nayif's life was one illustration of the new trend. Yet QAP ideology and tactics still had very limited social traction in Yemen, and QAP remained numerically limited to a few hundred at most – even if they tried linking into tribal society through marriage. What room for maneuver they were able to carve out was partly the result of the rugged terrain and the incomplete grip of the central government over parts of Yemeni territory. But central was the combination of economic crisis, comprehensive misgovernment and corruption, and the resulting exacerbation of the southern and northern conflicts, which drained resources and further undermined legitimacy while creating new spaces for QAP to maneuver. The government's approach to these conflicts did not help: both could be settled by addressing the socio-economic grievances at their heart. The 'Houthi' rebellion is neither revolutionary nor an Iranian proxy; the southern movement similarly is not an inevitable secessionist threat either. Neither has any truck with QAP: indeed, they could be natural allies against it. Meanwhile, QAP as of 2010 did present an increased threat (not least to Riyadh and Western interests), although not to the survival of the Yemeni and Saudi regimes. Apart from counter-terrorism aimed surgically at QAP alone, without American 'boots on the ground' and avoiding drawing tribal populations into the conflict, the key requirements for containment will be major economic assistance and serious governance reform: the latter is paramount, but also the biggest challenge of all.[43]

Other cases of non-violent Islamism

The cases of Turkey, Indonesia, Malaysia, Kuwait, Bahrain and Jordan all further demonstrate how a wide variety of Islamist movements can become integrated in a political game that imposes rules and limitations, which they then prove by and large to observe, even at the expense of single-minded pursuit of their original ideological aims. Not only do they appear to develop a stake in the system, however critical they may still be of aspects of that system; they also, in the right circumstances, end up competing with other variants of more or less radical Islamist or other ideologies – thus both diluting the overall strength of any comprehensive extremist tendencies, and indirectly tending to feed into further 'normalization' of their own political–ideological platforms. Especially if combined with effective government, the evidence seems strongly to suggest that the overall result includes the isolation of violent extremist strands and actors that remain: while individual voices and outrages cannot be excluded, their 'social traction' and overall impact becomes much reduced.[44]

Transnational networks and cross-border impacts

Much has been made of transnational networks, whether in non-state organizations such as al-Qaeda and its allies, or regarding the role of states such as Iran and Saudi Arabia, in explanations for terrorist activity in particular places, including in the Middle East. Certainly, the combination of local grievances, mobilizing conflicts such as Palestine, Iraq and Afghanistan, and ease of travel and communication have made cross-border influences and impacts very significant. These range from cross-border flows of activists and terrorists themselves – as between Yemen and Saudi Arabia, Iraq and Saudi Arabia, Iraq and Syria, Iraq and Lebanon, or indeed between the Mashreq and the Maghreb, and between Afghanistan and the Arab world as a whole – to the influence of 'recruiting themes'. As to the latter, it is clear that motivating factors for individuals being recruited to organizations using terror tactics do not always lie in the domestic scene, but that recruiters often initially use other themes to draw in new members of the group: thus, for instance, the evidence in Morocco is that well over 80 percent of violent Islamist groups' members were recruited for the ostensible aim of resisting the Iraq War, only for them then to be deployed in other ways. Similar stories are encountered in the case of Saudi recruits.[45]

Certainly, state authorities are right to be concerned about such flows of individuals and ideas, and indeed Saudi Arabia, long concerned about the potential return of jihadi fighters in Iraq, was growing increasingly worried at the time of writing about the influx of radicals from across the border in Yemen. It is equally clear that many of the most radical figures in jihadi violence across the region have been, or were in close touch with, veterans of the Afghan jihad against the Soviets, and that there has been a continued traffic of radical activists and fighters between Afghanistan and Pakistan on the one hand, and the Middle East and North Africa on the other – and thence from one state (not least Algeria) to others. Yet it should be noted that, while these figures have been able to inflict major damage in some places – one thinks in particular of Iraq and Algeria, for instance – this should be qualified primarily in two ways. First, the places where they had the greatest impact were suffering other weaknesses that made them into prime targets and fields of action. Second, where this was less the case, and also when the violent excess of such movements became felt by the population at large, they tended fairly quickly to run up against substantial local resistance, losing their room for maneuver. Foreign fighters have tended perhaps to be the most extreme, but they also remained, or ultimately became again, isolated from the local society they would need to thrive. The greatest threat has been where the most radical global 'brands' – in particular the al-Qaeda 'franchise' – have become merged with, or adopted by, local actors, especially if they are able to combine local and global 'causes' in their recruitment and mobilization. However, this is proving far from easy to sustain.

Finally, the oft-presumed role of 'state sponsors' merits a note. Clearly a range of states have used or attempted to use opposition groups in other regional states as proxies, and this sometimes has taken violent forms, including the use of terror tactics. Certainly governments have often complained of being so targeted: Saddam Hussein accused Iran, Iran accused the Iraq-supported Mujahidin-e-Khalq, Saudi Arabia has been accused of sponsoring violent Sunni groups from Yemen to Iraq and Lebanon, and Iran has been accused of being at the heart of a Shia network bent on subversion – with some of their protégés engaging in violence, including terror tactics. As to the Saudi role, undoubtedly the Saudi state and its religious establishment have inspired many and sponsored some Salafi groups around the world, and some of the funds channeled through charities have ended up being used by radical groups. Equally, the Saudi leadership aims to keep its links to, and influence in, Sunni groups and tribes in Iraq and elsewhere in the surrounding region, especially to try to contain the influence of Iran and other regional competitor regimes. But, ultimately, Saudi policy is aimed at stability, both at home and in the wider region – hence, among other things, the stricter controls on charities' financial flows that have been introduced, and the national campaign, using both official and religious authority, to stop young Saudis from going to fight in Iraq.[46]

As to Iran, the issue is complicated by the many actors within the system – both within the state apparatus proper and in the parastatal sphere of the *bonyads* (foundations). Certainly, Iran's Revolutionary Guards were instrumental in setting up Hezbollah in Iran, and equally certainly, Iranian links extend across the Shia parts of the Arab world (from the Gulf to Lebanon) but also to actors such as Hamas in Palestine. By the same token, regimes and parts of the Sunni population in the Arab Middle East feel threatened by a perceived network of Shia influence centered on Iran. Yet this needs to be qualified in two ways. First, support for Hezbollah and Hamas is viewed in Tehran – and, indeed, in much of the Arab world – as perfectly legitimate support for a national movement; as already suggested, it is in any case problematic to equate support for these movements with 'support for terrorism'. Second, the groups receiving Iranian attention or support are essentially rooted in and driven by their own local environment – even Hezbollah. However grateful some of them may be for the support, none of them are or would want to be controlled by Tehran: that is true of Hezbollah, but also of the Shia parties and movements in Iraq. In case of the Hamas–Iran relationship, this is simply a case of a Sunni group that found itself ostracized looking for tactical allies; while, for Tehran, supporting Hamas has been aimed at containing Israel and the US, and demonstrating Iran's potential for a leadership role beyond Shia Islam.

The Houthi rebellion in northern Yemen could certainly not be classified as 'terrorist'. Moreover, their Zaydism may be historically associated with Shiism, but is quite distinct in practice. Grievances over socio-economic marginalization and the state-enabled influx of Salafi-Sunni schools and funds were exacerbated by the government response. Some Houthi leaders looked – largely in vain – to Iran as a possible source of help. Painting the rebels as part of the putative 'Iranian-Shia' coalition in the region had a limited 'self-fulfilling prophecy effect', but Iranian involvement remained peripheral, and there is no credible evidence of significant arms supplies or military assistance.[47]

Of course, it is true that there are extensive Shia networks throughout the region, but these are not essentially political in nature, nor are they centralized: Shia populations everywhere are free to choose their own 'sources of emulation' – i.e. the Shia Grand Ayatollahs they look to for spiritual leadership. Many of these are in Iran, some key ones (such as Sistani) are not. And there is neither unanimity among these figures, nor indeed majority support for the principles of Iran's Islamic Republic as implemented under the Supreme Leader (*Velayat-e-Faqih*).[48] It is true that these networks may be an avenue for Shia populations that feel under threat to look for succor in Iran; and, equally, Iranian regime actors are likely to try to use such networks to attain influence. The networks, in other words, may be liable to politicized use in particular circumstances. But, given the diversity of the Shia populations across and within different countries, the diversity of the lines of authority within these networks, and their essentially non-political nature, there is not really any 'Shia crescent' to be concerned about – let alone one that could be controlled by Tehran.

Conclusion

While it is critical to have effective intelligence and security operations aimed at the most violent groups, including effective international cooperation, this cannot, by itself, provide the whole answer and may even make the problem worse in the medium and longer terms. Attention for the wider environment within which support for such movements grows, and for the grievances that underlie such support and tolerance, is crucial for success; first, because it drains away the pool of potential recruits and shrinks the room for maneuver for the violent, radical core; and second, because it can in turn help the effectiveness of intelligence and security operations. 'Hearts and minds' campaigns and co-optation are important tools, and, depending on the local social context, using the kinship and clan or tribal networks as part of this campaign can prove very useful. So can the use of credible, authoritative interpreters of Islam.

Putting broader opposition movements, be they Islamist or other, beyond the pale and attempting to exclude them from the socio-political debates can only be counter-productive. Integration into the political 'game', within certain rules, appears to be an effective means for 'taming' such movements. They will not necessarily give up all aspects of their programs that governments, outside powers, or other sectors of society dislike, but the extent to which they will be prepared, by using violence, to risk wrecking their own position in this game and the stake they thus build up, along with the support of their constituency that may be much less radical than the leadership, will be much reduced. The evidence of the MENA region is that constituencies can push movements toward compromise, that at least parts of these leaderships often do adjust their position when reassessing their options and interests, and that significant sections of the movements and their memberships can shift toward accommoda-tionist, or at least non-violent, stances if given a reason and way to do so. By the same token, misguided policies of absolute exclusion can have the opposite effect.

There is a built-in limitation to the domestic sustainability of the most irrec-oncilable and extreme terrorist movements: they tend to overreach themselves and to lose traction amongst the local population once casualties and visible cruelty affect that population sufficiently, especially if their own excesses are accompanied with smart security operations and intelligent 'hearts and minds' policies that avoid ostracizing others who can be detached from the violent irrec-oncilable core. This is what happened in Saudi Arabia, Iraq, Jordan, Lebanon and Egypt, among other places. Only violent and oppressive policies, and/or exceptional circumstances of state collapse combined with external occupation or military involvement, are keeping the suicide bombers in business and main-tain the critical mass of support or tolerance that makes the most extreme ideo-logues truly dangerous.

There are two related qualifications to these conclusions. The first is that even the best policies and general success will never guarantee 100 percent prevention of terror attacks. Second, there may always be some parts of radical movements' cores, and some small, un-reformable millenarian groups such as the key leadership of al-Qaeda, that remain bent on extremist violence. But the likeli-hood of such violence can be reduced as societal tolerance for those wanting to use such tactics shrinks, reducing their room for maneuver and support. They can then be the true target of all the more effective intelligence and security operations, which are much more likely to attract popular support.

Notes

1 D. Whittaker (ed.), *The Terrorism Reader* (London and New York: Routledge, 2001), p. 8; B. Hoffmann, *Inside Terrorism* (New York: Columbia University Press, 1998); G. Martin, *Understanding Terrorism* (London: Sage, 2003); A. Schmid and A. Jongman, *Political Terrorism* (Amsterdam: North Holland, 1988); C. Fettweis, 'Freedom Fighters and Zealots: Al Qaeda in Historical Perspective', *Political Science Quarterly*, 124:2 (2009), pp. 269–296.

2 T. Gurr, 'Political Terrorism: Historical Antecedents and Contemporary Trends', in T. Gurr (ed.), *Violence in America* (London: Sage, 1989), Vol. 2.

3 Hoffmann, *Inside Terrorism*, p. 43.

4 Fettweis, 'Freedom Fighters and Zealots', p. 270 (note 3). His rejoinder that so-called 'state terrorism' is simply 'repression' is both too narrow (states use terrorism outside their borders as well, for a variety of reasons) and beside the point, if one accepts that terrorism is a tactic.

5 See, for instance, R. Jackson, M. Breen Smyth and J. Gunning (eds.), *Critical Terrorism Studies: A New Research Agenda* (London: Routledge, 2009).

6 K. Dalacoura, 'Middle East Area Studies and Terrorism Studies', in Jackson *et al.* (eds.), *Critical Terrorism Studies*, pp. 124–137.

7 See Martin, *Understanding Terrorism*.

8 Adapted from ibid., p. 113. This purposely leaves out a category of 'international terrorism', as this refers merely to the area of operation rather than saying anything about the nature or drivers.

9 Whitaker (ed.), *The Terrorism Reader*, p. 33.

10 M. Abrahms, 'Why Terrorism Does Not Work', *International Security*, 31:2 (2006), pp. 42–78.

11 Fettweis, 'Freedom Fighters and Zealots'.

12 Ibid., p. 270.

13 On the Muslim Brotherhood, in all its political and geographical variation, see R. Leiken and S. Brooke, 'The Moderate Muslim Brotherhood', *Foreign Affairs*, 86:2 (2007), pp. 107–121; also the excellent brief piece 'The Muslim Brothers: Appease or Oppose?', *The Economist*, 10 October 2009, pp. 60–61; Z. Munson, 'Social Movement Theory and the Egyptian Muslim Brotherhood', *The Sociological Quarterly*, 42:4 (2001), pp. 487–510; S. Abed-Kotob, 'The Accommodationists Speak: Goals and Strategies of the Muslim Brotherhood of Egypt', *International Journal of Middle Eastern Studies*, 27:3 (1995), pp. 321–339.

14 Perhaps the most striking recent work on this has been that of O. Ashour, in *The De-Radicalization of Jihadists: Transforming Armed Islamist Movements* (London: Routledge, 2009), and 'Lions Tamed? An Inquiry into the Causes of De-Radicalization of Armed Islamist Movements: The Case of the Egyptian Islamic Group', *Middle East Journal*, 61:4 (2007), pp. 596–625.

15 Hoffman, *Inside Terrorism*, pp. 82–83, 92.

16 R. Hassan, 'Suicide Attacks: Life as a Weapon', *ISIM Newsletter*, 14 (June 2004), pp. 8–9.

17 R. Pape, 'The Strategic Logic of Suicide Terrorism', *American Political Science Review*, 97:3 (2003), pp. 343–361; and his book-length study *Dying to Win: The Strategic Logic of Suicide Terrorism* (New York: Random House, 2005).

18 The case of Aum Shinrikyo stands out; see Ian Reader, 'Dramatic Confrontations: Aum Shinrikyo against the World', in D. Bromley and G. Melton (eds.), *Cults, Religion and Violence* (Cambridge: Cambridge University Press, 2002), pp. 189–208.

19 D. Petraeus, *The U.S. Army and Marine Corps Counterinsurgency Field Manual*, available also at http://freeinfosociety.com/media/pdf/3095.pdf, and in a published edition with the University of Chicago Press, 2007; D. Kilcullen, 'Counterinsurgency Redux', *Survival*, 48:4 (2006), pp. 111–130; and 'Countering Global Insurgency', *Journal of Strategic Studies*, 28:4 (2005), pp. 597–617.

20 B. Riedel, *The Search for Al Qaeda: Its Leadership, Ideology and Future* (Washington: Brookings Institution Press, 2008[†]; G. Kepel, *The Trail of Political Islam*, revised edition (London: IB Tauris, 2009); G. Kepel, *Beyond Terror and Martyrdom* (New Haven: Harvard University Press, 2008); J. Filiu, *Les Frontières du Jihad* (Paris: Fayard, 2006); O. Roy, *Globalised Islam* (London: Hurst, 2004).

21 See, for example, R. Hinnebusch, 'Order and Change in the Middle East', in B. Buzan and A. Gonzalez-Pelaez (eds.), *International Society and the Middle East* (Basingstoke: Palgrave Macmillan, 2009), pp. 201–225.

22 See, for example, I. Harik, 'The Origins of the Arab State System', in G. Luciani (ed.), *The Arab State* (London: Routledge, 1988), pp. 1–28.

23 For a still relevant discussion of the mosaic model in the Arab world, and the whole legitimacy puzzle more broadly, see M. Hudson, *Arab Politics: The Search for Legitimacy* (New Haven: Yale University Press, 1979).

24 H. Beblawi and G. Luciani (eds.), *The Rentier State* (London: Routledge, 1988).

25 G. Nonneman, 'Political Reform in the Gulf Monarchies: From Liberalisation to Democratisation? A Comparative Perspective', in A. Ehteshami and S. Wright (eds.), *Reform in the Middle East Oil Monarchies* (Reading: Ithaca Press, 2008), pp. 3–45.

26 For an elaboration of this argument see Nonneman, 'Political Reform in the Gulf Monarchies', pp. 21–23.

27 See International Crisis Group, *Islamism, Violence and Reform in Algeria: Turning the Page* (Islamism in North Africa III), Middle East Report No. 29, 30 July 2004, www.crisisgroup.org/home/index.cfm?id=2884&l=1. For a useful brief discussion of the Tunisian and Algerian cases, see Dalacoura, 'Middle East Area Studies and Terrorism Studies', pp. 127, 131.

28 O. Ashour, 'Islamist De-Radicalization in Algeria: Successes and Failures', Washington: Middle East Institute, Policy Brief No. 21, November 2008.

29 *Al-Hayat*, 5 December 2009. Al-Hattab's video message was relayed through *Al Jazeera* TV (Arabic) on 9 February 2009 following a written statement to the Algerian press in January; the 2005 call was publicized in an interview *with Al-Sharq al-Awsat*, 15 October 2005.

30 David Kilcullen refers to the 'conflict ecosystem', in 'Counterinsurgency in Iraq: Theory and Practice', PowerPoint seminar presentation, Marine Corps Base, Quantico, 26 September 2007. Also see the analyses by the International Crisis Group, www.crisisgroup.org/home/index.cfm?id=2436&l=1; J. Yaphe, 'After the Surge', *Strategic Forum* (Washington: National Defence University), no. 230, February 2008; and the insightful on-going comment by Juan Cole at www.juancole.com. Specifically on the jihadist phenomenon see M. Hafez, *Suicide Bombers in Iraq* (Washington: USIP Press, 2007).

31 For Hizballah's manifestoes see http://moqawama.org (English version http://english.moqawama.org/). See also J. Gunning, 'Hizballah and the Logic of Political Participation', in Marianne Heiberg, Brendan O'Leary and John Tirman (eds.), *Terror, Insurgency and the State* (Philadelphia: University of Pennsylvania Press, 2007), pp. 156–186; A. Saad-Ghorayeb, *Hizbu'llah: Politics and Religion* (London: Pluto Press, 2001); J. Palmer Harik, *Hizbollah: The Changing Face of Terrorism* (London: I.B. Tauris, 2005); A.R. Norton, *Hizbollah: A Short History* (Princeton: Princeton University Press, 2007). Also the useful 'primer' by L. Deeb, 'Hizballah: A Primer', Middle East Report Online, July 2006, www.merip.org/mero/mero073106.html.

32 A. Tamimi, *Hamas: Unwritten Chapters* (London: Hurst & Company, 2007); J. Gunning, 'Social Movement Theory and the Study of Terrorism', in Jackson *et al.*

(eds.), *Critical Terrorism Studies*, pp. 156–177; J. Gunning. 'Peace with Hamas: The Transforming Potential of Political Participation', *International Affairs*, 80:2 (2004), pp. 233–255; K. Hroub, *Hamas* (Washington, DC: Institute for Palestine Studies, 2000); S. Mishal and A. Sela, *The Palestinian Hamas: Vision, Violence & Coexistence* (New York: Columbia University Press, 2000).

33 J. Gunning, 'Hamas: Socialisation and the Logic of Compromise', in Heiberg *et al.* (eds.), *Terror, Insurgency and the State*, pp. 123–154; Q. Wiktorowitz and K. Kaltenthaler, 'The Rationality of Radical Islam', in D. Caraley et al. (eds.), *Terrorist Attacks and Nuclear Proliferation* (New York: Academy of Political Science, 2007), pp. 49–73, at p. 53. See also Tamimi, *Hamas*; and Z. Chehab, *Inside Hamas: The Untold Story of Militants, Martyrs and Spies* (London and New York: I.B. Tauris, 2007). See also the Hamas government website http://www.pmo.gov.ps.

34 T. Gade, *Fatah al-Islam in Lebanon: Between Global and Local Jihad* (Oslo: Norwegian Defence Research Establishment, 2007), FFI-rapport 2007/02727, www.mil.no/multimedia/archive/00102/02727_102478a.pdf; and personal communication from a well-placed Lebanese observer, London, 2008.

35 Ashour, 'Lions Tamed?', pp. 609–612. Two of the most telling works by a group of historical leaders are Karam Zuhdi *et al.*, *Nahr al-dhikrayat* [River of Memories]; and *Istratijiyat wa tafjirat al-qa'ida: al-akhta' wa al-akhtar* [Al-Qaida's Strategy and Bombings: The Mistakes and Dangers] (both Cairo: Al-Turath al-Islami, 2003). On the Gama'a and radical Islam in Egypt in general, see also I. Al-Hudaiby, 'Trends in Political Islam in Egypt', in M. Emerson, K. Kausch and R. Youngs (eds.), *Islamist Radicalisation: The Challenge for Euro-Mediterranean Relations* (Brussels and Madrid: CEPS and FRIDE, 2009), pp. 25–51.

36 Ashour, 'Lions Tamed?', p. 612.

37 For the group's key statements and publications, see its website, www.egyig.com, esp. www.egyig.com/Public/articles/books_studies/index.shtml (partial English version at http://egyig.com/Public/enarticles/behaviours/index.shtml). See also, Ashour, 'Lions Tamed?', pp. 614–624; and Ashour, in *The De-Radicalization of Jihadists*.

38 Author's discussions with Saudi observers in Riyadh and various locations in Europe, 2004–2009; R. Meijer, 'The Limits of Terrorism in Saudi Arabia', in P. Aarts and G. Nonneman (eds.), *Saudi Arabia in the Balance* (London: Hurst, 2005), pp. 271–311; T. Hegghammer, 'Terrorist Recruitment and Radicalization in Saudi Arabia', *Middle East Policy*, 8:4 (2006), pp. 39–60; T. Hegghammer, 'Jihad, Yes, But Not Revolution: Explaining the Extraversion of Islamist Violence in Saudi Arabia', in *British Journal of Middle Eastern Studies*, 36:3 (2009), pp. 395–416.

39 Among other things, Al-Awda published a Ramadan letter to Osama bin Laden in October 2007, starkly criticizing him on religious grounds. The letter is on Al-Awda's website, *IslamToday*; for the English version, see www.islamtoday.com/showme2. cfm?cat_id=29&sub_cat_id=1521.

40 Discussions with Saudi observers, Riyadh, 2008–2009; C. Boucek, 'Saudi Arabia's Soft Counter-Terrorism Strategy', *Carnegie Papers*, 97 (Washington: Carnegie Endowment, September 2008). See also R. Lacey, 'Rehab the Terrorists – with Love', on *The Daily Beast*, 21 May 2009, www.thedailybeast.com/blogs-and-stories/2009–05–21/rehab-the-terroristshellipwith-love/?cid=hp:featureline.

41 The 2007 polling results, in a report by TFT, are based on a representative sample of 1,004 respondents across the country, www.terrorfreetomorrow.org/upimagestft/TFT%20Saudi%20Arabia%20Survey.pdf.

42 For the attack on Muhammad bin Nayif and the newly increased activity especially of cells based in Yemen, see B. Slavin and S. Carter, 'Saudi Royal Hurt by al Qaeda Suicide Blast', *Washington Times*, 29 August 2009; B. Riedel, 'Al-Qaeda's New Murder Plot', *The Daily Beast*, 24 October 2009, www.thedailybeast.com/blogs-and-stories/2009–08–28/al-qaedas-new-murder-plot/?cid=tag:all1; C. Murphy, 'Saudi Concern Rises of Al-Qaeda Activity in Yemen', *Christian Science Monitor*, 19 October

2009, www.csmonitor.com/2009/1019/p06s10-wome.html; and *Politics, Succession and Risk in Saudi Arabia*, Gulf States Newsletter Special Report, London, January 2010, pp. 12–13. QAP's own take was set out in its magazine *Sada al-Malahim*, 11, October 2009 (www.archive.org/details/Almalaahm_11).

43 See *CTC Sentinel* 'Special Issue on Yemen', January 2010 (http://ctc.usma.edu/sentinel/CTCSentinel-YemenSI-2009.pdf); QAP's statements and positions – occasional media releases apart – are issued roughly bimonthly since 2008 in *Sada al-Malahim*. See also I. Glosemeyer, 'Dancing on Snake Heads in Yemen' (Calgary: Canadian Defence & Foreign Affairs Institute, May 2009); G. Hill, 'Yemen: Fear of Failure', Chatham House Briefing Paper, January 2010 (update, London: Chatham House, 2010); C. Boucek, 'Yemen: Avoiding a Downward Spiral,' Carnegie Papers no. 102 (Washington: Carnegie Endowment, September 2009). On the shades and dynamics of Islamism in Yemen, see L. Bonnefoy, 'Varieties of Islamism in Yemen', *MERIA*, 13:1 (2009) (www.gloria-center.org/meria/2009/03/bonnefoy.html).

44 See the excellent recent analysis by A. Echagüe, 'The Radicalisation of Moderate Islamist Parties: Reality or Chimera?', in Emerson *et al.* (eds.), *Islamist Radicalisation*, pp. 108–125, which surveys the evidence on both moderation and potential re-radicalization, concluding that the danger of the latter has been overstated. Also M. Hafez, *Why Muslims Rebel* (Boulder: Lynne Rienner, 2003), M. Asseburg (ed.), *Moderate Islamists as Reform Actors: Conditions and Programmatic Change* (Berlin: Stiftung Wissenschaft und Politik, April 2007), SWP Research Paper no. 4; J. Piscatori, *Islam, Islamists and the Electoral Principle in the Middle East* (Leiden: ISIM, 2006); G. Krämer, 'The Integration of the Integrists', in G. Salamé (ed.), *Democracy Without Democrats? The Renewal of Politics in the Muslim World* (London: I.B. Tauris, 1994), pp. 200–226; F. Volpi and F. Cavatorta (eds.), *Democratization in the Muslim World* (London: Routledge, 2007). On Jordan and Yemen specifically, see J. Schwedler, *Faith in Moderation: Islamist Parties in Jordan and Yemen* (Cambridge: Cambridge University Press, 2006). On Bahrain, see K. Niethammer, 'The Paradox of Bahrain: Authoritarian Islamists Through Participation, Pro-Democratic Islamists through Exclusion?', in Asseburg (ed.), *Moderate Islamists as Reform Actors*. On recent trends in Indonesia, see *The Economist*, 'Toppled', 18 September 2009, www.economist.com/world/asia/displaystory.cfm?story_id=14483927 and its 'Special Report on Indonesia', 10 September 2009, www.economist.com/specialreports/displaystory.cfm?story_id=14391438. On Malaysia, see K. Abdullah, *The Politics of Islam in Contemporary Malaysia* (Bangi: Penerbit Universiti Kebangsaan Malaysia, 2003).

45 Confidential discussion with Moroccan intelligence personnel, Rabat, October 2008; Dominique Thomas, 'From Local to Global Jihad', presentation to conference on *The State of Saudi Arabia*, Princeton University, 12–14 November 2009.

46 Discussions in the context of the two Sciences-Po/Princeton conferences on *The State of Saudi Arabia*, in Menton (France), 6–8 June 2008, and Princeton, 12–14 November 2009; discussions with Saudi and British officials and observers, 2008–2009; and see G. Nonneman, 'Determinants and Patterns of Saudi Foreign Policy', in Aarts and Nonneman (eds.), *Saudi Arabia in the Balance*, pp. 340–343.

47 Discussions with Yemeni, European and US analysts, 2007–2010, and confidential exchanges on Gulf2000 network (hosted at Columbia University), 2009–2010. See also Glosemeyer, 'Dancing on Snake Heads in Yemen'; Hill, 'Yemen: Fear of Failure'; Boucek, 'Yemen: Avoiding a Downward Spiral'.

48 See, for example, L. Louër, *Transnational Shia Politics: Religious and Political Networks in the Gulf* (London and New York: Hurst & Columbia University Press, 2008).

3   Radicalism, extremism and government in North Africa

George Joffé

During the past two decades, all governments in North Africa have had to react to the radicalization and the growth in extremism amongst their populations linked to the increasingly important role of political Islam. This has conditioned domestic politics and security issues, but has also influenced foreign policy as well. Normally, such developments are analyzed in terms of dipolar antagonism, and the issue of antiphonal engagement between what appears to be polar opposites in political terms is rarely posed. Yet it is also the case that such tensions have provided governments with new opportunities for reasserting control through discursive deictic distinction and securitization, both in terms of domestic and external relations.

There can be little doubt that, since the beginning of the 1990s, every regime in North Africa has been challenged by radical opposition and threatened by extremist violence.[1] Algeria, between 1992 and 1999, had to contend with what was virtually a civil war, which reached a crescendo in 1995–1996 before being brought under control. Even today, marginalized extremism continues which, even if it no longer threatens the state, still disrupts the security of significant portions of the population. Tunisia, allegedly fearing an Islamist threat at the start of the 1990s, cracked down violently in 1991 and 1992 against the an-Nahda movement and, apart from the Djerba synagogue bombing in 1993, seems to have controlled potential threats, albeit at the cost of an extremely repressive political regime.

Yet, even here, the repression in Tunisia seems to have generated its own response, with incidents in December 2006 and January 2007 which led to the dismantling of the mysterious 'Soliman Group'. Libya faced a significant threat of anti-regime violence focused on Cyrenaica at the end of the 1990s, which the regime successfully crushed, despite several attempts on the life of its leader, Colonel Qadhafi. Even Morocco which, warned by the Algerian example of the dangers of extremism and comforted by its moves toward political plurality, believed itself to be sheltered from such violence, discovered in 2003 its own vulnerability to the wave of confrontation sweeping through the region.

The seriousness of the threat that this history of violence has posed to North African states cannot be underestimated. Yet, at the same time, it is noticeable that the governments and regimes concerned have been little given to introspection over its causes. They have tended to point toward the inherent irrationality and fanaticism of their opponents and to have complained about their own diplomatic isolation in the predicament they have faced. There has been a growing tendency in the Maghreb[2], despite the evidence, to attribute such events to the fact of transnational violence which has increasingly alarmed the West since the events in Washington and New York on 11 September 2001, if not long before as well.

Thus the claims by a major clandestine group in Algeria in 2003 and 2006 to be an affiliate of al-Qaeda have been gratefully seized upon by North African governments as a way of explaining their own political dilemma by pointing toward exogenous causes, rather than confronting their own longstanding social, economic and, above all, political crises. They have also blamed European states for their insouciance during the 1990s when the latter ignored complaints from the Maghreb that their indulgence of political extremism was largely responsible for the continuing challenges that states in the South Mediterranean region faced. Indeed, it could be argued that there has been a general tendency to seek in Europe's mistakes the explanation of the political crises they experience.

The problem with this approach is that it both trivializes the violence to which the Maghreb has been subjected and normativizes it into a discourse that fits into the dominant Western view of transnational violence during this decade. No attempt is made to understand the root causes of the phenomenon and of the alienation of Maghrebi populations; indeed, this approach renders such concerns irrelevant for it implicitly contains its own rationale. Nor is any attempt made to deconstruct the meaning of 'terrorism' within the North African experience, another essential component of any objective analysis of the history of the last decade.

It is the basic argument of this chapter that, quite apart from the undeniable reality and seriousness of the challenge to established political order throughout the Maghreb, North African states have also used the crisis to significantly change the terms upon which their relationships with Europe and the United States are based. In part, of course, they have been the unintended beneficiaries of the West's own discovery and experience of transnational violence. But they have also actively sought to redefine the relationship from one in which they have traditionally been the petitioners for Western attention to one in which, today, they are much more its partners, at least as far as security issues are concerned. It is this, far more than the objective reality of threat, that now explains the European security engagement across the Mediterranean or the United States' enthusiastic leadership of and participation in the Trans-Saharan Counter-Terrorism Initiative. The consequence has been that objective analysis of the phenomenon of regional violence has been neglected in favor of a normative view that is shared across the Mediterranean and the Atlantic. This chapter, therefore, also seeks to correct this bias.

Social movements, social networks and mass action

Before examining the question of the antiphonal engagement between challenges to regimes and their domestic responses, or their diplomatic manipulation of such challenges with third states, we need to establish the natures and dimensions of the challenges involved. Individual antagonism to the hegemonic discourse of a political regime, legitimized by its monopoly of state-instituted violence, has little chance of challenging, let alone modifying, regime behavior. It can only contribute to such a project within a formal political arena if the regime itself is prepared to respond to political opposition by engagement with its challengers. Even if this is possible, it requires mass, not individual, action so that individual opponents are forced into social movements that may or may not become formal political parties, depending on the regime's approach to the control of public space.[3] In this context, social movements are, in short, collective challenges to political authority which embody common purposes, usually develop in transitional societies where patterns of governance are often fluid and the nature of the transition process itself offers major challenges to government, and are usually initiated by catalytic events in terms of popular frustration, often being articulated through charismatic leadership.

The key question is, then, how the common purposes of such movements should be articulated; what are, in short, the drivers for the ideology or objectives that it formulates, so that the resources that it contains can be mobilized? Clearly, the way in which the issues that the social movement addresses are themselves addressed is crucial for, if this is not collectively accessible, the movement's coherence will disappear. In other words, the key to success is the way in which a movement frames its discourse of contention. Such 'frames of contention' are, therefore, interpretive schemata that provide a context for an ideological analysis which justifies contention and the social movement associated with it. They provide diagnoses of social disequilibrium, solutions to it and rationales for action to achieve this that have meaning and value for participants.

Such spontaneous patterns of resource mobilization can easily morph into more formal structures of contention such as political parties, as has tended to be the case with Islamic social movements in recent years. Indeed, social movements and political parties can co-exist as different patterns of mutually reinforcing contention, thus creating social-movement communities, as has been the case in Morocco and Algeria. Here, patterns of contention are diffused between formal and informal movements with flexible leaderships and fluid boundaries between them. This was precisely the pattern that developed in Algeria during the 1980s, and which contributed to the atmosphere in which country-wide riots developed in October 1988. These challenged the existing political system and initiated the changes that were eventually to lead to the civil war in the 1990s. In Morocco in the current decade, it has led to a formal political party and an informal social movement seeking similar political objectives of democratizing the political system despite the formal competition between them.[4]

Furthermore, insofar as such movements are rational and organized, they also require and therefore create bureaucracies or take over existing administrative structures. Indeed, it is for this reason that, in Islamic activist movements, the mosque can play a crucial role,[5] alongside informal Islamic institutions, such as charities, schools, societies and cultural centers. In fact, in the context of the Muslim world, political extrapolations of Islamic doctrine have emerged as the most appropriate framing ideology. In part this arises from the cultural context but it is also a conscious reaction to other ideological failures rooted in nationalism and secularist ideologies of liberation and development. Specific aspects of the Islamic corpus have become important, particularly those governing social and political organization such as the concept of a just society and sharia (Islamic jurisprudence), together with more atavistic and symbolic concepts, such as the recreation of the Caliphate.[6]

Such framing ideologies can, of course, be contested, either in terms of content and strategy or in terms of tactics, such that additional mechanisms are developed to impose a hegemonic discourse on the movement or to generate splits within it. It was this that lay behind the struggle between the GIA (Groupes Islamiques Armés – Jama'at Islamiyya Musalaha) and the AIS (Armée Islamique du Salut – Jaysh Islamiyya li'l-Inqadh) during the Algerian civil war in the 1990s. The frame can also be challenged from outside, particularly if the movement's major opponent, the state, has created its own hegemonic framing ideology. Thus the Moroccan monarchy's claim to be a caliphate and thus to dominate the domestic Islamic agenda challenges the discourse of groups such as 'Adl wa'l-Ihsan and the PJD (Parti de la Justice et du Développement – Hizb al-'Adala wa'l-Tanmiyya).[7]

Such challenges can produce one of – or a combination of – three outcomes, one organizational and the other two essentially ideological in nature; transformation into a social network, ideological and organizational exclusiveness or transnational ideological adherence, whether symbolic or operational. Networks share many of the characteristics of social movements, but are more purposive, in that they have specific agendas and restricted memberships. As Sageman suggests, 'social networks are complex communicative networks that create shared worlds of meanings and feelings, which in turn shape identity, perceptions and preferences.'[8]

They are structured as nodes and hubs linked by ties in which nodes consist of individuals or cliques[9] and hubs form key control nodes with the ties providing the interconnectedness generated by shared beliefs and common goals. As such they can cut across bounded groups and social categories within wider social movements as both *gesellschaft* and *gemeinschaft*, enjoying both shared values and structures. In essence, social movements are usually the domain of radicalism, whereas networks often reflect a progression toward extremism.

Ironically enough, membership of such networks is not apparently dependent on prior acceptance of a frame of contention. Sageman rejects recruitment explanations based solely on common social backgrounds, shared psychopathologies and specific circumstance, arguing instead that recruitment is part of a process, not a specific decision.[10] He points to analyses developed by Lofland and Stark with respect to the Moonies, by Della Porta for the Brigada Rossa in Italy and by Saad Eddin Ibrahim for the violent Islamist movements in Egypt to show that recruits are often alienated individuals and have prior affective links with their recruiters.[11] He concludes that the main driver is the peer pressure generated within cliques, alongside ideological frames of contention which may or may not be present.[12]

Such networks tend not to be hierarchical, for then action by the state can easily decapitate them and destroy their intercommunication facilities. Instead they are decentralized, maintaining organizational coherence through the dense interconnectivity of their nodes and hubs so that, even if hubs are destroyed, alternative routes exist to restore communication and operational effectiveness. They also tend to depend on their ability to embed within the surrounding social environment, either through their relationship to a wider social movement or because of their links to the wider society.

Indeed, loss of such embeddedness would imply vulnerability to hostile external action unless the network is sufficiently large for it to consider itself to be a virtual community in its own right; an 'imagined community' based on a shared sectarian ideology.[13] This is, after all, how a social movement views itself and it also seems to be the case in the transnational networks and the associated transnational social movements that have emerged in recent years.[14] The importance of this is that such virtual communities acting as networks also develop ideological frames that are not easily bounded by attitudes in the wider social movement or environment, as effective embedding would require.

They can thus become exclusive in terms of organization, membership and frame – they develop anti-system collective frames, as Hafez[15] suggests, which are innately hostile to the existing political order which they seek to replace. His primary concern, however, has been to explain the extraordinary brutality that characterized dissident networks – he regards them as social movements – during the Algerian civil war in the 1990s. Toward the end of the decade, a series of spectacular massacres of civilians took place which was conventionally blamed on these groups. There have since been well-authenticated claims of direct and indirect security-force involvement in the massacres, as part of a counter-insurgency strategy and for other, more disreputable, reasons.

Whether or not this is true, it is the case that dissident social networks have engaged in targeted violence against civilians. This is a feature that needs to be taken into account in any discussion of dissident networks in North Africa, for similar exclusivist violence has also occurred in Morocco and has even been threatened in Tunisia. For Hafez,[16] the violence was a consequence of a political process of radicalization as the result of the confluence of three separate conditions. These are the brutality of state repression, the reactive construction of an exclusive dissident organization and the consequent promotion of an anti-system collective frame[17] to justify violence against state repression. Such a frame, by rejecting reform of the state as impossible because the political system itself was corrupt, seeks to justify its overthrow instead.

The exclusive organizational structure, designed to counter the threat from the state and to exclude defectors, also thereby creates 'spirals of encapsulation'[18] in which insurgents are isolated from the wider society and lose touch with the political reality of that environment. It also rejects other dissident organizations as potential threats and insists on ideological discipline and commitment, seeing resistance as a justification in itself for violence designed to eliminate its opponents and ideological alternatives.[19] The network thereby becomes in itself an agent for further extremism of its beliefs and practices. Even neutrality becomes opposition[20] so that the population itself becomes a legitimate target for indiscriminate violence on the grounds that neutrality implies a return to jahiliyya[21] and therefore 'unbelief' (kufar), and thus apostasy, for which the legal penalty, according to sharia-based religious law, is death.

This analysis of social movements and networks aims to describe the lineaments of radicalism and extremism in the Maghreb. It is designed to provide an understanding of how individuals become opposed to government and then actively engage in attempts at its destruction quite independently of the ideologies they may profess. It highlights, at the same time, that the cultural environment in which such movements develop is bound to condition the ways in which they frame their antagonism to regimes-in-place. It also seeks to investigate the degree to which the two kinds of movement and the phenomena of radicalism and extremism are interlinked and interdependent such that the one may morph into the other, a development that may or may not be inevitable even though they have been treated as being analytically and antiphonally independent. It also emphasizes that the evolution of such movements is a consequence of the convictions of the individual actors that engage in them. By doing this, it does not exclude the more conventional explanations for contention, whether economic, social, political or psychological, it merely folds them into the mechanism by which they are expressed – the 'interpretive schemata' that form the crucial framing process that gives such movements ideological coherence and meaning.

Violent extremism, asymmetric warfare and the state

Networks of the kind described above engage in violence which has usually conformed to the pattern of asymmetric warfare that typifies the contemporary scene as well. The particular form of extremist asymmetric warfare that has been adopted is usually described as 'terrorist', a term that bears some analysis in itself. One of the problems with the term is the lack of its precise definition. Here it is taken to mean 'coercive intimidation', the definition used by Paul Wilkinson in his original study, *Terrorism and the Liberal State*.[22] This definition, which is equivalent to the use of coercive violence for political ends,[23] has the advantage that it is formally neutral, a consideration which is in itself important. This is because it removes events involving terrorism from the realm of the cultural. That is to say, if a terrorist act can be described in terms that apply to other, similar acts designed to achieve political outcomes, we can be fairly sure that it is itself an essentially political phenomenon that has nothing to do with cultures or civilizations, in particular with intrinsic Islamic values or with specific interpretations of Islam.[24] This is, after all, an argument that has been widely used in Europe and America, despite the denials of politicians, to explain the unique horror associated with terrorist events in the wake of the events of 11 September 2001, and to justify their response.

The major ambiguity involved with terrorism lies in its relationship to the state and in the definition of the moral status of terrorist acts. Terrorism is primarily the prerogative of non-state actors; groups and organizations that do not enjoy the advantages of states. Most importantly, they are not accorded the innate rights that establish states as the uniquely authorized mechanisms for imposing social order or the embodiment of collective identity[25] and that allow them to articulate the collective views of their citizens in the international arena. The state is, therefore, both the entity with the monopoly over the legitimate use of violence[26] and 'the actuality of the ethical idea'.[27] This is important because it allows the state to define what we may and may not do through a system of laws in which we are tacitly engaged and to which we implicitly assent. It also means that the state may sanction behavior of a kind that is normally forbidden in pursuit of its own interests. Thus it can legalize killing, as it does in times of war, an act that it would otherwise rigorously repress.

A problem arises, therefore, if this monopoly of the state over ethical and moral considerations and definitions is contested. What happens if you cannot morally accept the dictates of the state, as expressed through its government – which is, after all, one of the expressions of state power? What happens, furthermore, if you also believe that the principles on which the actions of the state are based cannot be changed by the normal political processes; by changing its government or government policy through public pressure or the democratic process – a particularly important concern if the state itself is not democratic? What happens, too, if you believe that you are subject to the dictates of another state to which your own government inclines and with which you morally cannot agree? And, finally, what happens if you believe that the state to which you are subject is inherently an immoral construct? These are, of course, profound personal dilemmas, but they can become collective drivers for the construction of an ideology of resistance and rejection if no alternative means of addressing the situation seem to exist.

This seems to be precisely the dilemma that terrorist groups in essence implicitly seek to articulate in their rhetoric, and why it is that their specific claims and concerns are also part of a wider class of political action. The essential point here is that action that appears intolerable to the victim is seen as acceptable, even necessary, to its perpetrator because of his or her perceptions of the moral status of the target. Thus the specific content of the rhetoric that movements use to justify what they do is, at this level, irrelevant, although it is of crucial relevance when we come to consider what the responses to it should be. In other words, the particular argument that such groups may have with states, be they Arab or Muslim states, or be they states in the West, is an example of a general phenomenon that has a long history and a universality that the proponents of the 'clash of civilizations' or the increasingly normative Western discourse do not recognize.

In essence, in all such situations the moral and ethical right of the state to act on behalf of its citizens is challenged by questioning its innate legitimacy, so that conflict between the state and non-state actors emerges. There is, of course, nothing particularly new about this; such conflicts have always existed and scholars of warfare have termed the resulting conflicts as 'asymmetric warfare' or 'low-intensity conflict'. Terrorism is undoubtedly within this class of conflict, alongside guerrilla warfare and national liberation struggles. It is, however, more than that, and has two unique characteristics that make it unmistakable despite the difficulty that specialists of the subject have had in trying to define it precisely.

The first is that, because the asymmetry is usually acute for terrorist groups, they make use of unbounded action. That is to say, the coercive aspect of their violence appears to be effectively indiscriminate, hence the victimization of civilians ostensibly unconnected with the cause of the violence itself. In fact, it can be argued that the violence used for coercive effect is not as indiscriminate as it is usually portrayed, but it is undoubtedly directed at persons who have no conceivable personal link with the grievance concerned. The classic response to this is to be found in the 'testament' of Emile Henry, an anarchist who bombed a café in Paris frequented by the French bourgeoisie in 1894 precisely because of their class identity.

His testament, in the form of a statement to the jury whose verdict enabled his sentence of death – he was executed in May 1894 – is a detailed and reasoned exposition of this argument.[28] Thus the apparently indiscriminate nature of terrorist violence in fact has certain specificity about it, for there are groups of people who are considered legitimate targets precisely because they are members of the group, not because of their individual actions. The principle, of course, can have much wider ramifications but, in the case of terrorism, it is an integral part of the process itself and, almost by definition, means that innocent individuals will be the intended targets and not simply unfortunate incidental victims.

This leads on to the second aspect of the phenomenon of terrorism that seems to be central. This is that there is really no such thing as a terrorist group, in the sense that this is its sole and bounded purpose. Terrorism is not an ideology in itself; it is simply a mode of action, designed to achieve a particular political result. In other words, there are only terrorist acts, not terrorist groups – although, of course, if the group solely or primarily engages in terrorist acts, we may be justified in referring to it as a terrorist group. This is important because, at some stage, those seeking to contain or eliminate the phenomenon have to address the reasons why terrorism occurs. If, for analytical purposes, the group's objectives are confused with the methods used to achieve them, then this process becomes extremely difficult, as the continuing crisis in Algeria demonstrates so clearly. Of course, common parlance does assimilate the group with the act, but this tends to create precisely the kind of absolutist dichotomy that makes effective analysis and resolution of the phenomenon so difficult.

Patterns of violence in the Maghreb

Thus, at the same time as defining the nature of opposition, it is essential to determine how, in practice, such movements emerge, and what their social and political effect may be. Despite current anxieties both within and outside the Maghreb, which tend to assume that the violence of the last two decades is exceptional, the simple fact is that, since independence, regimes in the region have frequently had to confront domestic violence that has often been extremist in nature. Thus the history of independent Algeria, for example, has been marked by a series of challenges to the state that reflect a widespread conviction that, in terms of the right to sovereignty earned through the war of independence, it has failed to achieve popular legitimacy, provoking as a result parallel experiences of social movements and violent exclusivist networks which latterly seek their own legitimacy through Islamic metaphors and paradigms. In Morocco, too, the monarchy has been shaken by threats to its own legitimacy, either from within the armed forces or through social movements seeking legitimacy through the role of Islam in the country's history and culture.

These challenges have been at their most explicit in the past two decades and have also sought frames of contention specifically rooted in Islam, so that it is the legitimacy of the state that has been challenged in each case, in terms of both its consonance with Islamic paradigms and its ability to provide social justice rather than just generating benefits for its political and economic elites. It is also alleged, by the states concerned and their Western backers, that radicalism and extremism are inextricably linked, so that the one is the progenitor of the other. This seems to be questionable, to say the least, as an examination of violence in North Africa demonstrates.[29] Thus, in Libya where the state implicitly lays claim to a hegemonic discourse of political supremacy legitimized by 'popular democracy', enshrined in the Jamahiriyah, that excludes any other political model, the late 1990s produced movements that directly challenged the Qadhafi regime, some of which were undoubtedly seeking to create a violent challenge to the regime; others were clearly not, but sought engagement with it instead.[30]

The violent movements, often derived from salafi-jihadism[31] and the experiences of Afghanistan, sought to replace the Jamahiri model despite its claimed consonance with Islamic principles. They were primarily located in Cyrenaica, a region noted for its hostility toward the tribally based and revolutionary formal political system. Although they operated in parallel with social movements within Libya derived from the Muslim Brotherhood and from secular paradigms which had long been in contention with the regime, there were no obvious antiphonal links between the two types of movement in terms of personnel or ideology.

The dominant extremist movement was the Libyan Islamic Fighting Group (LIFG – Jam'a Islamiyyah al-Muqatilah fi'l-Libiyya) which had grown out of the experience of war in Afghanistan against the Soviet Union in the 1980s. The LIFG, which rejected the transnational ideology of al-Qaeda, had moved, first to Sudan and then, in the late 1990s, into Cyrenaica itself. There, after several attempts on the life of the Libyan leader, it was eliminated from its two strongholds in Benghazi and Derna by the end of the decade and most of the group was imprisoned. Many of its members have now recanted and the LIFG has produced a refutation of its original salafi-jihadi doctrines as a token of recantation.

In Tunisia, on the other hand, social movements rooted in Islamic precepts and challenging the predominantly secular legacy of the political system developed by the then president, Habib Bourguiba, reached back to the 1970s and were centered around study groups at the Zitouna mosque in Tunis. They had all formally sought to share the political arena in order to contest the normative discourse of the state that had emerged at independence through established mechanisms of political engagement, despite the state's refusal to concede their right to do so. This had led to an increasingly bitter attempt to repress such movements, particularly the dominant one, led by Rachid Ghannouchi, the Mouvement de la Tendence Islamique (MTI).

In the wake of the replacement of Habib Bourguiba by Zine El-Abidine Ben Ali as president in 1987, the MTI had even sought, unsuccessfully, to establish itself as a political party, An-Nahda, within the formal political arena, despite its marginalization by the regime. By the start of the 1990s, however, the Ben Ali regime labeled it extremist and forced the party first underground and then into exile. In a series of trials in 1991 and 1992, the party was dismantled, with its leadership fleeing abroad in the wake of a torrent of accusations of its involvement in clandestine violent extremism. It has remained repressed in Tunisia ever since; yet, in reality, there has never been concrete objective evidence of its involvement with violence as an extremist organization, although the party has never hidden its determination to contest the legitimacy of the Ben Ali regime, but through peaceful, democratic engagement.

That is not to say, however, that small extremist movements did not emerge, particularly at the start of the 1990s. They, however, had no obvious links to the social movements that had preceded them, such as that which had metamorphosed into An-Nahda. Nor did such movements gain much purchase within the population in the decades that followed, even though violent evidence of them was to emerge in 2002, in the al-Qaeda-instigated bombing of the Djerba synagogue, and between the end of 2006 and the beginning of 2007, when the mysterious Soliman Group was alleged to have been planning attacks on foreign embassies in Tunis and to have been trained by extremists in Algeria. Such extremism seems to have been linked to far wider paradigms, reaching back to the experience of Afghanistan in the 1980s and Algeria in the 1990s, although the transnational dimension of violence that emerged there in the 1990s and in this decade also seems to have been absent, except for the Djerba synagogue bombing.

It is in Algeria that, superficially, the most obvious pattern of inter-linkage appeared to have taken place during the 1990s. Yet, early patterns of interaction between state and social movement had not resulted in significant terrorist violence. Thus the challenge to the state in 1963, just one year after Algerian independence, was a result of rejection by two of the *chefs historiques* of the Algerian revolution, Hocine Ait Ahmed and Mohamed Boudiaf, of the outcome of the coup organized by Ahmed Ben Bella, another *chef historique*, with the backing of the military commander, Houari Boumediènne. Boumediènne's own coup in 1965 was again really part of the argument within the elite in Algeria about the future of the revolutionary state, as was the unsuccessful coup organized against it by Colonel Zbiri in 1967.[32]

Even though the state that resulted from these events was generally construed as illegitimate, it was only in 1980 that a social movement deliberately and directly questioned its innate legitimacy in terms of political participation and historic legacy. The Berber rebellion in April of that year laid bare the nature of the Algerian state and ushered in the question of how the Algerian revolution had been sidelined by its aftermath, as sanctioned by the Algerian army. This was paralleled by an increasingly important but clandestine Islamist movement, based on the twin inspirations of the nineteenth century *salafist* movement and the *djazai'arist* arguments of Malek Bennabi.[33] Thereafter, challenges to the state were increasingly articulated in terms of the state's betrayal of the original promise of the Front de Libération Nationale (FLN) to embody the Islamic identity of Algerian society in its struggle for independence.

It was this failure that led, first, to Mustafa Bouyali's violent challenge to the Algerian state in the mid-1980s in the Blida region. Although it failed, with Bouyali himself being killed and his supporters being imprisoned, it underlined the growing sense of the way in which the state had failed to fulfill its own promises. This, in turn, set the scene for the events of October 1988 which forced the Bendjedid regime to concede a multiparty political system in which, eventually and against the regime's wishes, the Front Islamique du Salut (FIS) was to set the political agenda, not as a politico-religious alternative but as the embodiment of the true aspirations of the FLN at the end of the Algerian war for independence – hence the slogan, 'Le FIS est le fils de l'FLN.'

The banning of the FIS in 1992, after all, led directly to the appalling violence of the Algerian civil war between 1992 and 1999. There also seems to be little doubt that both the FIS itself and its successors in the Armée Islamique du Salut (AIS) and the GIA or in today's Groupe Salafiste du Predication et du Combat (GSPC), transformed since September 2006 into al-Qaeda in the Islamic Maghreb (AQIM) represent Islamic social movements and their extremist counterparts. That is, after all, the narrative upon which the Algerian government has based its own counter-insurgency strategies and that has been largely accepted in Europe since the start of this decade, as Europe itself securitizes its own relationship with its Mediterranean periphery.

Yet it is by no means clear that these assumed linkages operate or that the primary motivation for the decade-long crisis in Algeria was rooted in an Islamic contestation of the state or in a violent confrontation rooted in Islamic precept to replace it. This is not to deny that there was an attempt to challenge the Algerian regime's self-definition at the end of the 1980s and the beginning of the 1990s, nor that the state's repression of such a movement led to an extremely bloody confrontation by groups seeking to replace the state structures upon which it was based, or even that such initiatives sought legitimization through recourse to Islamic paradigms. It is, however, to question whether the movements were interlinked and antiphonal in nature, in that the suppression of the one led to the emergence of the other, and to raise the issue of what the real justifications argued for such movements really were.

Behind the formal Islamist frames of the FIS, for example, lay a very different narrative, as mentioned above, one of the failure of the Algerian revolution to honor the promises made during the revolution itself. In other words, the legitimacy of the social movement from which the FIS emerged was based as much on this sense of a revolution betrayed as it was on the Islamic rhetoric through which it was expressed. And it was to this that the institutions of the Algerian state reacted when, in 1991, they aborted the electoral process that the FIS was poised to win. The FIS itself had always endorsed political engagement and, despite its obvious origins in the long salafist traditions that had informed the political process throughout the long years of colonialism throughout North Africa, had also a democratic tradition that excluded it, as a movement, from endorsing a violent alternative of confronting the state rather than contesting its political behavior.

Even the violent movements that did emerge betrayed this political bifurcation, for the AIS really sought to force the Algerian state to reinstate the formal political process that it itself had interrupted in the 1992 coup. Eventually, when it could not do so, it compounded with the state and withdrew from the contest in October 1997. The tradition of violent confrontation with the state, with the explicit intention of destroying it and replacing it with an intolerant alternative based on a very specific interpretation of Islamic constitutional doctrine, was reserved for the collection of autonomous groups within the coalition known as the GIA.[34] Yet, even here, it was not always clear to what extent the normative objectives reflected the real objectives of these movements, as criminality partnered religious conviction and as counter-insurgency techniques became interspersed with extremist violence.[35] Nor was there significant inter-linkage in terms of chronology, ideology or personnel with the FIS which had preceded them.

This is not to deny, of course, that the rhetoric of such movements did not increasingly reflect Islamist paradigms as time passed. But it does raise the question of the extent to which origins of their political action were solely a product of such ideologies and to what extent such justifications were adopted to legitimize a much more classical kind of struggle against what was perceived as a repressive state, a struggle which would have occurred whether the Islamist trope for political action had emerged or not. Even the activities of the GSPC–AQIM today fall within the same strictures. And it needs to be remembered that the extent to which 'al-Qaeda' has become a branding that legitimizes political violence parallels, in much the same way, what occurred with the Marxism–Leninism of the New Left in the 1960s and 1970s.

In Morocco, the direct causality implied by the conventional assumption that Islamic social movements inevitably generate Islamist violence appears to be even more obscure. One reason for this is the peculiar relationship of the institution at the core of the Moroccan state, the monarchy, to the control of public space. It is of course the case that normative assumptions about the institutions of the state and the relationship of the state to the public arena – in which it exercises its monopoly of legitimate violence – are suffused throughout the Islamic world with presuppositions about the Islamic vision of social and political order at both the normative and the demotic levels.

However, in Morocco, the engagement of the central institutions of the state in this domain are based on the conscious assumption that such public space is not merely conditioned by Islamic precept but is sacralized by the nature of the institution itself, for the monarchy is also a caliphate and, as such, can claim a peculiar, specific and absolute justification for its right to condition public debate and action, even as it formally encourages political participation. Thus movements that wish to contest the hegemonic discourse of the state must also contest the monarchy itself, as Abdeslam Yacine did in 1974.[36] This has meant that it has been particularly difficult for social movements of contestation based on Islamic precept to find a purchase within the Moroccan body politic. One consequence of this has been the tendency for challenges to the state, whether secular or religious in inspiration, to have been violent, for contestation of the control of the public space has always been trumped by the monarchy's absolute claim of moral and political right.

Another consequence has been the ability of the state to co-opt groups normatively opposed to it or to marginalize those groups that refuse to be co-opted. Thus the violent Shabiba Islamiyya of the 1960s and 1970s was either forced into exile or co-opted to re-emerge as a legitimate political party in the 1990s – the Parti de Justice et du Développement (PJD). On the other hand, a movement that did contest the legitimacy of the king's control of the public space, 'Adl wa Ihsan, and whose leader, Abdeslam Yacine, committed the egregious offence in the 1970s of challenging the king's right to dominate the sacralized public arena, has always rejected co-option and is denied political legitimacy in consequence.

It is only in the last decade, starting with the violent incidents in Casablanca in May 2003, that the moral and religious status of the Moroccan state has been openly challenged through violence, derived from salafi-jihadi traditions. The subsequent discovery of clandestine networks of violent opposition in Casablanca, Fez and Tangier, the rumors of discrete groups training in the Middle Atlas and the evidence of links abroad, into Europe – the Madrid bombings and the Belliraj conspiracy, often intermixed with criminal networks as well – and elsewhere seem to recall the violent rejection of the Moroccan state in the 1960s and 1970s.[37]

Yet there has been no evidence of a linkage between such political extremism and the social movements that have increasingly become integral features of the formal Moroccan political scene. And, furthermore, these Islamic social movements, one co-opted and the other still outside formal political engagement, have moved further and further away from the Islamic roots and more and more into political engagement revolving around political paradigms involving democracy and human rights. In other words, here there seems to be a complete split between social movement and political violence. Moreover, it seems that the inspiration for the latter is rooted outside the Moroccan political tradition, in the transnational ideology of salafi-jihadism and in the experience of emigration to Europe.

Transnational links and securitization

This conclusion could apply with equal force to the other countries of the Maghreb for, since 2003, there has been an increasing acceptance within the international community that an al-Qaeda presence has developed in the Sahel and is linked into North Africa. It is a claim that has long been argued by North African states who insist that the domestic violence from which they have suffered is part of a transnational pattern involving networks stretching from Afghanistan into their domestic arenas. They have been very resentful of the fact that, until 2001, European states had not generally been prepared to take their claims seriously. This has now changed, although it is debatable that the new assumptions about transnational violence are any more accurate than were the original ones, certainly as far as North Africa is concerned.[38]

It has long been recognized that the extremist networks in North Africa share a common exclusivist ideology that is related to salafi-jihadism.[39] It has also been the case that claims have emerged in the past five years of the appearance of links between indigenous North African networks and the transnational structures of violence associated with al-Qaeda and associated groups. These, if true, would imply that there has also been an ideological shift from the 'near enemy' to the 'far enemy' as well.[40] One aspect of this has been repeated claims in Europe of support networks there providing logistical and financial support for extremist groups in North Africa.

This was a pattern that was established during the Algerian war for independence when the FLN created elaborate networks amongst migrant workers in France and used them to raise financial support for the struggle in Algeria itself. It also occurred with the FIS when a network amongst migrants, called the Fédération des Algériens en France (FAF), was created in Europe in the 1990s and was openly sympathetic to the FIS until it was dismantled by the French authorities. The French authorities suspected it of being linked to GIA networks in France that were engaged in violence, although many of these were later shown to have been mobilized by the Algerian security services as a counter-terrorist operation.

Other such networks in France and elsewhere in Europe were essentially imitative of the violent struggle in Algeria but autonomous from it. This was the case with the Chasse-sur-Rhône group which was dismantled in 1995 after a series of bombings on the RER rapid-transit system in Paris. It was also true of the group that carried out a spree of bombings and bank robberies in Morocco in the previous year, culminating in the shooting of two Spanish tourists in a hotel in Marrakesh. Such groups were recruited from amongst the alienated youth of the second generation of North African migrants in Europe, but were not directly linked to the groups inside North Africa itself.[41] Similar patterns have been repeated in the first decade of the twenty-first century, only this time basing themselves on the example of al-Qaeda. They were often accused by European security authorities of actually being linked to the parent organization, although the links frequently seemed tenuous and were often only virtual in nature.

One reason for such assumptions resided in the increasing homogenization of the ideological framing used to justify such actions. This, in turn, reflected an ever-increasing facility of access as salafi-jihadism exploited the Internet and satellite television, thus becoming instantly available to the new generation sensitized toward it, not only in Europe but also in North Africa. Its members were predisposed toward the explanations it offered for their own situations in Europe or North Africa, and for the crisis faced in the Middle Eastern region by the growing polarization of Muslim opinion in the aftermath of the invasion of Iraq in 2003 by Western forces led by the United States. This has produced a series of reactions, ranging from spontaneous and organized recruitment to wage jihad in Iraq[42] to recruitment into activist national networks such as the GSPC in Algeria.

Necessarily, such developments have an implication inside North Africa itself. It has been argued that the GSPC in Algeria has been undergoing an evolution in terms of its recruiting base in 2007, in that it has begun to seek adherents from a new youthful generation sensitized by the Internet. Thus, the bombings of the prime minister's offices and the ministry of the interior in Algiers on 11 April 2007 were said to have been carried out by representatives of urban youth, as was a subsequent bombing of a police station. These attacks differed from their predecessors in that they involved suicide bombers and urban youth recruited from the petty bourgeoisie in Algiers. As such, they represented a new, global threat to established government and indicated the way in which Algerian youth was being shaped by new forces of information and radicalization.

Whether or not this is a new trend is not fully clear, but it was also notable in Casablanca in Morocco in violent incidents that occurred in early March 2007, compared with the modus operandi in 2003. However, subsequent incidents in both Morocco and Algeria did not seem to demonstrate that this trend is coming to dominate the security scene, despite claims by both insurgent groups and government that this was the case. It remains to be seen to what extent they are the forerunners of a new wave of jihadi protest predicated upon youth and the Internet as a new virtual community of violence.

Similar uncertainty clouds the reality of alleged threats of transnational violence replacing the older patterns of national violence through the direct incorporation of activist networks in North Africa into the al-Qaeda fold. These claims go back to the start of this decade and the attacks upon New York and Washington on 11 September 2001. Shortly after these events, the United States, with the encouragement of the Algerian government – which, like the Libyan government, had hurried to provide information on known extremists to the Bush administration – began to investigate the potential of the Sahel and Saharan regions as possible al-Qaeda redoubts for the future. Such suspicions were given substance by the kidnappings of 33 European tourists in the Sahara in the first quarter of 2003. The tourists were eventually freed in mid-year, partly by military action and partly by negotiation and the payment of a ransom.

The incident, however, gave substance to Algerian claims and American suspicions of the growth of transnational terrorism, suspicions that were eagerly fanned by Algeria. It also fitted within the pan-Sahelian Initiative, an American program of aid and support for counter-terrorism activities in Mali, Mauritania, Chad and Niger that had started with $125 million over a five-year period and which was later to develop into the Trans-Saharan Counter-Terrorism Initiative, backed by a new military command for Africa, Africom, funded at $500 million over six years and extended to include Algeria, Nigeria, Senegal and Morocco within its purview. In fact, the distinction between such transnational violence and the activities of local smuggling networks in the Sahara was extremely difficult to make, as a subsequent kidnapping of two Austrian tourists in February 2008 and another of a small group of tourists attending a Touareg music festival in Mali in late 2008 were to make clear.[43] The conclusion must therefore be that the transnational dimension of its activities, like those of other groups within North Africa, is mere rhetoric and its arena remains substantially national in scope.

Yet the argument of North African states – that they are the victims of a transnational violent agenda, not the targets of domestic challenge and asymmetric warfare – continue to hold sway, particularly in Europe. The issue here is important because, certainly since 2001 and in some cases long before, European states have feared spill-over effects from North Africa, typified by their concerns over migration. Indeed, the first real example of a European Union foreign-policy initiative – only possible after the Maastricht Treaty went into operation in 1993, thereby creating the Common Foreign and Security Policy (CFSP) mechanism – was the Euro-Mediterranean Partnership, announced in Barcelona in 1995. Although the formal objective of the policy was to render inward migration into Europe from North Africa unnecessary by creating a 'zone of share peace, stability and prosperity', it also contained measures designed to advance the Union's Justice and Home Affairs agenda by engaging South Mediterranean states, through a process of externalization,[44] in security measures, designed to improve Europe's domestic security.[45]

This was all very well, but North African states – in the wake of the outbreak of the Algerian civil war – felt the bargain was very one-sided, for European states did not treat their concerns or arguments about asymmetric violence with much attention. Violence began to spill over into Morocco in 1994 and Libya in 1996, and there was a sudden rise in refugee and migrant flows to Europe which thereby unwittingly provided dissidents with sanctuary. This was to test the relevance of Europe's normative power as Southern governments began to call for cooperation over securitizing such flows as an extension of their domestic struggles.[46] Dissidents, they claimed, were using Europe as a sanctuary because of Europe's security laxity – even as it sought to apply normative values to deal with such security issues at their source in the South. It was only after the events in New York and Washington in 2001 that this began to rapidly change.

The beginnings of the change had predated these events (but was dramatically accelerated because of them) for a new security agenda was introduced into the Barcelona Process at the end of the 1990s as concerns about transnational violence began to grow. The new agenda involved migration directly and was related to both illegal migration and the phenomenon that was to be increasingly associated with it, transnational violence. In the end, it was to overshadow the normative objectives of the Barcelona Process. Indeed, ultimately, the exercise of the Union's normative power, together with the new norms it had meant to introduce – norms of governance and human rights – were not only overshadowed but seen, in retrospect, to have been consciously neglected as bilateral interests increasingly took precedence over the supranational objectives of the European Union, even if they continued to pay rhetorical loyalty to its normative principles.

In fact, when circumstances rendered security concerns the dominant issue, normative objectives were either marginalized or mobilized as part of the subsequent securitization process. They were mobilized to stigmatize political attitudes and behavior the Union considered antithetical to its security interests – an attitude often enthusiastically endorsed by its Southern partners. They were marginalized whenever they threatened to interfere with the prosecution of the new security agenda, again often with the encouragement of partner-states. The irony is that, through this process of securitization of normative policy, the object to which policy had originally been directed – the partner-states as the source of migration and, latterly, political violence – now became the partner in policy articulation. This has turned out to be a case of 'externalization-in-reverse', for the partner states had long insisted on the dangers of transnational terrorism as an emanation of the violence they claimed was inherent in political Islam. It was this that the EU had claimed could be marginalized and eliminated if only the Union's normative objectives were internalized into the political structures and behaviors of its Southern partners, and it was this that Europe – both the European Union and its member states – now abandoned as, throughout the first decade of the twenty-first century, they adopted the North African discourse of transnational violence and political Islam.

Notes

1 Radicalism here is seen as a process of contention of the hegemonic discourse of the controlling institutions of a state. It is usually expressed through a social movement. Extremism is the attempt to challenge and, if possible, replace the state itself through violence. Islamism refers to the political and/or social manipulation of Islamic concepts to establish a rhetorical or ideological tool through which to challenge established institutions.

2 The countries of Libya, Tunisia, Algeria, Morocco and Mauritania. The term has been used interchangeably with 'North Africa' which normally includes Egypt as well.

3 S. Tarrow, *Power in Movement: Social Movements and Contentious Politics* (Cambridge: Cambridge University Press, 2008), p. 10.

4 A. Spiegel, *Islamist Pluralism: Youth, Activism and the State in Morocco*, unpublished PhD (Oxford University, 2009).

5 Q. Wictorowicz (ed.), *Islamic Activism: A Social Movement Theory Approach* (Bloomington: Indiana University Press, 2004), p. 10.

6 Ibid., p. 16. This would also include the catchphrase, 'Islam is the solution' as a mechanism for rejecting ideological alternatives whether seen as secularist or as foreign cultural or political imports.

 7 G. Joffé, 'Politics in the Muslim World: Morocco, Iran and Indonesia', in L. Graham (ed.), *The Politics of Governing: A Comparative Introduction* (Washington, DC: QC Press, 2006).

 8 M. Sageman, *Understanding Terror Networks* (Philadelphia: University of Pennsylvania Press, 2004), p. 158.

 9 Ibid., p. 168. Sageman defines cliques as 'dense networks of nodes, each connected to every other', a situation which, at the extreme, would create social implosion as there could be no external links. He invokes 'brokers' as individuals mediating between cliques and networks who provide weak links outside the clique – a crucial factor for him in the construction of networks of networks that make up the modern transnational salafi-jihadi movement.

10 Ibid., pp. 69–95.

11 Ibid., pp. 127–134.

12 Ibid., pp. 152–153.

13 Ibid., p. 149.

14 Transnational social movements are 'mobilized groups recruiting across borders engaged in sustained contentious interaction with power holders in which at least one state is either a target or a participant' (S. Tarrow, 'Beyond Globalization: Why Creating Transnational Social Movements is So Hard and When is it Most Likely to Happen?'). The paper was originally published in 1999 in the *Global Solidarity Dialogue*. This is the version that has been consulted here: www.antenna.nl/~waterman/tarrow.html.

15 M.A. Hafez, 'From Marginalisation to Massacres: A Political Process Explanation of GIA Violence in Algeria', in Wiktorowicz (ed.), *Islamic Activism*, p. 41.

16 Hafez, 'From Marginalisation to Massacre', pp. 38–44.

17 'Condensed symbols of meaning that fashion shared understandings of the insurgent's world to legitimate and to motivate collective action' (Hafez, 'From Marginalisation to Massacres', p. 38).

18 D. Della Porta, *Social Movements, Political Violence and the State: A Comparative Analysis of Italy and Germany* (Cambridge: Cambridge University Press, 1995), p. 12.

19 V. Jabri, *Discourses of Violence: Conflict Analysis Reconsidered* (Manchester: University of Manchester Press, 1996), p. 7.

20 M. Crenshaw, 'The Effectiveness of Terrorism in the Algerian War', in M. Crenshaw (ed.), *Terrorism in Context* (College Park: University of Pennsylvania Press, 1995), pp. 447, 483–484.

21 'Jahiliyya' (state of ignorance) is the term conventionally used to describe the situation in the Arabian peninsula before the Islamic revelation, but it has been adopted by contemporary Islamists to describe the apparent abandonment of Islamic doctrine and praxis by contemporary Muslim society – a situation which they regard as culpable because this is done, not through ignorance as was originally the case, but with the full knowledge of the Islamic revelation available to the Muslim world.

22 P. Wilkinson, *Terrorism and the Liberal State* (London: Macmillan, 1986, 2nd edition), p. 51.

23 Effectively the British legal definition up to the 2000 Terrorism Act.

24 S.P. Huntington, 'The Clash of Civilizations?', *Foreign Affairs*, 72:3 (1993), pp. 22–49.

25 This refers not only to the concept of the nation-state as the political embodiment of the 'imagined community' of the nation but also to the idea of the legal personality of a state as embodied in the 1933 Montevideo Convention.

26 M. Weber, 'Politik als Beruf', in *Gesammelte Politische Schriften* (Munich, 1921), p. 397.

27 G.W.F. Hegel, *Elements of the Philosophy of Right* (Cambridge: Cambridge University Press, 1821, 1991), p. 275.

28 http://recollectionbooks.com/bleed/AnarchistTimeline2.htm or http://recollectionbooks.com/bleed/0212.htm.

29 This is described in detail in 'Informal Networks in North Africa', in D.M. Jones, A. Lane and P. Schulte (eds.), *Terrorism, Security and the Power of Informal Networks* (Cheltenham: Edward Elgar, 2009).

30 A. Pargeter, 'Qadhafi and Political Islam in Libya', in D. Vandewalle (ed.), *Libya Since 1969: Qadhafi's Revolution Revisited* (London: Palgrave-Macmillan, 2008), pp. 83–104.

31 The term denotes groups and networks that combine the literalist practices of the neo-salafi movement which refer to Islamic traditions of the Rashidun period with a modernized and activist interpretation of jihad as first practiced in Afghanistan and derived from the writings of Abdullah Azzam, Muhammad Faraj and, behind them, Ibn Taymiyya. See A. Azzam (ed.), *In Defence of Muslim Lands*, www.religioscope.com/info/doc/jihad/azzam and *Join the Caravan*, www.islamistwatch.org/texts/azzam/caravan/part1.html; M.A. Faraj, *The Absent Obligation* (Birmingham: Maktabah al-Ansaar Publications, trans. 2000).

32 M. Harbi, *Les archives de la Révolution Algérienne* (Paris: Editions Jeune Afrique, 1981), pp. 352–353.

33 The salafist movement, inspired by Jamal al-Afghani in the 1860s and propagated throughout North Africa by Muhammad 'Abuh at the turn of the nineteenth and twentieth centuries, argued that the Islamic tradition, especially those of the Rashidun period, contained what was necessary for the Islamic world to generate political, social and technological dynamism to parallel that of post-Industrial Revolution Europe. It had been the inspiration, in the 1930s, for the Association des Ulemas Algerians, which rejected the colonial vision of Algeria's integration and assimilation into France. This tradition of salafism has nothing to do with the neo-salafism of the 1980s and 1990s, although the latter was to inform the extremist movements that did emerge in Algeria. Malek Bennabi, a social and political analyst of the early years of independent Algeria, proposed that Algeria's Islamic identity and traditions should be the basis for the construction of a modernist society and polity based on political plurality and democratic principle. See S.J. Walsh, 'Killing post-Almohade Man: Malek Bennabi, Algerian Islamism and the Search for a Liberal Governance', *Journal of North African Studies*, 12:2 (2007), pp. 235–254.

34 The best source for this is B. Izel, J.S. Wafa and W. Isaac, 'What is the GIA?', in Y. Bedjaoui, A. Aroua and M. Ait-Larbi (eds.), *An Inquiry into the Algerian Massacres* (Geneva: Hoggar Books, 1999).

35 L. Martinez, *The Algerian Civil War 1990–1998* (London: Hurst and Co., 2000), pp. 119–146.

36 A. Yacine, *al-Islam aw't-Tufan: Risala Maftuha ila Malik al-Maghreb* (Salé, Morocco, 1974).

37 A. Pargeter, 'The Islamist Movement in Morocco', *Terrorism Monitor*, 3:10 (Jamestown Foundation, 19 May 2005).

38 E.G.H. Joffé, 'The European Union, Democracy and Counter-Terrorism in the Maghreb', *Journal of Common Market Studies*, 46:1 (2008), pp. 147–171.

39 Wiktorowicz, *Islamic Activism*.

40 The 'near enemy' are national governments in the Middle East and North Africa against which such groups operate within their own national arenas; the 'far enemy' are their Western backers in Europe and, particularly, the United States. The terminology is Muhammad Faraj's, and is discussed in detail by F. Gerges, *The Far Enemy: Why Jihad Went Global* (Cambridge: Cambridge University Press, 2005).

41 This alienation is typified by the comments of Khalid Kelkal, a leading member of the Chasse sur Rhône group. See D. Loch, 'Moi, Khalid Kelkal', *Le Monde*, 7 October 1995. The interview had been recorded on 3 October 1992.

42 The Algerian press, for example, has repeatedly reported on recruitment networks being dismantled, particularly in El-Oued, in the past year. That such networks tend to be spontaneous is revealed not only by press reports but by an interesting interview on Al-Jazeera in January 2008. See www.memritv.org/clip/en/1659.htm.

43 J. Keenan, 'Waging War on Terror: The Implications of America's New Imperialism for Saharan peoples', *Journal of North African Studies*, 10:3–4 (2005), pp. 619–647.

44 P.C. Schmitter, 'Three Neofunctional Hypotheses About International Integration', *International Organisation*, 23:1 (1969), pp. 161–166.

45 S. Lavenex, 'EU External Governance in "wider Europe"', *Journal of European Public Policy*, 11:4 (2004), pp. 680–700.

46 The term 'securitization', in this context, is taken to mean the process by which a policy tool or instrument becomes 'an instrument which, by its very nature or by its very functioning, transforms the entity … it processes into a threat' (T. Balzacq, 'The Policy Tools of Securitisation: Information Exchange, EU Foreign and Interior Policies', *Journal of Common Market Studies*, 46:1 (2008), pp. 75–100).

4 Strategic confusion

America's conflicting strategies and the war on terrorism

David Hastings Dunn and Oz Hassan

The unprecedented controversy generated by the foreign policy of George W. Bush has not ended with the President's return to Texas. Indeed, the battle to justify and vindicate his policies and to see their continuation under the new administration continues to animate the American foreign-policy debate. Through both the publication of documents professing *A Charge Kept* and concerted appearances by former Vice President Richard Cheney declaring that American should continue with Bush's War on Terror, the controversial goals, methods and policies of the Bush years remain central to the American debate on how it should relate to the world and the threats it faces. While President Obama has tried to move the country and the debate on, for President Bush's supporters any such change of course would not only demonstrate a lack of US will but would catastrophically endanger the American people.

One of the defining features of the narrative espoused by proponents of the Bush administration's foreign policy is that it represents the War on Terror as possessing a homogenous core. What President Bush termed the 'War on Terror' is therefore being framed as if there is an instruction sheet from which a route can in fact be mapped out. This chapter seeks to demonstrate that this is not the case. Rather, the 'war on terrorism' was the product of a remarkably dynamic process, which evolved rapidly after 11 September 2001 and continued to develop well into the Bush administration's second term in office. In its post-9/11 policies, the administration showed a remarkable tendency to re-evaluate definitions of what constituted a threat, and what response was required to deal with it. As a result, in analyzing Washington's response to the 9/11 attacks it is possible to identify three distinct strategies pursued by the administration:

Strategy One: The War of Terrorism as counter-terrorism.
Strategy Two: As pre-emption and pre-eminence.
Strategy Three: The 'Freedom Agenda' pertaining to democratic imperialism.

Notably, while these three strategies were distinctive in their policy focus, each new strategy represented an additional focus and response rather than a replacement policy. With each accumulative strategy building upon the one that preceded it, the conceptualization of the War on Terror was broadened, directly impacting on perceptions of how it should be fought. This point is of critical importance for understanding the Bush legacy, not least because it problematizes the notion of the War on Terror being based on a single unified strategy. This chapter sets out how and why these different approaches were adopted, and shows how Washington's conceptualization of the problem developed as a response both to events and its own internal policy processes. What is evident from such an analysis is that all three strategies were to some extent internally contradictory, while also contradicting one another.

To structure this analysis and demonstrate its key insights, it is useful to apply a series of questions to each of the three strategies;

1   'Who attacked our country'?[1] i.e. who are the enemy?
2   'Why do they hate us?' i.e. what is their motivation/why did they do it?
3   'How will we fight and win this war?' i.e. how shall we respond?

These three questions were originally articulated by President Bush in an address to a Joint Session of Congress and the American people on 20 September 2001. During this address the administration sought to answer its own questions both rhetorically and in policy terms. In setting out both these questions and an initial set of answers, the White House also provided a useful mechanism by which to evaluate the way in which the war on terrorism evolved, both rhetorically and substantively. By doing this it is clear that distinctive strategies were adopted.

Strategy One: countering terror and ridding the world of 'evil'

The initial response to the attacks of 11 September 2001 was rapidly decided. Without knowing who had in fact perpetrated the attacks, President Bush, on board Air Force One, told the Vice President, 'We're at war.'[2] In the days following the attacks, this was to become the dominant framing for the administration's construction of the events, as the President openly declared that 'The deliberate and deadly attacks which were carried out yesterday against our country were *more than acts of terror. They were acts of war.*'[3] Yet, in constructing a war the President was forced to answer a larger series of questions about the nature of that 'war'. A larger narrative had to be constructed, that 'grasped' together and integrated into a whole scattered events, therefore rendering them intelligible. It was explicitly to this task that the Bush administration turned to on 20 September 2001 as they began answering three distinct questions:

1   Who are the enemy? The administration's answer to this question was that the enemy was both terrorists and governments that support them:

> Our enemy is a radical network of terrorists, and every government that supports them.... Our war on terror begins with al-Qaeda, but it does not end there. It will not end until every terrorist group of global reach has been found, stopped and defeated.

2　Why do they hate us? In the initial aftermath of the attacks, the enemy was simplistically characterized as 'evil'. Indeed, this was a theme that Bush would make his own, especially in his less-scripted explanations of the attacks. On the night of the attacks, for example, his first response was that 'Today, our nation saw evil'.[4] Three days later, Bush expressed similar sentiments, 'Our responsibility to history is clear: to answer these attacks and rid the world of evil.'[5] Notably when Bush referred to the enemy as 'evil', this was more than just a term of strong disapproval. Rather, an explicitly ontological claim was being made which reflected Bush's assertion that 'We know that *evil is real*, but good will prevail against it'.[6] Evil in this context was portrayed as part of the moral furniture of the world, and was very much a component of the President's religiosity.

　　Characterizing the enemy in simplistic binaries also allowed the Bush administration to claim that the enemy was motivated by an atavistic rejection of modernity. The administration seamlessly transformed claims that 'Freedom and fear, justice and cruelty have always been at war, and we know that God is not neutral between them', to larger claims that

They hate what we see right here in this chamber [the US Capitol Building] – a democratically elected government.... They hate our freedoms – our freedom of religion, our freedom of speech, our freedom to vote and assemble and disagree with each other.... These terrorists kill not merely to end lives, but to disrupt and end a way of life.... They are the heirs of all the murderous ideologies of the twentieth century. By sacrificing human life to serve their radical visions – by abandoning every value except the will to power – they follow in the path of fascism, and Nazism, and totalitarianism.[7]

In sum, the administration's answer, explaining why the United States was attacked, was that they are evil, they hate our freedom, and they want to destroy us. Such an answer was firmly rooted in the identity of the attackers constructed by the Bush administration, which portrayed the threat as apolitical, even pre-political or pre-modern.

3　How to respond? Given the above, the administration's response was to 'bring our enemies to justice or bring justice to our enemies'.[8] This would be achieved by directing 'every resource at our command – every means of diplomacy, every instrument of law enforcement, every financial influence, and every necessary weapon of war – to the disruption and defeat of the global terror network.' And, as part of that process, 'we will pursue nations that provide aid or safe haven to terrorism ... any nation that continues to harbor or support terrorism will be regarded by the United States as a hostile regime.' The US response can be summarized as a desire to eliminate al-Qaeda, its associates and supporters since they were beyond negotiation or accommodation. As Bush remarked, 'I want justice. There's an old poster out west, as I recall, that said, "Wanted: Dead or Alive."'[9]

Strategy One in practice: the war on terrorism as counter-terrorism

The way in which the administration conceptualized the threat, as articulated by the answers to its own questions, signaled how US foreign policy would respond in the immediate aftermath of the 9/11 attacks. The model adopted for this strategy was traditional counter-terrorism techniques plus a policy focus on Afghanistan where the preferred approach was regime change. In practice, this meant a policy response typical in many ways to that which followed previous terrorist attacks: the identification and pursuit of the suspects internally and externally through the criminal-justice system, with the clear indication that if they lay beyond national and international legal reach then a military response could be expected. The level of the response, however, was different. There was an enormous effort to interdict and dismantle the financial side of the terrorist operation.[10] Groups and individuals also had their assets frozen. Al-Qaeda suspects and supporters were rounded up on a global scale (over 3,000 in number) and intelligence agencies worldwide were redirected toward the new threat priority.

The Bush administration also desired an approach that went beyond the typical pattern of responses that had characterized the 1990s. Frustrated at the way that terrorist attacks had been dealt with in the past, Bush had long made it clear that he wanted a more robust response to terrorism, stating, 'I'm tired of swatting flies. I'm tired of playing defense. I want to play offence. I want to take the fight to the enemy.'[11] What this meant in practice was a war on many fronts pursuing al-Qaeda and its associates using traditional instruments of American statecraft, diplomacy, aid packages, intelligence work, collaboration between traditional law-enforcement agencies on an international scale, and renewed efforts and concerns at counter-proliferation. Bush wanted a response that went beyond treating the acts as criminal. Consequently, the administration responded as if the attacks were an act of war, and deployed the full panoply of the national security establishment.

For an administration that had initially signaled the limits of America's international involvement, the events of 9/11 prompted a reordering of US international engagements. As one administration official observed, in the wake of 9/11, 'nothing now is in the category of unimportant. Small countries, failing states, all become crucial in the war against terror.'[12] The nature of the threat was global, and the government would need to enlist the entire international community in its fight to eradicate it. Thus, Congress was quick to vote its annual dues to the UN while the administration sought a UN Security Council Resolution condemning the attacks on the US. While the US became more internationally engaged, it did not, as many expected, become more multilateral in its approach. While it increased its involvement on the world stage, it was very clear that this was to be on its own terms. This was nowhere more apparent than in President Bush's often repeated statement in the immediate aftermath of the attacks that 'You are either with us or you are with the terrorists.'[13]

This bifurcated approach meant a shift in relations with certain key states, most notably Russia, China and Pakistan. While these relationships had formally been strained by concerns over regional issues, human rights and political freedoms, these were subordinated as the global war on terrorism became the overarching rationale in US foreign policy. Accordingly, Moscow's policy toward Chechnya was both downgraded as an issue and recast as part of the global problem of international terrorism. Additionally, the US decision to support China's branding of the East Turkestan Islamic Movement as a terrorist group was a move designed to establish reciprocal support in the war against terrorism.[14] In return for this support, Washington showed a new attitude toward China's hostility toward democracy in Hong Kong and Taiwan, and the deterioration of Russian democracy and free media.[15] Furthermore, the most dramatic bilateral transformation was evident in US–Pakistan relations, as the Bush administration chose to put aside concerns over proliferation, Kashmir, democracy and human rights, and embrace the Musharraf regime. This was in stark contrast to the 1990s, when Pakistan was the target of US economic sanctions and diplomatic censure, especially after it exploded a nuclear device in 1998. However, under the rubric of more pressing strategic goals of the War on Terror, Pakistan was to become one of the US's most important partners in its new campaign. In the words of Thomas Carothers, 'The cold shoulder that Washington turned toward General Pervez Musharraf after he seized power in 1999 has been replaced by a bear hug.'[16] Accordingly, by March 2004 the Bush administration granted Pakistan 'Major Non-NATO ally' status.[17]

The pattern of prioritizing more immediate interests, perceived through the original construction of the War on Terror, was indicative of the wider counter-terror strategy. In Uzbekistan and Kyrgyzstan, the establishment of US airbases took priority over concerns about human-rights abuses and political freedoms.[18] In the Philippines and in Indonesia, differences over human rights were controversially set aside and training missions established between local armies and the US military.[19] In the Middle East and North Africa, the administration forged more intimate ties with regimes in the region such as Tunisia and Algeria. In its support for anti-terrorism measures, the US has found itself condoning measures that suppress freedom of expression in those countries.[20] Indeed, a 2003 report for the United Nations Development Program was critical of the US-led War on Terror for 'giving ruling regimes in some Arab countries spurious justification for curbing freedom'.[21] What was true for Arab states was also true for America's approach toward Israel. Although Washington recognized the need to make progress on the Israeli–Palestinian issue, the logic of its own position meant that it was also loathe to condemn Israel for pursuing its own fight in the 'war against terrorism'. Thus, although Israeli military incursions into the Palestinian territories and its policy of assassinating the leadership of Islamic terrorist organizations was clearly stoking support for such radical Islamic groups, little was done to bring an end to these actions. Similarly, while the Bush administration announced its support for the creation of an independent Palestinian state and a renewal of the Middle East peace process, they were accompanied by a call for a new Palestinian leadership 'not compromised by terror'.[22] It was an approach that showed the limits of the Bush administration's *realpolitik* policy. While it was willing to compromise on many issues and interests in many of its international engagements, its approach to the war on terrorism was pursued in practice with as little nuance as the administration's 'with us or against us' rhetoric.

Identifying 'terrorism' as the enemy meant that the 'administration failed to differentiate between tactics and objectives'.[23] Instead, the administration pursued what Elliot A. Cohen referred to as the '9/11 rules', in which the dichotomous declaration that you are either 'with us or against us' led the administration to 'help our friends, punish those who impede us, and annihilate those who attack us'.[24] This level of parsimony, however, created serious complications in the task of dealing with al-Qaeda. In adopting this approach, it multiplied the number of its foes and unnecessarily limited the number of allies it could use in its fight against al-Qaeda. Such an inflexible approach failed to identify priorities, while treating states as uncomplicated unitary actors. Without nuance in the model, Iran was seen as the enemy due to its pro-Hezbollah position, despite being anti-al-Qaeda. Conversely, Israel was seen as an ally, and therefore the US failed to criticize it for its approach to the Palestinian territories. The approach failed to take account of the fact that winning the support of a government and condoning its authoritarian tactics may be counter-productive in the wider war of ideas.

The contradictions inherent in the limited application of the Bush administration's *realpolitik* approach, however, did not become immediately apparent in the application of the strategy, in part due to the pace of international events. The culmination of the implementation of the first strategy was the war in Afghanistan and the decapitation of the Taliban regime. The operation was conducted primarily with US Special Forces and airpower working together, with the Northern Alliance providing the forces on the ground. This combination resulted in the rapid fall of the Taliban regime in Kabul with negligible American casualties. It did not, however, provide the basis either for the apprehension of al-Qaeda and Taliban fugitives in the country or the establishment of a stable domestic order in Afghanistan. Indeed, American action dispersed rather than destroyed its enemy without significantly changing the milieu from which the terrorist groups emerged. Despite pledges of aid and assistance, the US showed little interest in nation-building beyond the establishment of new institutions in Kabul. The mission was more decapitation than democratization.

What is strikingly clear about this counter-terrorism strategy is that it was remarkable for its lack of political context and naivety. The construction of the 'war on terrorism' was apolitical, characterized as a product of 'evil' rather than as a symptom of a political problem, let alone a political grievance. There was no apparent attempt to identify or address underlying causes. This was a policy pursued as if there were a finite number of terrorists, who could be tracked down and eliminated. This 'scorecard' approach led the US to act as if it was engaged in a manhunt, with Osama Bin Laden paralleling a James Bond villain that existed in an apolitical universe. Asked what his approach would be in September 2001, Bush said, 'To kill the terrorists', and then as an afterthought, 'Or to capture them and bring them to justice.'[25] Accordingly, the administration did not demonstrate any appreciation that this was a dynamic, politically motivated enemy whose international support could be influenced by the way the US responded. The enemy became all terrorists, whether global Islamists or local or regionally ethno-nationalist, yet the fight was against a tactic rather than a specific enemy. This broadened America's task considerably, with few obvious net benefits. There were successes in disrupting al-Qaeda's financial operations and terrorist planning operations. Yet Afghanistan was a mixed success. Al-Qaeda training camps were shut down and the Taliban removed from power. However, as the Bush administration left office, conflict persisted and it was clear that whatever the President meant by 'bring our enemies to justice or bring justice to our enemies', it did not deliver Osama bin Laden, who remained beyond the reach of American power.

Strategy Two: pre-emption and pre-eminence

The rapid collapse of the Taliban regime in Afghanistan in late 2001 laid the foundations for the next evolutionary development of the war on terrorism. Al-Qaeda operatives had been routed (or at least dispersed) and the operation had also achieved regime change at a remarkably low cost. Indeed, with media outlets reporting how Afghans celebrated the removal of a tyrannical regime, the Bush administration was able to talk of the American military as liberators that would rebuild Afghanistan and turn a former enemy into an ally. Such a regime-change strategy was therefore perceived as an attractive model, which, following soon after Kosovo in 1999, led to 'a profound optimism that we can do it – we can invade a country halfway round the world and bring about a reasonable settlement'.[26]

Simultaneously to the Afghanistan experience was the White House's strategic assessment of the terrorist threat. Following 9/11, 'Cheney became the self-appointed examiner of worst-case scenarios' and began to 'think the unthinkable'.[27] Central to this approach was the assumption that 9/11 had been less a failure of intelligence than it was a failure of imagination. No one had thought of this threat and so new imagination had to be applied to threat assessment. It was an approach that led to the conflation of America's threats. What if, Cheney asked, America's enemies got together? What if rogue nations supply the material and al-Qaeda supplies the martyrs? The logic linking the two was simple. An enemy that sought weapons of mass destruction has attacked the US. At the same time, there were states which were enemies of the USA that were seeking to build weapons of mass destruction and were known to have armed terrorist groups in the past. In such circumstances, it was argued, it would be foolish to either wait for a positive connection between these two enemies to be proved or until after such an attack had occurred.[28] Thus, for the Bush administration, the answers to its own same set of questions began to change. They didn't replace the old ones, but they expanded their scope.

1   Who are the enemy? The enemy was still the terrorists and the governments that support them, but the definition was widened. The enemy became not

only all terrorists and the regimes that support them, but also tyrants with WMD and their rogue regimes.

2   Why do they hate us? This too was expanded. They attack us because they are evil, but also because of the nature of their regimes, and because America is an impediment to their ambitions. Indeed, as President Bush declared, 'Terror cells and outlaw regimes building weapons of mass destruction are different faces of the same evil. Our security requires that we confront both.'[29] This conflation was to find its most prominent articulation in the January 2002 State of the Union Address, under the title of an 'Axis of Evil'.

3   How to respond? The enemy needed to be hunted down and eliminated, but that was not enough. Regimes that harbor them need to be changed, as do states that might support them. A crucial difference here was a lowering of the threshold of reasonable doubt. States that were regarded as potential attackers became the focus of America's evolving strategy. Regime change and nation-building grew out of these answers, and the model was to be Iraq.

Strategy Two in practice: the war on terrorism as pre-emption and pre-eminence

In the 2002 State of the Union Address, the Bush administration provided its first public articulation of its second strategy in the War on Terror. The President identified three 'rogue' regimes as comprising what it described as an 'axis of evil arming to threaten the peace of the world': Iran, Iraq and North Korea. All three states had a record of supporting terrorism (but not al-Qaeda) and had embarked on programs to build weapons of mass destruction, including nuclear weapons and the long-range ballistic missiles to deliver them. All three were accordingly warned to desist from such activity or face serious consequences. It was a speech that signaled that America's tolerance of openly hostile states was radically reduced.

Whereas Iraq and the other 'Axis' states had formally been seen as regional problems that could be deterred and contained, they were now viewed as potential accomplices in the War on Terror. The rules of the game had fundamentally been altered. No longer was policy coming from Washington to be evidence led, but rather a dichotomy had been constructed between analysis and action. This disarticulation created a scenario where the *possible* was to be deemed more important to strategy than the *probable*. Or, as Sir Richard Dearlove, head of the UK intelligence agency MI6, noted before the Iraq war, 'the facts and intelligence' were being 'fixed round the policy'.[30] Indeed, as Paul Wolfowitz argued, 'Anyone who believes that we can wait until *we have certain knowledge* that attacks are imminent has failed to connect the dots that led to September 11.'[31] It is for this reason that Iraq's *potential* capability to build WMD and its *potential* to supply them to terrorists was latched upon as justification for its high threat status in Washington.[32] As Donald Rumsfeld would later confess:

The coalition did not act in Iraq because we had discovered dramatic new evidence of Iraq's pursuit of weapons of mass murder. We acted because we saw the evidence in a new light, through the prism of our experience on September 11th, 2001.[33]

The development of the pre-emption doctrine was in a sense the extreme expression of the 'with us or against us' test. Rumsfeld had been advocating pre-emption since shortly after the attacks. 'You can't defend at every place at every time against every technique,' he argued, 'you have to take it to them, and that means pre-emption.'[34] As an official policy, the strategy evolved throughout 2002, with an important address by Bush at West Point in June, reiterating that 'if we wait for the threat to materialize we will have waited too long', we need 'to take the battle to the enemy, to disrupt his plans, and to confront the worst threats before they emerge.'[35] What was new and radical in this approach was not America's willingness to contemplate pre-emption so much as the centrality of this option within the overall strategy. Deterrence and containment were being superseded because 'Deterrence – the promise of massive retaliation against nations – means nothing against the shadowy terrorist networks with no nation or citizens to defend.' Thus, 'Containment is not possible when unbalanced dictators with weapons of mass destruction can deliver those weapons on missiles or secretly provide them to terrorist allies.'

What was also novel was what the administration meant by 'pre-emption'. This was hinted at in the most formal statement of the pre-emption doctrine, the 2002 *National Security Strategy of the United States* (*NSS02*). Here the administration explained that while 'international jurists often conditioned the legitimacy of pre-emption on the existence of an imminent threat ... [w]e must adopt the concept of imminent threat to the capabilities and objectives of today's adversaries.'[36] Although left undefined in this document, the implication was that America would not limit its actions to the narrow circumstances prescribed within the definition of pre-emption where an attack was imminent and unavoidable, and would reserve onto itself the right to take *preventive* action. In doing this, however, the US was undermining the internationally accepted limits on the use of such a resort without adequately defining the scope and legitimacy of its new definition.

Reactions to this shift in strategic approach were swift and critical. Brent Scowcroft questioned the benefit of exulting to the status of declaratory policy an option that the US had long included in its list of policy responses, 'As a declaratory policy it tends to leave the door open to others who want to claim the same right. By making it public we also tend to add to the world's perception that we are arrogant and unilateral.'[37] This point was reiterated by Henry Kissinger who warned against the development of 'principles that grant every nation an unfettered right of pre-emption against its own definition of threats to its own security'.[38] For Heisbourg the adoption of an 'ill-defined and open ended strategy of forceful prevention' was likely to be corrosive of alliance relations given the reluctance of the European powers to replicate such an approach.[39] UN Secretary General Kofi Annan similarly warned that such action 'could set precedents that resulted in a proliferation of the unilateral and lawless use of force, with or without credible justification'.[40] Other concerns were more practical. The US intelligence community was concerned that a pre-emptive attack that threatened regime survival was more likely to induce use of WMD than any other scenario.[41] Still others were concerned about the reliance of such a strategy on intelligence which at the best of times is an inexact art. For James Dobbins, such a policy set a much higher threshold for the integrity of secret intelligence, concluding that, 'It is one thing to expand one's defences on the basis of inconclusive evidence; it is quite another to attack a foreign nation on that same basis.'[42]

The articulation of the pre-emption strategy, however, was a central aspect of the Bush approach. It was meant as a statement of intent and thus of deterrence. It was also a key component of the Bush administration's stated intention to establish and maintain security for itself and its values through military pre-eminence. The *NSS02* document put American power at the center of its strategy with the proclamation that 'We will defend the peace by fighting terrorists and tyrants. We will preserve the peace by building good relations amongst the great powers. We will extend the peace by encouraging free and open societies on every continent.'[43]

The document also stated the administration's hegemonic intentions, in its assertion that the US intended to maintain military dominance against all challenges and discouraging all rivals from even contemplating such competition. At the heart of this document, and indeed of the strategy, was an extraordinarily ambitious undertaking, the stated willingness, as Rhodes observes, 'to use American military hegemony not simply aggressively and unilaterally, but globally' in pursuit of a liberal empire.[44] It was, however, the pre-emption aspect of the strategy that gained most attention when the document was released, and while it was asserted as a general principle, it was clear from the outset that Iraq was the place where the new doctrine would be applied.

The administration was clearly intent on conflating al-Qaeda and the Saddam Hussein regime, claiming that,

> We know that Iraq and the al-Qaeda terrorist network share a common enemy – the United States of America. We know that Iraq and al-Qaeda have had high-level contacts that go back a decade. Some al-Qaeda leaders who fled Afghanistan went to Iraq. We've learned that Iraq has trained al-Qaeda members in bomb making and poisons and deadly gases. And we know that after September 11, Saddam Hussein's regime gleefully celebrated the terrorist attacks on America.[45]

Furthermore, for the Vice President, regime change was necessary because the American calculus had changed. Thus Cheney warned that Iraq might use the threat of its WMD capability to blackmail the world and thus 'seek domination of the entire Middle East' and 'take control of a great portion of the world's energy supplies'.[46] For Cheney, the 'thing that is different about Iraq' was 'its government and its regime and its past history. The fact that he [Saddam

Hussein] has launched ballistic missiles against Saudi Arabia, Kuwait, Israel, Iran. He's twice invaded his neighbours.'[47] As far as the Bush administration was concerned, therefore, it was the nature of the regime – which it regarded as hostile and beyond diplomatic engagement – that constituted the nature of the threat. It was on this basis that Washington concluded that 'regime change' in Iraq was both desirable and necessary.

The construction of the Iraq threat as the embodiment of the doctrine of pre-emption provides a variety of interesting perspectives of the second strategy of the war on terrorism. Not least of these was the fact that Iraq became Washington's target of choice not because it was strong but because it was weak. It was less because it was an immediate threat than because it was immediately vulnerable. After 12 years of sanctions and no military modernization during the period following the decimation of its army in 1991, war, when it came, was guaranteed to be one-sided. The only possible force equalizer that the Iraqis possessed was the recourse to chemical or biological munitions. Interestingly, this was a threat that Washington regarded as manageable, and the war was fought in the context of that threat. The administration's expectations about how American forces would be greeted after the fall of the regime, and about how easily Iraq could be transformed at little cost into a model secular, democratic Middle Eastern state, also informed its focus on Baghdad.

Of equal interest in this threat construction, as with other past threat-construction exercises, was the narrowness of the focus. The process was narrow even by the administration's own terms. Of the three Axis of Evil states, Iraq was arguably the most contained militarily by the (extended) no-fly zones and economically by the UN sanctions regime. Iran, by contrast, is well advanced in its nuclear ambitions and was as heavily involved in the sponsorship of Palestinian suicide bombers as Iraq. Like Iraq, North Korea was in breach of its international obligations with regard to its WMD programs, but the manner of those breaches has been more blatant and aggressive than any statement from Baghdad. Furthermore, in contrast to Iraq, Pyongyang has succeeded in developing a small nuclear arsenal and is an active proliferator of ballistic missiles. Like Iraq, both Iran and North Korea are openly hostile to Washington's international agenda and clearly fail the 'with us or against us' test. While the deterrent effect of Pyongyang's nuclear weapons may explain the absence of American attention toward it, the same cannot be said for Iran.

The theory set out in the *NSS02*, was put into practice between March–May 2003 as Operation Iraqi Freedom was executed. The swift American military victory and the collapse and disappearance of the old Iraqi regime appeared to vindicate the Bush strategy. Exuberance and hubris led the administration to assert 'Mission Accomplished', while certain sections of the Washington political community called for similar military action elsewhere. Iran and Syria were touted as obvious next candidates. 'Everyone wants to go to Baghdad, real men want to go to Tehran'[48] became the boastful line of the neo-conservatives. Yet several factors checked this momentum and gave cause to question the continued validity of an American doctrine of pre-emption worth its name. The most immediate of these impediments to the further application of this strategy was the failure of the Americans to discover the WMD on which the case for the immediate invasion of Iraq was justified. The lack of any evidence of nuclear, chemical or biological weapons, or even of any ongoing programs to produce them, was widely seen as undermining the American case for war. The second factor was the inability of the American occupiers to provide security, civil amenities and a semblance of order. The faulty assumptions on which Operation Iraq Freedom were built and justified, were a setback for the Bush administration in both practice and in principle. The popularity of the occupation forces continually declined as support for the insurgents increased, resulting in what was just short of a full-blown sectarian civil war. As a result, the continued US military presence in Iraq consumed America's political, economic and military resources on a grand scale.

The strategy of pre-emption was designed to deter and defeat America's enemies, and the invasion of Iraq was the clearest expression of that intent. Yet the question must be asked, was it anything more than a strategy designed specifically for Iraq? At a rhetorical level, the administration never wavered from its commitment to pre-emption and the pre-eminence strategy. Indeed, it claimed that Libya's decision to abandon its quest for WMD and the subsequent dismantling of its chemical and nuclear programs as evidence of the coercive effect of the American strategy. In terms of its own actions, however, the administration's policies gave a different impression. In its approach to Syria, an array of sanctions on Syria's government and banks became the preferred strategy after Syrian officials were implicated in the former Lebanese Prime Minister Rafik Hariri's killing. State-authorized terrorism was met with sanctions and not force. With North Korea, the administration engaged regional powers in a multilateral diplomatic initiative to share the pressure on Pyongyang and the responsibility if further action should be necessary. Indeed, the Chinese were quick to illustrate how intelligence failures over Iraq should urge caution toward North Korea.[49] With regard to Iran, too, the US allowed the United Nations to take a prominent role in outlining what was acceptable within Tehran's treaty obligations, while Iran challenged Washington's 'assumption train', rebutting claims that its nuclear program was weapons-related.

Given such circumstances, by the time the Bush administration left office, Iraq looked more like a demonstration of the limits of American power than its ability to shape events. Regime change was the easy part when compared to the Herculean task of creating a functioning and secure order thereafter. In this respect, both Afghanistan and Iraq – vastly expensive and difficult undertakings – have not provided models worthy of emulation. Far from proving an additional front to defeat the terrorists, America's action, especially in Iraq, clearly exacerbated the situation. Despite President Bush's calls to 'bring 'em on', America's occupation of Iraq, together with some of its actions there, encouraged more Islamic radicals to take up arms against its military with negative results. Paradoxically, rather than being a reaction to the supposed links between Iraq and al-Qaeda, the invasion and occupation proved to be a self-fulfilling prophecy in creating Islamic militancy and al-Qaeda-linked terrorism. Similarly, rather than inducing caution in the capitals of rogue states, the threat of pre-emption may well have increased the threat from some states. According to Thomas Friedman, the Syrians were 'so convinced that they [we]re next on the Bush hit parade that they have been easing the entry of anti-US guerrillas into Iraq – because the more preoccupied the US is there, the less likely it is to invade Syria.'[50] In the wake of Iraq, and the regional impact it had, it can be seriously doubted whether Bush's pre-emption doctrine was worthy of the name.

Strategy Three: the Freedom Agenda and the forward strategy

The Bush administration's third strategy in the War on Terror can be seen as an implicit recognition of the limitations of preceding national strategies. In effect, the Bush administration's 'Freedom Agenda' was the quintessential expression of a liberal grand strategy for the Greater Middle East, characterized by its emphasis on the domestic nature of other states as vitally important for the attainment of American security and material interests. For this third strategy, promoting both American self-interest and values, in the form of 'freedom' and 'democracy', was seen to be symbiotic; enhancing both American global influence and creating the conditions for peace, prosperity and freedom throughout the region. Such thinking was an expansion of the logic laid out in the *NSS02*, where it was argued that there was a linkage between democracy promotion and pre-emption in both theory and practice.[51] That is, the willingness to strike down rogue states was seen to provide an obligation to replace the old regimes with representative governments, which would produce democratic states. Successful or not, Afghanistan and Iraq were seen to be paradigm examples of this. Indeed, the Bush administration continuously espoused the idea that the removal of both regimes would create a 'domino effect' and promote democratization throughout the greater Middle East more broadly.[52] Notably the qualitative difference between democracy promotion, envisioned under the 'Freedom Agenda', and the 'domino effect' espoused as part of the justification for the Iraq War, was that the Bush administration was now placing democracy-promotion as both a method for engaging with the Middle East, and for countering terrorism, not as a subsidiary result of the pre-emption strategy. This became evident in November 2003 when President Bush argued that the United States would pursue a 'forward strategy of freedom in the Middle East'.[53] Under this strategy, the administration acknowledged, as the President himself later declared, that 'We cannot rely exclusively on military power to assure our long term security.'[54] This was a clear indication that the Freedom Agenda was the product of the evolving and expanding answers to the administration's three questions.

1   Who are the enemy? The enemy was still the terrorists and the governments that support them, but now included tyrannical and authoritarian regimes that repressed the democratic aspirations of their populous.

2   Why do they hate us? They hate 'us' because 'they' are evil, but they are
    evil because of the lack political and economic freedom. That is to say, that
    the form of terrorism that manifested itself on 11 September 2001 was a
    symptom of the political and economic conditions within authoritarian states
    in the Greater Middle East.
3   How to respond? Through counter-terrorism, pre-emption and regime
    change if necessary, but also by bringing about the political, social and eco-
    nomic transformation of the Greater Middle East.

Strategy Three in practice: Freedom Agenda and the forward strategy

The evolution of the Bush administration's thinking about the causes of terrorism was at its most developed in the promulgation of the Freedom Agenda. This
stood in sharp contrast to the initial denunciations of al-Qaeda as an 'evil' that
could be caught or killed. This avowedly liberal strategy, notable for its ideological underpinnings, offered both an explanation of the causes of terrorism and
its solution. The diagnosis was that 'As long as the Middle East remains a place
where freedom does not flourish, it will remain a place of stagnation, resentment
and violence ready for export.'[55] Consequently, to solve such a problem, the
administration argued that, 'If the Middle East joins the democratic revolution
that has reached much of the world, the lives of millions in that region will be
bettered and the trend of conflict and fear will be ended at its source.'[56]

Interestingly, President Bush employed both his own religiosity and 'democratic peace theory' to legitimize the notion that promoting democracy in the
Middle East was in America's national interest,

> The freedom agenda is based upon our deepest ideals and our vital inter-
> ests.... We believe that freedom is a gift from an almighty God, beyond any
> power on Earth to take away. And we also know, by history and by logic,
> that promoting democracy is the surest way to build security. Democracies
> do not attack each other or threaten the peace.[57]

In short, Bush's third strategy was arguing that 'the advance of freedom leads to
peace'.[58] This was in sharp contrast to the first strategy that treated terrorism as
if it emerged and popped like glittering bubbles from a swamp; instead, the third
strategy wanted to drain it. That is to say, the Freedom Agenda attempted to go
beyond dealing with the symptoms of the problem, the terrorists and their sponsors. It was a strategy seeking to address the causes of terrorism and other dis-
contents. It was adopted partly in recognition of the scale of the problem, made
even more obvious after events in Iraq, and partly as a realization that, with the
present state of the Middle East, 'it would be reckless to accept the status quo'.[59]
It was also unusually self-critical of previous American foreign policy toward
the region, but also paradoxically, by implication, of its own initial and concur-
rent strategy in the war on terrorism, stating that 'Sixty years of Western nations
excusing and accommodating the lack of freedom in the Middle East did nothing

to make us safe, because in the long run stability cannot be purchased at the expense of liberty.'⁶⁰ And furthermore,

> We must shake off decades of failed policy in the Middle East ... [since] in the past [we] have been willing to make a bargain: to tolerate oppression for the sake of stability. Long standing ties often led us to overlook the faults of local elites. Yet this bargain did not bring stability or make us safe.... As recent history has shown, we cannot turn a blind eye to oppression just because the oppression is not in our own backyard. No longer should we think tyranny is benign because it is temporarily convenient.... We will consistently challenge the enemies of reform and confront the allies of terror. We will expect a higher standard from our friends in the region.⁶¹

At a rhetorical level, this amounted to strong implied criticism of both Egypt and Saudi Arabia in particular. Yet the announcements of the new strategy also included caveats. 'The movement of history will not come quickly' Bush cautioned, stating, 'we must be patient with others' and recognize that 'the Middle East countries have some distance to travel',⁶² plus, 'working democracies always need time to develop ... and this makes us patient and understanding as other nations are at different stages of this journey.'⁶³ These caveats lowered both the force and immediacy of the other statements. Indeed, as the Middle East Partnership Initiative (MEPI) was launched, Secretary of State Colin Powell was eager to emphasis the 'partnership' element of this flagship democratization program.⁶⁴ Moreover, as a senior Bush administration official hastened to add, the US was not planning 'to abandon long-term allies such as Saudi Arabia and Egypt because of their lack of democracy', but would offer 'positive reinforcement for emerging reform trends'.⁶⁵

Problematically, while the Bush administration was eager to assert that 'Our part as free nations is to ally ourselves with freedom wherever it occurs',⁶⁶ the ambiguity of such statements made it extremely difficult to operationalize. Ultimately, the administration was deploying essentially contested terms, such as 'freedom' and 'democracy', which made translating rhetoric into praxis difficult at best; offering ideological convictions was no substitute for detailed empirical subscriptions. With a lack of strategic guidance, the Freedom Agenda took one step forward before taking two steps back. In turn, this led to MEPI funding projects in a 'hodgepodge' and near-sporadic manner.⁶⁷ Indeed, as J. Scott Carpenter confessed in his role of overseeing MEPI:

> We don't know yet how best to promote democracy in the Arab Middle East. I mean we just don't know. It's the early days.... I think there are times when you throw spaghetti against the wall and see if it sticks.⁶⁸

By 2006 it became highly evident what exactly had 'stuck' as an approach. Namely the Bush administration had adopted a policy of conservative radicalism.⁶⁹ The approach was *radical* to the extent that it insisted on political democracy, yet *conservative* in its desire to safeguard the socio-economic privileges and power of the established order to secure regional stability. However, what was noticeable about such a strategy was that the radical side was being targeted at regimes that opposed US influence in the region, while the conservative side was the approach adopted for friendly allies in the MENA. As the Bush administration oscillated between emphasizing both of these elements, it enabled double standards in the Freedom Agenda to emerge.

For regimes that challenged American influence in the region, such as Iran and Syria, the price of such opposition was the Freedom Agenda's radical side. This insisted on regime change and political democracy. This was not to be done through military intervention, as in Iraq, but rather the State Department in conjunction with the Defense Department set up a new Iran–Syria Operations Group; the aim of which was to couple diplomatic pressure with the Iran Democracy Program and the Syria Democracy Program. These programs utilized MEPI funds and personnel to bolster internal dissidents and exile groups wanting US-supported regime change.[70] However, the acme of the radical side was targeted at the Palestinian territories. Having been surprised by the electoral success of Hamas in 2006, the Bush administration speedily overturned its dedication to democracy promotion and set about its archetypal response to the rise of an Islamist regime. Despite being democratically elected, the US, along with the European Union, responded swiftly by cutting off aid to the Palestinian Authority and refused to work with the Hamas-led government.[71] More problematic, however, was the covert initiative from within the Bush administration to supply new weapons and training to Fatah, designed to remove the democratically elected Hamas-led government from power.[72] While this attempt failed, leading to a civil war in the Palestinian territories, it demonstrated a guiding rule underpinning the Freedom Agenda strategy. The United States would aspire to promote democracy in the Middle East if, and only if, the results of this did not challenge its influence and other interests in the region. Thus demonstrating how 'making other people free is said to be the goal of US foreign policy; but the natives are expected not only to accept the offer of freedom but also to show their gratitude.'[73]

Conversely, regimes that helped to maintain American influence in the region were offered the *conservative* side of the conservative–radicalism dyad. This aspect of the Freedom Agenda was designed to generate stability through liberalization, with democratization being a secondary long-term goal. Indeed, this distinction is crucial because, while 'democratization' signifies a move toward greater degrees of political participation in existing governmental systems, 'liberalization' can mean any reform that enhances the individual freedom enjoyed by a citizen. Thus, unlike Iran, Syria and the Palestinian territories, when it came to regimes such as Saudi Arabia, Egypt, Jordan, Kuwait, Morocco and Yemen, the Bush administration never advocated regime change through military action, democratic populism or civil disobedience. Indeed, this was reflected in the Freedom Agenda programs, which showed an overwhelming emphasis on low-risk gradualist policies that emphasized promoting evolutionary reform of existing status-quo regimes. This was not democratic reform as much as it was the promotion of the conditions for eventual democratic reform, highlighting that the Freedom Agenda was a strategy that construed democracy as a long-term project emerging out of a 'social and economic context that should be prepared'.[74] Indeed, when MEPI was launched to operationalize this policy, it was criticized for its timidity in the way it spent its budget, most of which went toward helping governments promote free trade.[75] This led some US officials to argue that MEPI was more a 'philosophical commitment' to democracy promotion than a radical new approach.[76] Despite such a euphemism, it was clear that the Freedom Agenda, as Amy Hawthorne of the Carnegie Endowment for International Peace argued, was not 'really designed to press for reforms. The stated purpose is to promote "reform" in Arab countries, but it also is designed to support pro-American governments and pro-American policies.'[77]

Conspicuously, when the radical side of the agenda was emphasized, the Bush administration portrayed 'freedom' and 'democracy' as entities that could be created from outside. Stress was placed on the universality of freedom, which merely required tyrannical regimes to be removed and the natural aspirations of the 'human spirit' to come forth. Yet, with the conservative side of the approach, it was implicitly acknowledged that the inherent nature of democracy meant that it could not be imposed from the outside; it was a gradual process that America simply didn't have the power to decree. Given this juxtaposition, it became highly evident that the Bush administration placed an economic strategy at the heart of its conservative approach. Indeed, it relied on a modernization thesis to legitimize a 'gradualist' and 'sequential' understanding of how political economy related to democratization in the region. Upon launching the Middle East Free Trade Area (MEFTA), President Bush argued that

> The Arab world has a great cultural tradition, but is largely missing out on the economic progress of our time. *Across the globe, free markets and trade have helped defeat poverty, and taught men and women the habits of liberty.* So I propose the establishment of a U.S.–Middle East free trade area within a decade, to bring the Middle East into an expanding circle of opportunity, to provide hope for the people who live in that region.... *By replacing corruption and self-dealing, with free markets and fair laws, the people of the Middle East will grow in prosperity and freedom.*[78]

Within this schema, economic 'freedom' was paramount. Capitalism was seen as the heart of democracy because it would produce wealth that, it was assumed, would 'trickle down' and lead to higher levels of mass consumption. In turn, this would produce a well-educated middle class that would demand cultural changes favorable to democracy, such as increased secularism, and therefore weaken the role of Islamic identities. In effect, a theory of political change was consistently put forward that posited modernization as a functionalist and economistic outcome of capitalism. This was not a radical challenge to friendly regimes, but rather provided them with a policy they desired to prevent their regimes facing legitimation crises.[79]

The appeal of this approach was located in the manner in which it appeared to favor both parties. Middle Eastern regimes were able to accept such an agreement in the belief that economic reforms would allow them to alleviate the poor social conditions that threaten their power; the US was able to pursue a strategy that many believed would dilute the appeal of Islamist groups and move the region slowly to stable liberalized democracies. This apparently symbiotic relationship was appealing because of its gradualist emphasis in which the US need not directly challenge friendly regimes, consequently allowing cooperation to ensue on security and other economic concerns. In effect, it provided the default foundations upon which the Freedom Agenda was constructed, by offering the illusion of a 'silver bullet' to Middle East reform. Accordingly, it mirrors Edward Ingram's insight about pax-Americana, which favors 'trade and investment without rule whenever possible, but with rule when unavoidable'.[80]

The Freedom Agenda, however, was undermined from its very conception by the first two strategies. After 9/11, the US embarked on a policy of 'extraordinary rendition', which sent contradictory messages to secure more immediate goals in the War on Terror. This raised serious credibility issues regarding the sincerity of the Freedom Agenda to observers in the Middle East and beyond. Not only was the Bush administration willing to curtail international law, but the notion that it was promoting 'freedom' in the Middle East appeared ironic given that the CIA was utilizing Middle Eastern prisons for 'torture, indefinite detentions, and disappearances'. Indeed, as former CIA agent Bob Baer argued:

> If you want a serious interrogation, you send a prisoner to Jordan. If you want them to be tortured, you send them to Syria. If you want someone to disappear – never to see them again – you send them to Egypt.[81]

Similar sentiments were expressed by Michael F. Scheuer, the former Chief of the CIA's Bin Laden Unit, in which he stated:

> There were no qualms at all about sending people to Cairo and kind of joking up our [the CIA] sleeves about what would happen to those people in Cairo in Egyptian prisons.... I don't care what happens to the people who are targeted and rendered.... Mistakes are made.... They are not Americans. I really don't care.... I never got paid, sir, to be a citizen of the world.[82]

Such a serious contradiction did not, however, go unnoticed, with Representative Bill Delahunt, Chairman of the Subcommittee on International Organizations, Human Rights and Oversight, arguing that

> These extraordinary renditions are utterly inconsistent with our broader foreign policy goals of promoting democracy and the rule of law, the very foundations of civil society. These practices have brought us universal condemnation and have frustrated our efforts to work in a concerted way with our allies in fighting terrorism.[83]

The case of extraordinary rendition not only demonstrated a dependency on the very regimes the Bush administration claimed to want to reform by promoting democracy and freedom, but more problematically under the rubric of security demands, the Bush administration utilized for its own purposes the very conditions it claimed were the cause of terrorism. If this was not tragic enough, the assault on Iraq brought with it other serious credibility problems as the pictures of abuses at Abu Ghraib demonstrated.[84] This was a far cry from President Bush's claim that 'the torture chambers and secret police are gone forever'.[85] Accordingly, it is little wonder that, despite all the grand rhetoric that accompanied the Freedom Agenda, this third strategy was largely met with derision and cries of hypocrisy.

The Bush legacy and the Obama administration

The Bush administration's approach to the war on terrorism proved remarkably dynamic. It evolved from a narrow conception of the enemy to definitions and strategies that became progressively broader and more ambitious in scope. The questions that the administration set itself in identifying who and why it was fighting after September 2001 provided a useful framework for evaluating how the administration's thinking, strategies and polices developed. As such, the administration demonstrated not only a willingness to adopt approaches in response to the dynamics of events, but also a willingness to question the very basis of its foreign policy approach. Yet, with three competing strategies – one based on *realpolitik*, the second on the doctrine of pre-emption and pre-eminence, and the third based on 'democratic imperialist' ideas or what Pier Hassner described as 'Wilsonianism with boots'[86] – it is little wonder that the Bush administration's approach to the war on terrorism was riddled with contradictions. This in turn creates a very confusing milieu in which to judge the Bush legacy. Far from passing the Obama administration a homogenous approach to be followed, the new administration has inherited a bewildering set of policies that it is both pursuing and seeking to untangle.

Despite campaigning with the slogan 'Change we can believe in', however, the Obama administration has already demonstrated that it has not radically broken with its predecessor. The current administration's counter-terrorism strategy, unsurprisingly, has strands of both continuity and change. The Obama administration has rejected the use of torture and harsh interrogation tactics, while also ordering the closure of the Guantanamo Bay detention facility. However, while this dealt with one of the most controversial facilities, others such as Bagram Airbase in Afghanistan have remained open. Moreover, the Obama administration has continued to grant the CIA authority to carry out renditions, in which suspects are picked up and often sent to a third country for questioning. The logic of this was asserted by an administration official who argued:

> Obviously you need to preserve some tools – you still have to go after the bad guys.... The legal advisors working on this looked at rendition. It is controversial in some circles and kicked up a big storm in Europe. But if done within certain parameters, it is an acceptable practice.[87]

Evidently the Obama administration has decided to retain some of the practices adopted as part of the Bush administration's first strategy in the War on Terror. Indeed, with a refocusing on Afghanistan, which Obama has called the 'central front on terror', the Obama administration is in fact expanding the first strategy. This is not only demonstrated in the doubling of the US military presence in the country, but also with regards to US policy toward Pakistan.[88] The current administration has been willing to adopt a unilateral policy that targets suspected terrorists within sovereign Pakistani territory.[89] This is part of Obama's strategy of letting Islamabad know that he will be making greater demands than his predecessor, and if needed will curtail US military aid. Such a strategy is the embodiment of Bush's first realpolitik strategy, with some tinkering at the edges. As such, Obama's policy has not signaled that 'Bush's war on terror comes to a sudden end', as some *Washington Post* headlines have suggested.[90]

Similarly, despite predictions that the Obama administration would abandon the Freedom Agenda, this has not been the case. There has certainly been a more cautious approach to asserting the need for democratization in the Middle East, namely because of the manner in which the Freedom Agenda has been so closely associated with the war in Iraq. Thus, as President Obama has asserted:

> I know there has been controversy about the promotion of democracy in recent years, and much of this controversy is connected to the war in Iraq. So let me be clear: No system of government can or should be imposed by one nation on any other.[91]

However, the President, who has demonstrated his desire to place democracy promotion at the heart of US foreign policy since sponsoring the 2005 ADVANCE Democracy Act (ADA),[92] hastened to add:

> That does not lessen my commitment, however, to governments that reflect the will of the people. Each nation gives life to this principle in its own way, grounded in the traditions of its own people.... But I do have an unyielding belief that all people yearn for certain things: the ability to speak your mind and have a say in how you are governed; confidence in the rule of law and the equal administration of justice; government that is transparent and doesn't steal from the people; the freedom to live as you choose. These are not just American ideas; they are human rights. And that is why we will support them everywhere.

Notably, where President Bush articulated the promotion of freedom with his own religiosity, the Obama administration has shifted to viewing it as a human-rights issue. While both Presidents have shared a common belief that the values of freedom and democracy are universal, there are points of departure over how these values should be promoted. Where Bush pronounced the use of free markets to deliver Middle Eastern states to its 'single sustainable model', the Obama administration has been eager to signal an alteration by using foreign assistance for 'dignity promotion'.[93] This is certainly not a radical departure from the sentiments that lay behind MEPI, and given the global financial crisis it is not clear how this signal will be translated into praxis. Moreover questions over exactly how serious the Obama White House will pursue its promise of foreign assistance have been raised, especially given the prolonged failure to nominate a new director of the US Agency for International Development (USAID). This has been a source of tension between the White House and the Department of State, with Secretary of State Hillary Clinton arguing that 'It's hard to justify not having our full government in place six months after we started.'[94] Moreover, with Obama arguing that 'Our problems must be dealt with through *partnership*',[95] it is difficult to see any far-reaching shift between Bush's Freedom Agenda and that set by the new administration; the conservative side of the conservative radicalism dyad has remained.

The greatest political change from the Bush to Obama transition, however, has come in the form of the latter's rejection of radicalism. Indeed, it is perhaps best to characterize Obama's foreign policy as one of 'conservative pragmatism'; characterized by an emphasis on diplomatic engagement rather than regime change. Indeed this shift was signified in Obama's inauguration, when he argued that 'we will extend a hand if you are willing to unclench your fist'.[96] This has certainly been an approach adopted toward Syria, in which the Obama administration has decided to send an ambassador, ending a four-year isolationist policy. This followed a series of high-level meetings between the administration's special envoy for the Middle East, George J. Mitchell, and the Syrian President Bashar al-Assad.[97] Moreover, while President Obama has elected to keep sanctions against Syria in place, Assad has informally invited Obama to Syria for talks, demonstrating that relations between the two countries may be thawing.[98]

A policy of engagement has also been extended toward Iran. Indeed, despite the disputed 2009 Presidential elections in Iran, leading to the Iranian government clamping down on mass demonstrations and opposition, the Obama administration has sought to maintain the promise of an open door for discussions. As President Obama confirmed after these events:

> We've got some fixed national security interests in Iran, not developing nuclear weapons, in not exporting terrorism, and we have offered a pathway for Iran to rejoining the international community.... We will have to assess in coming weeks and months the degree to which they are willing to walk through that door.[99]

Similarly, Vice President Biden has added, 'If the Iranians respond to the offer of engagement, we will engage.'[100] Yet, with the Iranian regime facing the most severe internal challenges since the rise of the Islamic Republic in 1979, it appears that the Obama administration may have to heed Harold Macmillan's warning about 'Events, dear boy. Events.'

Despite this apparent new era of engagement, it is not entirely legitimate to claim that this is a radical break with the Bush administration. Indeed, having failed to get its own way by the exercise of its unilateral power, the Bush administration did embrace a more multilateral policy as its time in office drew to a close. Over North Korea the administration engaged the regional powers in a multilateral diplomatic initiative to share the pressure on Pyongyang, while with regard to Iran, the US allowed the United Nations to take a prominent role in outlining what is acceptable within Tehran's treaty obligations. This was an admission of powerlessness in the face of the intransigence of these recalcitrant regimes. Moreover, with the Iraq War, amongst other policies, demonstrating that America simply is not powerful enough to stand alone in the world, the Bush administration was forced to realize that being isolated internationally is a position from which very little can be achieved. Accordingly, the implications of the Iraq invasion on American foreign policy more broadly are considerable. This is a legacy that greatly curtails and shapes the policy options available to Obama.

The legacy of the Iraq War has not been lost on the new President. Indeed, as Obama tries to repair America's damaged international reputation, he has made some bold public admissions, the acme of which was that 'Unlike Afghanistan, Iraq was *a war of choice*', and that 'events in Iraq have reminded America of the need to use diplomacy and build international consensus to resolve our problems whenever possible'.[101] This is a bold admission that Iraq has severely curtailed America's room for diplomatic maneuver. Moreover, with the Obama administration setting out a timetable that withdraws all American troops from Iraq by 2012, it is clear that this administration is accepting the limitations of American power. As President Obama set out this new timetable, he made it clear that

> What we will *not* do is let the pursuit of the perfect stand in the way of achievable goals. We cannot rid Iraq of all who oppose America or sympathize with our adversaries. We cannot police Iraq's streets until they are completely safe, nor stay until Iraq's union is perfected. We cannot sustain indefinitely a commitment that has put a strain on our military and will cost the American people nearly a trillion dollars.[102]

What this amounts to in sum is that the Bush legacy lives on through the Obama administration, with elements of the first and third strategies set out by Bush being accepted. It is the same wine being poured, although perhaps a little more matured and certainly served in a better-packaged bottle. Yet, because of the inherently problematic nature of the second strategy, the Obama administration has been forced to accept the limits of American power and is trying to reconstruct international perceptions of America as a benign exemplar, in a world that is increasingly becoming multi-polar. Whether this strategic confusion, packaged as policy change, can survive its own contradictions for long remains to be seen.

Notes

1 All quotations in this section are from President Bush's 'Address to a Joint Session of Congress and the American People', 20 September 2001, unless otherwise indicated, http://georgewbush-whitehouse.archives.gov/news/releases/2001/09/20010920-8.html.
2 See B. Woodward, *Bush at War* (London: Simon and Schuster, 2002) pp. 17–18.
3 President Bush's 'Remarks in a Photo Opportunity with the National Security Team', http://georgewbush-whitehouse.archives.gov/news/releases/2001/09/20010912-4.html.
4 He used the word 'evil' a total of four times in his four-minute address. Cited by I. Daalder and J. Lindsay, *America Unbound* (Washington, DC: Brookings, 2003), pp. 87–88.

5 Ibid.
6 President Bush's 'Address to the United Nations General Assembly', http://georgewbush-whitehouse.archives.gov/news/releases/2001/11/20011110–3.html.
7 Ibid.
8 President Bush's 'Address to a Joint Session of Congress and the American People', 20 September 2001.
9 President Bush's 'Guard and Reserves "Define Spirit of America"', http://georgewbush-whitehouse.archives.gov/news/releases/2001/09/20010917–3.html.
10 See 'Financing Islamist Terrorism: Closing the Net', *IISS Strategic Comments*, 9:10 (December 2003).
11 Cited by Daalder and Lindsay, *America Unbound*, p. 76.
12 F. Zakaria, 'Bush, Rice and the 9/11 Shift', *Newsweek*, 16 December 2002.
13 www.youtube.com/watch?v=-23kmhc3P8U&NR=1.
14 E. Eckholm, 'Branding of China Muslim Group as Terrorist is Disputed', *International Herald Tribune*, 14–15 September 2002.
15 See J. Mann, 'For Bush, Realpolitik Is No Longer a Dirty Word', *New York Times*, 12 April 2004, and T. Carothers, 'Promoting Democracy and Fighting Terror', *Foreign Affairs*, 82:1 (January/February 2003), p. 89.
16 Carothers, 'Promoting Democracy and Fighting Terror', p. 85.
17 This status allows greater access to American military technology, surplus defense equipment and training. D. Rohde, 'US Will Celebrate Pakistan As a "Major Non-NATO Ally"', *New York Times*, 19 March 2004.
18 For details of central Asian human rights concerns, see the Human Rights Watch website, www.hrw.org/wr2k1/europe/uzbekistan.html. See also Carothers, 'Promoting Democracy and Fighting Terror'.
19 For Carothers, with regards to Indonesia:

> the willingness of the US government to enter into a partnership with a security force that just a few years ago was involved in a horrendous campaign of slaughter and destruction against civilians sends a powerful negative message throughout the region and beyond.
>
> (Ibid., p. 85)

20 R. Khalaf and G. Dinmore, 'Reforming the Arab World: "The US is Serious – it Wants to Change the Middle East But it Doesn't Know How"', *Financial Times*, 23 March 2004.
21 G. Smyth, 'Terror War "Holding Back Arab Societies"', *Financial Times*, 21 October 2003.
22 George W. Bush: 'I call upon the Palestinian people to elect new leaders not compromised by terror', 25 June 2002, *Independent*, see http://www.independent.co.uk/news/world/americas/george-w-bush-i-call-upon-the-palestinian-people-to-elect-new-leaders-not-compromised-by-terror-606605.html.
23 Ibid.
24 E. Cohen, 'Iraq Can't Resist Us', *Wall Street Journal*, 18 December 2001; p. A16.
25 Refer to note 1.
26 Philip Gordon, cited by G. Baker, 'Missing in Action', *Financial Times*, 1–2 February 2003.
27 B. Woodward, *Plan of Attack* (New York: Simon and Schuster, 2004), p. 29.
28 A. La Guardia, 'Time for All Nations to Act', *Daily Telegraph*, 7 November 2002.
29 President Bush 'Outlines Iraqi Threat', http://georgewbush-whitehouse.archives.gov/news/releases/2002/10/20021007–8.html.
30 See M. Rycroft, 'The Secret Downing Street Memo', *Sunday Times*, 1 May 2005.
31 Paul Wolfowitz speech at IISS, 2 December 2002, cited by F. Heisbourg, 'A Work in Progress: The Bush Doctrine and Its Consequences', *Washington Quarterly*, 26:2 (2003), p. 76.

32   Richard Perle was candid in his answer to this question. 'We cannot know for sure', he reasons.

> But on which side would it be better to err? How would a decision to do nothing now and hope for the best look when Saddam has nuclear weapons and he makes another run at Kuwait or succeeds Afghanistan as terrorist headquarters of the world?
>
> (R. Perle, 'Why the West Must Strike First Against Saddam Hussein', *Daily Telegraph*, 9 August 2002)

33   V. Allen, 'Rumsfeld: We "Saw evidence in a Dramatic New Light"', *Reuters*, 9 July 2003, http://abcnews.go.com/sections/wnt/World//iraq030708_wmd.html.
34   Woodward, *Plan of Attack*, p. 34.
35   Ibid., p. 132.
36   Cited by Heisbourg, 'Work in Progress', p. 77.
37   Brent Scowcroft, cited by Daalder and Lindsay, *America Unbound*, p. 126.
38   H. Kissinger, 'Consult and Control: Bywords for Battling the New Enemy', *Washington Post*, 16 September 2002, cited by Daalder and Lindsay, ibid.
39   Heisbourg, 'Work in Progress', pp. 82–3.
40   'This logic [he continued] represents a fundamental challenge to the principles on which, however imperfectly, world peace and stability have rested for at least 58 years.' See I. Williams, 'A Story of Two Speeches: Kofi Annan and George W. Bush', *Foreign Policy in Focus*, 3 October 2003. See www.fpif.org.
41   For the CIA, Iraq

> appears to be drawing a line short of conducting terrorist attacks with conventional or chemical and biological weapons against the United States. Should Saddam conclude that a US-led attack could no longer be deterred, he probably would become less constrained.
>
> (George Tenet, cited by Daalder and Lindsay, *America Unbound*, p. 127)

42   J. Dobbins, 'A Perilous Dialogue of Pessimists', *Financial Times*, 4 February 2004.
43   See www.globalsecurity.org/military/library/policy/national/nss-020920.pdf.
44   E. Rhodes, 'The Imperial Logic of Bush's Liberal Agenda', *Survival*, 45:1 (2003), p. 136.
45   Cited by T. Friedman, 'Long Spoon Diplomacy', *New York Times*, 9 October 2003.
46   D.E. Sanger, 'The Debate Over Attacking Iraq Heats Up', *New York Times*, 1 September 2002.
47   M.R. Gordon, 'In Bush's "Axis of Evil", Why Iraq Stands Out', *New York Times*, 9 September 2002.
48   See David Renwick, War Without End, *The New Yorker*, 14 April 2003, available at http://www.newyorker.com/printables/talk/030421ta_talk_remnick. See also David Hastings Dunn, Real Men want to go to Tehran: Bush, Pre-emption and the Iranian Nuclear 'Challenge', *International Affairs*, 83:1 (2007), pp. 19–38.
49   According to US diplomats, China has argued that, 'If you missed this much in Iraq, how are we supposed to believe that the North Koreans are producing nuclear weapons?' D.E. Sanger, 'Bush's Pre-emptive Strategy Meets Some Untidy Reality', *New York Times*, 12 July 2004.
50   Friedman, 'Long Spoon Diplomacy'.
51   G. Dinmore, 'Hawks Set Out Bold Postwar Vision of World', *Financial Times*, 23 March 2003.
52   For Under Secretary of Defense for Policy Douglas Feith, a free Iraq would give 'tens of millions of people an alternative way to look at the future', P. Grier and F. Bowers, 'The Mideast as Arc of Freedom or False Hope', *The Christian Science Monitor*, 4 December 2003. Also see O. Hassan, 'Bush's Freedom Agenda: Ideology and the Democratization of the Middle East', *Democracy and Security*, 4:3 (2008), pp. 268–289.
53   'In Bush's Words: "Iraqi Democracy Will Succeed"', full text of President Bush's Remarks on the 20th Anniversary of the National Endowment for the Promotion of

Democracy.' Reprinted in the *New York Times*, www.nytimes.com/2003/11/06/politics/06TEXT-BUSH.html.

54 'Bush's Words to Britain: "Both Our Nations Serve the Cause of Freedom"', text of the speech at Whitehall Palace, London, 19 November 2003, reprinted in the *New York Times*, www.nytimes.com/2003/11/20/international/europe/20PTEX.html.

55 Bush, National Endowment speech, p. 8.

56 Bush, Whitehall Palace speech, p. 5.

57 Bush, National Endowment speech. See also Hassan, 'Bush's Freedom Agenda'.

58 Bush, National Endowment speech, p. 3.

59 Ibid., p. 8.

60 Ibid.

61 Bush, Whitehall Palace speech, p. 5.

62 Ibid.

63 Bush, National Endowment speech, p. 6.

64 C. Powell 'A Strategy of Partnerships', *Foreign Affairs*, 83:1 (January/February 2004), pp. 22–34.

65 See M. Ottaway, 'The Problem of Credibility', in T. Carothers and M. Ottaway (eds.), *Uncharted Journey: Promoting Democracy in the Middle East* (Washington, DC: Carnegie Endowment for International Peace, 2005), p. 182.

66 Bush, National Endowment speech, p. 5.

67 See *Statement of Amy Hawthorne, Independent Middle East Democracy Promotion Specialist*; House Committee on International Relations; Hearing on 'Redefining Boundaries: Political Liberalization in the Arab World', 12 April 2005.

68 See D. Finkel, 'U.S. Ideals Meet Reality in Yemen', *Washington Post*, 18 December 2005, p. A01.

69 See Hassan, 'Bush's Freedom Agenda'.

70 A. Ganji, 'Money Can't Buy Us Democracy', *New York Times*, 1 August 2006. See also J.M. Sharp 'Syria: Background and US Relations', CRS Report for Congress: Order Code RL33487 – updated 11 March 2009.

71 See M. Turner, 'Building Democracy in Palestine: Liberal Peace Theory and the Election of Hamas', *Democratization*, 13:5 (2006), pp. 739–755.

72 See D. Rose 'The Gaza Bombshell', *Vanity Fair*, April 2008. See also H.D.S. Greenway, 'Once Again, U.S. Policy Lies in Shambles', *New York Times*, 19 June 2007.

73 E. Ingram 'Pairing Off Empires: The United States as Great Britain in the Middle East', in T.T. Petersen (ed.), *Controlling the Uncontrollable? The Great Powers in the Middle East* (Norway: Tapir Academic Press), p. 3.

74 T. Cofman Wittes and S.E. Yerkes, 'What Price Freedom? Assessing the Bush Administration's Freedom Agenda', The Saban Centre for Middle East Policy at the Brookings Institute.

75 F. Stockman, 'Autocratic States Gain from US Democracy Promotion Fund', *Boston Globe*, 7 July 2004. Referenced at www.iht.com/articles/528252.html on 15 July 2004.

76 J.M. Sharp, 'The Middle East Partnership Initiative: An Overview', CRS Report for Congress: Order Code RS21457 – updated 8 February 2005.

77 Ibid.

78 See President Bush, 'President Bush Presses for Peace in the Middle East', 9 May; Remarks by the President in Commencement Address at the University of South Carolina; Columbia, South Carolina, http://georgewbush-whitehouse.archives.gov/news/releases/2003/05/20030509–11.html.

79 See R.Z. Lawrence, 'A U.S.–Middle East Trade Agreement: A Circle of Opportunity?', Peterson Institute for International Economics (2006).

80 Ingram, 'Pairing Empires', p. 7.

81 In S. Gray, 'America's Gulag', *The New Statesman*, 17 May 2004, www.newstatesman.com/200405170016.

82 Joint Hearing Before the Subcommittee on International Organizations, Human Rights,

and Oversight and the Subcommittee on Europe of the Committee on Foreign Affairs, House of Representatives. *Extraordinary Rendition in U.S. Counterterrorism Policy: The Impact on Transatlantic Relations*. First Session. 17 April 2007.

83 Ibid.
84 These included

>   1,325 images of suspected detainee abuse, 93 video files of suspected detainee abuse, 660 images of adult pornography, 546 images of suspected dead Iraqi detainees, 29 images of soldiers in simulated sexual acts, 20 images of a solider with a swastika drawn between the eyes, 37 images of Military Working Dogs being used in abuse of detainees and 125 images of questionable acts.
>   (See S.F. Eisenman, *The Abu Graib Effect* (London: Reaktion Books, 2007), pp. 123–124)

85 K. Williams, *American Methods: Torture and the Logic of Domination* (Massachusetts: South End Press, 2007), p. 7.
86 See Daalder and Lindsay, *America Unbound*.
87 See G. Miller 'Obama Preserves Rendition as a Counter-Terrorism Tool', *Los Angeles Times*, 1 February 2009.
88 K. Deyoung, 'Afghan Conflict will be Reviewed', *Washington Post*, 13 January 2009.
89 R. Jeffery Smith, '2 U.S. Airstrikes Offer a Concrete Sign of Obama's Pakistan Policy', *Washington Post*, 24 January 2009, p. A01.
90 D. Priest, 'Bush's War on Terror Comes to a Sudden End', *Washington Post*, 23 January 2009, p. A01.
91 B. Obama, 'Remarks by the President on a New Beginning', Cairo University, 4 June 2009, www.whitehouse.gov/the_press_office/Remarks-by-the-President-at-Cairo-University-6–04–09.
92 See J. Traub, *The Freedom Agenda: Why America Must Promote Democracy [Just Not the Way George Bush did]* (New York: Farrar, Straus and Giroux, 2008), pp. 226–229. However, please note that, while Traub asserts that this never came into law, this is not the case. On 3 August 2007, as part of H.R.1. *Implementing Recommendations of the 9/11 Commission Act of 2007*, ADA was ratified.
93 See Obama and Biden Campaign, 'Fact Sheet: Strengthening Our Common Security by Investing in Our Common Humanity', www.barackobama.com/pdf/issues/Fact_Sheet_Foreign_Policy_Democratization_and_Development_FINAL.pdf.
94 M. Landler, 'For Clinton, '09 Campaign Is for Her Turf', *New York Times*, 15 July 2009.
95 Obama, 'Remarks by the President on a New Beginning'.
96 B. Obama, 'Inaugural Address', 2009, www.nytimes.com/2009/01/20/us/politics/20text-obama.html?Pagewanted=3.
97 M. Landler, 'Obama Will Send Envoy to Syria, Officials Say', *New York Times*, 24 June 2009.
98 See *Continuation of the National Emergency with Respect to the Actions of the Government of Syria*, www.whitehouse.gov/the_press_office/Continuation-Message-to-Congress-from-the-President-and-Federal-Register-notice-concerning-Syria/; see also 'Syria's Assad Offers Informal Invitation to Obama', *Independent*, 3 July 2009, www.independent.co.uk/news/world/middle-east/syrias-assad-offers-informal-invitation-to-obama-1730188.html.
99 D.E. Sanger, 'Despite Crisis, Policy on Iran Is Engagement', *New York Times*, 5 July 2009.
100 Ibid.
101 Obama, 'Remarks by the President on a New Beginning'.
102 K. Deyoung, 'Obama Sets Timetable for Iraq: Withdrawal Is Part of Broader Regional Strategy, President Says', *Washington Post*, 28 February 2009.

5   American counter-terrorism through the Rewards for Justice Program, 1984–2008

Steve Hewitt

After the attacks of 11 September 2001, a dual-headed consensus emerged in various quarters: that human intelligence (HUMINT) was crucial in aiding counter-terrorism efforts against al-Qaeda and that the United States for a variety of reasons had failed to generate the required HUMINT. To address the perceived problem on the domestic front in 2002, the administration of President George W. Bush introduced a new program to, in effect, enlist millions of Americans as potential informers.[1] The program, the Terrorism Information and Prevention System (TIPS) sparked a firestorm of political protests, including comparisons to the former German Democratic Republic, stretching from the left side of the American political spectrum all the way to the right. Congress quickly killed the plan before it could be enacted.[2] Meanwhile, another program for recruiting informers from outside of the United States to supply information about terrorists and terrorism that predated TIPS, the Rewards for Justice Program, expanded dramatically in the aftermath of 9/11, paying out tens of millions of dollars to informers, while facing little in the way of scrutiny, particularly with respect to its effectiveness.

It is the second of these programs, the Rewards for Justice Program, which is the focus of this chapter. Despite its long history, the program remains largely unexamined. The significance of Rewards for Justice in terms of American counter-terrorism is multifold: it reveals the limitations of the human intelligence capabilities of American intelligence agencies both well before and after 9/11; it potentially represents an American challenge to the sovereignty of other countries; it demonstrates a flawed conceptualization on the part of the US government toward al-Qaeda and related ideologically motivated terrorism; it speaks to the evolution in American conceptualizing of counter-terrorism, particularly within a criminal law framework, since the early 1980s.[3] Finally, it raises important questions about how complex addressing terrorism can be, and how difficult it can be in assessing the success of counter-terrorists efforts.

The HUMINT gap

One of the apparent consensuses in the aftermath of the attacks of 11 September 2001 was the need for increased HUMINT regarding terrorism.[4] In turn, there was criticism of the reliance of American intelligence, specifically the Central Intelligence Agency (CIA) on technological collection of information, Signals Intelligence (SIGINT) (used here in a generalized way to represent all collection through technology), in its pre-9/11 counter-terrorism efforts.[5] According to one post-9/11 study that appeared in 2003, the CIA has a 'deteriorated human-intelligence capability that makes it almost impossible to penetrate key targets such as terrorist organizations and cripples U.S. efforts to detect and prevent terrorist attacks.'[6] Concerns about the CIA's HUMINT capabilities are not new, having existed since at least the 1970s. Indeed, a component of this critique was ideologically motivated as it provided an opportunity to blame Democratic presidential administrations, specifically those of Jimmy Carter and Bill Clinton, for 9/11.[7] In the case of the former, this related to his CIA Director, Admiral Stansfield Turner, who prioritized technological collection over human intelligence.[8] With the latter president, the focus was on the so-called 'Deutch rules', restrictions on the recruitment of informers put into place by then CIA Director John Deutch in 1995 after it emerged that a CIA asset had been connected to the deaths of an American citizen and the spouse of an American citizen in Guatemala.[9]

The critique of an overreliance on technology and its implications for counter-terrorism reflected in some ways the profound difference between the two forms of intelligence collection. To use a generalized fishing metaphor, SIGINT represents a trawler pulling a driftnet at sea and thus churning up everything in its path, including both the preferred fish and those that need to be discarded. In discussions surrounding the expanding power of the state to conduct surveillance, especially since the end of the Cold War, an entire body of literature and even popular culture has been born to warn of the death of privacy through the use of electronic surveillance.[10] Hollywood films such as *Minority Report* and *Enemy of the State*, in some ways echoing the more subtle 1970s film *The Conversation*, portrayed a state and its agencies rendered omniscient through advanced technology.[11] The films imagined the state as using its intelligence functions to create the panopticon as envisioned originally by Jeremy Bentham and written about more recently in detail by Michel Foucault. For Foucault, such technology represented 'disciplinary power' that was 'bi-directional' in its impact. An American academic described this technological power as embodying 'postmodern social control ... that ... tends to be systematic, methodical, and automatic in operation'. He added that it is usually 'impersonal' because the watcher is 'rarely' observed.[12]

In contrast, because it often involves, especially in liberal-democratic societies, participants within targeted organizations, HUMINT is more precise – the equivalent of a fishing line containing a kind of bait designed to attract a particular type of fish. Informers in the shape of individuals recruited from within an organization or transplanted from the outside have in theory a greater ability to pursue specific information in a far more direct way than more technological solutions will allow. This, of course, has special relevance to tightly knit terrorist organizations. The then head of the CIA's Directorate of Operations told a public gathering in April 2002 that the one factor that could have prevented the attacks of 9/11 was someone well-entrenched within al-Qaeda providing information to security agencies of the United States.[13]

Seeking more human intelligence, however, is not the same as acquiring it. There was shallowness to the calls for increased human intelligence regarding terrorism, in particular as practiced by those loyal to or inspired by al-Qaeda. Questions left unasked included how informers in terrorist cells could be recruited or infiltrated in from the outside, and what would motivate them to cooperate with the American state. One source that introduced a note of realism into the debate actually appeared just prior to 9/11 when Reuel Marc Gerecht, a former CIA member, quoted a CIA Near East Division operative on the difficulties the CIA was having in the Middle East and Central Asia:

> The CIA probably doesn't have a single truly qualified Arabic-speaking officer of Middle Eastern background who can play a believable Muslim fundamentalist who would volunteer to spend years of his life with shitty food and no women in the mountains of Afghanistan. For Christ's sake, most case officers live in the suburbs of Virginia. We don't do that kind of thing.[14]

Gerecht offers an even more succinct statement from another CIA member about the difficulties in developing HUMINT about al-Qaeda: 'Operations that include diarrhea as a way of life don't happen.'[15]

Two other practitioners offered equally cautionary, if less colorful, notes about the ease of generating human intelligence about al-Qaeda. Paul Pillar, who served as the head of the CIA's Near East Division from 2000 to 2005, points out that terrorist groups are frequently divided into cells and that those with the most knowledge are the least likely to betray. He adds that religiously motivated groups like al-Qaeda are much more difficult to penetrate than previous terrorist groups.[16]

An even more cautionary note challenging simplistic calls for more human intelligence came from Michael Scheuer, former head of the CIA's bin Laden team. In a piece entitled 'Why It's So Hard to Infiltrate Al-Qaeda', Scheuer contrasted HUMINT recruitment within al-Qaeda with similar efforts carried out against the Soviet Union:

> Here's the challenge that al-Qaeda and other Sunni militant groups pose: In such organizations the old Soviet scenario is exactly reversed – the militants who are least ideologically committed (and therefore most easily recruited by our spy agencies) are found at the edges of the groups, among the ranks of those who perform gunrunning, human smuggling, and narcotics trafficking. Once we've recruited these people, their value to us increases as they move toward the center of al-Qaeda. The problem is that the higher a would-be spy rises in al-Qaeda's ranks, the greater the ideological and theological commitment of his associates; Sunni leaders are often (though certainly not

always) the devout and courageous men their media organizations claim them to be. Career advancement in al-Qaeda tends to wash away much of the mercenary hypocrisy found at the entry level – and therefore, in effect, to unrecruit those cultivated by our intelligence agencies.[17]

Scheuer concludes on a distinctly pessimistic note: 'The odds of our ever having an informant among the senior al-Qaeda decision-makers are remote.'[18]

The birth of Rewards for Justice

The difficulty the American intelligence community had well before 9/11 led to the creation of the original version of Rewards for Justice in the 1980s. The program's roots lay with the first major experiences of the United States as a target of terrorism in the post-World War II period. On 18 April 1983, a suicide bomber targeted the US Embassy in Beirut, Lebanon, killing 63 people. Then, on 23 October 1983, a suicide bomber at the wheel of a truck packed with explosives drove it into the barracks of a group of US Marines who had been stationed in Lebanon by the administration of President Ronald Reagan. A total of 241 American military personnel died as a result.

Although it received little media attention at the time, and has been largely ignored in histories of American counter-terrorism that have tended to focus on discussions within the Reagan administration over how to respond militarily to the attacks,[19] the legislative response to these major incidents of terrorism against Americans and American targets would arrive almost exactly a year later, when Congress passed 'An Act to Combat International Terrorism'. President Reagan quickly signed it into law, proclaiming that it would

> provide the resources and authorities essential in countering the insidious threat terrorism poses to those who cherish freedom and democracy.... This nation bears global responsibilities that demand that we maintain a world-wide presence and not succumb to these cowardly attempts at intimidation.[20]

Although to this day not labeled as such, one aspect of the new law effectively established an informer-recruiting program. It offered a reward of up to $500,000 to 'any individual who furnishes information regarding an act of terrorism directed against a U.S. person or U.S. property'.[21]

'An Act to Combat International Terrorism' required the approval of the President for the payment of any rewards above $100,000, although this would soon rise to $250,000.[22] Eventually, a detailed system would emerge with the President no longer needing to have the final say. The granting system still in place involves an interagency committee with representatives from the CIA, the Department of Justice, the National Security Council, the Department of State's Office for Counter-terrorism and the FBI. The State Department's Bureau of Diplomatic Security, the body that administers the program, supplies the committee chair. The committee decides on the legitimacy of an award. Any rec-ommendation for payment then arrives on the desks of the Secretary of State and the Attorney General for a final determination.[23] The criteria for determining the amount of the reward to be paid is based on the quality of the information, the level of threat represented by the terrorist being informed on, and by the extent of the danger the informer faced for supplying the information.[24]

This new counter-terrorism tool was slow to be used by the Reagan adminis-tration. A year after the legislation became law, Palestinian terrorists hijacked the Achille Lauro cruise ship and murdered American tourist Leon Klinghoffer. Five US senators wrote to Secretary of State George Schultz requesting that a reward of $500,000 be offered for information leading to the arrest of the leading individual behind the hijacking. Reflecting a view of terrorism as essentially a criminal activity and not an act of war against the United States, Republican Senator Alphonse D'Amato of New York made it clear that the money would only be paid out if the operation's mastermind ended up facing the American criminal-justice system.[25]

In style, the new program resembled a crime-fighting initiative called Crime Stoppers that began in Albuquerque, New Mexico, in July 1976, and which offers rewards for information that leads to criminal convictions.[26] While offer-ing rewards to generate information is not a unique phenomenon, and recruiting informers through financial reward is a common practice, there was a uniquely American aspect to the effort.[27] This emanates from a particularly American tendency to personalize larger threats to the nation or to the wider social order. Since 1950, the Federal Bureau of Investigation (FBI) has produced 'Ten Most Wanted Fugitive' lists to promote the Bureau through the media while using the offer of rewards to generate public assistance in tracking down fugitives.[28] Within the US, the Fox Network has been airing since 1988 *America's Most Wanted*, a popular television show offering over 1,000 profiles of fugitive crimi-nals who were subsequently captured.[29] More recently, the US military produced prior to the 2003 invasion of Iraq a deck of cards featuring the 52 most wanted members of Saddam Hussein's regime.[30]

The new Reagan administration program had a 'reactive policing'[31] quality to it in that it sought information after terrorist attacks had occurred. The emphasis on rewards to induce the supplying of information about terrorism reflected some of the competing and complex discourses surrounding terrorism in the 1970s and 1980s as governments interpreted the meaning of terrorism: a criminal act, an act of war, or a combination of the two.[32] Offering a criminal-justice type reward also suggested that if terrorism represented a crime, then counter-terrorism required policing methods. Studies of police informers conducted by criminolo-gists and sociologists such as Malin Åkerström and Gary T. Marx have shown that the key motivator for those who become informers is monetary reward.[33] 'Money talks' was how one State Department official justified the emphasis on a monetary reward for helping the United States – appeals to justice or to helping the United States for altruistic considerations apparently were not of equal weight.[34]

The program was significant in several other respects. The need for a rewards program in the first place reflected an obvious inability on the part of the American intelligence community, especially the CIA, to develop human sources of its own in its pursuit of terrorists. In the 1980s, for example, Brent Scowcroft, a senior official in both the Reagan and George H.W. Bush administrations, expressed frustration at the lack of human intelligence available about Americans kidnapped in Lebanon.[35] The fact that the payments would only occur if the terrorism targeted Americans indicated a certain global view. Moreover, the use of an international bribery program potentially allowed the US to circumvent domestic policing and security agencies in some of the targeted countries that might be more reluctant to cooperate.[36]

There was a certain difficulty, however, with generating intelligence about terrorism through a program focused on cash rewards. The approach essentially said that everyone had his or her price. This philosophy was problematic as a recruiting tool for members of small terrorist cells with ideologically committed members prepared to die for the cause or, as one observer put it, 'individuals who forged their ties over decades in the dust of Palestinian refugee camps, the chaos of Beirut or the killing fields of Afghanistan'.[37] Focusing on monetary rewards was, to a certain extent, the opposite of the model frequently applied to espionage in the first few decades of the Cold War where the expectation was, in the aftermath of spies like the 'Cambridge Five', that people would spy for ideological reasons. This ideological motivation disappeared later in the concluding decades of the Cold War when spies such as Aldrich Ames and Robert Hanssen burned the CIA and FBI respectively for cold hard cash.[38]

Perhaps because of the nature of the approach, the program was invisible for its first few years and, by the end of 1988, had paid out not a cent for information in six terrorist cases for which a reward was on offer.[39] This prompted a reform of the program. Ironically, the State Department announcement of the revisions occurred almost to the minute that a bomb on board Pam-Am flight 103 was bringing it down over Lockerbie, Scotland, on 21 December 1988, killing 270 people. The alterations expanded the program to not only cover the arrest and conviction of those involved in terrorist attacks that had already occurred, but also to cover 'payment for information that leads to the prevention, frustration or favorable resolution of terrorist acts against US persons or property overseas'. As part of this expansion, the US State Department began an advertising campaign, distributing posters about the rewards in a variety of languages to its embassies around the world, while emphasizing that the 'identities of informants' would be protected.[40]

The bombing of Pan-Am 103 prompted an additional reform to the program. Congress, specifically the Senate, raised the maximum reward offered under the program from $500,000 to $2,000,000, and President George H.W. Bush signed the bill into law in December 1989. Still, the response to the program remained slow, with only one payment of $500,000 having been paid out by the time that Secretary of State James Baker held a State Department briefing in October 1990, some six years after the start of the program. He unveiled yet more changes to the

Rewards for Terrorism Information Program, as it was then called, including the change of its name to the 'Heroes Program'.[41] This re-branding reflected an effort to portray informing on behalf of the state, generally viewed in a negative light, as an act of heroism. Furthermore, the Secretary of State publicized a state–private partnership in the program, an angle that would expand after 9/11.[42] For terrorist attacks on civil aviation, the Air Transport Association and the Air Line Pilots' Association each agreed to contribute up to $1 million in matching funds to the maximum $2 million already offered by the US government.[43]

Related to the increase in reward money, and in an effort to generate more of a response, a new advertising campaign began. The US began to distribute matchbooks and over 7,000 posters advertising the program. Additionally, television and radio spots featuring Hollywood actors Charlton Heston, Charles Bronson and Charlie Sheen were created and aired both within the US and abroad, including in the Middle East, with subtitles in local languages. The choice of actors was telling beyond offering a muscular projection of America. Their masculine presence presented informing as heroic. So did the actual ads which extorted 'ordinary people' to do 'extraordinary things'. Anyone who called the English-language hotline even received his or her recorded instructions from Heston.[44]

The combination of the expanded program and high-profile terrorist attacks led to the payment of more rewards. By November 1995, the US government had distributed $3 million in a handful of cases where rewards were on offer.[45] Two-thirds of that amount related to one prominent incident, the 1993 attack on the World Trade Center (WTC). In emphasizing the successes of the program, US officials turned a single individual, Ramzi Yousef, into the program's poster boy. Yousef was the direct organizer of the 26 February 1993 bomb attack on the WTC that left six people dead and over 1,000 injured. He quickly fled the US after the attack and became involved in the planning of other terrorist attacks with his uncle, Khalid Sheikh Mohammed, the mastermind of the 11 September 2001 attacks. While operating in Pakistan, he recruited a South African Muslim who in 1995 gave Yousef up to American authorities for the $2 million reward. Although the US government had spent $100,000 to publicize the amount, the individual who turned in Yousef had read about the reward in *Newsweek*.[46] The Yousef arrest proved a landmark for this counter-terrorist effort and the US government over subsequent years would repeatedly cite his case as a demonstration of the usefulness of the effort.[47]

By 1997, the program had paid out $5 million and its website was receiving 50,000 hits a month. The latter fact was boasted of by a State Department spokesman who noted the way the new technology allowed the US to circumvent the sovereignty of other countries:

> we have now the ability, through the Internet, to reach countries which are state sponsors of terrorism and which in the recent past have not allowed the Department of State to take out advertisements in their newspapers to advertise the Heroes program.

He added that he was specifically referring to 'Iran, Iraq, Libya, and Syria'.[48] Another official emphasized the successes:

> We believe this program has saved thousands of innocent lives through people coming forward, providing us information that helped us resolve or prevent acts of terrorism worldwide.... Through our program two-dozen terrorists have been jailed or killed in shootouts with authorities.[49]

In contrast to the pre-emptive rhetoric, the program appears to have been more reactive than proactive in that cases with claimed rewards tended to be in the aftermath of terrorist acts having been committed and not to disrupt operations already in the pipeline. This was true in the case of Mir Aimal Kansi who killed two people outside the CIA headquarters in 1993 and was later arrested in Pakistan in 1997 after a tip.[50] In 1998, after the bombings of US embassies in Tanzania and Kenya, for the first time the program targeted Osama bin Laden with the offer of a $5 million reward for information leading to his arrest. Yet another advertising campaign to publicize the program was also initiated.[51]

Despite some genuine triumphs, by 2000 only $6 million had been paid out in 20 cases, with approximately one-third of that amount having gone to the informer who turned in Ramzi Yousef. This reality, coupled with another serious terrorist attack, this time against the USS *Cole* in Yemen, led to another expansion of the program. A proactive quality was emphasized even more with the slogan: 'We Can Give You 7 Million Reasons To Stop Terrorism.'[52] The increase in the top reward on offer appeared to reflect an underlying philosophy that any lack of response was due to payments not being high enough.

The State Department also revealed some details about the program. Most tips arrived via the Internet. They then underwent evaluation by experts as to their validity – if deemed legitimate, follow-up visits on the part of US diplomatic security officials would ensue. Most of those who supplied information had connections to the terrorist groups in question, reflecting the fact that those doing the informing were hardly innocent bystanders.[53] Moreover, the nature of those supplying the information had a deeper significance in that it demonstrated the Catch-22-like nature of such a program: only those involved in the terrorist activities possessed truly inside information; in turn, such individuals tended to be ideological motivated and, thus, more reluctant to cooperate with the US government.

All of this represented a prologue to a different program that would emerge in the aftermath of 9/11 as part of the Bush administration's War on Terror. Reflecting the gravity of the attack, the value of the rewards would rise dramatically, and advertising would occur within the US. The state–private element would become more significant as business entrepreneurs invited ordinary Americans to contribute money to the system of rewards being offered to recruit informers abroad. Finally, what the reward was for would also change – ensuring the arrest and conviction of a terrorist was no longer a priority – now it became simply about aiding the American state to track down its targets, in the words of President Bush, 'dead or alive'.[54]

Rewards for Justice after 11 September 2001

In some respects, the impact of the attacks of 11 September 2001 mirrored previous major terror incidents in the sense that the US government responded in a reactive way by increasing the amount of the enticement offered to potential informers. The Uniting and Strengthening America By Providing Appropriate Tools Required to Intercept and Obstruct Terrorism Act of 2001 (Patriot Act), passed in October 2001, increased the maximum reward to $25 million. A pattern was clearly on display: the more audacious the attack, the more dramatic the reforms to the counter-terrorist response, in this case through Rewards for Justice. Another consistent reaction, as in the past, was to launch a new advertising campaign.

Part of the publicity involved encouraging ordinary Americans to participate in the program, not by supplying information to the authorities but through tax-deductible donations to sweeten the financial inducements on offer to potential informers. This state–private approach mirrored efforts made during the Cold War against communism. In this case, two businessmen, Joe Rutledge, an ad executive, and Scott Case, one of the founders of priceline.com, spearheaded the effort. Less than a month after 11 September 2001, they announced a plan to allow ordinary Americans to contribute directly to the War on Terror through the tax-deductible Rewards for Justice Fund; reaching $100 million was the stated goal; they provided $1 million from their own resources as start-up capital and other private companies joined in with additional money.[55] Ordinary citizens could donate directly or through the purchase of 'United We Stand' license plates in six US states.[56] The businessmen's efforts in the fall of 2001 were closely coordinated with those of the State Department. Indeed, Charlotte Beers, a former advertising executive, who served as Under Secretary for Public Diplomacy and Public Affairs from October 2001 to March 2003, invited them to redesign the State Department's website for the program at www.rewardsforjustice.net.[57]

Both Case and Rutledge received a wave of publicity for their efforts as they appeared across American television and radio. Rutledge even officially began the program during an appearance on the *Today Show*. Their rhetoric was revealing. In announcing the program, Rutledge declared that

> [o]ne of the most powerful weapons in the war against terrorism can be found in every American home: the US dollar. This new fund will make sure every American has the opportunity to use that weapon as fully as possible, to help root out terrorists and bring them to justice.[58]

Together they repeatedly hailed the program as one of the most effective tools in fighting terrorism[59] since it used 'rewards dollars to turn terrorist supporters and sympathizers into terrorist informants'.[60] In introducing the new effort, Rutledge, bringing a cost–benefit mentality to the issue, suggested that the only impediment to success was a lack of resources: 'if $8 1/2 million has, over the last 16 years, helped bring 22 terrorists to justice, if we can raise far more, the program can be that much more effective'.[61]

Only rarely did the scheme of the businessmen receive critical analysis. In particular, a *Philadelphia Inquirer* story a year after 11 September 2001 offered a pertinent point about the program: 'It seems a curious business: Raising money for the U.S. government, which has a $2.1 trillion budget and a collection agency, the IRS, that doesn't have to rely on the kindness of strangers.' By that time, the program had added a lobbyist and fundraiser to its payroll. Case's enthusiasm was unbounded: 'Pay your taxes. Support our troops. But at the end of the day, this is the way that you as an individual can really make a donation toward fighting this particular war.'[62] The emphasis on the individual was important – it was individualizing the War on Terror by encouraging private citizens to aid in recruiting informers. Ultimately, the entire effort was a complete failure. The founders announced its conclusion in January 2008 after it raised only $1.5 million.[63]

As part of the advertising campaign that emerged after 11 September 2001, Rewards for Justice focused not just on foreign audiences but on domestic ones as well. Clearly, however, the target was not all Americans, but on Muslim and Arab Americans. One poster employed an image of Egyptian Mohammed Atta, the lead hijacker on 11 September 2001, as a selling point. 'He was spotted in Hamburg, Prague, Florida and Maine', it warned. 'And if someone had called us, his picture wouldn't be spotted in this ad.... [He] lived among us, attending classes, shopping at the mall, eating pizza, going out now and then with friends.'[64]

The domestic emphasis sparked scrutiny and even criticism of Rewards for Justice. At a State Department press conference, fronted by Colin Powell, on 13 December 2001, to announce the details of the program and preview an accompanying advertising campaign, the press asked Charlotte Beers several questions about its emphasis, including:

> But it's in the subtext of your questions that if it's an Arab American or a Middle Eastern-looking person who's asking these questions which otherwise might not be suspicious, then that's who you want to – you want someone to drop a dime on them.[65]

In a similar vein, the head of the Arab American Anti-Discrimination Committee complained:

> We've just heard too many cases in which people have reported that somebody is suspicious because they are Middle Eastern-looking or they seem to be Arab or, 'I think the man down the street is an Arab.' It basically becomes a kind of pattern of guilt by ethnicity. We have seen that and, as a matter of fact, we've heard complaints about that from law enforcement.[66]

Rewards success in generating informers with information about al-Qaeda was another story. Domestically, by April 2002, the FBI had received at least 20 reports of sightings of Osama bin Laden in Utah.[67] Abroad, between September and November 2001, the State Department received over 22,000 separate tips about the whereabouts of bin Laden and other senior al-Qaeda members, most via telephone or email. A State Department official dismissed the validity of much of what arrived by noting that not many telephones or computers existed in the areas where bin Laden was likely hiding. In reality, many of what flooded in involved individuals relaying that Osama bin Laden was somewhere near the Pakistan–Afghanistan border and then requesting their reward.[68]

Renewed campaigns abroad began in 2004 and, in a tactic previously tried, the US distributed thousands of matchbooks in Pakistan and Afghanistan showing Osama bin Laden's face on them.[69] In March 2004, the House of Representatives unanimously passed legislation allowing Rewards to pay out up to $50 million for individuals such as Osama bin Laden and devoting even more money to using radio and television to disseminate information about the program. The Senate followed suit in July 2007 when it also passed a motion calling for bin Laden's reward to grow to $50 million.[70] The State Department launched additional advertising campaigns in Pakistan and Afghanistan in the first half of 2005, with the Pakistan leg generating 242 tips between January and June 2005.[71]

There was another change in Rewards that mirrored a broader shift in American counter-terrorist operations. Whereas in its initial incarnation the program had stressed that money would only be paid out if the individual was arrested and convicted of terrorism-related offences in the US, now this requirement had been weakened:

> Rewards also may be paid for information leading to the arrest or conviction of terrorists attempting, committing, conspiring to commit, or aiding and abetting in the commission of such acts or *to the identification or location of an individual who holds a key leadership position in a terrorist organization.*[72]

As a number of sources have documented, the Bush administration made fundamental decisions after 11 September 2001 that dealing with terrorism would no longer have a criminal justice emphasis.[73]

The scale of the program grew as well, and so did the payouts. In 2003, the two largest disbursements in the history of the program occurred. One of $27 million, which included $2 million in relocation aid to help him move his family, went to an Egyptian al-Qaeda member who supplied information that led, in a key success of the program, to the capture of Khalid Sheikh Mohammed, the apparent mastermind of the 11 September 2001 attacks.[74] The new record under Rewards for Justice later surpassed that amount: $30 million for the information that led the US military to locate and kill Saddam Hussein's sons ($15 million for each). No one noticed that instead of using Rewards for Justice to locate terrorists, it had been employed to finance the discovery of men associated with a repressive regime toppled by the US. The program would later emphasize that it also seeks information about war criminals and narco-criminals, but Saddam's sons remain listed on the official Rewards' website as being examples of people caught through information 'that prevented international terrorist attacks or helped bring to justice those involved in prior acts'.[75] Elsewhere, payments went to Filipinos who aided in the pursuit of an Islamist group Abu Sayyaf[76] – in one case a US Embassy official handed over a suitcase containing $1 million to a masked informer. This event received extensive coverage on US diplomatic websites in a clear effort to encourage others to step forward by demonstrating that money would be paid.

Conclusion

Despite over 25 years of activity and considerable publicity, the overall effectiveness of Rewards for Justice in efforts against terrorism remains unclear. Supporters legitimately point to high-profile arrests as clear victories because of the program. However, 74 percent of all money paid out in the history of the program was for two cases, including the biggest single payout, the $30 million for the tip that led to the discovery of Saddam Hussein's non-terrorist sons.[77]

In turn, the program has the potential to damage American counter-terrorism efforts by alienating allied countries through American hegemonic encroachment. Although it received little attention in the US, the Rewards program in other key countries has caused controversy. In the Philippines, there have been complaints about the program's infringement of Filipino sovereignty.[78] Pakistani and Indonesian officials also have expressed concern, with the then vice president of Indonesia going so far as to state publicly that stopping terrorists 'must be done through an institution-to-institution cooperation of the countries involved. It shouldn't be an institution giving rewards to individuals.'[79] In December 2005, Republicans in the House of Representatives passed by voice vote legislation to allow the US government to pay money to officials in foreign governments (not previously allowed under Rewards) who supply the US with information, much to the chagrin of some American allies and also American officials who viewed the move as counter-productive.[80]

The major problem, however, with Rewards for Justice relates to its effort against al-Qaeda. Specifically, the premise on which it is seeking to motivate individuals to become informers is based on a criminal model in which criminals are essentially corrupt and can be subject to bribery. How would this apply to terrorists motivated by ideology? A 2002 question from a reporter to a Bush administration official at a news conference touched upon this:

> Some of these informants that you hope to get information from as part of this new program are part of whatever terrorist network that you are targeting at the moment. Unfortunately, they are willing – 9/11 showed that they are willing to die for their cause. Can you talk about the challenges in terms of trying to get information from these people who are so loyal, so patriotic to bin Laden or whoever their terrorist leader is, and they'll be not very likely therefore to sell out?[81]

It is a point Osama bin Laden himself raised in an interview with Al Jazeera about the reward being offered about him:

> [they] left the world and came to these mountains and land, leaving their families, fathers and mothers. They left their universities and came here under shelling, American missiles and attacks. Some were killed.... These men left the world and came for the jihad. America, however, which worships money, believes that people here are of this [same] calibre. I swear that we have not had the need to change a single man from his position even after these reports [about the US offering a multimillion reward].[82]

One response to the criticism is that the program is not just directed at those closely involved in terrorism, but to those who might have any knowledge and thus be less inclined to be motivated by ideology. Thus, it was and is about getting more marginal and less-committed players to come forward. This point perhaps explains the program's success in the Philippines, where members of Abu Sayyaf have less of an ideological commitment.[83] There is also the program's potential to encourage paranoia on the part of terrorists as trust in their colleagues diminishes while security precautions increase.[84]

Some American politicians appeared to recognize the limitations of the program or, at least, found themselves frustrated with the seeming lack of information related to al-Qaeda actors such as Osama bin Laden. In March 2004, the House of Representatives unanimously passed legislation allowing the US government to offer up to $50 million for individuals such as bin Laden; it also put more money into television and radio advertising. A Republican Congressman and proponent of Rewards observed that free publicity is one of the purposes of increasing the bounty on bin Laden's head: 'Each round you raise the price is more free media for the reward.'[85] The Senate followed suit in July 2007.[86]

Raising rewards, however, could be counter-productive. In the aftermath of the death of the leader of al-Qaeda in Iraq, Abu Musab al-Zarqawi, it emerged that the US military in Iraq had requested that the $25 million offered for him be reduced because his significance was in decline. A high reward thus afforded him more credibility than he deserved.[87] Terrorism expert Marc Sageman portrays the entire Rewards program as a failure that was responsible for turning 'nobodies into heroes'.[88] Within the US government, recognizing the limitations of money as an inducement to inform has led some to propose different types of rewards such as wells, livestock and tractors. One State Department official said, 'We can't come up with 70 virgins, but we can come up with goats.'[89] Although, as terrorism expert Bruce Hoffman points out, anyone using a new tractor or suddenly owning additional goats would raise suspicion and cause themselves to be 'marked' for elimination.[90]

In the end, the Rewards for Justice Program is problematic to say the least, particularly in terms of its effectiveness. Indeed, reports by a *Washington Post* journalist in 2008 found the program lacking in several respects, particularly in its ability to generate high-level al-Qaeda informers. In that respect, the terrorist group remained more impenetrable than the Kremlin during the Cold War.[91] In some ways Rewards is an effective tool for promoting a particular approach to US foreign policy in the way that it emphasizes personality and individuals instead of promoting a deeper consideration of the so-called 'root causes' of terrorism, or even a clearer understanding of the American War on Terror. The fact that payments were made from the fund for the individual who provided the US military with the location of Saddam Hussein's sons is evidence of this. Overall, the program seems less about combating terrorism than it is about appearing to combat terrorism. Hence, the frequent media campaigns, the introduction of private money after 9/11, and the continual raising of some of the rewards being offered. Collectively, it represents a 'throw money at the problem to solve it' attitude that is profoundly reactive. Terrorism expert Brian Jenkins famously said that 'all terrorism is theatre'.[92] The Rewards for Justice Program suggests that the same point may apply to some aspects of counter-terrorism.

Notes

1 'Informer' here is defined as anyone who secretly supplies information to a government agency. This definition would not include witnesses in trials.
2 N. Hentoff, 'The Death of Operation TIPS', *Village Voice*, 13 December 2002.
3 For more on counter-terrorist approaches, see R. Crelinsten, *Counterterrorism* (London: Polity, 2009), p. 90.
4 By terrorism, I mean the threat or use of violence for political reasons, such as to influence government policy, against civilians and non-combatants by non-state actors (this does not deny the existence of state terrorism but that is something separate). For discussions about defining terrorism, see W. Laqueur, *No End to War: Terrorism in the Twenty-First Century* (New York and London: Continuum, 2003), pp. 237–238; L. Richardson, *What Terrorists Want: Understanding the Terrorist Threat* (London: John Murray, 2006), pp. 19–25.
5 C. Fusco, 'Spies Lost in Cold War in a New Age of Terror', *Chicago Sun-Times*, 23 September 2001; M. Aid, 'All Glory is Fleeting: SIGINT and the Fight Against International Terrorism', in C. Andrew, R.J. Aldrich and W.K. Wark (eds.), *Secret Intelligence: A Reader* (London: Routledge, 2009), p. 47.
6 M.D. Villaverde, *Structuring The Prosecutor's Duty To Search The Intelligence Community For Brady Material*, Cornell Law Review, 88 (2003), pp. 1527–1528.
7 For prime examples of this genre, see B. Gertz, *Breakdown: How America's Intelligence Failure Led to September 11* (New York: Plume, 2003); A. Roberts, 'Bring Back 007', *Spectator*, 6 October 2001; Laqueur, *No End to War*, pp. 120–122.
8 T. Naftali, *Blind Spot: The Secret History of American Counter-terrorism* (New York: Basic Books, 2005), p. 143.
9 For more on the impact of the 'Deutch Rules' on human intelligence, see S. Hewitt, '"Operations That Include Diarrhea as a Way of Life Don't Happen": The CIA, Human Intelligence, and the War on Terror', unpublished paper presented at CIA and US Foreign Policy Conference, Clinton Institute for American Studies, University College Dublin, Dublin, February 2009.
10 For a selection, see S. Garfinkel, *Database Nation: The Death of Privacy in the 21st Century* (Cambridge: O'Reilly, 2000); W.G. Staples, *The Culture of Surveillance: Discipline and Social Control in the United States* (New York: St. Martin's, 1997); J. Rosen, *The Unwanted Gaze: The Destruction of Privacy in America* (New York:

Vintage Books, 2000); C.J. Sykes, *The End of Privacy: The Attack on Personal Rights – at Home, at Work, on-Line, and in Court* (New York: St. Martin's Griffin, 1999).

11 Francis Ford Coppola, director, *The Conversation*, 1974; Tony Scott, director, *Enemy of the State*, 1998; Steven Spielberg, director, *Minority Report*, 2002.

12 Staples, *The Culture of Surveillance*, p. 4.

13 D. Pasternak, 'Squeezing Them, Leaving Them', *U.S. News and World Report*, 133, 2, 8 July 2002, p. 12.

14 R.M. Gerecht, 'The Counter-Terrorist Myth', *Atlantic Monthly*, July/August 2001.

15 Ibid.

16 P. Pillar, *Terrorism and US Foreign Policy* (Washington, DC: Brookings Institute Press, 2001), pp. 110–111.

17 M. Scheuer, 'Why It's So Hard to Infiltrate Al-Qaeda', *Atlantic Monthly*, April 2005.

18 Ibid.

19 The legislation does receive extensive attention in the relevant histories of counter-terrorism during this period. Timothy Naftali, *Blind Spot: The Secret History of American Counter-terrorism* (New York: Basic Books, 2005), p. 138; David C. Martin and John Walcott, *Best Laid Plans: The Inside Story of America's War Against Terrorism* (New York: Harper & Row, 1988); Marc A. Celmer, *Terrorism, U.S. Strategy, and Reagan Policies* (Washington, DC: Greenwood Publishing Group, 1987); David C. Wills, *The First War on Terrorism: Counter-Terrorism Policy During the Reagan Administration* (New York: Rowman & Littlefield, 2003), p. 18.

20 R. Reagan, 'Statement on Signing the 1984 Act to Combat International Terrorism', 19 October 1984, www.reagan.utexas.edu/archives/speeches/1984/101984a.htm.

21 US Congress. *A Bill to Combat International Terrorism*. H.R. 6311, 1984.

22 B. Koerner, 'Do Terrorist Informants Have to Pay Taxes?', *Slate*, 13 March 2003.

23 C. Suellentrop, 'Could the Taliban Collect the $5 Million bin Laden Bounty?', *Slate*, 20 September 2001.

24 'Big Rewards If US Citizens Dob in a Potential Terrorist – War on Terror: The Final Phase', *Daily Telegraph*, 15 December 2001.

25 D. Iacono, 'International', *United Press International*, 17 October 1985.

26 'Our History', Crime Stoppers International, www.c-s-i.org/OurHistory.aspx.

27 Israeli security is a leading example of the use of human sources for intelligence against Palestinian terrorism. B. Hoffman, 'The Logic of Suicide Terrorism', *Atlantic Monthly*, June 2003; G. Gorenberg, 'The Collaborator', *New York Times Magazine*, 18 August 2002. For more on the recruitment of informers as part of counter-terrorism, see S. Hewitt, *Snitch! A History of the Modern Intelligence Informer* (New York: Continuum, 2010).

28 'The FBI's Ten Most Wanted Fugitives', www.fbi.gov/wanted/topten/tenfaq.htm#3.

29 *America's Most Wanted*, www.amw.com/.

30 Anonymous (Michael Scheuer), *Imperial Hubris: Why the West is Losing the War on Terror* (Washington, DC: Brassey's, Inc., 2004), p. 222.

31 Crelinsten, *Counterterrorism*, p. 90.

32 A report on terrorism in the 1970s by National Security Council member William Odom argued that 'When it [terrorism] happens here, it is a crime. When it happens abroad, it is war.' The latter, of course, was predicated on the idea of a state sponsor of the act of terrorism. Naftali, *Blind Spot*, p. 101. A police force in the form of the Federal Bureau of Investigation already was the lead agency for counter-terrorism within the United States and would take charge of future attacks abroad against Americans.

33 T. Williamson and P. Bagshaw, 'The Ethics of Informer Handling', in R. Billingsley, T. Nemitz and P. Bean (eds.), *Informers: Policing, Policy, Practice* (Uffculme: Willan Publishing, 2001), pp. 59–60; R. Billingsley, 'Informers' Careers: Motivations and Change', in Billinsley, Nemitz and Bean (eds.), *Informers*, p. 86; G.T. Marx, 'Thoughts on a Neglected Category of Social Movement Participant: The Agent

Provocateur and the Informant', *American Journal of Sociology*, 80:2 (1974), pp. 414–417; M. Åkerström, *Betrayal and Betrayers: The Sociology of Treachery* (New York: Transaction Publishers, 1991), p. 22; C. Dunninghan and C. Norris, 'A Risky Business: The Recruitment and Running of Informers by English Police Officers', *Police Studies*, 19:2 (1996), p. 4.

34 S. Ellis, 'U.S. Offers up to $7 Million for Tips on Terrorists', US Department of State, 2000.

35 Naftali, *Blind Spot*, 208.

36 International law required the US to seek the permission of those countries it was seeking to conduct investigations in. Villaverde, 'Structuring the Prosecutor's Duty to Search the Intelligence Community for Brady Material', pp. 1516–1517.

37 R. Scheunemann, as quoted in A. Roberts, 'Bring Back 007', *Spectator*, 6 October 2001.

38 S.A. Taylor and D. Snow, 'Cold War Spies: Why They Spied and How They Got Caught', *Intelligence and National Security*, 12:2 (1997), pp. 101–125; D. Wise, *Spy: The Inside Story of How the FBI's Robert Hanssen Betrayed America* (New York: Random House Books, 2003). See also K.L. Herbig, 'Changes in Espionage by Americans: 1947–2007', United States Department of Defense, March 2008, www.fas.org/sgp/library/changes.pdf.

39 The six were: the 28 June 1988 murder of the US Defense Attaché in Athens ($500,000); terrorist bombing of TWA Flight 840 on 2 April 1986 ($250,000); the assassination of four US Marines and two US civilians in San Salvador on 19 June 1985 ($100,000); the hijacking of TWA Flight 847 on 13 June 1985 ($250,000); the hijacking of Kuwaiti Airlines Flight 221 on 4 December 1984 ($250,000); and the hijacking of the cruise ship Achille Lauro on 7 October 1985 ($250,000). P. Oakley, 'From the State Department (Expansion of Rewards Program)', State Department Briefing, 21 December 1988.

40 Ibid.

41 Kyodo News Service, 'U.S. Offers Reward for Information on Terrorism', 8 June 1990.

42 For more on the concept of the state–private relationship in an American context, see S. Lucas, *Freedom's War: The American Crusade Against the Soviet Union* (New York: New York University Press, 1999).

43 J. Baker, 'Rewards for Terrorism Information Program', Washington, DC: State Department, 22 October 1990.

44 Ibid.

45 'State Dept. Offers $2 Million Reward', *United Press International*, 24 November 1995.

46 S. Balman, Jr., 'U.S. Offers $2 Million for New York Bombing Suspect', *United Press International*, 23 July 1993; Naftali, *Blind Spot*, p. 242; A. Laine, Interview by D. Zwerdling, 'State Department Rewards', *NPR Weekend All Things Considered*, 9 November 1998.

47 US Fed News, 'Rewards for Justice Program Pays Three Filipinos $1 Million for Information on Abu Sayyaf Leaders', *US Fed News (HT Media)*, 26 October 2004.

48 N. Burns, 'State Department Regular Briefing', Washington, DC: State Department, 30 January 1997.

49 As quoted in Warren Richey, 'Checkbook Justice: Police Snag Fugitives Using Big Bounties', *Christian Science Monitor*, 28 October 1997.

50 'State Department Rewards'; Richey, 'Checkbook Justice'; J. Stein, 'Convicted Assassin: "I Wanted to Shoot the CIA Director"', *Salon*, 22 January 1998, www.salon.com/news/1998/01/22news_kasi.html.

51 Laine, interview with Zwerdling; 'Rewards Program: Release of Public Service Announcement', Department of State, 1999.

52 R. Boucher, 'Rewards for Justice Program – Prevention of Terrorism Advertising Campaign', Washington, DC, 2000; S. Ellis, 'U.S. Offers up to $7 Million for Tips on Terrorists', US Department of State, 2000.

53 Ibid.

54 'Bush Pledges to Get Bin Laden, Dead or Alive', *USA Today*, 14 December 2001.

55 'NeuStar and the Rewards for Justice Fund Partner to Support Anti-Terrorism Cause', *Newswire*, 4 September 2002.

56 'United We Stand What More Can I Give; a Concert for Washington D.C. And America', *Business Wire*, 20 October 2001; 'Florida License Plates Supporting Rewardsfund.org Are America's Latest Weapon in Nation's Drive Against Terrorism', *Business Wire*, 30 October 2001; J. Gordon, 'Hitting the Road for a Patriotic Cause', *New York Times*, 1 September 2002.

57 'U.S. State Department and Rewards for Justice Fund Launch New Websites Allowing All Americans to Contribute to War On Terrorism', *Business Wire*, 13 December 2001; 'E-Government: Feds Solicit E-Commerce Experts for Design Help', *National Journal's Technology Daily* (2001). For more on Charlotte Beers involvement in US public diplomacy after 11 September 2001, see L. Kennedy, 'Remembering September 11: Photography as Cultural Diplomacy', *International Affairs*, 79:2 (2003), pp. 315–326.

58 'US Citizens Asked to Contribute 100 Million Dollars for Terrorist Bounty', *Agence France Presse*, 2 October 2001.

59 'Importance of New "Rewards for Justice Fund" Underscored by U.S. Secretary of State Colin Powell', *Business Wire*, 10 October 2001.

60 'Transcript of Interview with Scott Case and Joe Rutledge', *Hannity and Colmes*, Fox News, 15 October 2001.

61 Katie Couric interviews Joe Rutledge, *Today Show* transcript, 1 October 2001.

62 Eugene Kiely, 'Nonprofit's Money to Aid U.S. Program: Fueling the Fight Against Terrorism', *Philadelphia Inquirer*, 16 September 2002.

63 www.rewardsfund.us.

64 'U.S. to Expand Terrorist Bounty to Palestinians, New Ad Campaign', *Agence France Presse*, 13 December 2001.

65 State Department, 'Special State Department Briefing', *Federal News Service*, 13 December 2001.

66 Hussein Ibish, as quoted in M. Kelemen, 'Rewards for Justice Program Expands to Encourage Reporting of Information about Possible Terrorists Domestically', *NPR Weekend All Things Considered*, 15 December 2001.

67 'Harper's Index for April 2002', www.harpers.org/HarpersIndex2002–04. html#230553581536753.

68 E.J. Lake, 'How the Bounty on bin Laden Works', *United Press International*, 21 November 2001; K. Whitelaw, 'Just a Phone Call Away', *U.S. News and World Report*, 31 January 2005, p. 32.

69 B. Gertz and R. Scarborough, 'Inside the Ring', *Washington Times*, 23 January 2004.

70 K. Haskell, 'Turning in Terrorists: Take the Money and Run', *New York Times*, 28 March 2004; 'Senate Doubles Bin Laden Bounty to 50 Million Dollars', *Japan Today*, 14 July 2007.

71 A. Whaidullah, 'First War, Now PR to Get bin Laden', *The Times Union*, 3 September 2005.

72 'Rewards for Justice Program', Department of State, 13 December 2001.

73 See, for example, J. Risen, *State of War: The Secret History of the CIA and the Bush Administration* (New York: Free Press, 2004); R. Suskind, *The One Percent Doctrine: Deep Inside America's Pursuit of its Enemies Since 9/11* (New York: Simon & Schuster, 2006); J. Mayer, *The Dark Side: The Inside Story of How the War on Terror Turned into a War on American Ideals* (New York: Doubleday, 2009).

74 B. Koerner, 'Do Terrorist Informants Have to Pay Taxes?', *Slate*, 13 March 2003.

75 'Powell Signs Off on 30 Million Reward to Saddam Sons Informant', *Agence France Presse*, 31 July 2003; 'Rewards Paid', Rewards for Justice, www.rewardsforjustice. net/index.cfm?page=success_stories&language=english.

76 'Rewards for Justice Program Pays Three Filipinos $1 Million for Information on Abu Sayyaf Leaders', *State News Service*, 26 October 2004.

77 'Powell Signs Off on 30 Million Reward to Saddam Sons Informant.'

78 J.O. Valisno, with F.F. Salvosa II, 'US Offers $5m Each for Five Bandits (Military Says Bounty to Help in Fight to Eliminate Abu Sayyaf Group)', *Business World*, 30 May 2002; 'Talking Points', *Philippine Daily Inquirer*, 31 May 2002.

79 'Allies Object to U.S. Idea to Pay Officials for Terrorism Tips', *Bloomberg News*, 1 March 2006, www.bloomberg.com/apps/news?pid=10000100&sid =a_uiMWAylJw0&refer=gemany.

80 Ibid.

81 'News Conference with Jimmy Gurule, Treasury Undersecretary for Enforcement and Frank Taylor, State Department Coordinator for Counter-terrorism', *Federal News Service*, 13 November 2002.

82 Bin Laden, as quoted in Richardson, *What Terrorists Want*, p. 64.

83 M. Bowden, 'Jihadists in Paradise', *Atlantic Monthly*, March 2007.

84 S. Hudson, 'Zarqawi Bounty May Go Unpaid but Rewards Aid Fight', *Reuters*, 9 June 2006.

85 Representative Mark Kirk, as quoted in E.J. Lake, 'Forces Asked That Price on Zarqawi's Head Be Reduced', *New York Sun*, 14 June 2006.

86 Haskell, 'Turning in Terrorists'.

87 Lake, 'Forces Asked That Price on Zarqawi's Head Be Reduced'.

88 M. Sageman, *Leaderless Jihad: Terror Networks in the Twenty-First Century* (Philadelphia: University of Pennsylvania Press, 2008), p. 151.

89 K. Whitelaw, 'Just a Phone Call Away', *U.S. News and World Report*, 31 January 2005, p. 32.

90 Koerner, 'Do Terrorist Informants Have to Pay Taxes?'

91 C. Whitlock, 'After a Decade at War with West, Al-Qaeda Still Impervious to Spies', *Washington Post*, 20 March 2008; C. Whitlock, 'Bounties a Bust in Hunt for Al-Qaeda', *Washington Post*, 17 May 2008.

92 B. Jenkins, 'International Terrorism: A New Mode of Conflict', in David Carlton and Carlo Schaerf (eds.), *International Terrorism and World Security* (London: Croom Helm, 1975), p. 16.

6 British armed forces and European Union perspectives on countering terrorism

Major General Graham Messervy-Whiting

The aim of this chapter is to outline a British armed forces perspective on countering terrorism since World War II, within the frameworks of their approach to intelligence and security in general and of overall British government policy in this field. The chapter then outlines how the British have worked with their colleagues inside the European Union to meet the challenge of current terrorist threats in a networked world. The first snapshot provides one bottom-up perspective, the second one top-down one; there are of course many others.

A British armed forces perspective on countering terrorism

British military intelligence is composed of several bodies. The British Army is the only Service to have a full-time body of professional 'intelligencers', the Intelligence Corps. The skills they are trained in include all aspects of how to develop intelligence from people (human intelligence, or HUMINT). This has been the traditional focus of armies down the ages and the British are currently recognized as amongst the best in the world at it. Personnel are also trained in how to develop intelligence from imagery intelligence (IMINT) and various forms of electronic signals (SIGINT). Increasing emphasis has recently been given to developing as much intelligence as possible from open sources (OSINT). They are also trained in all the defensive aspects of the intelligence business.

The Royal Navy has a number of establishments that have an intelligence function, and trades which specialize in aspects of intelligence, such as the sound signatures of vessels. The Navy has been in the signals intelligence field for a very long time. Most naval vessels are capable of being platforms for undertaking a range of intelligence collection tasks. The Royal Air Force (RAF) set-up in the intelligence business currently lies somewhere between those of the Army and of the Royal Navy, like the Navy with a traditional strength in knowledge of potentially threatening platform and equipment signatures. The RAF has historically majored in the imagery intelligence field, but its aircraft also provide the platforms for other forms of intelligence collection.

Since World War II, much of the British military intelligence effort has been conducted on a tri-service ('joint') basis. The Defence Intelligence Staff was the first major part of the Ministry of Defence (MoD) to become truly joint. Nowadays, the Defence Intelligence and Security Centre carries out most of the intelligence training in the various disciplines for all three Services, a number of British civilian agencies and for a wide variety of foreign military and civil services. The UK's national strategic imagery and interrogation establishments are both military and have been joint almost since inception.

Military intelligence has a close working relationship with each of the UK's three secret services. The Security Service (MI5) and the Secret Intelligence Service (SIS or MI6) grew out of Army military intelligence branches in and around World War I; Government Communications Headquarters (the signals intelligence service – GCHQ) out of the military-run Bletchley Park after World War II. Today, armed-forces personnel and specialist units still provide a substantial part of the civilian-run GCHQ's workforce and capabilities; SIS and, to a lesser extent, MI5 are still dependent on several forms of specialist armed-forces assistance. Much of the military intelligence effort, particularly in the technical fields, has also been conducted on a very close basis with the UK's main intelligence allies from the 1940s (USA, Australia, Canada and New Zealand) and, more recently, with other allies who are undertaking a particular military operation with the UK (a 'combined' operation), such as within NATO, the European Union or within ad-hoc coalitions of the willing.

The defensive side of security, 'protective security', is often viewed as the least glamorous aspect of the military intelligence business: the Intelligence Corps professionals are engaged in the security of personnel, of information and of materiel against the threats of subversion, espionage, sabotage and terrorism; they carry out security education and training and security surveys to help the customer to identify areas for improvement; and they advise commanders and their staffs on threats and risks. All of this constitutes key aspects of 'risk management', in today's boardroom jargon.

The offensive side of security has developed dramatically since the 1960s. Traditionally for the Army, it used to be focused on 'field security'. So, for example, in addition often to being the last out when the Army was withdrawing from operations, to ensure that no high-value people, information or materiel was being left behind, the field security teams were often amongst the first in during an advance, in order to facilitate the capture of the enemy's high-value people, information and materiel. This task has since been wrapped into the concept of 'operational security', nowadays linked in with 'force protection'. But what the intelligencers' limited resources have been increasingly being focused on since the 1960s has been 'security intelligence': bringing particular human intelligence skills to bear in the counter-intelligence and, increasingly, counter-terrorist fields. Here, they are of course always working closely with, and often in direct support of, all the relevant civilian agencies; if the case is big enough, its direction will normally be taken over by the competent national agency. So, for example, in Germany in the 1970s and 1980s, working with various combinations of the local German police special branches (SBs), regional and national-level security agencies and the UK's MI5 and SIS, intelligencers mounted a number of covert surveillance operations and human source recruitment operations. Their main targets were hostile intelligence services operating against British armed forces targets, then the Provisional IRA terrorist group when they started operating against British targets on the Continent. They started mounting what were called 'composite' security intelligence operations, trying to make best use of all the intelligence tools that could be made available. For example, they might start off with a major security vulnerability in a high-value target, identified by the protective security process, mount a speculative security intelligence operation to monitor any hostile exploitation of that vulnerability, then, if they found exploitation, bring some of the more expensive human and technical resources to bear.[1]

Turning to the perspective of British armed forces on countering terrorism since World War II, the narrative often starts with the successful Malayan counter-insurgency campaign, although terrorism was perhaps first used as a deliberate tactic against British security forces in the 1940s by Zionist extremist groups such as Irgun and Lehi ('The Stern Gang'), in Palestine. In the Malaya (1947–1960), Kenya (1952–1960), Borneo (1962–1966), Oman (1962–1975) and Cyprus (EOKA-B 1971–1974) campaigns, terrorism was a tactic mainly directed against particular ethnic groups (including British settlers), tribes or villages. By contrast, earlier in Cyprus (EOKA 1955–1960) and in Aden (1964–1967), terrorist acts were also directed as a matter of policy against British forces.

In Palestine, the terrorist threat was conceptualized by the British, acting at that time under a UN mandate, as a tactic used by Zionist extremists attempting to unravel a UN peace process in order to establish a state of Israel on their terms and as quickly as possible. The British intelligence setup in Palestine looked comprehensive on paper: a Defence Security Office (or DSO – an MI5 outpost) watching over the intelligence work (led by the Political Branch of CID) of the British-officered and well-armed Palestinian Police Force. The British Army acted mainly in support of the police, on unpopular tasks such as guarding key points, curfew enforcement, riot control, and cordon and search operations. Intelligence Corps units, both area-based and also embedded with Army formations at divisional-level and above, were focused mainly on the field security function, including plain-clothes HUMINT operations in areas where it was difficult for the Army to conduct uniformed patrols. One of several exceptions to this was the existing Combined Services Detailed Interrogation Centre (CDIC – located in the Suez Canal Zone) which was authorized to carry out this HUMINT function on behalf of the Police CID. This campaign period (1945–1948) cannot be viewed as any sort of British success: while the security forces acted by and large with determination and efficiency in what they were tasked to do, they made few serious inroads into Irgun and Lehi's capability[2] against the backcloth of the disastrous political 'no win' mess into which they were thrust, a mess which remains as one of the world's most intractable flashpoints. However, it can be argued that some useful lessons were learned by the counter-insurgency operators on the ground, many of whom went on after the British withdrawal in

1948 to establish the special constabulary in Malaya and thence on to Kenya and other hotspots of the shrinking empire.[3]

In Cyprus, the terrorist threat posed by Grivas' EOKA in the late 1950s was seen as a tactic in the pursuit of the political goal of *enosis* (union with Greece). Unlike in Palestine, the British in Cyprus now re-organized their command and control structure along the lines of that of the successful Malayan campaign: an overall Director of Operations was appointed, with authority over the counter-insurgency policy, plans and operations of the administration, the Police and the Army, and a joint intelligence organization was similarly established.[4] The Intelligence Corps role was again primarily a field security one, with personnel embedded with the police special branch and working closely with Royal Navy and RAF personnel on port and airport security, and travel control. Significant numbers of personnel were also engaged on the island in the imagery and signals intelligence functions.[5] One big difference, though, from Palestine was that Army force levels rose significantly at the start of this period, mainly because of the administrative relocation to Cyprus of headquarters and units that had been based in post-war Egypt; helicopters also became available for operational use on the island from around 1957. This fortunately enabled the British security forces to dominate the area of operations much more effectively than in Palestine. The counter-terrorist strategy was embedded into the criminal-justice system, with emergency legislation enabling measures such as collective punishment, deportation and a broadening of the death sentence. This campaign can be seen as a British success: despite the Suez distraction, a police force that was less than wholly non-partisan, and often being the 'meat in the sandwich' between Greek and Turkish Cypriot factions, the British security forces did succeed in making serious inroads into EOKA; and the political aim was maintained, leading to negotiations with Greece and Turkey and an agreement enabling the end of British rule and an independent Republic of Cyprus.[6]

In Aden, the Yemen-based National Liberation Front (NLF) started to focus on an urban terrorist campaign from late 1964, targeting British forces and their families as well as members of the local security forces and others associated with the nascent British-fostered Federation of South Arabia (FSA). The British visualized the NLF threat as a largely cross-border insurgency stoked up by foreign powers inimical to British intentions in the area.[7] A second group of nationalist insurgents, the Front for the Liberation of Occupied South Yemen (FLOSY), opened their terrorist campaign in late 1966. By November 1967, the date announced for British withdrawal, drew nearer, the NLF and FLOSY also started fighting each other for the control of Aden. The local security forces started to waiver and some, such as the Aden special branch, were almost completely wiped out. At this stage, the British armed forces found themselves having to assume many of the security functions normally carried out by civil authorities, to the extent needed to secure an 'across the beach' withdrawal. The Army mounted operations such as patrols, road blocks, cordon and search, and house searches.[8] The Intelligence Corps' Counter-Intelligence (CI) Company in Aden had to assume many of the normal police SB functions, against the backcloth of the campaign of intimidation making it particularly difficult to gather HUMINT from the local population.[9] For the British, the Aden campaign ended up as a militarily successful damage-limitation withdrawal, which had been marred by a particularly poor match between political aims and military action on the ground.

The British Army's longest campaign in modern times was its 38 years of supporting the civil authorities in Northern Ireland (Operation BANNER 1969–2007). Their initial task was in essence to support the local civil authorities and in particular the local police force, at that time the Royal Ulster Constabulary (RUC), in maintaining public order, then countering the terrorist threats posed by extremists on both sides of the 'tribal' divide. The British government's overall strategy was to buy time for an eventual political solution; within this, the role of the armed forces was to hold the ring. The counter-terrorist strategy was to view terrorist acts as criminal acts, to be dealt with under the criminal-justice system, with that system being progressively extended by the passing of emergency legislation, to encompass 'temporary measures' such as no-jury trials and detention without trial.[10]

The Army was, throughout the campaign, in the armed forces lead, but the other Services played important roles.[11] The Royal Navy and Royal Marines provided principally the maritime and inland security dimensions, plus helicopter, special forces and, in the cases of the Marines, straight infantry-role support. The RAF provided principally helicopter but also some special forces and infantry-role support. The 'joint' dimension was fairly nominally provided, under the lead of the Army General Officer (GOC) commanding Northern Ireland and his Commander Land Forces (CLF), by their receiving liaison from the Senior Naval and Senior RAF Officers Northern Ireland. The 'combined' dimension was provided, certainly towards the end of the campaign, by increasing cooperation between the British and Irish security forces.

It quickly became apparent to Army commanders that they needed reliable sources of intelligence which were not totally dependent on the RUC since, although the RUC was key to the solution, some elements were seen as a part of the 'tribal' problem.[12] The area-based Intelligence Corps unit in Northern Ireland was expanded to encompass both sub-units embedded with the deployed Army brigades and more detailed theatre-level support to the Northern Ireland HQ, such as in the field of weapons intelligence.[13] Personnel were also involved in the developing in-theatre imagery and signals intelligence operations. Some intelligence functions were hived off to new specialized intelligence units, which were rapidly expanded by the recruitment and training of volunteers from other parts of the armed forces, the Intelligence Corps being too small to do other than provide a kernel of expertise and experience. Another such unit took on the running of those human sources recruited by the armed forces,[14] another the function of plainclothes covert passive surveillance operations. Some of these new intelligence units worked very closely with the deployed special forces sub-units.[15]

That all these arrangements were being established by the armed forces in a part of the UK was not without controversy, and indeed opposition, from other government departments and agencies. Over the course of the campaign, the three main British secret services also weaved their way through this unfamiliar and complex intra-state counter-terrorist situation with major inter-state dimensions. MI5 claimed the lead, and spent time and effort defending primacy against all-comers, but SIS also had a very important role to play and GCHQ successfully re-orientated itself, away from its classic Cold War strategic role and towards supporting more closely the operational and tactical levels of armed forces command.

Several efforts were made to bring all counter-terrorist policy, plans, intelligence and operations under more effective command and control, along the lines of the Malayan model. None of these efforts succeeded to the same degree as in Malaya, perhaps inevitably owing to the primarily domestic nature of the Northern Ireland campaign and therefore the closeness of the issue to the British organs of state. Nevertheless, the armed forces successfully held the ring until a political solution could be agreed by all parties and new political, legal, administrative, police, military and intelligence arrangements are in the process of coming into effect. For example, following the coming into being of the new Police Service for Northern Ireland (PSNI), MI5 at long last in October 2007 officially achieved the lead for national security and intelligence gathering in Northern Ireland.[16]

Moving from the historical experience to the current counter-terrorist challenge post-9/11, the lead government departments are the Home Office for domestic issues, and the Foreign and Commonwealth Office (FCO) for overseas issues, coordinated by the Cabinet Office. The main strands of the strategy are 'the four Ps': pursue, prevent, protect and prepare. 'Pursue' covers the stopping of terrorist attacks; 'Prevent' – stopping people from becoming terrorists or supporting violent extremism; 'Protect' – strengthening protection against attack; and 'Prepare' – mitigating the impact of attacks that cannot be stopped. The strategy was first issued in 2003 and revised in March 2009.[17]

Within this framework, the armed forces play a strong supporting role. At home, their contribution is limited to providing capabilities that are unique to the military, such as explosive ordinance disposal, to support the civil authorities in dealing with the most challenging of threats. Examples include the use of special forces in support of the civilian police in ending the 1980 terrorist siege of the Iranian Embassy in London and assistance to the civil authorities in Manchester after the Provisional IRA's 1,200 kg bomb there in 1996. In the wake of the London bombings of 7 July 2005, it emerged that armed forces specialists had been supporting a hard-pressed Metropolitan Police Service (MPS) in the covert passive surveillance role;[18] volunteer reservists also helped to run a number of the emergency centers that were set up.[19]

The MoD's main focus, however, is on the overseas dimension, aiming to fight the battle 'upstream' by developing partnerships and helping partners to build their counter-terrorist capacity. Examples include training the trainers in specialist activities such as forensics and counter-IED (improvised explosive devices). The armed forces also contribute through their current operational activities in the fields of intelligence, the disruption of terrorist capability and stabilizing failed or failing states.

Turning to measuring the success of British counter-terrorism strategy, the British government and the security services state[20] that, under 'Pursue', over a dozen attacks have been successfully disrupted since 2001; the impact of the 'Prevent' strand is only likely to be detectable in the longer term; the 'Protect' strand has been focused on protecting critical national infrastructure (in much the same way as counter-sabotage protection was focused on 'key points' during the Cold War, but with the inclusion now of places where large numbers of people congregate) and has led to the creation of a new agency dedicated to this task;[21] 'Prepare' has focused on putting into effect the many lessons drawn from the 2005 London attack to improve the effectiveness of all the responding agencies and the communication and coordination between them.

A European Union perspective

In addressing the challenges of counter-terrorism post-9/11, the EU has conceptualized threats within the framework of the overall European Security Strategy; the response, in the shape of the EU's Counter-Terrorism Strategy, is firmly based on respect for human rights and international law, and placed within the overall framework of a European area of freedom, justice and security. Importantly, the EU has developed metrics, through its action plan, for development and implementation to be evaluated frequently and regularly at Heads of State and Government level.

The EU started to develop its security dossier, in the broadest sense, under the Justice and Home Affairs (JHA) banner. Member States began to cooperate in the JHA area in the mid-1970s on an informal, intergovernmental basis outside the Community framework. This arrangement was formalized with the entry into force of the Amsterdam Treaty in the late 1990s. Two main subsequent events took place to widen this approach.

First was the advent into EU business, starting in 1999, of the Common Foreign and Security Policy (CFSP) dossier, including its European Security and Defence Policy (ESDP) component. Second were the events of 11 September 2001 in New York and Washington, subsequently reinforced for Europeans by the events of 11 March 2004 in Madrid, and 7 July 2005 in London.

The advent of CFSP and ESDP progressively added an outward-looking dimension to the task of meeting the security challenges. Some of the key events since the new millennium have included the development of a strong intelligence team in the EU's Military Staff. This team has secure links with the defense intelligence organizations of the Member States, which provide it with classified assessed defense intelligence products, thus allowing the EU Military Staff to supply its customers with timely and accurate EU defense intelligence assessments. The development of a joint (in this context, meaning a joint civil–military) Situation Centre (SITCEN) then enabled joint assessments to be disseminated.

Second was the mounting, in 2003, of the EU's first three ESDP operations: a police mission in Bosnia and Herzegovina, and two military missions, one in the Former Yugoslav Republic of Macedonia and one in the Democratic Republic of Congo. Some 23 missions on three continents are, at the time of writing, underway or have been completed.

Finally was the adoption by the EU's Heads of State and Government in December 2003 of a European Security Strategy. The strategy lists the key threats as: terrorism, the proliferation of weapons of mass destruction, regional conflicts, state failure and organized crime. It goes on to list what the EU has done so far to tackle the threats, and what it must now work towards. This includes that 'better coordination between external action and JHA policies was crucial in the fight against terrorism and organized crime'.[22] The implementation of the strategy was reviewed and reinforced by Heads of State and Government in December 2008.[23]

Politically, the EU reacted very quickly indeed after the 2001, 2004 and 2005 attacks. Following 9/11, the Council of Ministers reached decisions on sanctions against named international terrorists and terrorist organizations, and an overall action plan, since supplemented by a detailed roadmap, for the first time pulling together all the strands across the EU's areas of responsibility including: legal, financial, police, border, diplomatic, military, cooperation with the private sector, trade and aid, and so on. The elements in this plan led, for example, to the adoption of a European arrest warrant; better coordination of cross-border investigations by a new agency called EUROJUST;[24] the establishment of a Police Chiefs' task force; steps to attack terrorist financing, including legislation on the freezing of assets; and an agreement on mutual legal assistance with the United States, including the exchange of liaison officers and of intelligence between US law-enforcement agencies and EUROPOL.[25]

After the 2004 Madrid attacks, a draft package was prepared, within four days, of ten measures to enhance the EU's work on combating terrorism, including political commitment to a solidarity clause;[26] a revised action plan, followed by a comprehensive implementation plan; a new post of 'Security Coordinator';[27] enhanced intelligence cooperation; guidelines for a common approach to fighting terrorism; increased EU/UN coordination on terrorism; new actions directed at the financing of terrorism; the reinforcement of practical cooperation; implementation of existing measures; and enhanced relations with third countries. After preparatory meetings of Justice and Home Affairs and Foreign Ministers, a comprehensive package was adopted by the EU Heads of State and Government on 25 March 2004, in its 18-page declaration on combating terrorism.[28]

All this was done within the framework vision of 'a European area of freedom, security and justice'; in other words, meeting the challenge of benefiting from the free movement of people, goods and capital generated by the internal market, while taking all reasonable and sensible steps to minimize the security threats. The need for global partnerships was stressed, of course with the United States but also with new near neighbors, such as Russia and Ukraine.

Counter-terrorist clauses were now to be written by the EU into all agreements with third countries, such as on trade.

Following the 2005 London attacks, EU Justice and Home Affairs Ministers reached an agreement[29] on an overall EU Counter-Terrorism Strategy;[30] together with a strategy for combating radicalism and recruitment to terrorism; and a progress report, including a scoreboard, on the implementation of the action plan by Member States. EU Heads of State and Government formally review the implementation of the strategy at least once per year.[31]

The EU's Counter-Terrorism Strategy is based on respect for human rights and international law, and covers four strands of work: preventing radicalization and recruitment and the factors behind them; protecting potential targets; pursuing terrorists; and responding to the aftermath of an attack. In this, it is not dissimilar to the main thrusts of the UK's '4Ps', but there are differences in emphasis and nuance. For example, unsurprisingly, it lists the 'protection' strand ahead of 'pursue'. Some practical developments since 2005 under the 'Prevent' strand have included initiatives by EUROPOL and Member States to address radicalization in prisons and to counter violent radicalization through the Internet; EU aid projects to third countries, such as in the Western Balkans, Algeria and Morocco, in the field of good governance and the rule of law, to address factors that can contribute to radicalization and recruitment; and the formation of an expert group on violent radicalization by the Commission in 2006.

Under the 'Protect' strand, practical developments have included measures to improve the protection of borders, such as the directive on the inclusion of biometric features in EU passports; measures to improve the security of transport, such as the ports security directive and initiatives to improve the security at European airports, following the aborted 2006 attack on transatlantic aircraft in the UK; wide-ranging measures to improve the protection of critical infrastructure, including a directive establishing a procedure for the identification and designation of European critical infrastructure, and a European rapid alert system to respond to emergencies; and, for the first time, the inclusion of security-related research and development in the EU's research program. The Seventh Research Framework Program (2007–2013) has earmarked €1.4 billion for this purpose and several cross-border studies on radicalization have been commissioned.[32]

The 'Pursue' strand has seen the European Arrest Warrant increasingly being employed as a tool against terrorism and other forms of major crime; initiatives to combat the financing of terrorism, including the Third Money Laundering Directive (2005), the Regulation on cash couriers requiring disclosure of cash or equivalent in excess of € 10,000 (2005), and the Regulation on funds transfers (2006); and several measures aimed at strengthening information exchange. For example, a common position to improve information sharing on lost and stolen passports, including with Interpol, was adopted in 2005. A directive on the retention of data was adopted in 2006, as was a framework decision on simplifying the exchange of information and intelligence between law-enforcement agencies. Efforts continue to integrate the Treaty of Prüm (2005), which allows national law-enforcement authorities access to databases in other Member States (including of fingerprints and DNA), and which facilitates cross-border police cooperation.[33] Finally, EUROPOL and EUROJUST are each involved in around 20 ongoing terrorism-related investigations. An agreement strengthening information exchange between EUROJUST and the US Department of Justice was agreed in 2006, and the European Police College (located at Bramshill) has initiated counter-terrorism training programs for senior police officials.

Under the 'Respond' strand, practical developments have included initiatives to improve consular protection of EU citizens in case of terrorist attacks or natural disasters in third countries; military assets and capabilities having been identified that could support coordinated EU disaster-response efforts. They include strategic transport (air/sea), tactical transport (helicopters), medical units, field hospitals and logistics; and the holding each year of multinational exercises to test the readiness of Member States to assist each other in case of man-made or natural disasters.

Additionally, the EU has focused on international cooperation in pursuit of its strategy. Such initiatives included cooperation with the United Nations in order to back the EU's increasing role in combating terrorism. The UN Security Council has established a Counter-Terrorism Committee (CTC)[34] and recruited experts to support, advise and assist it. The EU continues to push for a comprehensive UN convention against terrorism, and in its relations with third countries, the EU consistently urges the ratification and implementation of the existing 16 UN conventions and protocols against terrorism

The EU also holds annual high-level political dialogues on counter-terrorism with the United States, Russia, India, Pakistan, Australia and Japan. In the framework of the Asia–Europe Meetings (ASEM), the EU has co-hosted regional conferences on inter-faith dialogue. Since 2004, the EU has co-organized an annual dialogue to combat terrorist financing with the countries of the Gulf Cooperation Council. Cooperation against terrorism is also being mainstreamed into the Union's external agreements, such as the Revised Cotonou Agreement, the Euro-Mediterranean Code of Conduct against Terrorism and the agreement on counter-terrorism and non-proliferation with Pakistan. Cooperation in the field of counter-terrorism has also been included in the 11 action plans under the EU's Neighbourhood Policy. Finally, the EU has launched counter-terrorism capacity-building initiatives with Algeria, Indonesia and Morocco. The Commission has also supported a range of counter-terrorist-related projects, notably in the fields of border protection and countering of terrorist financing, in regions ranging from the Balkans to South-East Asia. The Stability Fund (2007–2013) is enabling the Union to significantly increase its counter-terrorism capacity-building assistance to third countries. The first CFSP Joint Action on terrorism was in 2007 and consisted of financial aid to the African Union's Centre for Counter-Terrorism in Algiers.

Despite the myriad initiatives in the field of counter-terrorism post-9/11, the 2008 review of the European Security Strategy highlighted some important areas where improvements were still needed.[35] These included tightening coordination arrangements for handling a major terrorist incident, in particular using chemical, radiological, nuclear and bioterrorism materials; further work on terrorist financing, along with an effective and comprehensive EU policy on information sharing, taking due account of protection of personal data; and doing more to counter radicalization and recruitment, by addressing extremist ideology and tackling discrimination. In this area, inter-cultural dialogue, through such fora as the Alliance of Civilizations (AoC), had an important role.[36] The AoC was established in 2005, at the initiative of Spain and Turkey, and now works under the auspices of the UN to mobilize concerted efforts to promote cross-cultural relations among diverse nations and communities

Conclusion

These two perspectives on countering terrorism – a British armed forces one and an EU one – have provided a juxtaposition between one bottom-up and one top-down view. Taking the bottom-up UK armed forces perspective first, their considerable experience since World War II has included being landed in one no-win political mess (Palestine) and one mismatch between political aims and military actions (Aden); and two successes, where the political aim was maintained and eventually led to agreements between the parties ('Cyprus one' in the 1950s and Northern Ireland). In both the successes, the British counter-terrorist strategy was embedded into the criminal-justice system, albeit with emergency legislation enabling measures such as collective punishment, deportation and a broadening of the death sentence (Cyprus); and detention without trial and trial without jury (Northern Ireland). In Palestine, one practical challenge (not unlike the current situation within the UK perhaps) was that the terrorist was often indistinguishable from the security forces themselves, having been British trained, dressed and equipped and sometimes of British nationality. In Aden, British armed forces found themselves being drawn into filling serious gaps – including intelligence gaps – in the capability of the local police, not, perhaps, unlike the earlier years in Northern Ireland.

The jury is perhaps still out on the success to date of Britain's overall counter-terrorist strategy – within which the armed forces play an important supporting role. Although, under the 'Pursue' strand, over a dozen attacks may well have been successfully disrupted since 2001, one major attack – London in 2005 – was not; the impact of the 'Prevent' strand is only likely to be measurable in the longer term; the 'Protect' strand has focused on protecting critical national infrastructure; 'Prepare' has focused on putting into effect the many lessons drawn from the London attack to improve the communication and coordination between all the responding agencies. Certainly there is a pressing need, across all the strategy's strands, for more than lip service in implementing a truly comprehensive approach across government departments, to include training and working more closely together; this need remains very visible where the armed forces intervene overseas in what are now being termed 'S&R' (stabilization and reconstruction) operations.

This leads on to a thought about the distinction made between 'insurgency' and 'terrorism'. British military doctrine defines insurgency as: 'an organised movement aimed at the overthrow of a constitutional government through the use of subversion and armed conflict.'[37] Analysts have drawn attention to the reluctance of state authorities to acknowledge insurgencies and to call them terrorism instead.[38] After 2001, there might also be a tendency for government and non-government actors to categorize as counter-terrorism all that might possibly qualify for the very large funding streams available under this heading.

Although the strategy emphasizes that all actions are firmly within the rule of law, the law has been significantly extended in a number of fields. There are now widespread concerns, not just from human rights NGOs but also from politicians, judges, officials and academics, that the essential balance within a democracy between the rule of law, security and human rights is, in the UK, becoming skewed by the way the counter-terrorist strategy is being interpreted in its implementation. For example, in addition to the plethora of 'surveillance society' incidents in the public domain, such as the use of counter-terrorist provisions by local councils in fields like waste collection and school catchment areas, and by civil servants and the police in relation to political leaking, former counter-terrorist practitioners have also stated that the boundaries of the law are on occasion being crossed.[39]

Turning to the top-down EU's perspective, the threats have been firmly conceptualized within the framework of the European Security Strategy. The response – the EU's Counter-Terrorism Strategy – has been squarely based on respect for human rights and international law, and placed within the framework of the European area of freedom, justice and security. The EU has developed metrics for progress to be evaluated regularly and frequently at the highest possible level.

It can be argued[40] that the British government's reaction to terrorism used to be 'smarter' than the US administration's reaction after September 2001: less heavy in terms of the defensive measures and more agile in terms of the offensive ones. It might currently be argued that the UK has now moved away from its traditional criminal-law-framed response and closer to the US model, certainly in the domestic strand of its strategy. Yet it is ironic that, within the EU, the UK has played a key role in helping to design a counter-terrorist strategy that looks much like the traditional British one.

Notes

1 Drawn from author's background interviews with former practitioners.
2 Many of whom had been British trained and fought with the Allies during World War II.
3 For an authoritative analysis of this period, see D.A. Charters, *British Intelligence in the Palestine Campaign, 1945–47, Intelligence and National Security*, 6:1 (1991), pp. 115–140.
4 For a detailed account in the public domain, see P. Dimitrakis, 'British Intelligence and the Cyprus Insurgency, 1955–1959', *International Journal of Intelligence and Counter-Intelligence*, 21:2 (2008), pp. 375–394.
5 For the detail of the organization and role of the Intelligence Corps in Cyprus, see A. Clayton, *Forearmed – A History of the Intelligence Corps* (London: Brassey's, 1993), chapter 13.

6 The Zurich and London Agreement, signed on 19 February 1959.
7 See C. Jones, *Britain and the Yemen Civil War 1962–65: Ministers, Mercenaries and Mandarins; Foreign Policy and the Limits of Covert Action* (Sussex: Sussex Academic Press, 2004).
8 See J. Walker, *Aden Insurgency: The Savage War in South Arabia 1962–1967* (Staplehearst: Spellmount, 2005).
9 Clayton, *Forearmed*.
10 As of June 2009, the emergency legislation for no-jury trials had not yet been repealed.
11 See M. Dewar, *British Army in Northern Ireland* (New York: Weidenfeld & Nicolson, 1997), and N. Van Der Bijl, *Operation BANNER: The British Army in Northern Ireland 1969–2007* (Barnsley: Pen & Sword Military, 2009).
12 See, for example, the subsequent 2003 report of the Stevens Enquiry, http://news.bbc.co.uk/1/shared/spl/hi/northern_ireland/03/stephens_inquiry/pdf/stephens_inquiry.pdf and the Police Ombudsman For Northern Ireland's report of 22 January 2007, http://news.bbc.co.uk/1/shared/bsp/hi/pdfs/22_01_07_ballast.pdf.
13 Drawn from author's background interviews with former practitioners; very little authoritative analysis on the military intelligence function during Operation BANNER is as yet in the public domain.
14 Sean Rayment's *Daily Telegraph* article of 4 September 2007 makes reference to this unit's former work in Northern Ireland. In the context of its operations in Iraq, see www.telegraph.co.uk/news/uknews/1541542/Top-secret-army-cell-breaks-terrorists.html.
15 Peter Taylor's three-part BBC2 TV series *The Brits* (May 2000) included interviews with former members of these units, see http://news.bbc.co.uk/1/hi/uk/749453.stm.
16 Margaret Gilmore, 'No Way Back? Examining the Background and Response to the Rise of Dissident Terrorist Activity in Northern Ireland', *RUSI Journal*, 15:2 (2009), pp. 50–55.
17 *The United Kingdom's Strategy for Countering International Terrorism* is available at http://security.homeoffice.gov.uk/news-publications/publication-search/general/HO_Contest_strategy.pdf?view=Binary.
18 Evidence before the inquiry and inquest into the subsequent killing by the MPS of the Brazilian Jean Charles de Menezes.
19 Drawn mainly from FANY (PRVC), see www.fany.org.uk/.
20 In the March 2009 update of the UK counter-terrorist strategy.
21 The Centre for the Protection of National Infrastructure (CPNI), see www.cpni.gov.uk/.
22 See www.consilium.europa.eu/uedocs/cmsUpload/78367.pdf.
23 See www.consilium.europa.eu/ueDocs/cms_Data/docs/pressdata/EN/reports/104630.pdf.
24 See www.eurojust.europa.eu/.
25 See www.europol.europa.eu/.
26 Since incorporated in the Treaty of Lisbon as Article 188R:

> The Union and the Member States shall act jointly in a spirit of solidarity if the Member State is a victim of terrorist attack or natural or man-made disaster. The Union shall mobilise all the instruments at its disposal, including the military resources made available by the Member States.

At the time of writing, the Treaty's ratification process has been fully completed by 23 of the 27 Member States.
27 Currently Gilles de Kerchove (See EU Council document S256/07 dated 19 September 2007).
28 http://ue.eu.int/cms3_fo/showPage.asp?id=248&lang=en&mode=g, click 'The Fight against Terrorism', click 'Key Documents'.

29 JHA Council of 1–2 December 2005 (EU Council documents 82757–58 dated 1 December 2005).
30 See http://register.consilium.eu.int/pdf/en/05/st14/st14469-re04.en05.pdf.
31 See http://register.consilium.europa.eu/pdf/en/09/st09/st09715-ad01re01.en09.pdf and http://register.consilium.europa.eu/pdf/en/09/st09/st09715-re01.en09.pdf for the June 2009 reviews.
32 See, for example, the European-Commission-sponsored study *Recruitment and Mobilisation for the Islamist Militant Movement in Europe* (ICSR/KCL, October 2008), http://icsr.info/paper.php?id=9.
33 For one analysis of the Treaty, see the House of Lords report *Prüm: an Effective Weapon Against Terrorism and Crime?* at www.statewatch.org/news/2007/may/eu-hol-prum-report.pdf.
34 See www.un.org/sc/ctc/.
35 See EU Council Secretariat document S407/08 dated 11 December 2008.
36 See www.unaoc.org.
37 Joint Doctrine Publication ADP 0–01.
38 See, for example, J. Kiszely, 'Learning about Counterinsurgency', *Military Review*, 87:2 (2007), pp. 7–12.
39 See, for example, episode 3 of the BBC2 TV program *Who's Watching You: The Intelligence Race*, broadcast on 8 June 2009.
40 As, for example, the author did in *Intelligence and National Power: the Role of the Military* (lecture at St Antony's College, Oxford, 4 June 2003).

7　The development of the UK intelligence community after 9/11

Sir Francis Richards

This chapter aims to describe the response of the UK intelligence community to the events of 9/11 and its subsequent development. It looks first at the state of the agencies immediately before 9/11, and at how far they were already focused on international terrorism as a priority target. It looks briefly at how far the extremist threat to the UK is part of a generic international threat, and what features it has which are specific to the UK. It then considers how that threat has shaped the organizational and cultural changes which the agencies have made to meet it; how this response fits into the UK government's overall CT strategy; and, finally, how its success can be evaluated, and whether that success comes – as regards the agencies – at a price. Given the limited amount of information on these themes that is in the public domain, it makes no claim to be an authoritative or comprehensive account; it draws heavily on subjective personal impressions and anecdotal evidence.

Changes after the Cold War

The Cold War left the UK intelligence community in urgent need of change. For decades it had focused primarily on the Soviet target abroad, and on Northern Irish terrorism and counter-espionage at home. It had developed great expertise in these areas, at the expense of flexibility. The author recalls being asked by an African farmer the day the Berlin Wall came down, 'What are you people going to do now you are out of a job?' The question was even then not difficult to answer; events in the Gulf and in former Yugoslavia were already moving in a direction that would make the 1990s a decade of continuous and increasing overstretch for the British armed forces and all those working on security issues. But that did not prevent there from being a general perception that the world was now a safer place, and that defense and security should occupy a lower place in national spending priorities; governments were determined to collect the 'peace dividend'. Between 1994/1995 and 1998/1999 the Single Intelligence Vote (SIV), which included the funding for all three UK intelligence agencies, shrank from £855.1 million to £695.4 million – a very substantial decline when the impact of inflation is taken into account.[1]

The advent of a new Labour administration in 1997 was followed by a 'zero based' review of the tasks and needs of every department of government. The

Strategic Defence Review represented the first radical rethink of Britain's security needs since the end of the Cold War. It concluded that the world had become a more unpredictable and in many respects more dangerous place, and that the armed forces needed to restructure themselves to achieve the flexibility and mobility needed to deal with the unexpected. It emphasized the importance of better cooperation between the services, and better teaming between the armed forces and other parts of government. A similar and parallel review of the Single Intelligence Vote came up, not surprisingly, with very similar conclusions. It pointed to the need for intelligence on a new range of global threats – nuclear proliferation, narcotics, money laundering and other serious crime, and counter-terrorism. But counter-terrorism was only one among these new priorities, and not the highest; there was little perception of a major non-Irish terrorist threat to British interests abroad until the East African embassy bombings in 1998, and little sense of a threat to the UK homeland until 9/11. This review also – inevitably, given the funding climate at the time – stressed the need for more efficiency, not least through increased joint working.

The review did mark at least the beginning of the end of the 'peace dividend'. Funding increased modestly to £743.2 million in 1999/2000 and remained more or less constant in cash terms until 9/11.[2] This meant of course a slow continuing reduction in real terms; the Treasury continued to require annual 'efficiency savings', which meant that the agencies – like other parts of government – were expected to produce undiminished outputs with (given the impact of inflation) endless resources each year, at a time when advances in technology steadily increased the price of success, above all for GCHQ as the communications intelligence agency. The agencies did their best. All three launched ambitious modernization programs, involving major cultural change as well as moves into new accommodation, with the aim of achieving the operational flexibility and ability to work across organizational boundaries called for in the SIV review – and in GCHQ's case to cope with the digital revolution in communications technology. They worked hard to demonstrate achievement against the new global threats, and had some notable successes. But intelligence production is demand-led, and demand for intelligence against traditional targets was slow to diminish. The Defence Intelligence Staff continued to devote a high proportion of their effort to Russian targets, both because there was little faith in the permanence of positive political changes in Russia and because Russia continued to supply military hardware to a wide range of countries with the potential to threaten Western interests. Irish dissident republican terrorism remained a major preoccupation; the major bomb attack by dissident republicans in Omagh took place within a few days of the East African embassy bombings, and the Security Service was still devoting 33 percent of its effort to Irish CT work in 2001–2002. Supporting military operations in the Balkans and the containment of Iraq consumed further effort, and demand for some new priority work was slow to develop; in the late 1990s, the police were heard to complain that one agency was producing too much intelligence on serious crime for their analysts to cope with. Given the background of steadily reducing resources, it is hardly surprising that by 9/11 the reorientation of effort was far from complete, and that capacity had been lost against targets (e.g. in Afghanistan) which had ceased to feature as strategic priorities for the UK, but which were to prove crucially important for the future. An efficiency adviser was appointed after the SIV Review to promote joint working between the agencies, but it is hard to point too much in the way of harvest from his efforts – not through lack of effort or goodwill, but because the tasks of the agencies remained sufficiently distinct for there to be limited scope for useful change. The agency chiefs were genuinely committed to greater cooperation, but there were also significant cultural obstacles to overcome. The relationship between the agencies had traditionally been competitive, with each seeking to claim credit for more intelligence triumphs in order to maximize its share of the Single Intelligence Vote at the next spending review. This zero-sum game came to an end with the more collegiate approach of the late 1990s, but eradicating the negative stereotypes that each agency tended to harbor of the others did not happen overnight.

At the same time, the end of the Cold War had a negative impact on established intelligence-liaison relationships. There was a perception among all of the UK's traditional intelligence allies that national priorities were starting slowly to diverge, and that there was no major common threat to be faced. This was particularly the case in Washington, where the UK's attempt to breathe some life into EU military cooperation was seen by many in the Pentagon and in parts of the US intelligence community as evidence that the UK had reached a fork in the road, and had chosen to give European defense cooperation priority over the transatlantic relationship. This perception was mistaken, but persisted despite efforts to counter it; while it did not have immediate dramatic consequences, its impact was beginning to be felt by the end of the old millennium in the appearance of small bureaucratic obstacles to routine cooperation. Long-established relationships continued, but their long-term future value started to be increasingly questioned.

On the eve of 9/11, therefore, the agencies had the flexibility to react swiftly to events. But the work of making non-Irish CT the overriding operational priority had to be done from scratch, and was to prove to require faster and more radical changes than anybody would then have predicted.

The impact of 9/11

It was significant that the way Tony Blair chose to demonstrate solidarity with the US was by immediately dispatching an aircraft with the chiefs of the three agencies to Washington; 9/11 for almost the first time moved the agencies to the center of the political stage. Virtually everything that was known about al-Qaeda came from secret intelligence, and for the first time in recent memory all meetings of the 'war cabinet' were attended by all three agency chiefs and by the chairman of the Joint Intelligence Committee, and every meeting began with an intelligence briefing.

9/11 had an impact on almost every aspect of government. Among its immediate consequences were an immediate increase in demand for, and resources for, intelligence; intensified pressure for better coordination across organizational boundaries; a fresh emphasis on foreign intelligence relationships; a much increased requirement for support to military operations and to the police; a new sense of vulnerability, both of government and of society and the economy; pressure for changes in the law to help combat terrorism.

As time passed, all of these effects came to be encompassed in a comprehensive counter-terrorism strategy – CONTEST. Before considering how the agencies fitted into that, it is worth pausing first to look at how the threat of extremist terrorism presented itself to the UK – which aspects were simply part of a global threat to the West and its allies, and which were specific to the UK. The UK was at risk for three main reasons: first, it was seen – indeed, was at pains to present itself – as the US's most loyal and enthusiastic ally. Though its government never held the same Manichean view of the Muslim world as the US administration, seeing it in shades of gray rather than black and white, this did not communicate itself to Muslim opinion abroad or in Britain. Blair's attempts to get the US to make a determined push for a settlement in Palestine an integral part of its strategy had little obvious impact, and in due course the UK's high-profile involvement in the Iraq intervention seemed to many to complete the justification of its demonization by bin Laden. Other European countries felt less obviously threatened, and none gave the same kind of immediate extra attention to CT work – at least until after the Madrid bombings in March 2004. Second, it offered a more concentrated and softer target than the US, which after the shock of 9/11 was able to implement more draconian measures to strengthen its border controls and other external defenses than the UK, with its traditionally liberal (and imperfectly enforced) immigration controls, could easily adopt. Finally, like most other European countries – but unlike the US – it had a large, economically disadvantaged and geographically concentrated Muslim minority population, which had been providing recruits for armed jihad (initially in Chechnya, later in Afghanistan and other areas of conflict) since the mid-1990s. The feature of this population which was unique to Britain was the large element – well over half a million – of Pakistani (and, more specifically, Kashmiri) origin, which maintained close links with Pakistan and was vulnerable to the extreme religious views being propagated there. The US Muslim population, by contrast, was more diverse, more dispersed and more economically successful, and for all these reasons was better integrated – so that it was possible for the US to treat extremist terrorism as essentially an external threat. For the UK, it evolved from being an external threat with domestic connections to being a primarily domestic threat with external connections. 2005 saw the coordinated 7/7 bomb attacks on the London transport system. In 2006, three separate but related plots, including an alleged major planned attack on flights out of Heathrow, appeared to show a strategic AQ approach to the British target. Until 2006, most young UK radicals became active terrorists through the Pakistan connection, and this remains their primary source of inspiration to violence, though from 2006 on we have also seen them processed through three more hubs – Iran/Iraq, the Levant and East Africa.

The CONTEST strategy has been under development since 2001, but although its conceptual framework was fairly quickly established, initial progress in putting flesh on the bones was slow, as the very small staff in the Cabinet Office initially assigned to driving it encountered all the institutional obstacles that bedevil any attempt to develop a centrally driven strategy in Whitehall. In consequence it was not rolled out publicly until 2006, and its implementation only really gathered pace when, in 2007, responsibility for it was transferred to a well-staffed and genuinely interdepartmental Office of Security and Counter Terrorism (OSCT) within the Home Office, which packed enough punch – and was able to distribute enough money – to give it coherence and momentum. The National Security Strategy, which provides a wider context for CONTEST and is intended to produce a badly needed improvement in the coherence of all government policies and departments dealing with issues relevant to security at home and abroad, was published after a long and difficult gestation only in March 2008. It has been widely seen as a missed opportunity. It describes all the components of the national response to security challenges without seriously analyzing its weaknesses, or appearing to establish strong enough machinery to give the same coherence to wider national security policy that OSCT has brought to CONTEST. The CT strategy was reissued in a revised form in March 2009. This is a much better-presented and more substantial document than its predecessor, with solid analysis of the threat and a wealth of fresh detail on implementation. The main features of the strategy it describes are unchanged, but increased emphasis is placed on disrupting the overseas links of terrorism and on preventive action at home. A refreshed version of the National Security Strategy is also promised for 2009, but seemed unlikely at the time of writing to prove much more ambitious than its predecessor.

CONTEST is a comprehensive CT policy, and not surprisingly its main elements are not dissimilar to those of CT strategies in other countries. It has four strands: Pursue (detecting, catching and disrupting active terrorists), Prepare (improving national resilience in the face of attack through better contingency planning and preparation), Protect (which covers such things as reducing the vulnerability of the critical national infrastructure, restricting access to potentially hazardous materials and improving border controls) and Prevent (addressing the huge task of making violent extremism less attractive to young Muslims in Britain and abroad). The main contribution of the agencies has of course been to the 'Pursue' strand; however, they are actively involved in all four, in different degrees and in different ways, and this involvement has brought about profound changes within the agencies, in their relationship with each other, and – perhaps most significantly of all – in their relationship with the rest of the public service. The change in their resourcing after 9/11 was dramatic. The Single Intelligence Account (SIA) increased initially by about 7 percent per annum in real terms over the next three years.[3] This enabled a substantial expansion of all three agencies. The Security Service began growth which – increasing in pace after the London bombings of 2005 – will see its size double by 2011, with a new network of offices in major cities throughout the country.[4] GCHQ received the funds it needed to develop intelligence access to digital communications, and to provide operational support to the other agencies and the armed forces – a particularly challenging requirement given the disproportionately rapid growth in the size and needs of the Security Service. SIS increased its size, expanding both its own operational CT effort and its program of assistance to other countries (see below, pp. 00–00). Expenditure on CT and intelligence overall has expanded from £1 bn in 2001 to £2.5 bn today, and will reach £3.5 bn by 2011.[5] Growth in the Single Intelligence Account (i.e. agency funding alone) has been steady throughout the period since 2001; while the 2005 London bombings and the alleged plot against airliners in 2006 gave fresh impulsion to CT work, this did not result in sudden step changes in funding, if only because the ability of the agencies to absorb increased resources without waste was finite. This expansion was accounted for almost entirely by the increase in work on international terrorism, which in the case of the Security Service – the only agency to have made a proportion public – increased from 16.4 percent of its operational effort in 1997–1998 to 70 percent in late 2006, with further measures in train to bring this total to 80 percent (more still if the resources devoted to protective security – largely terrorism related – are taken into account).[6] For all three agencies, increased resources made it possible to significantly accelerate the pace of organizational and cultural modernization.

Focus on a common overriding priority produced an immediate acceleration in improving coordination and cooperation – initially between the agencies, but, as CT strategy developed, also with the police and other government departments. The intelligence responsibilities of the Cabinet Secretary (Head of the Civil Service) were delegated in 2002 to a newly appointed deputy who, at the time, combined the functions of advising the Prime Minister on intelligence and security with chairmanship of the Joint Intelligence Committee and heading the secretariat responsible for coordinating the work of the three agencies; to these was added overall responsibility for delivering the government's CONTEST strategy. One of the early – and very successful – actions of Sir David Omand, the first occupant of this job, was to centralize responsibility for assessing terrorist threats in a new body staffed jointly by all the agencies, the police and 16 other government departments – the Joint Terrorism Analysis Centre (JTAC). His aim was to achieve a critical mass of analytical effort by bringing together resources hitherto scattered, not only across the agencies but also in the police and in other parts of government. Joint working was intensified in many other areas, and was supported by increased secondments of staff between agencies. Increased contact, together with the new blood which expansion injected into the senior ranks of the agencies, brought its own dynamic of cultural change, so that the prejudices that had earlier resulted in some institutional resistance to joint working rapidly vanished. The opening of regional Security Service offices has produced a sea change in the quality of relationships between the Security Service – and, through them, the intelligence community as a whole – and local police forces; its last Director General has pointed to the improved three-way teamwork with such forces and the Metropolitan Police.

Foreign intelligence relationships received a huge boost from the appearance of a clear common threat, and from the immediate recognition that this threat was global and required a response with global reach which was far beyond the unaided capacity of even the largest Western intelligence agencies. Initially, this served mainly to revitalize relationships with such traditional intelligence allies as the US, Canada and Australia. Other bilateral relationships, with European and Muslim countries, would clearly be of great importance, but had in many cases to be developed from a much lower base. In fact, intelligence coverage of many high-priority parts of the Muslim world suffered in the very short term after 2001, as scarce Arabic-speaking resources were diverted to build up the effort against al-Qaeda targets in the Middle East and South Asia. But SIS was quick to recognize that effective international cooperation would require not just intelligence sharing, but help for some key liaison countries to build their own CT capacity. Multilateral intelligence sharing was and remains inhibited by security considerations, but there was a new emphasis (which continues) on building up coordination on counter-terrorist measures in the EU and other organizations. Bilateral cooperation with European countries is a high priority. But, as already indicated, it was not until after the March 2004 Madrid bombings that important progress began to be made in most of these relationships.

Military operations in Afghanistan and police demands at home produced an immediate requirement for CT intelligence to be available in a form that could be given quickly and securely to those – military commanders, police and foreign partners – who need to take action on it. This accelerated work that was already in progress on producing 'usable' intelligence. In practice this means that intelligence from sensitive sources can be issued in a 'tearline' form, with a summary attached that contains the actionable information without source information and can be released at a lower classification to people (e.g. police officers) with no intelligence clearances both in Britain and, when appropriate, in partner countries. This is an essential condition for implementing a national CT strategy that makes effective, coordinated and timely use of all security resources. Information technology makes it possible to place intelligence (e.g. on a threat whose nature is known, but which may materialize anywhere) in the hands of law-enforcement country-wide as soon as it has been received and evaluated, provided that bureaucratic delays entailed in moving information between organizations can be eliminated in this way. When the author asked a very senior member of one of the agencies recently what was the most important single lesson the intelligence community had learned since 9/11, he replied without hesitation 'dare to share' – meaning that it is worth accepting a somewhat greater level of risk of exposing intelligence in order to get it into the hands of those who can make best use of it, at home and abroad.

Pressure for changes in the law did not come primarily from the agencies, which in general have been satisfied with the authorities given by existing legislation. However, 9/11 did renew the old debate about the use of intercept material in court cases, favored by the police as likely to help secure terrorist convictions, but bitterly opposed by GCHQ and SIS as liable to lead to the exposure of methods of collection. Such changes in the law as have been made so far were mainly requested by the police to promote conviction and deportation of terrorist suspects (and some of these have proved of limited value, as their use is in practice often struck down by the courts as conflicting with human rights). But the march of technology (e.g. Voice Over Internet Protocol and – further ahead – the prospect of 'cloud' computing) will bring the needs of the agencies into the Parliamentary and public spotlight as the requirement for legislation to cover new forms of data retention becomes urgent; there is, for example, little point in seizing terrorist laptops if their owners' files are all sitting in a remote server beyond the reach of the law. The reaction to the first cautious mention of this in The Queen's Speech in the autumn of 2008 showed just how contentious this is likely to prove.

Finally, the Northern Irish experience has turned out to be of limited relevance to the new CT environment. It has given the UK well-established habits of managing the risk of attacks on governmental and military targets – although primarily from bomb and rocket attack, not, for example, from indiscriminate attacks against civil aviation – and good technical intelligence and surveillance skills. But the UK has not until now had to deal with a movement with no negotiable political objectives, which can deploy volunteers ready to sacrifice their lives in suicide attacks.

The cumulative effect of all these changes on the agencies has been radical – as radical as the shift from the targets of World War II to those of the Cold War. Internally, it has meant major restructuring as – in the case of SIS and GCHQ – CT work has moved from the periphery of their operational priorities to the center, and in the case of the Security Service, with evolution from a London-based to a nationwide-dispersed organization. Within the intelligence community, it has, as already noted, produced a culture of systematic and widespread joint working in place of the coordination and ad hoc cooperation of the immediate post-Cold War period. And beyond it, there has been an unprecedented degree of integration between the agencies and other parts of the public service engaged in delivering elements of CONTEST, with agency staff filling for the first time senior positions in a number of Whitehall departments on secondment, and joint working extended in centers like JTAC in such a way that civil servants, police and agency staff work permanently alongside one another rather than teaming for a temporary and finite task. This development has perhaps been less dramatic for the Security Service, with its traditionally domestic focus, than for the two external intelligence agencies. With expansion has come a much raised profile – particularly for the Security Service, whose Director General is now better known to the public through his public statements and interviews than any Whitehall Permanent Secretary. Indeed, he is more well-known than the Cabinet Secretary himself, given the traditional rule that it is for Ministers and not officials to speak publicly on issues of policy (which in practice has normally included performance). This is presumably because Ministers feel that, when potentially unpopular legislation on extending the reach of the state into the lives and records of its citizens needs to be justified, this comes better from a non-political professional than from themselves (a calculation perhaps not very different from that which led to the Joint Intelligence Committee putting its name to the much-vilified dossier on the eve of the invasion of Iraq). But greater openness is not confined to statements; all three agencies now recruit through advertisements and websites – a far cry from the traditional tap on the shoulder in an Oxford corridor, and one which is driven by the need for staff not only in greater numbers than before, but from a much wider range of backgrounds and ethnic origins.

Evaluating the success and cost of the changes

The universal verdict is that the immediate gains in effectiveness have been very significant. The agencies would certainly not claim victory over terrorism in Britain – indeed, with over 2,000 individuals and 200 networks with known terrorist sympathies and objectives currently being monitored, they would not even claim that the threat has stopped getting worse. But there has been no significant successful attack since 7/7, and that must be the main short-term measure of success for the 'Pursue' strand, which is where the agencies' main responsibilities lie. Measuring the success of the strategy as a whole is more difficult – particularly as the 'Prevent' strand is still in its infancy. Its declared objective is 'to reduce the threat from international terrorism, so that people can go about their daily lives freely and with confidence'. But that is more a mission statement than a satisfactory measure of success; most people would say that the efforts of the police and the agencies in the 'Pursue' strand alone have been so far successful, so that most citizens do indeed go about their lives with many worries higher on their list than fear of being the victim of a terrorist attack. Indeed – as already noted – the government sometimes finds it necessary to talk up the threat in order to persuade the public to accept the need for expensive or intrusive measures, thus on the face of it frustrating achievement of their own objective. But the implied objective of the whole strategy is surely something more ambitious – to create an environment in which the overwhelming majority of every significant community in the UK actively rejects violent extremism and those who espouse it, and seeks to further its aims only within the democratic process. That is a very long way off. Indeed, as an objective it suffers from one of the same difficulties as Allied aims in Afghanistan. Given that (as the Prime Minister recently commented) some 75 percent of known terrorist plots in this country have their origins in Pakistan,[7] as long as Britain remains umbilically linked to Pakistan (which it will be as long as British people of Pakistani origin want to maintain their present close relationship with the country), and Pakistan itself still has a substantial violent extremist problem, it will be difficult if not impossible to insulate Britain (or, for that matter, Afghanistan) entirely from that problem. And, as long as the threat has therefore to be managed rather than eliminated, the main burden will continue to fall on law-enforcement and the intelligence agencies.

The agencies are certainly not only larger but immensely more capable, as well as more diverse, than they were. They are well run, recruitment is good and morale is high. Their achievement against the threat has been impressive, and has come without any apparent lessening in public confidence in, and support for, the agencies' work. However, when evaluating the price paid (by this I do not mean the increasing intrusions of the state into individual privacy, or the inconvenience of enhanced security measures to the travelling public; that is too large a subject area to be addressed here, and in any case relates more to the actions and requirements of law-enforcement than of the intelligence agencies), within the agencies themselves there have been – inevitably – some changes that have not been for the better, and some which may turn out to have side-effects which it is still too early to assess. The Intelligence and Security Committee has expressed concern in its report for 2006–2007 that 'aspects of key intelligence and security work are suffering as a consequence of the focus on counter-terrorism priorities', and suggested that more funding might be needed to redress this.[8] Like the armed forces, the agencies have been compelled by immediate operational priorities to sacrifice much of the flexibility and versatility emphasized in the reviews of the late 1990s. Work on serious crime has been a particular casualty, only partly compensated for by the new capability of the Serious and Organised Crime Agency (SOCA). Given that most of the agencies' new funding has come specifically tied to CT work, the problem of ensuring that CT occupies no more than its appropriate place in priorities for intelligence collection is not one that the agencies can themselves do much to resolve; even if intelligence assessment is not policy driven, it is right that its priorities should be. It is, however, legitimate to ask whether, in the light of experience over the period since 1990, the process of setting priorities gives enough weight to resourcing tomorrow's requirements. It is almost inevitable in a democracy that requirements, even when foreseen, are rarely properly resourced until they become critical. But a stronger and more capable ownership within government for national-security strategy might do something to help. The agencies themselves pursue new ideas and technology energetically – but almost entirely in relation to the targets they are tasked and funded to address.

There is arguably a second downside to some of the positive developments described above. There has been a strong tradition in Britain of maintaining a strict separation between policy and intelligence, so that government will be told what it needs to hear rather than what it would like to hear. That has been the whole point of the Joint Intelligence Committee; if we have not always managed to achieve intelligence-driven policy, we have usually been free of the evil of policy-driven intelligence. Chiefs of the agencies have usually been in their last jobs, with no further preferment to look for. Their staff have accepted that the price of their life on the inside of events is less than their due in the way of public recognition and obvious worldly success; they have looked for no rewards beyond those that their own chiefs can dispense. Their motivation and ethos have been profoundly different from those of the normal civil servant – closer perhaps to those of the military, with whom they share the task of pursuing their country's interest by means which would be unacceptable when used by anyone else. This is now changing, largely in consequence of the focus on counter- terrorism. Intelligence officers are not only integrated to an unprecedented degree in the work of Whitehall departments, but are already starting to fill senior positions in those departments, with policy responsibilities and the kind of regular contact with ministers that they would been most unlikely to have in the past.

Moreover, the use of intelligence to make the case for the Iraq War – inevitable given the pre-emptive nature of the operation – has shown how difficult it is in such circumstances to keep intelligence and policy separate to the satisfaction of Parliament and the public. However necessary and beneficial the changes of the past decade have been, they do create new risks for the intelligence community. There is no evidence yet of specific adverse consequences; indeed, they may take many years and a generational change to emerge – if they ever do. But managing these risks will take strong leadership within the agencies and strong oversight outside them. The agencies are now so much larger, and their profile is so much higher, that the maintenance of public trust is bound to be both more important and more difficult – particularly at a time when more informal ways of doing business have made the boundaries between politicians and those who serve them much harder to demarcate clearly than in the past. An intelligence officer is not and should not be just another civil servant.

Conclusion

Britain has a counter-terrorism strategy which is comprehensive and well-coordinated. The intelligence community has reorganized itself and its relationship with the rest of government so as to give highly effective support to the implementation of that strategy. They and law enforcement have managed the immediate risk of attack well. But the combination of Britain's history and its close alignment with the United States along with its population's links with Pakistan place it uniquely at risk among Western countries, and it may be a generation or more before the real success of its strategy can be judged. Meanwhile, if we do not want to risk being taken by surprise by the next major threat to national security, the agencies do need to be resourced and tasked adequately to address known threats other than extremist terrorism, and to scan the horizon for new ones. That seems unlikely to happen until those in the national-security community who task the agencies include a powerful stakeholder for those future threats.

Notes

1 *Annual Report of the Intelligence and Security Committee* (ISC) for 1998–1999.
2 *Annual Report of the ISC* for 1997–1998. Outturn figures for later years varied slightly from the projections in that report, and headline figures were increased by the change to resource accounting, but without changing the overall trend.
3 *ISC Annual Report* 2002–2003. Real growth in the years after 2001 is set out in a useful table in the ISC's report for 2006–2007.
4 National Security Strategy, March 2008.
5 Ibid.
6 *Annual Report of the ISC* 2006–2007.
7 Prime Minister's Joint Press Conference in Islamabad, 14 December 2008.
8 *Annual Report of the ISC* 2006–2007.

8   Israel and the al-Aqsa intifada

The *Conceptzia* of terror

Clive Jones

While still shocking in their visual and emotional impact upon Israelis, the events of 9/11 were regarded by many in the Jewish state as but a part, albeit of a magnitude hitherto unknown, of a global, Islamist-inspired terrorist threat, a terror that brooked no compromise with the West in general and Israel in particular. This existential interpretation of events was understandable. With the outbreak of the al-Aqsa intifada in September 2000, suicide-bomb attacks inside the Green Line, culminating with an attack on a hotel in Netanya on 28 March 2002 that murdered 28 Israelis on the eve of the festival of *Pessach*, was proof enough that the conflict with the Palestinians had gone beyond a clash of nations and territory. Such attacks, seemingly indiscriminate in their choice of targets, demonstrated an animus, inspired and justified in the name of Islam, that could never be satiated by territorial compromise, however generous.

Not atypical of this Israeli perception of existential threat were the remarks of the former Israeli Chief of Staff, Lieutenant General Moshe 'Boogie' Ya'alon. In an interview with the daily newspaper *Ha'aretz*, he noted of the Palestinians that they would have to internalize the fact that terrorism would not 'defeat us, will not make us fold'. He continued:

> If that deep internalization does not exist at the end of the confrontation, we will have an existential threat to Israel. If that is not burned into the Palestinian *and* [my emphasis] Arab consciousness, there will be no end to their demands on us.... That's why this confrontation is so important. There has not been a more important confrontation since the War of Independence.[1]

Accordingly, Israel's reoccupation of the main Palestinian urban areas of the West Bank during 'Operation Defensive Shield' in April 2002, designed to root out the Palestinian 'terrorist infrastructure', met with widespread public approbation among Israelis.[2] Even when the use of force by the IDF was excessive, most notably the assassination in Gaza of Salah Shehadah, a leading figure in the military wing of Hamas, Izz al-din al-Qassem in July 2002, which resulted in the deaths of 15 Palestinians, nine of whom were children, few in Israel expressed immediate concern over the use of such deadly force. Not all observers remained so sanguine about such human collateral damage. Nowhere was this more apparent than in the dominant narrative used to apportion blame for the outbreak of the violence: the outright rejection by Yasser Arafat at the Camp David meeting of September 2000 of proposals put before him by former Israeli Premier Ehud Barak that would have led to the establishment of a Palestinian state in all but a small part of the Occupied Territories, with a capital established in East Jerusalem.[3] Arafat's actions at the summit may well have *occasioned* the outbreak of the al-Aqsa intifada, but the *causation* of the violence to which Israel itself had contributed remained hidden for many Israelis amid the carnage visited by Palestinian bombers on their streets.[4] As such, the idea that the al-Aqsa intifada had become a war of no choice – *en brera* – allowed policy-making in Israel to be driven by military considerations and military solutions. It became a conflict that pitted the strength of absolute state power against the fragmentary nature of the Palestinian Authority, its warlords, and against a Palestinian people who had begun to feel they had little to lose by recourse to the bomb and gun. Simply put, Israel's description of the conflict in absolute terms, and the use of overwhelming force to crush the Palestinian militias, meant that political options to curtail the violence remained subservient to the pursuit of total military victory.

This, in essence, is the *Conceptzia* this chapter seeks to explore and how the policy prescriptions that flowed from this mindset – the total destruction of Palestinian terror groups, and, more broadly, the diplomatic isolation of *Rais* Arafat – were helped by (1) the permissive acceptance by Israelis of Palestinian culpability for the violence and (2) association with Washington's wider war on Islamist-inspired terror. The former allowed a war-fighting strategy to be unleashed upon the Palestinian Authority that included targeted killings, mass detentions without trial and long-term curfews. While Israeli as well as international human rights organizations and peace groups protested against such human rights violations, the logic of the *Conceptzia*, with its siren-like appeal to a polity in need of physical assurance, isolated such liberal dissent to the margins of society. With regard to the latter, Washington did voice open disquiet at the use of a one-ton bomb to kill Shehadah. Nonetheless, concord with the Bush administration over the malfeasance of Arafat and his role in encouraging acts of terror against Israelis, both inside Israel and the Occupied Territories, allowed Israel a permissive environment to launch an all-out onslaught against the Palestinian Authority, its symbols, institutions and leaders. This chapter makes no judgment on the moral efficacy of the *Conceptzia*. Rather, it traces how the practical implementation of its key tenets, which enjoyed widespread support among Israelis, produced a new political reality, both in Israel and in its wider relations with the Palestinians.

The origins of *Conceptzia*

The deregulated though networked nature of the al-Aqsa intifada has been compared to so-called 'Fourth Generation Warfare' (4GW), defined by Thomas Hammes as the sum total of political, economic, social and military variables that impact adversely on strategies and political objectives set by state elites. Democratic states are ill-suited to prosecuting this type of conflict, Hammes argues, since it involves compromising over the very values that such polities claim as underpinning their own social orders. As he notes, 4GW is '[P]olitical, socially (rather than technically) networked and protracted in duration. It is the antithesis of the high-technology, short war the Pentagon is preparing to fight.'[5] Both the Sunni insurgency in Iraq and, more recently, the ongoing war against an emergent, more diffuse Taliban clearly demonstrate the efficacy of such thinking. Certainly in the case of Afghanistan, hopes that the strategic aim – the establishment of an effective form of government where legitimacy is derived from popular support, thereby allowing 'human security' to take root and flourish – have been undermined by an insurgency that enjoys clears transnational links across recognized but physically porous borders.[6]

This is akin to the view expressed by Rupert Smith, that conflict is now defined as 'war among the people', the delineated battlefields of the past that marked inter-state warfare being increasingly confined to the annals of military history, and where the developed state will often struggle to impose a decision upon technologically inferior entities or groups in alien domain.[7] Afghanistan and Iraq remain apposite examples, not least because the concept of human security which now informs in large part Western approaches to counter-insurgency, with its emphasis upon a secular construct of popular political participation and human rights, runs counter to traditional mores and values among societies where legitimacy is derived from custom, religion and tribe. In short, who governs has as much credence as how one is governed.[8] Attempts, however well meant, to enforce change under the simplistic mantra of 'hearts and minds' have therefore foundered in both Iraq and Afghanistan because of the failure by the United States and its allies to understand that the very conceptual basis of its own counter-insurgency strategy, with its incumbent liberal ideals, remain anathema to the fabric of societies where legitimacy often rest with the strong patriarchal leader, rather than any idea of popular participation. Thus, while Washington offered up the success of national and regional elections in Iraq as testament to the appeal of democratic politics, the United States military ultimately remained dependent upon suborning the tribes in Al-Anbar province in attempts to curb the worst excesses of al-Qaeda and its affiliated groups from 2006.[9]

However, the case of Israel and its response to the al-Aqsa intifada would suggest that, in this particular instance, a state, with its proud if contested claims to democratic governance, has, at least in strategic terms, imposed a military decision on a fragmented Palestinian polity and in the process created new political realities. One should of course be wary of drawing exact parallels with the response of other democratic states to insurgency. First, the violence of the al-Aqsa intifada remained constrained by geography within tightly controlled political boundaries. Put simply, the porous borders that allowed men and material to filter from Syria and Pakistan to Iraq and Afghanistan, respectively, simply had no parallel in the case of the Palestinians. Aside from one well-publicized failure of Iran to smuggle arms to the Palestinian Authority in Gaza by sea, the so-called 'Karine A' affair, Arab support for the Palestinians remained restricted for the most part to rhetorical flourishes. Both Cairo and Amman ensured that strict border security measures prevented arms and explosives reaching Palestinian militias. Second, despite incurring heavy casualties in both Iraq and Afghanistan, both Washington and London cannot claim that the existential security of the state, at least in the short to medium terms, is or was at stake. Indeed, while clearly wanting to ensure the stability and long-term survival of friendly regimes in Kabul and Baghdad, the claim that British or United States troops have to be in Afghanistan to prevent, in the longer term, the destabilization of Pakistan and extremist acts in Britain or the United States carries overtones of a domino theory discredited in the aftermath of the Vietnam War.

As such, distance, be it function of security or geography, never came to define Israel's response to the al-Aqsa intifada once it was construed as an existential threat to the very existence of the state. Aside from its first four months, the violence that broke out across the Occupied Territories in September 2000 bore little resemblance to the mass street demonstrations and stone throwing that marked the intifada of 1987 to 1993. The proliferation of militias under the auspices, though never the full control, of the Palestine Authority (PA) resulted in the conflict evolving through a number of consecutive stages: popular uprising in Palestinian Areas 'A'; attacks upon Israeli military targets and settlements in the Occupied Territories and East Jerusalem; attacks upon Israeli civilian targets within the Israel's pre-1967 border; Israel's massive response in Areas A and targeted attacks on individuals, infrastructure and symbols deemed responsible for the ongoing violence. Arafat's incompetent and often corrupt authority allowed for a myriad groups and militias to emerge under enigmatic leaders able and willing to mobilize support for anti-Israel activities. This was akin to an emergent warlordism, defined here as the appeal of a strong individual or group within a given geographical confine and removed from the control of a strong or reliable overarching authority.[10]

Between September 2000 and January 2005, some 3,529 Palestinians and 1,030 Israelis had been killed in violence related directly to the al-Aqsa intifada.[11] When broken down into specific time periods, the figure given for Israeli fatalities demonstrated a specific learning curve in the tactics and strategies used to counter Palestinian terror attacks. According to research conducted by Nadav Morag, the first year of the intifada resulted in approximately 200 Israeli deaths. From September 2001 to September 2002, around 400 fatalities were incurred, dropping back to under 300 in the following period. Between September 2003 and July 2004, only 24 Israelis were killed, evidence, Nadav argued, of 'the success of Israel's antiterrorism policies at the tactical level'.[12]

These anti-terrorism policies were essentially intelligence led, with Agaf Mod'in (AMAN or Military Intelligence) and the Sherut Bitachon ha'Klali (Shin Beth/Shabbak, or the General Security Service – GSS) carrying the main intelligence burden with regard to the Palestinians. Human intelligence (HUMINT) remained at a premium in this conflict, with the pressing need for preventative intelligence requiring the GSS to re-establish networks of informers across the West Bank and Gaza Strip that had fallen into abeyance following the signing of the Oslo Accords in 1993.[13] The mass round-ups of Palestinian men in both March and April 2002 afforded the GSS the opportunity to recruit assets held at the Ketziot detention center in the Negev, using the not-so-subtle blend of access to work permits, exploitation of family or tribal grievances, as well as ignoring the more nefarious activities of drug pushers and other criminals, as inducements to supply information.[14] While much credit was rightly claimed by the GSS in thwarting terror attacks, the sharp reduction in the number of actual suicide attacks inside Israel's Green Line had as much to do with the styptic presence of IDF troops in and around the main Palestinian towns and cities of the West Bank, and, as importantly, the construction of Israel's controversial security barrier.

But the view that the conflict was strategic, indeed, *existential* became the dominant conceptual prism – the *Conceptzia* – determined its prosecution.[15] It eschewed a criminal-justice approach toward countering Palestinian terrorism or, indeed, any association with human security in preference for a war-fighting model. The clearest manifestation of this approach was in the widespread use of 'targeted killings'. Here, the perception of an existential threat overrode the normative legal principles adhered to by democratic states – the right to life, innocence unless proved otherwise through a fair trial – as Israel consciously adopted a war-fighting model as its preferred means of countering terrorism. Its application was justified by the IDF Advocate General Menachem Finkelstein, who invoked the IDF's right of self-defense in fighting hostile elements in the territories and where, devoid of other alternatives, such action can help save lives. Aside from its operational impact, the *Conceptzia* had a wider societal message. It bolstered public moral by countering, according to Avi Kober, a primary objective of the terrorists: a dilution of trust by Israelis in their own government that, in turn, would sow dissent against the prevailing political order.[16]

Strong in its emotional appeal and cogent in its legal reasoning, the *Conceptzia* effectively proscribed any alternative political options to resolve the conflict, or indeed, cast doubt on the widely held assumption that Arafat had planned the violence. For example, a Saudi peace plan, agreed upon by Arab League states at a Beirut summit in May 2002, a plan which entailed full diplomatic recognition of Israel in return for a withdrawal from Palestinian Areas 'A' in the West Bank and progress toward final status negotiations, was never seriously discussed by Israel's Cabinet, despite its obvious historic significance. As Ya'alon remarked, only complete 'regime change' among the Palestinian leadership, something that should stand comparison with the process of de-Nazification in post-war Germany, would suffice.[17]

To be sure, some within Israel's military establishment did question the *Conceptzia* and the narrative that led to its formulation: that Ehud Barak, as Prime Minister, had made a generous offer to Arafat at Camp David and that its rejection by the Palestinian revealed an unrepentant terrorist bent on the destruction of the Jewish state. Major General Amos Malka, the Director of Military

Intelligence during Barak's tenure of office, claimed that analytical reports produced by the Research Division of Aman prior to the Camp David talks supported the view that Arafat preferred diplomacy over violence to achieve his aims. Claiming Palestinian violence was usually a response to what was regarded as Israel's diplomatic recalcitrance, Malka noted that:

> We [Aman] assumed that it is possible to reach an agreement with Arafat under the following conditions: a Palestinian state with Jerusalem as its capital and sovereignty over the Temple Mount [Harem al-Sharif]; 97 per cent of the West Bank plus exchanges of territory on the ratio of 1:1 with respect to remaining territory, some kind of formula that includes the acknowledgement of Israel's responsibility for the refugee problem and a willingness to accept 20–30,000 refugees. All along the way ... it was Aman's assessment that he [Arafat] had to get some kind of statement that would *not* depict him as having relinquished this [the Palestinian right of return] but would be prepared for a very limited implementation.[18]

Malka went on to state that even after the outbreak of the al-Aqsa intifada, all Israel's main intelligence agencies continued to argue that diplomacy remained Arafat's preferred option to achieving an independent Palestinian state. Malka's account does remain controversial, not least because other members of military intelligence, most notably the former head of the Research Division of Aman under Malka, Brigadier General Amos Gilad, argued that the floundering of the Camp David meeting on the very issue of the right of return negated Israel's right to exist. Even so, 'No one, including Gilad himself, argued that Arafat's expectations [at Camp David] included an Israeli agreement to accept 300–400,000 refugees in the framework of the right of return.' The numbers, according to Malka, would have remained purely symbolic.

Malka's views, however, did not reflect the prevailing sentiment among the military hierarchy. Doubts had developed among Israel's General Staff concerning the fidelity of Arafat to the Oslo Process long before the failure of the Camp David talks. The catalyst for such concerns was the widespread Palestinian violence across the Occupied Territories in September 1996, sparked ostensibly by the decision of the then Prime Minister, Binyamin Netanyahu, to allow an access tunnel to be opened under the Temple Mount/Harem al-Sharif. The incident led to the deaths of over 100 Palestinians and Israelis. The impact of the violence on the consciousness of the IDF was magnified by the fact that Palestinian Security Forces under the control of Arafat used firearms, allowed under the terms of the Oslo Accords, to attack Israeli security personnel. Such acts led the outgoing IDF commanding officer for Central Command, Major General Gabi Offer, to conclude that any repeat of such violence would elicit a real show of force by the IDF, designed to '[M]ake the rioters understand the heavy price they would have to pay for the continued violence, and that would cool their ardor at once'.[19]

The metaphorical water used to cool such ardor was the phenomenal expenditure of ammunition by the IDF in the first few days of the al-Aqsa intifada.

According to Malka, over 1,300,000 rounds of ammunition were fired at rioters, an expenditure justified by the belief held by senior IDF officers, including the former Chief of Staff Lieutenant General Shaul Mofaz, that Arafat's 'foray' into negotiations was merely a subterfuge designed to lead to Israel's destruction. According to Reuven Pedatzur:

> Mofaz, with the support of his senior aides, did not plan to bring about the end of the conflict at its very onset.... [H]e had an opportunity to finally 'beat' the Palestinians, to 'vanquish' them and lead them to negotiations in a weakened and exhausted state. This is the origin of the 'burned into their consciousness' thesis, which became the cornerstone of the IDF policy in the [Occupied] Territories.... This is the only way they are best off coming to terms with their inferiority and accepting Israel's demands.[20]

The paucity of such thinking was soon revealed. The mass street protests and rioting that marked the first intifada soon gave way to unrestrained violence as Palestinians took up arms that had been bequeathed to them under the Oslo agreements. In short, far from having the desired deterrent effect, the IDF's use of overwhelming force and the disproportionate casualties incurred by the Palestinians only acted to reinforce a more militant stance among a people who felt they had little to lose.[21] Thus, on assuming office in February 2001, Prime Minister Sharon's determination to fragment and destroy the security organs, institutions and leadership of the Palestine Authority, re-establish Israeli military hegemony over the West Bank and Gaza, and reconstitute a more compliant Palestinian political order found a receptive audience, as the interview with Ya'alon demonstrates, among senior members of the General Staff.[22]

Some Israeli commentators regard this as the recrudescence of a military culture in the decision-making process that had, in the aftermath of Oslo, been in apparent retreat. Other observers of civil–military relations in Israel believed such claims of subservience on the part of the executive to the dictates of the military were simplistic, preferring instead the more symbiotic descriptor 'political–military partnership'.[23] The totem of an existential threat has, nonetheless, always had a unifying effect on a society long fragmented along social, ethnic and religious lines. The noted social commentator Aluf Benn argued that the preference for military solutions cannot be reduced solely to the immediate exigencies of countering Palestinian terrorism. There remained a strong determination among senior IDF officers to recover the prestige of the army and its credibility as an effective deterrent following its unilateral withdrawal from south Lebanon in May 2000. This was seen as particularly important since the various Palestinian militias came to be viewed as trying to ape the success of the Hizb'allah. Given that the conflict has been termed 'existential', the IDF, according to Benn, perceived itself as having a mission that negated, a priori, any serious consideration of the means employed to subdue Palestinian terror, irrespective of the wider political impact this could entail.[24] This was most violently demonstrated in the policy of targeted killings.

Between 2000 and 2004, Israel carried out 159 targeted killing operations. The methods used have ranged from the use of helicopter gunships launching missiles into cars and homes, or explosive devices hidden in mobile phones, to the use of snipers. Such killings undoubtedly relied on precise operational intelligence and, indeed, the success of such operations did much to restore the self-esteem of the GSS, tarnished previously by its public failure to protect Yitzhak Rabin from assassination.[25] Few in Israel demonstrated public distaste for such operations, it being relatively easy for such killings to be justified in preventative terms. The horror of suicide bombings in Tel Aviv, Netanya, Haifa, Hadera, Nahariya and Jerusalem denied both time and space for moral scruples to be aired in public.

While targeted killings remained part of the repertoire of operational planning in the Occupied Territories, they moved beyond Israel's immediate security concern of curtailing terrorist activity. The killing of Mustafa Zibri, more popularly known as Abu Ali Mustafa, was a watershed in relations between Israel and the Palestine Authority. Zibri was a founding member of the PLO and the political leader of the Popular Front for the Liberation of Palestine (PFLP) who had openly renounced the use of violence as a condition for Israel allowing his return to the West Bank in 1999. His death on the 27 August 2001, the most high-profile of a Palestinian by Israel since the killing of Abu Jihad in Tunis in 1988, was justified by Tel Aviv on the grounds that Zibri was responsible for two bomb attacks in Jerusalem, a claim that Palestinians continue to deny vehemently. Of crucial importance, however, was the signal sent by Israel derived from the actual location of his death. His office in Ramallah where he met his bloody fate was only 500 meters from Arafat's headquarters in the city. For many, it was a clear warning that even those Palestinians with an international profile could not expect their fame to act as a protective shield if Israel felt retribution was justified. Indeed, in June 2003, Ya'alon openly admitted that the Israeli government had discussed the possibility of killing Arafat, though assurances given to President George W. Bush by Sharon that the Palestinian Rais would not be harmed meant that such a measure would have only been taken in *extremis*.[26]

For some analysts, such actions are more akin to a policy of outright political assassination rather than targeted killing. For example, the use by the United States of unmanned aerial vehicles or drones to target al-Qaeda operatives across the Middle East enjoyed an international legal approbation, however subjective, derived from Washington having made a formal declaration of war against Bin Laden and his associates. As such, the killing in Yemen on 4 November 2002 of Salim Sinan al-Harithi, a senior al-Qaeda operative deemed responsible for the attack on the USS *Cole* in Aden harbor, was consistent with the laws of war, irrespective of the fact that such an attack appeared to violate Yemeni sovereign territory.[27]

By contrast, Israel's use of the term 'targeted killing' to describe its actions rests upon recourse to a moral relativism that dilutes the role of international law. The former director of the Mossad, Danny Yatom declared, 'We don't take pride in liquidating terrorists. We are in the midst of a battle, in the midst of a war against terrorism and in this war we must strike at those who threaten Israel.' But despite such statements reinforcing the existential nature of the conflict, Israel never formally declared war against the PA. A state of war can only exist between two sovereign states, and a formal declaration of war would no doubt have been seen as de facto recognition of a Palestinian state. Colonel Daniel Reisner of the IDF's legal branch preferred the more nebulous terms 'unconflict' or 'active hostilities'.[28] But whatever names are applied, it cannot disguise the fact that domestic pressure, as well as a limited ability to apply less-lethal means of apprehending terrorist suspects, underpinned the continued use of assassination as a tool of state policy. Moreover, utilitarian calculations informed Israel's policy of targeted killing; the precise use of proportionate force helped to save innocent lives while reducing collateral damage among the Palestinian populace. Israeli decision-makers eschew the idea that such attacks are about punishment; rather, they are about either prevention or pre-emption, which Israel justifies under the customary right of nation-states to self-defense and under Article 51 of the United Nations charter that permits the right of self-defense to a state after an attack. Palestinian culpability for the outbreak of the al-Aqsa intifada is seen in this regard, though of course, the relevance of Article 51 to non-state actors, even if such culpability is accepted, remains a moot point.

Irrespective of such moral concerns, retaliatory measures against terrorists, and those that gave support – be it financial, logistic or even moral – have always enjoyed wide public support in Israel. Unlike the struggle against terrorist groups in Europe that has, for the most part, been dealt with through law-enforcement agencies, Palestinian terrorism, and particularly that associated with Islamist groups, remained a potent reminder of the atavism of much of the Arab world. Accordingly, rather than attempting to see such terrorism as, first and foremost, a manifestation of criminality, Israelis, perhaps understandably at an emotional level, came to view the situation as an outright war, a perception reinforced by the very public use of F-16 fighter jets, anti-tank attack helicopters and heavy armor to subdue the more active Palestinian militant groups and their supporters. Thus, despite some high-profile cases brought before the Supreme Court and ongoing debates within the confines of academe, discussion in Israel regarding the efficacy of the methods used to subdue Palestinian terrorism has prompted little discussion, leading Ariel Merari to conclude that 'The readiness [of the Israeli people] to use massive force is, undoubtedly fed by an existential threat to personal and national security.'[29]

The question remains, however, as to the effectiveness of targeted killings. Some have argued that their use merely radicalized Palestinian opinion, providing a steady stream of recruits wishing to visit vengeance upon the Jewish state and, in turn, contributing to a cycle of violence. There is certainly evidence to support such claims, particularly where those targeted were lower-level operatives. As Kober notes, the killing of 'military operatives' associated with Hamas and Islamic Jihad is akin to 'mowing a lawn', with the deaths of militants merely adding luster to the idea of martyrdom among Palestinian grass-roots support for such bloody actions. Evidence suggests that targeted killings did little to disrupt the cohesion of militia groups whose very decentralization worked to their advantage. However, after 2004 Israel specifically began to target the political leadership of groups such as Hamas. To be sure, this was a risky strategy. The killing of the spiritual leader of Hizb'allah, Shaykh Abbas Mussawi in 1992, marked the transformation of the organization into a more effective militia. But the assassination of the spiritual leader of Hamas, Shaykh Yassin in March 2004, soon to be followed by Abdel Aziz Rantisi in April, is akin to what strategists refer to as hitting the enemy's 'center of gravity'. It has been seen by some observers as effective in that it has forced Hamas toward a unilateral embrace of a *hudna* in June 2004. Indeed, since its overthrow of Fatah throughout Gaza in 2007, the responsibilities of power have seen Hamas temper its more extreme rhetoric and accepting Israel as a *fait accompli*, though stopping short of outright acceptance of its right to exist.

Israel, the United States and the global War on Terror

Throughout the al-Aqsa intifada, Washington expressed public understanding for the principles, if not always the intensity, of the methods employed by Israel, in prosecuting its war on Palestinian terrorism. Israelis certainly believed that their struggle was of a piece with the Bush administration's war on global terror. Major General Ahron Ze'evi, Director of Military Intelligence, certainly claimed as much publicly. Speaking during the course of a lecture delivered to the Jaffee Centre for Strategic Studies at Tel Aviv University in May 2002, he argued that the events of 11 September 2001 had led the United States to support 'Israel in every way possible [and] recognises its [Israel's] right to extirpate terror and protect its citizens'.[30]

Until his death in November 2004, the diplomatic isolation of Arafat was deemed proportionate by the Bush administration in light of events such as the '*Karine A* affair', and the capture of documents from Palestinian militias in the course of Operation Defensive Shield, documents that Israel circulated as widely as possible in Europe and Washington to demonstrate the malign intent of Arafat.

The '*Karine A* affair' in particular had a major impact in Washington, not least because it suggested Palestinian collusion with Iran and its Lebanese progeny, Hizb'allah, in an attempt to escalate the al-Aqsa intifada to the strategic level. The *Karine A* was a cargo ship that was intercepted and boarded by Israeli Special Forces 500 kilometers south of the port of Eilat on 3 January 2002. Laden with 500 tons of arms and ammunition, including Katyusha rockets and Sagger wire-guided anti-tank missiles, reports speculated that the nefarious haul would have been offloaded along the coast of the Sinai peninsula and, from there, smuggled into Gaza.[31] Despite denials of the Palestinian Rais of any knowledge of or involvement with the arms shipment, the '*Karine A* affair' was grist to the mill of those in Washington who viewed Arafat as an unreconstructed terrorist bent on the ultimate destruction of the Jewish state.

Partly in response to the '*Karine A* affair', but driven by the public outrage following the homicidal bombing in Netanya, Sharon authorized 'Operation Defensive Shield', the mass incursion by the IDF that shattered the illusion held by the PA that Israel lacked the political will to enter and reoccupy Palestinian cities on the West Bank. For the GSS and AMAN, the operation yielded an intelligence treasure trove of documentation, described by one GSS officer as 'the wettest dream I've ever dreamed'.[32] In the immediate aftermath of Defensive Shield, the research division of AMAN made documents seized during the operation available to Western embassies and intelligence agencies.[33] Sometimes referred to as the *Mukataa* documents, they provided forensic detail on the organization and terrorist operations of members of the Fatah-affiliated Tanzim and al-Aqsa Martyrs Brigade, as well as the activities of Hamas and Palestinian Islamic Jihad. These documents also had a clear propaganda value. Following widespread accusations of a massacre of Palestinian civilians in the aftermath of the IDF assault on the Jenin refugee camp, AMAN produced a detailed document highlighting the extent to which the camp had sheltered a terrorist infrastructure responsible for 28 suicide attacks. As one Fatah memorandum reproduced by AMAN stated, the Jenin refugee camp

> is characterized by an exceptional presence of fighting men who take the initiative (on behalf of) the national activity. Nothing will beat them and nothing worries them. Therefore they are ready for self-sacrifice with all the means. And therefore, it is not strange that Jenin (has been termed) *A'simat al-Istashidin* (the martyrs' capital).[34]

Of crucial importance was the emphasis placed by Israeli officials on the radical Islamist dimension of these documents. This placed the al-Aqsa intifada above and beyond the widely held perception that it was but a continuation of a nationalist struggle, locating instead its essential dynamic as of a piece with global Jihad. According to Major General Aharon Ze'evi, the attacks of 9/11 had sharpened the distinction between the values of the West and those of the Arab–Islamic world and that, accordingly, Islam remained the main source of terrorism in the contemporary world. Continuing with this 'Huntingtonian' thesis, Ze'evi noted:

> American policy towards Iraq and Iran, both of which are 'members' of the 'Axis of Evil' and the branding of Hizbollah [sic] as a terrorist organisation, have provided fertile ground for tightening American–Israeli co-operation. United States policy in this area is important for Israel's own struggle against its local 'Axis of Evil'.[35]

In light of the speech by President Bush on 22 May 2002, when he lambasted Arafat's failures both as a statesman and political leader, and consequently declared him to be *persona non grata* in Washington, Israel assumed considerable latitude in imposing its own solution to the al-Aqsa intifada. This culminated in the August 2005 withdrawal from the Gaza Strip and the continued construction of the security fence. In this regard, Israel appeared to be a net beneficiary of the March 2003 invasion of Iraq. At any other time, the build up to war in Iraq would have dominated political and public debate in Israel. The duration and ferocity, however, of its own War on Terror meant that events elsewhere were, if not remote, then certainly removed from the immediate strategic horizon of most Israelis. Sharon made it clear to President Bush that should Israel be subjected to attack by Iraqi weapons of mass destruction it reserved the right to strike back with overwhelming force. More immediately, Israel heightened its state of readiness along its northern border with Lebanon lest its erstwhile nemesis, Hizb'allah, chose this moment to demonstrate, however symbolically, its fidelity to the idea of Arab unity. Concurrently, Palestinian towns and villages in the West Bank, already suffering under draconian restrictions as a result of the al-Aqsa intifada, were placed under curfew.[36]

The war itself was seen as a means by which the regional order could be recast to Israel's benefit; few Israelis evinced much sympathy for the mass public demonstrations against the war seen across the globe. Shimon Peres captured the national mood when he declared

> There is no greater killer in our time than Saddam Hussein. I'm not impressed by the demonstrators. When Saddam gassed 100,000 innocent Kurds nobody demonstrated. When he attacked Iran and a million people lost their lives, nobody demonstrated.... Where was public opinion during all the massacres, all the dictatorships, all the killings, all the terror?[37]

Such moral rectitude on the part of Israel's elder statesman masked a more realist expediency on the part of the Jewish state's more hardline government ministers. In the absence of any credible evidence to the contrary, it is doubtful if the mass expulsion of Palestinians from the West Bank – despite the more alarmist predictions in some of the Arab press – was ever considered as a policy option at Cabinet level. But Sharon was instructed by Washington not to use the outbreak of the conflict to remove Chairman Arafat from the Muqata'a in Ramallah – either through physical expulsion or assassination – lest it inflame regional passions still further.[38]

In the realm of military support, however, Israel remained keen to offer any assistance it could to the United States. With the belief that their forces would be involved in urban combat operations, Pentagon officials remained keen to draw on the experience of IDF officers involved in operations against the various Palestinian militia groupings in the towns and cities of the West Bank, including the use of real-time intelligence gleaned from the use of Unmanned Aerial Vehicles and undercover operations. While Israeli officers briefed their American counterparts in the United States, not all US intelligence officials were happy with what one unnamed officer summarized as advice on how to set up 'an assassination program'.[39] Though such collaboration curried favor with the United States on a purely military level, the broader ramifications of the fall of Saddam worried some Israeli commentators. By its very physical presence in Iraq, the United States became a Middle East power in its own right, a fact that was not lost on Israeli decision-makers. Despite the undoubted esteem in which the administration of George W. Bush held Israel, Tel Aviv remained concerned that, as a newly constituted Middle East power, Washington had its own agenda, an agenda in which Israel's role would be greatly diminished. As Aviad Kleinberg argued:

> [The] threat [from Iraq] has been removed, more or less. However, the invasion of Iraq dramatically lowers Israel's stock as a strategic asset. And not because Israel is not loyal to Uncle Sam; on the contrary, it is a most obedient and faithful vassal. It's just that Israel is not really needed. Israel's great strategic weight stemmed from its ability to act – or to constitute a potential threat – in a region in which the United States did not want to intervene directly.... If American involvement becomes direct, there is no further need for mediators.[40]

Such fears of regional redundancy have yet to be realized, but the impact of the Iraq War had a more immediate impact on Israel's strategic environment and, by extension, the very discourse surrounding Zionism itself. By the very removal of Saddam Hussein and the Ba'athist regime, Washington and London removed at a stroke *the* strategic rationale for continued occupation of the West Bank: the retention of this territory as a buffer against any Iraqi incursion through Jordan aimed at the state of Israel. This argument had long been used as an umbrella under which settlement construction had been allowed to continue apace, creating a synergy between those in Israel – mainly associated with the Likud bloc, who merged historic claim and strategic necessity in justifying Israel's retention of the West Bank and Gaza Strip – and those who, on purely eschatological grounds, refuse to abrogate their covenant with God by handing back land to an alien sovereignty.[41]

Shorn of this wider strategic rationale, but unwilling to abandon the main settlement blocs in the West Bank (including East Jerusalem), knowing the attendant civil disorder this would undoubtedly entail, the continued construction of the security fence offered attractive strategic and political solutions, at least to many Israelis. Strategic because it has reduced substantially the number of homicide attacks inside Israel; political because, however distressful it may be to those settlers who view the West Bank in its entirety as their rightful dispensation, the trail of the security fence meant that most settlements would remain inside Israel, allowing a Jewish majority to be maintained. Given that demographic trends have long favored the Palestinians, such enforced unilateral separation remains the only way in which Israel can remain both Jewish and democratic, the very basis of the Zionist ideal.[42] It is here perhaps that the cumulative impact of the al-Aqsa intifada has been most profound. Faced with a Palestinian population which, for the most part, remains bloodied but unbowed while enjoying the diplomatic forbearance (and indeed, at times, indulgence) of the Bush administration, former Prime Minister Olmert and his predecessor Ariel Sharon had, albeit by default, begun the process of closure that began over a century ago: defining the physical, as well as the political boundaries of Zionism.

Conclusion

No one should underestimate the suffering that Palestinian terrorism has inflicted upon Israelis, both in terms of its scale and its psychological impact. The base fears that such attacks arouse indicate for many a base recidivism among Palestinians, unwilling and unable to accept the reality of the Jewish state within their midst. Such existential concern lay at the very heart of the *Conceptzia* and was readily shared by a majority of the Israeli public. As such, discussion over the *Conceptzia* of tackling Palestinian terrorism – ranging from the moral efficacy of targeted killings to the building of the security fence – remained, for the most part, conspicuous by its absence. Moreover, the perception that Israel was at war and that the enemy, while at the gates, had not overrun the citadel, meant that, for the most part, the threat to civil liberties *inside* Israel proper was never an issue. This may be cold comfort to those 14 Palestinian Arab citizens of Israel who lost their lives protesting against the overwhelming use of force by the IDF at the very beginning of the al-Aqsa intifada. But precisely because the violence and, indeed, the enemy were external to the state, political and civil rights for Israeli citizens at least remained untouched, something for which many in Israel take great pride.

Thus, while the Israeli Supreme Court did force amendments to the route of the fence where it was deemed to impact unnecessarily on Palestinian livelihoods, the actual legality of the fence, let alone the use of assassinations as a tool of state policy, elicited little discussion beyond the immediate confines of academe in Israel. As the Roman sage Cicero noted, '*inter arma silent leges*' ['in battle, the laws are silent'].[43] Thus, when Israel launched 'Operation Cast Lead' in December 2008, a massive offensive into Gaza designed to destroy the military infrastructure of Hamas, few in Israel questioned the sagacity of a mission that resulted in a Palestinian death toll of 1,500, mostly civilians, over a three-week period. The continuous shelling of the Israeli town of Sderot by Islamist militants over a period of eight years – shelling perceived as an attempt to ultimately force Israelis from their homes – was enough to convince the majority of Israelis that such mass use of force was not only justifiable but indeed necessary.[44]

This approach, with its preference for war-fighting, has enjoyed considerable sympathy, if not total support, from the United States. Washington's own preference for a war-fighting model to counter the global terrorist threat nonetheless conflates neatly with that of Israel, not least because the demands of Islamist-inspired groups such as Hamas and Hizb'allah are seen in absolute terms that brook no compromise. This was visibly demonstrated in March 2004 when a twin homicide attack in Beersheva killed 16 Israelis and injured more than 100 others. In response, Israel launched air attacks deep inside Syrian territory against targets associated with Hamas and Hizb'allah, former Prime Minister Sharon arguing that, as Damascus sponsored and sheltered these groups, it could not remain immune from retribution.[45] Given that Washington had long suspected that Syria had been too indulgent of insurgents fighting their own troops in Iraq, its rebuke of Israel's action was conspicuous by its absence. This is unfortunate since, while undoubtedly motivated by particular, indeed radical, interpretations of Islam, Hizb'allah and Hamas do remain nationally based organizations, setting them apart from the global jihadists associated with al-Qaeda, its groups and affiliates. Even so, the evidence to date from Israel's counter-terrorist methods would suggest that Palestinian violence has been successfully managed, if not defeated outright. In this process, targeted killings played a crucial role.

Washington would undoubtedly prefer Tel Aviv to abide by the provisions of the roadmap, but Israel's continued construction of the security fence, unfettered by regional or international opprobrium, exposed, at the very least, a benign indulgence of Israel as it continues to impose its concept of unilateral separation. It should be noted that this has nothing to do with Palestinian rights or, indeed, with reaching any form of negotiated accommodation with the Palestinian Authority. It has, however, everything to do with Israel's very raison d'etre: Zionism. The paradox of the *Conceptzia* therefore remains this: it has effectively countered what it believed to be the worst excesses of Palestinian terrorism and in the process has challenged those who believe that democratic states remain ill-prepared to reach a military decision in the war among the people without undermining their own values and sense of moral probity. But, equally, in the process of confronting the Palestinians, Israel has been forced to recognize the limits of its own ideological dreams and, with it, impose a physical reality of what it must do to survive demographically as a Jewish state in the contemporary Middle East.

Notes

1 A. Shavit, 'The Enemy Within', *Ha'aretz Magazine* (in English), 30 August 2002.
2 M.A. Heller 'Operation "Defensive Wall": A Change in Israeli Strategy?', *Tel Aviv Notes* (Tel Aviv University – Jaffee Centre for Strategic Studies/Moshe Dayan Centre for Middle Eastern and African Studies), 34:4, April 2002.
3 Exactly what was offered by Barak and rejected by Arafat remains the subject of a heated debate. While much has been written on the failure of the summit, the most revealing interviews appeared in a series of articles in the *New York Review of Books* (*NYRB*). See B. Morris, 'Camp David and After: An Exchange. 1. An Interview with Ehud Barak', *NYRB*, XLIX:10 (13 June 2002), pp. 42–45; R. Malley and H. Agha, '2. A Reply to Ehud Barak', *NYRB*, XLIX:10 (13 June 2002), pp. 46–48. The belief that Israel's version of events at Camp David had benefited from a news blackout imposed during the conference itself is made by A. Ben, 'The Selling of the Summit', *Ha'aretz* (in Hebrew), 27 July 2001.
4 For example, see N. Lochery, *Why Blame Israel: The Facts Behind the Headlines* (Cambridge: Icon Books, 2004), pp. 178–179.

5 T.X. Hammes, 'War Evolves into the Fourth Generation', *Contemporary Security Policy*, 26:2 (August 2005), p. 190.

6 For a detailed study of the Iraq Insurgency, see A.S. Hashim, *Insurgency and Counter-Insurgency in Iraq* (London: Hurst, 2006). The networked nature of the ongoing insurgency in Afghanistan is described in some detail in A. Guistossi, *Koran, Kalashnikov and Laptop: The Neo-Taliban Insurgency in Afghanistan* (New York: Columbia University Press, 2008). The concept of 'Human Security' remains a contested issue but came to inform the United Nations Development Report in 1994 and posited a shift from state-centric security beloved of Realism to 'people-centered' security, its central components being the freedom of individuals and communities from fear and want. It defined security in far more expansive terms than hitherto expressed, and has come to inform the foreign and development policies of Canada, Norway and the UK. See, for example, R. Paris, 'Human Security: Paradigm Shift or Hot Air?', *International Security*, 26:2 (2001), pp. 87–102.

7 General Sir R. Smith, *The Utility of Force: The Art of War in the Modern World* (London: Penguin/Allen Lane, 2005), pp. 278–280.

8 For greater elaboration of this argument, see M. Fitzsimmons, 'Hard Hearts and Open Minds? Governance, Identity and the Intellectual Foundations of Counterinsurgency Strategy', *Journal of Strategic Studies*, 31:3 (2008), pp. 337–365.

9 The role of tribes and other surrogates has increasingly come to inform debate on insurgency and counter-insurgency. See G. Hughes and C. Tripodi, 'Anatomy of a Surrogate: Historical Precedents and Implications for Contemporary Counter-Insurgency and Counter-Terrorism', *Small Wars and Insurgencies*, 20:1 (2009), pp. 1–35. See also R.L. Taylor, 'Tribal Alliances: Ways, Means and Ends to Successful Strategy', *Strategic Studies Monographs* (August 2005), p. 20, www.strategicstudies-institute.army.mil/pubs/display.cfm?pubID=619.

10 This interpretation is borrowed from the work of S.L. Woodward. See her chapter, 'Failed States: Warlordism and "Tribal Warfare"', in R.H. Schultz Jr. and R. Pfaltz-graff Jr. (eds.), *The Role of Naval Forces in the 21st Century* (Washington, DC: Brassey's, 2000), p. 105.

11 I. MacKinnon, 'Quiet Man of Palestine Prepares to Step Out of Arafat's Shadow', *The Times*, 8 January 2005. In addition, 28,399 Palestinians and 6,966 Israelis had been wounded.

12 N. Morag, 'Measuring Success in Coping with Terrorism: The Israeli Case', *Studies in Conflict and Terrorism*, 28:4 (2005), p. 310.

13 The importance of Intelligence in Israel's undercover war in the Occupied Territories was shown in the BBC TV *Correspondent* program, 'Israel Undercover', broadcast on 15 February 2002. For the transcript, see http://news.bbc.co.uk/1/hi/programmes/correspondent/1820862.stm.

14 For a detailed account of the techniques of entrapment used, see G. Gorenberg, 'The Collaborator', *New York Times*, 18 August 2002.

15 The term '*Conceptzia*' was first used to describe the prevailing mindset held by the Israeli military intelligence on the eve of the Yom Kippur War in October 1973. The dominant *conceptzia* held that because of Israel's clear military superiority, it remained highly unlikely that Egypt would be capable of launching any attack to regain the Sinai peninsula. See U. Bar Joseph, *Hatzofeh Shenirdam: Hafta'at Yom Ha'Kippurim Umekoroteha* (*The Watchman Fell Asleep: The Surprise of Yom Kippur and its Origins*) (Tel Aviv: Zmora Bitan, 2001).

16 A. Kober, 'Targeted Killing During the Second Intifada: The Quest for Effectiveness', *Journal of Conflict Studies*, 28:1 (2007), www.lib.unb.ca/Texts/JCS/bin/get.cgi?directory=Summer07/&filename=jcs27art06.html.

17 A. Shavit, 'The Enemy Within', *Ha'aretz Magazine* (in English), 30 August 2002.

18 A. Eldar, 'Popular Misconceptions', *Ha'aretz* (in English), 14 June 2004.

19 J. Pressman, 'The Second Intifada: Background and Causes of the Israeli–Palestinian Conflict', *Journal of Conflict Studies*, 22:22 (2003), p. 123.

20 R. Pedatzur, 'More Than a Million Bullets', *Ha'aretz* (in English), 29 June 2004.

21 Pressman, 'The Second Intifada', p. 125.

22 Sharon's aims were outlined by Joseph Alpher, a former member of Mossad and now a strategic analyst. See L. Hockstader, 'Sharon's Scorecard', *Washington Post*, 7 May 2002.

23 Y. Peri, 'The Political–Military Complex: The IDF's Influence over Policy Towards the Palestinians Since 1987', *Israel Affairs*, 11:2 (April 2005), p. 328.

24 A. Benn, 'In Israel, Too Much to Leave to the Generals', *Washington Post*, 18 August 2002.

25 A. Oren, 'More Intelligent Intelligence', *Ha'aretz* (in English), 12 May 2002.

26 A. Harel, 'Ya'alon: Killing Arafat was Debated', *Ha'aretz* (in Hebrew), 23 June 2003.

27 See E. Patterson and T. Casale, 'Targeting Terror: The Ethical and Practical Implications of Targeted Killing', *International Journal of Intelligence and Counterintelligence*, 18:4 (2005), pp. 645–647.

28 Reisner's comments are quoted in Y. Stein, 'Israel's Assassination Policy: Extrajudicial Executions', *B'Tselem* (January 2001), www.btselem.org/Download/extrajudicial_killings_Eng.doc.

29 A. Merari, 'Israel Facing Terrorism', *Israel Affairs*, 11:1 (January 2005), p. 229.

30 Major General A. Ze'evi (Farkash), Head of IDF Intelligence, 'Israel's Strategic Environment', *Strategic Assessment* (Tel Aviv: Tel Aviv University – Jaffee Centre for Strategic Studies), 5:2 (August 2002), www.tau.ac.il/jcss/sa/v5n2p7Zee.html.

31 A. Oren, 'The Old Man and the Sea', *Ha'aretz* (in English), 11 January 2002; E. Silver, 'Arafat Was Behind Arms Shipment, Says Sharon', *Independent*, 7 January 2002.

32 R. Bergman, 'The Ra'is Will Sign and Approve', *Yediot Ahronot* (in Hebrew), 12 July 2002.

33 AMAN already had access to documents before the mass incursions into the West Bank that detailed the strength of militant Palestinian groups in the Jenin refugee camp. A. Oren, 'More like Mogadishu than Kosovo', *Ha'aretz* (in Hebrew), 26 March 2002.

34 'Jenin: The Capital of the Palestinian Suicide Terrorists', IDF/Military Intelligence, document TR2–302–02, 18 April 2002, p. 2. Hereafter referred to as 'Jenin' TR2–302–02 (IDF/MI).

35 Major General A. Ze'evi (Farkash), 'Israel's Strategic Environment'.

36 A. Philps, 'States in the Cauldron: Israel', *Daily Telegraph Special Report*, 18 March 2003.

37 B. Russell, 'Peres Claims Defeat of Saddam Will be Welcomed by the Arab World', *Independent*, 3 April 2003. *Gush Shalom* (Peace Block) did organize peace vigils in Tel Aviv but these attracted little in the way of public support.

38 A. Harel, 'Ya'alon: Killing Arafat was Debated', *Ha'aretz* (in Hebrew), 23 June 2003.

39 P. Prier, 'Americans at the Israeli Urban Warfare School', *Le Figaro* (in French), 6 April 2003; J. Borger, 'Israel Trains US Assassination Squads in Iraq', *Guardian*, 9 December 2003.

40 A. Kleinberg, 'The War's Implications for Israel', *Ha'aretz Special Edition – War in Iraq*, www.haaretz.com/hasen/pagesShArtWar.jhtml?itemNo=282891&contrassID=33&.

41 T. Friedman, 'Breaking and Entering', *New York Times*, 11 December 2003.

42 Despite his reputation as being a champion of Jewish settlement in the Occupied Territories, Sharon was reputed to have been heavily influenced by the work on demographic projections by Professor Arnon Soffer of Haifa University. Soffer posited an

Arab majority between the Mediterranean and the Jordan River by 2020 and, accordingly, has long argued for physical separation between Israeli Jews and the Palestinians. See A. Soffer, *Israel, Demography 2000–2020: Dangers and Opportunities* (Haifa: National Security Studies Centre/University of Haifa, 2001), pp. 59–71.

43 The Israeli government would, undoubtedly, dispute this claim, arguing that its approach to tackling terror remains subservient to the law. See, for example, *Judgements of the Israel Supreme Court: Fighting Terrorism Within the Law* (Jerusalem: Israel Supreme Court, 2005), p. 210.

44 Y. Evron, 'Deterrence: The Campaign Against Hamas', *Strategic Assessment*, 11:4 (February 2009), www.inss.org.il/publications.php?cat=21&incat=&read=2656.

45 B. Burston, 'Israel's War on Hamas Takes a Turn Toward Syria', *Ha'aretz* (in English), 9 March 2004.

9 Russia and counter-terrorism

A critical appraisal

Cerwyn Moore and David Barnard-Wills

The roots of Russia's contemporary counter-terrorism policies derive from the end of the Cold War. As the Cold War ended, Russian troops withdrew from a bloody Afghan conflict, which created the environment in which a generation of militant fighters, who had successfully fought a defensive jihad against Communist forces, could refine their combat skills. In the immediate post-Cold War period, the West focused on ensuring that Russia's nuclear arsenal did not fall into the wrong hands, while contemplating the implications of vast political change in the former Soviet Union. Politically the West sought to provide a roadmap for the integration of former Soviet states in Eastern Europe into military organizations such as NATO. The newly emergent Russian political framework, the Commonwealth of Independent States (CIS), was itself a nascent organization with interim aims. There was clear pressure to hold this framework together, although by 1993 unrest in both Central Asia and the Caucasus increasingly threatened the coherence of the CIS. In newly independent Tajikistan in Central Asia, a civil war erupted, while two former Soviet republics, Tatarstan and Chechnya, were agitating for secession in the Caucasus, the latter escalating to a full-scale conflict between 1994 and 1996. Russian forces effectively lost the first war in Chechnya, and this led to a period of de facto Chechen independence, as well as introspection and opposition to the liberal policies within Russia.

Russia itself suffered economic turmoil in 1998 as markets crashed. The Yeltsin administration sought out a political replacement, identifying the former KGB officer Vladimir Putin as a suitable successor. Putin was promoted to Deputy Prime Minister on the 9 August 1999, enabling him to be appointed acting Prime Minister of the Government of the Russian Federation by President Boris Yeltsin. Throughout 1998 and 1999 Russian political elites – known as the *siloviki* – began to assert control over many areas of social, political and economic life, coalescing around a policy of recentralizing power in the Kremlin, a process endorsed and led by Putin. One aspect of this policy focused on re-establishing a dominant political narrative, which included a desire to deal with irredentism, insecurity and the threat of banditry, Islamism and terrorism emanating from the North Caucasus. To bolster this program of political reform and restore the position of Russia on the world stage, the Putin administration –

and the *siloviki* within it – established a distinctive counter-insurgency doctrine, which included a sub-policy designed to combat terrorism. Another aspect of political and military reform was the careful labeling of the campaign designed to counter separatism in Chechnya, which the Putin administration branded a 'counter-terror operation'. This labeling can be deconstructed and challenged, but the terms in use need to be taken as meaningful within Russian security discourse as a political logic and justification, while highlighting the political (and ideological) function this labeling serves. Such labeling is political and plays a particular role in the politics of Russian counter-terrorism, gesturing toward a return to imperial and Soviet-style policies of centralized control.

This chapter presents an introductory overview of developments in Russian counter-terrorism since 9/11. The chapter offers a preliminary discussion of counter-terror policies related to Chechnya before moving on to assess and analyze the centrality of information warfare within a broader policy of combating terrorism – a position between counter-terrorism and counter-insurgency. This includes traditional propaganda, but is really focused upon attempting to control and manage flows of information. While it also encompasses restrictions on press freedoms, in the modern world this necessarily includes an information-technology dimension and an analysis of the use of information technology and new media. In the Russian case, information warfare was bolstered by a clear military strategy, put in place as the Putin administration assumed control of the Kremlin throughout 1998; the aim was to rehabilitate the status of, and pride within, the Russian military following the 'humiliation' and defeat at the hands of Chechen separatists, while also aiming to eventually renovate the Russian security complex characterized by multiple competing agencies. As part of this process, Russia has also adopted the narrative and language of the War on Terror. However, Russia had *already* been fighting a campaign of counter-terrorism with a significant military dimension prior to 9/11. The militarized situation in several of the republics across Russia's southern security flank, the plethora of organizations involved in counter-terrorism, the radicalized politics of counter-terror in Russia and the strong 'tough guy' persona of Vladimir Putin have all contributed to this compatibility between the so-called Russian and Western 'wars on terror'. However, perhaps unique to the Russian War on Terror in the Putin era are two deeply engrained philosophical themes – *dervzhavnost*, the belief that Russia is, and should maintain its status as a great power; and *gosudarstvennost*, a longstanding belief that Russia should be run by a centralized state, in order to suppress irredentism and ensure it maintains its territorial integrity.

Historical background

Without attempting to construct a model of 'waves' of terrorism in Russia, the following historical perspectives provide a number of vignettes that shed light on the evolving practices of counter-terrorism in Russia. These examples contextualize contemporary counter-terrorism activity, and show that terrorism and counter-terrorism in Russia is not a new phenomenon, but one with historical antecedents affecting the contemporary policy environment.

Russia is associated with the development of the modern concept of terrorism as part of the revolutionary political violence in the struggle against Tsarism, prior to World War I and the Russian Revolution. The aim of terrorism in this context was the overthrow of Tsarist tyranny and the establishment of new, desired political institutions. Ideologically, expressed by theorists such as Nicholas Morizov, this violence was to be not vengeful or unconstrained, but rational, targeted and temporary – striking directly at the pillars of the political regime.[1] The particular favored weapon – dynamite – was chosen because it would distinguish their activity from simple murder.[2] Morozov believed that terror was:

> a war of strength against strength, of equals; a war of bravery against oppression, science and learning against the bayonet and the gallows. It endows individuals with the strength of the mighty, to perform deeds which are almost beyond the power of mortals. Never was there in history so convenient a situation for a revolutionary party and such successful methods of fighting.[3]

Narodnya Volya ('People's Will') emerged out of splits within the populist organization Zemlya I Volya, with the majority adopting terrorist tactics, with the assassination of the Tsar as their first goal. The minority faction 'Black Partition' disavowed terrorist tactics, preferring instead a supposedly purer form of populism.[4] Narodnya Volya's first success was the shooting of the governor of St Petersburg by Vera Zasulich in 1878. Then, in 1881, it launched its most significant attack – the assassination of Tsar Alexander II. However, the movement was largely destroyed by 1884 due to a combination of arrests, exiles and executions of its relatively small membership. Both the Narodniks and later the Bolsheviks relied on an elitist model of revolutionary change where a small group of educated, committed militants would serve as the active motor of social change. Nonetheless, the Mensheviks and the Bolsheviks opposed what they termed anarchist 'individual terror' in favor of class struggle.[5]

During the early Soviet period, the civil war drove the Bolshevik government to use terror in an attempt to defeat 'counter-revolutionary' forces. This is an example of what Duvall and Stohl call 'governance by terror' – 'terrorism practiced by "legally" constituted governments of nation-states'.[6] Both sides in the civil war made use of terror tactics. The Socialist Revolutionary campaign included the assassination of prominent Bolsheviks and the injury of both Lenin and Bukharin in 1918. The reprisals caused the newly formed Cheka (the All-Russia Extraordinary Commission for Combating Counter-Revolution and Sabotage) to engage in the Red Terror in pursuit of 'counter-revolutionary crime'.[7] This temporary, expedient response became institutionally embedded in the KGB.

Mapping terrorism and counter-terrorism within Russia during the Cold War period is problematic. During this period, the USSR was perceived in the West as being responsible for funding, arming, or indirectly supporting various 'red' terrorist movements. Evidence for this involvement, however, suggests an opportunistic exploitation of existing conflicts and circumstances rather than a coordinated and centrally controlled strategy.[8] Pluchinsky argues that terrorism was not a major security problem for the USSR as the 'authoritarian nature of the political and social systems made it difficult for such activities to surface, primarily due to strict government controls on the media and strong travel restrictions on foreigners'.[9] While we should be skeptical about the strong claim that authoritarian politics makes terrorism less likely, we can accept the weaker claim that it makes the transmission of information about terrorist events more problematic, and complicates reporting and analysis of these. Activities that would currently be termed 'terrorism' were encompassed under a broad rubric of 'counter-revolutionary' crimes in early Soviet jurisprudence, along with sabotage, espionage, anti-soviet agitation and aid to the international bourgeoisie.[10] The 1958 Law of State Crimes re-codified and updated the terminology of many of these crimes into the framework of 'state crimes'. This framework placed crimes with a political motive under the rubric of 'especially dangerous' crimes. Terrorism is divided into two categories, Terrorism ('political violence against public men') and Diversion/Wrecking ('political violence against public property').[11] Terrorism was highly subjective, dependent upon the public purpose the victim served, and necessitating a deep, invasive investigation of the suspect's political and private life. For example, one notable event in the latter part of the Cold War – the bombing of a Moscow subway train in 1977 which killed 30 people – was blamed on Armenian nationalists.

Terrorism and counter-terrorism proved a more pressing concern for Russian authorities in the years immediately after 1991. This was partly due to the cultural, legal and social transformation of Russia, which made it difficult to locate a meaning for acts of terrorism, but also because terrorism and symbolic acts of violence were used by different groups. The most pronounced examples stem from the first Russo-Chechen War of the 1990s (1994–1996). By the middle of 1995, Russian forces had successfully pacified a considerable portion of Chechnya, given their military superiority. Throughout early 1995, Chechen forces opted for a protracted guerrilla war, and what Chechen military leaders such as Aslan Maskhadov called 'war along the lines of communication' (*dorozhnaia voina*), mining convoy routes and exerting psychological pressure on the Russian war effort.[12] The highland towns and villages were well-defended, and, initially at least, afforded the Chechen forces a valuable foothold to mount a sustained guerrilla war. Yet Russian air superiority threatened the Chechen war effort, and by the late spring of 1995, Russian units had forced Chechen units to withdraw from a key highland town, Vedeno. In late June, a group of around 150 Chechens, led by Shamil Basayev, launched a raid deep into the Russian-controlled Stavropol region, beyond the boundaries of Chechnya. The style of the raid – a *nabeg* – harked back to an era when lightning raids were used by many groups in the Caucasus to capture cattle or hostages, often generating fear and panic due to the speed of the attack. Basayev, from a village near Vedeno, launched the raid on Budyonnovsk without permission from the Chechen military command, initially attacking a local police compound in the town. Chechen forces withdrew from the town center, and occupied the local hospital, taking local police and patients as hostages. The attack created chaos, exposing differences between the Russian public perception of the war in Chechnya and the discourse of the state authorities, compelling the Russian government to react. Despite numerous attempts to break the siege, the symbolic act of violence, drawn out over three days and broadcast worldwide, eventually forced the state authorities to negotiate with Basayev. His demands, a cessation of the conflict in Chechnya leading to negotiations on the status of the republic, and safe passage back to the highlands seemed outlandish. Nonetheless, they were granted. The raid on Budyonnovsk gave Chechen forces much-needed respite, forcing the Russians to the negotiating table, eventually turning the tide of the war, and profoundly damaging Russian morale. Moreover, part of the negotiations to end the siege took place live on Russian TV, publicizing the Chechen cause, granting Basayev mythic status in the resistance movement.

Another militarized *nabeg* took place in January 1996, when a group of around 150 raiders, led by Khunkar-Pasha Israilapov and Salman Raduyev, attacked a military base in the Russian-controlled Dagestani town of Kizlyar. Russian authorities managed to surround the withdrawing Chechen attackers in the town of Pervomaiskoye. Anatoly Kulikov of the Interior Ministry and Mikhail Barsukov took personal control of the operation designed to eradicate the Chechen attackers, and claimed an important victory. Again the raid was not sanctioned by Maskhadov, nor even by other field-commanders such as Basayev. The ensuing siege in Pervomaiskoye lasted for two days, as Chechen groups and their hostages dug into positions. The Russian military launched repeated Special Forces attacks, simultaneously making spurious claims that 'Raduyev had begun shooting hostages'.[13] Maskhadov's units launched a series of diversionary raids in Chechnya, and other Chechen units seized a number of Russian hostages in Grozny, in an attempt to aid the surrounded men. However, two days after the raid, news started to emerge that a considerable portion of Chechen fighters – including Israilapov and Raduyev – had actually broken out of the encirclement and made it safely back to Chechnya. Like Budyonnovsk, the raid 'humiliated' the political and military elite in Russia, generating much-needed international news coverage of the Chechen cause.

The upsurge of symbolic acts of spectacular violence in Russia by Chechen groups was compounded by another hostage-taking incident, this time in Turkey. The hijacking of an Istanbul-to-Sochi ferry by a group of Chechen sympathizers occurred in January 1996, against the backdrop of the siege in Pervomaiskoye. The hijackers were led by Mohammed Tockan who had, along with Basayev, participated as a volunteer in the Abkhaz War. The ferry passengers were mainly Russian and the boat was in Turkish national waters when it was seized, giving the Russian authorities a series of political and strategic dilemmas. The aim of the attack was to draw attention to the plight of the Chechens and demand an end to the war, drawing support from the large Diaspora community in Turkey who disagreed with Russian policies in Chechnya. After three days, the hostages were released and the hijackers arrested, but not before the Chechen issue had, once again, created front-page news.

While we will return to many of the issues raised, these historical examples shed light on the evolving use of terrorism, and indeed, the changing policy options, changing governmental procedures and processes of globalization that impacted on Russian counter-measures, particularly as they have evolved in the post-9/11 world. Understanding the logic behind these attacks through a strategic reading of terrorism also helps to shed light on the evolution of a Russian CT strategy that predates 9/11 but which gained momentum after the attacks on the World Trade Center and the Pentagon in 2001.

After the period of de facto independence from 1996, the situation in Chechnya slowly deteriorated as rival political and religious factions, criminal groups and warlords and their paramilitaries, vied for power and influence. Reconstruction of the republic was slow and, by early 1999, former Sufi loyalists had split from the nominally secular Chechen President Aslan Maskhadov, while other criminal and paramilitary groups – beyond the control of the Maskhadov administration – effectively controlled portions of Chechnya. Then, in late August 1999, the situation in the region rapidly deteriorated as one group – the Islamic Peacekeeping Battalion (IPB) – led by Shamil Basayev and Ibn Khattab, and supported ideologically by Movladi Udugov, Supyan Abdullaev and Zelimkhan Yandarbiyev – launched a large-scale military operation to unify the peoples of Chechnya and Dagestan. Although the incursion into Dagestan was routed – and led to calls by local groups for large-scale intervention by the Russian authorities – it gave the Yeltsin administration a pretext for preparing a military campaign to re-establish law and order in Chechnya. In 1999, the situation deteriorated further when a series of bomb blasts at a military barracks in Dagestan (Buinaksk, 4 September), and at apartment blocks in Volgodonsk (16 September) and Moscow (9 and 13 September) killed scores. The blasts, and a further failed attack in Moscow, were immediately attributed to Chechen militants.[14] However, in contrast to his usual claims of responsibility for attacks, Basayev maintained a stance of indifference, consistently discounting Chechen involvement in the attacks in Moscow. He stated shortly after the Beslan school siege that his group were 'in no way responsible for the blasts in Moscow or Volgodonsk'.[15] Interestingly, Basayev did not mention the attack on the military barracks near Buinaksk. Subsequent trial proceedings and reports implicated sympathizers in Dagestan, linked to the Nogai Battalion, an affiliated group which had pledged allegiance to Basayev. It seems plausible that the attack in Buinaksk was an act of reprisal, for the use of fuel air-explosives by federal forces when routing the IPB incursion into Dagestan.[16] Nonetheless, the apartment bombings can be understood as 'Russia's 9/11', not in the sense of any objective similarity, and not without a critical reading of what this category entails, but in the sense of '9/11' being used to construct a particular narrative – a narrative with shared outcomes in terms of hard-line, heavily militarized responses, an articulation of support from and defense of the polity, and further securitization of both discursive and physical security practices.

Between counter-insurgency and counter-terrorism

Wyman argues that the appointment of Putin as Prime Minister and the second period of military operations in Chechnya were actually a response to opinion polls prior to the State Duma elections suggesting the vote was likely to go against established Kremlin insiders.[17] Putin's reputation as a strong, decisive man with a KGB background formed part of a naked appeal to Russian national pride.[18] Additionally, the military action may have been, in part, a response to NATO operations in Kosovo in 1999. The NATO intervention occurred against the backdrop of Russian objections, leading to fears of military vulnerability, security marginalization and further potential interventions in areas of the CIS experiencing ethnic conflict within the Russian military and political elite.[19] Moreover, the feeling of impotence with regard to Chechnya, also linked to what was called the 'Afghan syndrome' – a fear of intervention in Islamic states, which emerged following the Soviet withdrawal from Kabul in 1989 – created a nationalist sentiment, coupled with a nostalgia for Great Power status, which encouraged officials to adopt assertive and demonstrative positions,[20] while the series of terrorist incidents in 1999 increased support for hard-line law-and-order positions.[21]

Military operations in Chechnya, in response to the IPB incursion into Dagestan 1999 and apartment bombings, resulted in significant bloodshed on both sides of the conflict. Grozny, the Chechen capital, was effectively leveled in a sustained air and artillery bombardment.[22] Despite taking control of Grozny in early 2000 and most major towns by mid-2000 (and Vladimir Rushailo declaring that 'the military phase of the anti-terrorist operation in Chechnya is drawing to a close' in early March),[23] providing a significant boost in public support for Putin,[24] Russian forces were unable to prevent a series of ambushes and attacks, and were unable to effectively eliminate armed resistance. Kramer argues that the Russian strategy, in the first years of the second conflict, took the form of 'standard counter-insurgency operations'.[25]

In the first war, Chechen national resistance was mobilized around a more vivid historical memory of resistance to Russian imperialism. The deportations of 1944, regarded as genocide, were in living memory for a significant number of Chechens.[26] The entire population of Chechnya was deported to Kazakhstan, Siberia and Kyrgyzstan, resulting in the deaths of thousands. They were only able to return after the death of Stalin, and the experience is strongly memorialized.[27] Similarly, not all acts of violence in the region should be regarded as purely ideologically motivated. There is a strong culture of blood feuds in the Caucasus, and experiences of the first war are still recollected and revenge likely sought.[28] However, in the second war, although enveloped within a broader regional anti-colonial narrative, anti-Russian resistance has been more fragmented with two different channels of control organizing military operations between 1999 and 2002. The first group, affiliated to Basayev, Udugov and Yandarbiyev, had a number of affiliated units such as the Islamic Battalion of the Akhmatov Brothers and Arbi Barayev's Special Purpose Islamic Regiment

(SPIR), which ran operations through the Majli us-Shura, while the Chechen President Aslan Maskhadov headed the more moderate group under the aegis of the State Defence Committee. There is also a high level of criminality in the region, which is a source of violence, and which has been used to label separatists as 'bandits'. Finally, the Putin administration sought to use the label of Wahhabi as a catch-all term to refer to the widely different groups from secular separatists, moderate Sufi groups, sub-ethnic groups in the North Caucasus, criminals, as well as Islamists and Salafi volunteers, all fighting under the aegis of an anti-Russian narrative. This did much to blur the differences between these groups, although the policy gained momentum after 9/11.

During the period from December 1999 through to June 2002, the ability of the 'Islamic Battalions' under the command of the Akhmatov brothers and the SPIR, led by Arbi Barayev, to counter the federal forces had diminished. This forced these groups to adopt radical tactics, including coordinated suicide truck-bomb attacks. By this time, the Russian authorities had skillfully manipulated inter-clan rivalries, exchanging patronage for the loyalty of the Sufi Qadiriyya tariqa. The first wave of suicide attacks largely targeted federal installations, and had support from the likes of Movaldi Udugov.[29] The amnesties and defections hindered further the operational capacity of these groups, and by the end of 2001 key figures in both networks, including Barayev himself, had been captured or killed. In response, remnants of these groups, some of whom had been integrated into Shamil Basayev's units, launched an audacious mass-hostage-taking attack in Moscow, in what became known as the Nord Ost theatre siege.

On 23 October, a group of around 40 hostage-takers took control of Dubrovka theatre house, in the Russian capital, Moscow. The attack aimed to disorientate the Russian people, affect Russian public opinion by demonstrating the war in Chechnya was not over, and challenge the authority of the Putin administration. Although not a suicide attack, many of those involved in the Nord Ost mass-hostage-taking were prepared to die for their cause.[30] Less than three days after the initial assault, Russian special services incapacitated those left in the theatre using a sedative gas, before storming the building, killing all of the hostage-takers. Following the attack, Basayev resigned from his post as the head of the military wing of the resistance, although he remained in charge of groups of loyal fighters. Others such as Zelimkhan Yandarbiyev also nominally broke from Maskhadov, although they also retained a degree of influence over the resistance, due to contacts with Middle Eastern donors. In truth, the radical wing of the resistance continued to be led by Basayev, Udugov and Yandarbiyev, who controlled a considerable portion of the resistance movement.

The theatre siege was intended to take the cause of the Chechen separatists to Russia's capital, employing the method of hostage-taking in order to garner extended news coverage. Although the central aim of the hostage-takers was the cessation of violence in Chechnya, the raid had the subsidiary aim of garnering more financial support from Middle Eastern donors. Symbolically, the attack on the Moscow Theatre was designed to undermine the sense of security in Russia's civilian population, and thus heighten fear and create disorientation in the center of Russian power, Moscow.

Operation Boomerang and Russian counter-measures

Events from late 2002 to September 2004 provide evidence of a concerted effort to deploy a broad wave of 'retaliation' sanctioned by Shamil Basayev and off-shoots of the radical wing of the Majli us-Shura. In June 2002, elements of the radical wing of the Chechen resistance adopted a strategy designed to disorientate federal forces, escalate the resistance campaign both in scope and depth, by broadening the military campaign into Russia and the North Caucasus, and fundamentally altering the political landscape, providing a long-term strategy designed to counter the federal campaign in the North Caucasus. As indicated, the first wave of suicide attacks had largely been organized by groups from Urus-Martan and Alkhan-Khala, as part of the broader war effort. Attacks were primarily directed at federal targets including checkpoints, military and police compounds, often using truck or car bombs, as federal forces surrounded the strongholds of warlords, restricting the ability of the insurgents to operate.

The radical wing of the resistance sanctioned terrorism, partly due to a deep sense of frustration that their message was not being heard. Dramatic attacks – along with the creation of military jamaat structure (a system of small groups designed to act in support of a broader guerrilla campaign) across the North Caucasus – were the key aims of the resistance. The meeting in late June of the State Defense Committee and Majli us-Shura in the Vedinsky district led to the centralization of military strategy under the leadership of Basayev, as Shura and the State Defense Committee were combined. Nonetheless Maskhadov, who retained the role as the political leader of the movement, still lacked the ability to control independent military operations undertaken by a number of radical field commanders.

It appears that Maskhadov did not sanction the use of terrorism. Instead, he was faced with internal radicalization in the anti-Russian movement, portions of which had adopted an even more religious tenor by late 2002. The strategy of the radical wing of the movement focused on a steady escalation of terrorism, initially using spectacular attacks to get their message heard in 2002, before moving toward a more protracted campaign of terrorism in 2003 and 2004 to react to the policies of normalization in Chechnya. Each spectacular attack from October 2002 fitted into a narrative of retaliation – a theme signaled earlier that year when Rabbani Khallilov, then head of the Dagestani Shar'ia jamaat, bombed the Victory Day military parade in Kaspiask, Dagestan.

The first spectacular attack in the second wave of suicide terrorism took place in December 2002, when two truck bombs blew up the pro-Kremlin Chechen administration building in Grozny, killing and wounding scores of people. In May 2003, Basayev made an official statement announcing 'Operation Boomerang' – a campaign of terrorism designed to set the Putin administration a number of challenges to which it had to react.[31] The strategy of 'provocation' was clearly aimed at making the Russian and federal authorities react in ways that could undermine its authority, while also creating the conditions in which an appropriate military and political movement in the North Caucasus could evolve.

This escalation of the terror campaign led to a cluster of new attacks. The first were targeted assassinations directed against federal forces, police and the pro-Russian Chechen authorities. Initially the attacks took the form of truck bombs, as in December 2002. This tactic changed in the period from May through to July, as bomb attacks were used in attempted assassinations and in attacks on the federal forces in and around Chechnya. The campaign escalated further in July, when a series of attacks took place in Moscow. Russian forces had put measures in place – such as the arrest and detention of men of fighting age, the use of fixed and mobile checkpoints and the target hardening of buildings – to disrupt and displace attacks, as part of the counter-insurgency. Equally, attempts were made to isolate and eliminate bomb-makers, to disrupt communication between key figures in the Chechen resistance, and dismantle the infrastructure of the insurgency. As part of this process, federal forces used disinformation to blacken the cause of the radicals and disrupt their activities, while intelligence was gained on key resistance figures by pro-Kremlin Chechen allies. Thus Russian counter-insurgency operated alongside a broader campaign of counter-terror, which included operations in neighboring regions such as Dagestan, Ingushetia and Georgia.

In order to circumvent these measures, Operation Boomerang drew on the support networks of the Stavropol and Shelkovsky jamaats, made up of remnants of the Nogai battalion, who could operate throughout the North Caucasus, given their status as an itinerant sub-ethnic group, located both inside and outside of Chechnya. Operation Boomerang also drew on the capacity of the Ingush jamaat, and small support groups in Kabardino-Balkaria and North Ossetia, who were linked through the system of military jamaats. Although operating clandestinely, the jamaats in Urus-Martan, Grozny, Shali and in villages and towns in the highlands such as Vedeno, took an active role providing support and participants for attacks. Russian counter-measures focused on military sweeps or *zachistkas* in which towns and hamlets were surrounded, sometimes over a period of two or three days, and searched. Unmarked vehicles containing masked gunmen were used at night to apprehend suspects as the psychological war intensified.[32] By 2004, the skeleton of the military jamaat structure was in place while Russia had successfully arrested or killed a number of important figures.[33] Units loyal to Basayev attempted to assassinate the Ingush President, Murat Zazykov, using a suicide bomber in April 2004, and killed a number of military leaders including the Chechen President, Akhmed Kadyrov, in a bombing at the Victory Day parade in Grozny in May. This was followed by an audacious raid on the Ingush city of Nazran in late June, killing scores of Russian military personnel, and expanding the conflict zone.

Russian counter-terror measures were focused on undermining the financial and logistical infrastructure of the Chechen resistance, including the arrest of suspects in the North Caucasus, but also the targeting of individuals abroad. The most notable effect of this move was the killing in April of Zelimkhan Yandarbi-yev by Russian agents in Qatar in 2004, and the killing of the head of the Arab mujahideen, Abu Walid, in Chechnya. One aspect of Russian policy was the arrest or detention of suspects under criminal law. Newspaper reports throughout 2003, 2004 and 2005 include references to the arrest of members of 'illegal armed formations'. This military policy was combined with an aggressive policy of granting amnesty to former rebels, while murkier operations, including the use of counter hostage-taking, also became a common feature of the counter-insurgency.[34] The Russian authorities bolstered military operations with local and regional constitutional change, aiming to centralize power in what has become known as a *vertical*, a centralized system of command and control. At the same time, the Russian authorities created federal districts to enable the control of agencies in different regions; they centralized law-making procedures, using the federal system as a benchmark. The process of political reform gained further momentum after the attacks at the Victory Day Parade (April), the raid on Nazran (June), and after the events leading up to the elections for a new Chechen President in the autumn of 2004, including Beslan. The suicide attacks on internal airliners and the suicide bombing in Moscow in late August, along with the mass hostage-taking at School number one in Beslan, were the last acts of Basyaev's terror network, the Riad us-Salihyn, and the last acts in Operation Boomerang. They had served to broaden the zone of conflict from Chechnya to the North Caucasus. Thereafter, the cause of the insurgents in the North Caucasus had been tainted by terrorism, forcing Maskhadov to call a moratorium on combat operations. On the one hand, then, Operation Boomerang created problems for the Russian and federal authorities, insofar as they were fighting an insurgency which included a component of terrorism.

Structures of Russian counter-terrorism

The structures of Russian counter-terrorism are highly complex, with a large number of militarized bureaucratic state agencies with some measure of responsibility and capacity. This increases the difficulty of coordination, but also creates a problem of accountability and oversight.[35] Baev argues that Putin instrumentally used Russian counter-terrorism policy to perform regime consolidation, but also to attempt to transform Russian military structures.[36] The legacy of Soviet-era institutions and 'divide and rule' approaches led to the creation of a plethora of agencies, both at the strategic and tactical levels. Counter-terrorism operations frequently include members of various units and agencies, often without formal identification. Amnesty International reports that it is often difficult to determine which security forces are involved in a counter-terrorism raid. The wide range of soldiers in Chechnya include the Ministry of Defense, several forces under the Interior Ministry, the State Security Service FSB and contract soldiers – effectively mercenaries, retired soldiers and policemen.[37]

In Chechnya in particular, there is a reliance upon pro-Russian Chechen militia and the strength of local leaders, as part of an attempt at a 'Chechinization' of the conflict. This structure is bolstered by an amnesty offered to militants if they swore allegiance to the pro-Russian Chechen President Ramzan Kadyrov and joined his personal security force. These personal guarantees contribute to instability in that Kadyrov's death could lead to amnestied militants once again changing sides. In January 2007, more than 500 militants surrendered to authorities as part of an amnesty following the 2006 death of Shamil Basayev, the military leader of what was, by then, a regional anti-Russian movement.[38]

Following the June 2004 attacks in Nazran, in the neighboring republic of Ingushetia, Russian authorities sought to create operational and control structures to coordinate CT operations. The measures were designed to improve interdepartmental coordination, precisely because a number of MVD and FSB officers had been targeted and executed in the Nazran raid, while federal forces based nearby received no instructions to counter the attack. The discussions brought together top officials, the head of the MVD (Nurgaliyev), the head of the FSB (Patrushev) and the Chief of the Defense Ministry (Ivanov), and led to the establishment of working groups to coordinate organizational reform. The working groups operated in 15 zones, and included additional input from representatives of the Ministry and Affairs of Civil Defense, Emergency Situations, and Elimination of Natural Disasters (known as the MChs). The key aim was to organize operational command and control (or GOU) groups to counter the threat posed by what were described as 'Ingush-type' attacks. The GOU zones included St Petersburg and Moscow, although they were focused primarily on the Southern federal districts. News reports indicated that a meeting took place in Rostov-on-Don as part of the Anti-Terrorist Commission on Federal Components. The meeting was chaired by the Chief of the Internal Troops, Nikolay Rogozhkin, and included input from Dimitry Kozak, President Putin's representative in the southern federal districts, deputy representatives and, latterly, the Head of the MVD, Nurgaliyev. The meeting also consisted of a series of exhibitions, to highlight the capacity of the GOU. Although the GOU was in its embryonic stages, and indeed led to considerable internal debate, it quickly became clear that it sought to counter attacks against particular facilities. That is to say, the structural reforms led to a division of labor, stemming from the specifications and targets of terror attacks in Russia. For example, if a significant regional facility was seized, the response was to be coordinated by the MVD; however, if hostages were taken, the FSB would take charge of the CT operation.

Counter-terrorism and human rights

Crelinsten identifies what he perceives as Russia's shift from a potential failed state to an authoritarian one, due to increased oil wealth and Putin's widespread domestic popularity, leading to a lack of protection for certain groups.[39] He is just one of several authors that draw attention to human rights concerns in Russia which can be critically linked to counter-terrorism practice. Amnesty International's report 'The Russian Federation: Denial of Justice' traced a picture of human rights abuses associated with the Chechen–Russian conflict. They found that 'Russian forces have been responsible for widespread human rights violations such as "disappearances", extrajudicial executions and torture, including rape'; violations that would be considered breaches of the Geneva Conventions.[40]

Federal Law on Counter-action of Terrorism, No. 35-FZ, 6 March 2006, allows for various controls over communication, without requiring judicial authorization. It also allows the President to appoint the commander of a counter-terrorism operation and, in practice, this authority is entrusted to the Federal Security Services. It allows far reaching powers of search, seizure of homes and correspondence, again without judicial authorization. Immunity powers included in the law significantly limit accountability. Finally, the law grants the president the authority to order counter-terrorism operations outside the territory of the Russian Federation, without parliamentary authorization.[41] This package of anti-terrorist laws, which gained renewed momentum following the acts of terrorism that year (the bombing of two internal airliners, the late-August Moscow bombing, and the Beslan hostage-taking incident), also focused on tougher registration regulations, as well as the heightening of border operations and security sweeps in airports and rail stations. The International Commission of Jurists heard evidence in its Russian panel that the Russian Federation had participated in parts of the international program of extraordinary rendition.[42]

Renz identifies a combination of structural factors, including a lack of clear legal guidelines to counter-terrorism activity, the failure of the justice system to cope with large-scale military-style operations, the existence of unofficial detention centers, the brutalization and hazing of Russian military conscripts and recruits combined with poor treatment, limited levels of education, and insufficient attempts to root out human rights abuses, as responsible for the mistreatment of detainees during the Chechen War. Racism was not identified as a primary driver, as ethnic Chechen forces were deemed responsible for the majority of human rights abuses.[43]

However, government and media-led anti-Chechen propaganda since the mid-1990s has contributed to a rise in anti-Muslim sentiment. An opinion poll conducted in early 2000, prior to the launch of the US War on Terror, found that 80 percent of those polled considered Islam to be 'a bad thing', a marked rise from only 17 percent in 1992.[44] Amnesty finds that minority ethnic groups within Russia have been stereotyped by law-enforcement as 'terrorists', resulting in widespread racial profiling and discriminatory policing.[45] The Russian authorities have placed controls on many Muslim institutions, including charities, many of which have closed, with a resulting drop in publishing and educational programs.[46] This demonstrates one of the side-effects of information war strategies and discursive contestation adopted as part of Russian counter-terrorism.

Information war

One element of the second conflict, which has its roots in the latter part of the 1990s, and which became a key aspect of both Russia's counter-insurgency and counter-terror policy, was the information war. This comprised a combination. We argue that Russia wages its own particular War on Terror through a combination of traditional propaganda tactics and the use of modern information technology and methods of cyber-warfare, to attempt to control the flow of information about the conflict. Russia is relatively advanced in the field of information warfare, combined with military methods – countering propaganda and Chechen narratives with its own, and making use of traditional and electronic warfare methods to assist the information component and tilt the discursive balance in its favor. There are three main discursive strategies in use as part of Russian counter-insurgency. First, the silencing of opposition voices; second, the labeling of insurgents as terrorists, bandits and criminals; and finally, the linking of the Russian 'counter-terrorist' activity with the wider narrative of the War on Terror. These moves attempt to delegitimize Chechen activity while legitimizing Russian counter-terrorism operations.

The 'picture economy' – be it in the use of visuals, symbols and imagery by the state – does, of course, evolve from within particular genres. However, it has been transformed further through explicit use as part of campaigns of propaganda, which are themselves enveloped in changes associated with globalization. The increasing importance of the media (and its assorted network reach), various means of communication and dissemination, and associated institutions, as a key element of countering terrorism, have also impacted upon terror campaigns themselves. As part of a strategic reading of terrorism, given the key aims of disorientation — be it through panic, fear and chaos – the 'picture economy' has itself become a tool in the arsenal of terrorists. Some use videos to generate shame, when, for example, organizing suicide attacks or military campaigns (such as the media campaigns by the LTTE or Hamas in 2008 and 2009 respectively).

Even though groups such as the Liberation Tigers of Tamil Eelam or Hezbollah (and, more recently, Hamas) have a long history of using media imagery, and the use of video footage has become synonymous with al-Qaeda,[47] the case of Chechnya is crucial in understanding the development of this aspect of both strategic terrorism and insurgency– and, for that matter, measures designed to counter it. Sandwiched between the use of imagery in the 1980s and the use of images in the Israeli–Palestine conflict (particularly martyr videos) in the late 1990s, as well as the horrific footage of attacks from Afghanistan and Iraq, were the two Chechen conflicts of the 1990s. As the first Russo-Chechen conflict gained momentum in early 1995, Chechen separatists sought channels to convey their message to the outside world, to seek support from sympathetic groups including their Diaspora community, and also to influence domestic Russian public opinion. The burgeoning market freedoms in Russia had created a nascent community of local media. The Chechen separatist movement had in its ranks a number of influential and highly capable media activists.

Chechen groups have been at the forefront of the use of imagery as part of their respective war and terror campaigns. Movladi Udugov, a spin-doctor in the first Chechen War (1994–1996), pioneered the use of satellite technology to allow US news channels to conduct 'live' interviews with Jokhar Dudayev, the then leader of the Chechen resistance. Udugov, Ibn Khattab (the leader of the Arab mujahideen in Chechnya) and Shamil Basayev all became adept at using many forms of imagery, pioneering the filming of attacks for pay or to raise funds for their cause through the sale of graphic videos and DVDs,[48] and within particular acts of terrorism, such as the Dubrovka Theatre Siege and the Beslan School siege. These campaigns were facilitated by cheap video equipment from VHS onwards and increased in reach, although not necessarily efficacy, by the ease of digital broadcasting. This group also saw the potential for dissemination through the Internet, setting up the Kavkaz news organization in the late 1990s and the portals supporting the Arab mujahideen in Chechnya such as Quoqaz. com and Azzam.com.

The network of Chechen-controlled and allied websites such as Kavkaz.org, qoqaz.net (and its internationally hosted mirrors, www.qoqaz.net.my, www. qoqaz.de and www.qoqaz.com) allowed dissemination of images, news items, videos and interviews with Chechen fighters and leaders.[49] They also made use of independent video-sharing websites such as YouTube.com which has the advantage of being relatively safe from intervention and widely available. Footage on YouTube includes attacks, operations and attempts to humiliate Kadyrov.[50] These sites demonstrate a tension between revealing Russian human rights abuses in a manner similar to that of an NGO, and also featuring footage of Chechan acts of violence.

In their account of terrorism, the strategic rationale behind it and policy measures that stem from their critique, Peter Neumann and M.L.R. Smith recognize the importance of stemming the flow of information from such groups. While it is well-known that jihadi portals provide forums which groups actively use, including the likes of al-Qaeda, and its video and production arm Al Shabab, little analysis exists of Russian attempts to counter the threat from the use of imagery by radical groups in Russia, or the use of cyber-terrorism by groups traced to Russia, nor indeed, the significance of Chechnya in the development of this aspect of both terror campaigns and insurgency. In this section of the chapter, we will explore each of these aspects, beginning with the role of Chechnya as a catalyst for a reformulation of the use of information campaigns by both states and insurgencies.

Throughout the late 1990s the Russian information war was hindered by the infighting within the Kremlin between oligarchs, and the lack of a coherent Russian policy toward the North Caucasus. The economic crisis in Russia in 1998 further eroded any sense of an effective Kremlin policy for the North Caucasus. The strategy became more focused throughout 1998, with the conflict labeled as a counter-terror operation, designed to eradicate 'bandits, criminals and terrorists' linked to Chechnya. As a dominant political actor, with strong public support, Putin's government was able to effectively securitize the Chechen insurgency – demonstrating the capacity to socially and politically constitute a threat and present separatism as an existential threat to Russia. It was clearly a war directed against Chechnya, which evolved in 2003 to a counter-insurgency and then a counter-terrorism operation across the North Caucasus. Following the outset of the second war, the repression of moderate elements of the Chechen political and religious elite was ruthless, efficient and total. While the second war was largely focused on Chechnya, as we have noted, the conflict always had a broader remit and included CT operations in parts of Dagestan and in Ingushetia. The information campaign did, however, do much to place these operations under the remit of criminal investigations. The chain of equivalential subject positions generated by Russian security discourse includes bandits, criminals and terrorists. Separatists of any sort are made equivalent to terrorists, an old and familiar rhetorical move. Kramer argues that Putin's position of 'no negotiation with terrorists' effectively means 'no negotiations with any political actors in Chechnya other than officials in the pro-Russian government'.[51]

Baev sees the attempts to deny Chechen access to independent media, so that official propaganda could remain unchallenged, as part of a broader strategy to keep the conflict consistently isolated, thus allowing Moscow to select the type of victory it would pursue.[52] This is contrasted with the perceived failure to do so during the first conflict. Control of media and communication enables and enhances efforts to achieve discursive hegemony, limiting exposure to other ways of potentially suturing the social space, enabling the dominant discourse to give meaning to events, and create and apply identities for social actors. The definition of 'state secret' under the Law on States Secrets has been expanded over recent years, to prevent publication of information on emergency situations, crime and human rights violations – including by government.[53] Reporter Andrei Babitsky was detained for trying to report on renewed fighting in Chechnya.[54] This appears to be part of a broader campaign to intimidate independent journalists.[55] Kramer notes that the Putin administration increased state control over television and other news media, undercut rival parties and 'greatly narrowed the room for political debate and competition in Russia', and the second war has not been significantly discussed on television or in parliament.[56]

The information campaign has a technological dimension, with the Russian authorities demonstrating interest and capability in technological information warfare directed both at separatists and neighboring nation-states. Russia is implicated in a series of electronic warfare attacks in Estonia, a massive distributed denial of service attack, using a series of remotely controlled computers across 76 different countries to overload the capacity of Estonian government and media websites.[57] Developments in this field will be explored in the following section.

Cyber-war and information counter-terrorism

There is a distinct information-technological dimension to Russian counter-terrorism activity. This is beset by a usual set of problematic definitions and terminology regarding 'cyber-terrorism' and 'cyber-warfare'. These two terms have some purchase in the wider literature on terrorism; however, the authors prefer the more neutral, although sufficiently broad, technologically based term 'attacks on information systems' as this allows identification of the actual activity that is occurring separated out from associated motives and information war. 'Cyber-terrorism' is an especially problematic term as it is often inflated to include any use of information technology by groups designated as terrorist – for example, a group using a website to communicate with supporters, or using email to communicate between members. Terming this cyber-terrorism would be akin to defining a terrorist simply driving in a car as a case of 'automotive-terrorism'. Furedi identifies the expansion and trivialization of the term itself as a contribution to feeding fear.[58] It also perpetuates the discursive strategy of labeling certain groups as terrorists and is therefore not politically neutral. Similarly, there is significant hype in the field and a danger of becoming fixated upon novelty and technological determinism. The Russian Federation has been involved in a series of information-warfare events, including the use of information warfare as part of proactive counter-terrorism operations.

There appear to be two main components of Russian cyber-warfare. First, to shape the information landscape, largely in support of the discursive strategies outlined above. There can never be total control, but strategies are devised to increase the level of influence. Second, the attempt to draw supporters into a wider assemblage of security actors. Both Russia and China have a history of citizen-armies, and can currently draw upon technologically literate and nationalistically motivated groups outside the government to participate in electronic warfare and in support of strategic priorities.

Relatively little has been written about Russia as a victim of cyber-terrorism in this technically defined sense. Chechen 'Cyberunits' have recently claimed successful attacks against Russian and 'apostate' websites through hacking and distributed denial of service (which comes from more than one computer, and overwhelms the target computer by sheer volume of traffic), or DDoS, attacks to prevent an 'enemy resource' from spreading 'lies and slanders'.[59] Cyber-terrorism as a threat to national security or critical national infrastructure has been discussed for over a decade, identified as being an increasing risk due to the interconnection and reliance of society upon information technology.[60] However, the impact on any country of attacks on information systems by non-state terrorist groups has so far been limited. Keith has analyzed coverage of cyber-terrorism and found that those authors that write as if cyber-terrorism is a looming threat provide an exaggerated assessment of the threat posed in comparison to those that argue that cyber-terrorism has already occurred, but that its effects have been minimal.[61] *Jane's Intelligence Review* identifies Russia as having strengths in the field of electronic protection, and of continuing to develop capacity in this area.[62] Computer and information experts have been hired for the FSB academy, which in 1999 set up a new administration with responsibilities for the field. The FSB had been attempting to re-incorporate FAPSI – the Federal Agency of Governmental Communication and Information – by RF, the equivalent of the American NSA or British GCHQ, using the increased funding and responsibility for combating terrorism placed upon it by the War on Terror;[63] FAPSI was dismantled by presidential decree in March 2003.[64] A 2004 report from Dartmouth Military College made the assessment that:

> The Russian technology sector and academic community, in conjunction with the Russian military, have developed cyber warfare doctrine beyond what any other country, save the U.S. possesses. The Russians recognize that information warfare requires the simultaneous conduct of offensive and defensive measures in order for cyber warfare to be successful.[65]

Russia also appears to have been involved in information warfare attacks of significant scale and impact on systems in Estonia, Georgia and Kyrgyzstan, which could potentially be regarded as terroristic. They are certainly attacks of some sort, and appear to have a political motive. Responsibility for many of these attacks has been directed at Russia, or to computers based in Russia. Allegations range from inaction to prevent these attacks and to locate the perpetrators, or to direct involvement of state agencies in these attacks.[66]

Russia has a developed computing and information technology sector, despite its economic difficulties. This includes a substantial hacker sub-culture or underground that has displayed noticeable patriotic and pro-government attitudes. Prior to the attacks on Estonia in 2007, which shut down the Estonian government's communication systems as well as those of many Estonian media outlets,[67] messages posted on Russian Web forums gave details of how to contribute to the attacks, including how to download and use software to do so, and gave reasons to participate based upon the slight to Russian veterans of World War II by the planned removal of a Soviet-era Red Army memorial in Tallinn.[68]

There is greater evidence of Russian use of information-warfare techniques as part of its overall counter-terrorism strategy. Jeffrey Car, who runs information security project 'Grey Goose', an attempt to identify those responsible for the cyber-attacks on Georgia that coincided with the Russian invasion of Ossetia in 2008, identifies the Russian cyber-attacks on Chechnya in 2002 as the first concrete example of a developing pattern of cyber-war in the region – the combination of attacks on servers with more traditional military strikes.[69] Chechen rebels claimed that kavkaz.org and chechenpress.com crashed due to attacks by the FSB, timed to coordinate with the storming of the Moscow Theatre. Chechenpress.com was taken down through a brute force denial of service attack, while it appears that hackers took down Kavkaz.org by changing the domain registration of the site and deleting data from the hosting servers based in the US.[70] This use of IT for counter-terrorism is supported by Oleg Gordievsky, former London KGB section head, who identifies groups of organized criminals associated with the FSB as hacking into pro-Chechen sites in the late 1990s. The authorities had put in place a plan to dismantle the Arab mujahideen and support networks in Chechnya (probably as far back as 1998). The plan led to the poisoning of Ibn Khattab in March 2002, and coincided with the attacks on the Internet portal of the Arab mujahideen. However, there might also have been some luck involved, insofar as the US authorities were by then clamping down on radical funding networks linked to the jihadi movement. Finally, assassinations have been linked to the pictures of leaders displayed on pro-Chechen websites, and McGregor identifies a recent reduction in militant videos as a result of growing amnestied militia presence, able to identify former comrades and use those videos for intelligence and targeting.[71]

Russia and the War on Terror

Many analyses of counter-terrorism after 9/11 identify the importance of the language of war, as well as the policy implications of adopting a war model of counter-terrorism.[72] Crelinsten uses the Moscow Theatre Siege and Beslan as examples of the failure of the military model of coercive counter-terrorism – showing that in such events hostages are much more likely to be killed in a rescue attempt than by their captors, and that military strikes can escalate violence or trigger revenge attacks.[73] He argues that since 9/11 the trend to adopt a war model, emphasizing military control over root causes and long-term solutions, has been exacerbated.[74] Cronin argues that the growing international characterization of the conflict in Chechnya as another front in the War on Terror may have impacted upon the relationship between Chechen tactics and Russian responses. She also sees this as having negative implications for the development of post-Soviet democracy.[75] There exists a tension between a campaign consistently dubbed an 'internal matter', yet is articulated within an international War on Terror.[76] This campaign has gained momentum, particularly after 9/11 and the inauguration of the US-led War on Terror. It gained further momentum following the US-led invasion of Iraq. In both instances, it granted the Russian authorities a measure of autonomy to continue the Kremlin campaign of disinformation and the broader restructuring of the power *vertikal* in Russia proper, and to mollify international opinion.

A number of different power ministries in Russia quickly adopted the language of the global War on Terror to legitimize their actions on the ground in its southern security flank. Baev argues that the War on Terror has been used as an instrumental political lever by the Putin government to deal with a bureaucracy he describes as post-Soviet neo-feudalism. In support of this, he identifies the expanding role of the FSB in relation to other ministries, and the spread of former FSB members to other agencies as they set up specialist units with counter-terrorism responsibilities. For Baev, the War on Terror is a camouflage for state centralization, supported due to the way that Vladimir Putin adopted counter-terrorism as his own personal crusade, and in doing so gained widespread popular support within Russia.[77]

Of particular note was the growth of discourse explicitly linking Chechen networks with the radical group known as al-Qaeda. Even though the likes of Khattab were not members of al-Qaeda, nor even were Saudi members of the Chechen Salafi jihadi movement, broad messages of support for the Salafis were exploited by Russian officials. While a concerted campaign of disinformation was ratcheted up, this aimed to place all foreign fighters within the orbit of al-Qaeda, overlooking the role of the Diaspora community and the broader Salafi movement within which the Arab mujahideen operated. For example, the Chechen Diaspora community in Jordan, Syria and Turkey all played a significant role in the foreign-fighter movement, with Basayev claiming that a Jordanian jihadi had, for example, taken part in the Beslan school siege. Other regional groups also played a role, with Azerbaijan, Dagestan and Ingushetia, as well as sub-ethnic groups such as the Nogai, Kist Chechens, smaller support networks in the Pankisi Gorge, in Kabardino-Balkaria and Karachevo-Cherkessia and small numbers of Central Asian jihadis offering support. In fact, by 2000 the Arab foreign-fighter movement in Chechnya was on the decline, as local groups rejected the Islamists as the violence became more internecine. This forced the remnants of the Arab movement underground.

The discursive strategy sought to label all foreign religious groups as Wahhabi in an attempt to link Islamic revivalism, and the threat it posed to stability to Russia's North Caucasus, with militancy stemming from Saudi Arabia. In contrast, many of the groups and foreign emissaries who based themselves in Chechnya and Dagestan were jihadi fighters following Sheikh Fathi and Ibn Khattab, operating within a broader Salafi movement. A sub-group were indeed of Wahhabi stock, including the influential Saudi financier and ideologist Abu Omar al-Sayf, the ascetic Saudi jihadi fighter Abu Walid al-Ghamidi, the shadowy Kuwaiti financier Abu Zaid, and Gulf State Arab logistics expert Abu Keutyba. Nonetheless the radical Islamic movement was at odds with other networks and Wahhabi groups in the Salafi movement such as al-Qaeda, which had formed in the mid-1990s in Afghanistan. The Chechen movement adopted Khattab's narrative of defensive jihad merged with elements of the national movement, making the location of the Chechen campaign as part of a wider arm of al-Qaeda problematic.[78]

The campaign of disinformation has blurred the complex relations between Chechen groups, foreign fighters from the Diaspora community and neighboring regions, and the Arab mujahideen.[79] The campaign sought to highlight the importance of particular Arab fighters and ideologues, explicitly linking them to al-Qaeda after 9/11. This has gone some way to create the impression that numerous Chechen's operate as 'guns for hire' or al-Qaeda operatives in jihadi hotspots – in Afghanistan, Iraq and even as far afield as the horn of Africa. While it is likely that some former fighters may have made their way to other fronts, no Chechens were captured or imprisoned in Guantanamo Bay. It is as likely that members of the Turkic community from the North Caucasus as a whole have been killed, and given their Russian passports, have been labeled as Chechens, reinforcing the disinformation campaign expounded by Kremlin officials. The impact of the information campaign by radicals, which has included the production of DVDs and the use of websites publishing information in Russian, Turkish, Arabic and English, has also been to downplay the importance of the Sufi component of the broader campaign of resistance. While moderates loyal to Maskhadov have themselves created online information portals, the differing strategies of dissemination have principally affected Maskhadov's ability to portray the Chechen separatist cause in the years after 9/11. In effect, by connecting into broader narratives, Udugov has helped the Russian authorities to place the Chechen cause into the basket of threats associated with the War on Terror.

Conclusion

As well as providing an overview of Russian counter-terrorism, this chapter has hoped to demonstrate the importance of information warfare for government and terrorist activity. It has demonstrated the importance of language in terms of labeling, silencing and rhetorical strategies involved in discursive contestation of the meaning of political violence. It has shown how these strategies are combined together, mixing a picture economy with a militarized logic of a War on Terror, by a state with limited respect for human rights and democratic norms. It has also questioned the dominant accounts that assume that the multiplier effect of information technology will primarily be leveraged by weaker states and groups by showing how a powerful state can multiply its counter-terrorist activity through targeted information warfare. We have also shown how the threat of terrorism evolved and changed, as Russia put in place counter-measures. This led to political reforms, in an attempt to centralize control and create a power *vertical*. Russian counter-terrorism operations have predominantly focused on Chechnya; however, since 2003, they have sought to address the threat from across the North Caucasus as a result of the establishment of a system of military jamaats.

Notes

1 Z. Iviansky, 'The Terrorist Revolution: Roots of Modern Terrorism', in D. Rappaport (ed.), *Inside Terrorist Organizations* (London: Routledge, 2002), p. 142.
2 Z. Iviansky, 'Individual Terror: Concept and Typology', *Journal of Contemporary History*, 12:1 (1977), p. 47.
3 Ibid., p. 54.
4 Iviansky, 2001, p. 147.
5 Iviansky, 1977 p. 44.
6 R. Duvall and M. Stohl, 'Governance by Terror', in M. Stohl (ed.), *The Politics of Terrorism* (3rd ed.) (Danvers: CRC Press, 2008), p. 241.
7 K.M. Sweet, 'Russian Law Enforcement under President Putin', *Human Rights Review*, 3:4 (2002), p. 20.
8 G. Wardlaw, *Political Terrorism: Theory, Tactics, and Counter-Measures* (2nd ed.) (Cambridge: Cambridge University Press, 1989), p. 56.
9 D.A. Pluchinsky, 'Terrorism in the Former Soviet Union: A Primer, A Puzzle, A Prognosis', *Studies in Conflict and Terrorism*, 21:2 (1998), p. 120.
10 P.B. Taylor, 'Treason, Espionage and Other Soviet State Crimes', *Russian Review*, 23:3 (1964), p. 247.
11 Ibid., p. 252.
12 A. Maskhadov, 'Interview' (1999), p. 7, www.smallwarsjournal.com/documents/maskhadovinterview.pdf.

13 G.B. Smith, 'Russia and the Rule of Law', in S. White, A. Pravda and Z. Gitleman (eds.), *Developments in Russian Politics 5* (Houndmills: Palgrave, 2001), p. 212.

14 Tatyana Andrianova, *Nezavisimaya Gazeta*, 2 September, 2004.

15 Shamil Basayev, 'Chechen Rebel Leader Urges Putin to Resign, Blames Security Troops for Beslan "Slaughter"', *Kavkaz Tsentr*, 17 September 2004.

16 Aleksandra Larintseva, *Kommersant*, 16 March 2004. Tellingly, throughout 2003 and 2004, Russian Special Forces targeted the Stavropol and Shelkovsky jamaats, established in part by the remnants of the Nogai battalion. This, in turn, led to a spate of suicide attacks. See C. Moore and P. Tumelty, 'Foreign Fighters and the case of Chechnya: A Critical Assessment', *Studies in Conflict and Terrorism*, 31:5 (2008), pp. 412–433.

17 M. Wyman, 'Elections and Voters', in S. White, A. Pravda and Z. Gitleman (eds.), *Developments in Russian Politics 5* (Houndmills: Palgrave, 2001), p. 66.

18 Ibid., p. 67.

19 A. Pravda, 'Foreign Policy', in S. White, A. Pravda and Z. Gitleman (eds.), *Developments in Russian Politics 5* (Houndmills: Palgrave, 2001).

20 J.P. Willerton, 'The Presidency: From Yeltsin to Putin', in S. White, A. Pravda and Z. Gitleman (eds.), *Developments in Russian Politics 5* (Houndmills: Palgrave, 2001), p. 39.

21 Smith, 'Russia and the Rule of Law', p. 127.

22 M. Kramer, 'Guerilla Warfare, Counterinsurgency and Terrorism in the North Caucasus: The Military Dimension of the Russian–Chechen Conflict', *Europe–Asia Studies*, 57:2 (2005), p. 212.

23 Ibid., p. 213.

24 Willerton, 'The Presidency: From Yeltsin to Putin', p. 39.

25 Kramer, 'Guerilla Warfare, Counterinsurgency and Terrorism in the North Caucasus'.

26 J. Hughes, 'From Federalisation to Recentralisation', in S. White, A. Pravda and Z. Gitleman (eds.), *Developments in Russian Politics 5* (Houndmills: Palgrave, 2001); B.G. Williams, 'Commemorating "The Deportation" in Post-Soviet Chechnya: The Role of Memorialization and Collective Memory in the 1994–1996 and 1999–2000 Russo-Chechen Wars', *History & Memory*, 12:1 (2000), pp. 101–134.

27 Williams, 'Commemorating "The Deportation" in Post-Soviet Chechnya', p. 105.

28 Phuchinsky, 'Terrorism in the Former Soviet Union'.

29 Commentators and even academics who do not understand the insurgency often over-zealously attribute the use of suicide attacks to foreign, particularly Arab, influence. Such accounts often fail to address the organizational dynamics in the Chechen resistance, the strategic and tactical rationale for the use of suicide terrorism, or extrapolate the fact that different waves of attacks and failed attacks have occurred, let alone the differences between individual acts of revenge. For a more nuanced reading of Chechen suicide terrorism, and the role of the Arab mujahideen, see C. Moore and P. Tumelty, 'Foreign Fighters and the Case of Chechnya: A Critical Assessment', *Studies in Conflict and Terrorism*, 31:5 (2008), pp. 412–433; C. Moore, 'Suicide Bombing and Strategy: Chechnya, The North Caucasus and Martyrdom', *Europe Asia Studies* (forthcoming, 2010).

30 A. Nivat, 'The Black Widows: Chechen Women Join the Fight for Independence and Allah', *Studies in Conflict and Terrorism*, 28:5 (2005), pp. 413–419.

31 C. Moore, 'Suicide Bombing and Strategy: Chechnya, the North Caucasus and Martyrdom' (forthcoming, 2010).

32 Amnesty International, *The Russian Federation: A Denial of Justice* (London: Amnesty International, 2002).

33 V. Barinov, 'Russian Response to Gunmen Leader al-Walid's Reported Death', *Gazeta*, 19 April 2004, p. 1.

34 Cerwyn Moore, 'Combating Terrorism in Russia and Uzbekistan', *Cambridge Review of International Affairs*, 20:2 (2007), pp. 303–323.

35 R. Thornton and B. Renz, 'Russian Counter-Terrorism', unpublished conference paper ISA, San Francisco (2008).
36 P. Baev, 'Putin's Counter-Terrorism: The Parameters of a Strategic Dead-End', *Small Wars and Insurgencies*, 17:1 (2006), p. 2.
37 Amnesty International, *The Russian Federation*, p. 58.
38 Office of the Co-ordinator for Counter-Terrorism, *Country Reports on Terrorism 2007: Europe and Eurasia Overview* (US Department of State, 2008), www.state. gov/s/ct/rls/crt/2007/103707.htm.
39 R. Crelinsten, *Counterterrorism* (Cambridge: Polity, 2009), p. 37.
40 Amnesty International, *The Russian Federation*, p. 50.
41 International Commission of Jurists, *Assessing Damage, Urging Action: Report of the Eminent Jurists Panel on Terrorism, Counter-Terrorism and Human Rights* (International Commission of Jurists, 2009), http://icj.org/IMG/EJP-report.pdf, pp. 72–3.
42 Ibid., p. 81.
43 B. Renz, 'The Status and Treatment of Detainees in Russia's Chechen Conflicts', *Centre for Diplomatic and International Studies Research Seminar Series* (2008), pp. 6–20.
44 V. Tolz, 'Values and the Construction of National Identity', in S. White, A. Pravda and Z. Gitleman (eds.), *Developments in Russian Politics 5* (Houndmills: Palgrave, 2001), p. 277.
45 Amnesty International, *The Russian Federation*, p. 33.
46 A. Yarlykapov, 'Separatism and Islamic Extremism in the Ethnic Republics of the North Caucasus', *Russian Analytical Digest*, 22:7 (2007), p. 10.
47 Hafez shows how a culturally astute framework is used to perpetuate a mythology and to allow terrorists actors to appear as moral agents and deactivate norms against violence. This includes a strategic use of emotional narratives to define a political problem (the oppression of Muslims by 'crusaders and Zionists') and provide an immediate and necessary solution to that problem: redemption through sacrifice. M.M. Hafez, 'Martyrdom Mythology in Iraq: How Jihadists Frame Suicide Terrorism in Videos and Biographies', *Terrorism and Political Violence*, 19:1 (2007), pp. 95–115.
48 G. Derlugian, *Bourdieu's Secret Admirer in the Caucasus: A World Systems Biography* (Chicago: University of Chicago Press, 2005); C. Moore, 'Hostage-Taking and Counter Hostage-Taking: Reflections on Recent Developments in the North Caucasus' (Central Asia – Caucasus Analyst, August 2006).
49 C. Billo and W. Chang, *Cyber Warfare: An Analysis of the Means and Motivations of Selected Nation States* (Institute for Security Technology Studies at Dartmouth College, 2004), p. 113.
50 A. McGregor, 'YouTube: The New Video Front for Chechnya's Mujahideen', *North Caucasus Analyst*, 8:12 (2007).
51 C. Coker, *War in an Age of Risk* (Cambridge: Polity, 2009), p. 216.
52 Baev, 'Putin's Counter-Terrorism', p. 3.
53 Smith, 'Russia and the Rule of Law', p. 126.
54 Ibid.
55 T.L. Thomas, 'Manipulating the Mass Consciousness: Russian and Chechen "Information War" Tactics in the 2nd Chechen–Russian Conflict', *Foreign Military Studies Office*, Fort Leavenworth, http://fmso.leavenworth.army.mil/documents/chechiw.htm.
56 M. Kramer, 'The Russian–Chechen Conflict and the Putin–Kadyrov Connection', *Russian Analytical Digest*, 22:7 (2007), p. 3.
57 Ibid., p. 75.
58 F. Furedi, *Invitation to Terror: The Expanding Empire of the Unknown* (London: Continuum, 2007), p. 7.
59 www.kavkazcentre.com/content/2009/06/30/10782.shtml.
60 Crelinsten, *Counterterrorism*, p. 167.

61 S. Keith, 'Fear-Mongering or Fact? The Construction of 'Cyber-Terrorism' in US, UK and Canadian News Media', *Safety and Security in a Networked World: Balancing Cyber-Rights and Responsibilities* (Oxford Internet Institute, September 2005), p. 15.
62 *Jane's Intelligence Review*, 'Asia Focus: Chart 4 – Summary of IW Capabilities', December 2000.
63 Baev, 'Putin's Counter-Terrorism', p. 6.
64 www.gazeta.ru/2003/03/11/Putinmakessw.shtml.
65 Billo and Chang, *Cyber Warfare*, p. 111.
66 Greylogic, *Project Grey Goose Phase II Report: The Evolving State of Cyber Warfare* (2009), www.scribd.com/doc/13442963/Project-Grey-Goose-Phase-II-Report.
67 I. Traynor, 'Russia Accused of Unleashing Cyberwar to Disable Estonia', *Guardian*, 17 May 2007.
68 J. Davis, 'Hackers Take Down the Most Wired Country in Europe', *Wired Magazine* (15 September 2007), www.wired.com/politics/security/magazine/15–09/ff_estonia.
69 D. Bradbury, 'The Fog of Cyberwar', *Guardian*, 5 February 2009, www.guardian.co.uk/technology/2009/feb/05/kyrgyzstan-cyberattack-internet-access.
70 Billo and Chang, *Cyber Warfare*.
71 McGregor, 'YouTube: The New Video Front for Chechnya's Mujahideen'.
72 R. Crelinsten, 'Analysing Terrorism and Counter-Terrorism: A Communication Model', *Terrorism and Political Violence*, 14:2 (2002), pp. 77–122; P. Bobbit, *Terror and Consent: The Wars for the Twenty-First Century* (London: Allen Lane, 2008).
73 Crelinsten, *Counterterrorism*, p. 80.
74 Ibid., p. 210.
75 A.K. Cronin, 'Russia and Chechnya', in R.J. Art and L. Richardson (eds.), *Democracy and Counter-Terrorism: Lessons from the Past* (Washington, DC: US Institute of Peace Press, 2007), p. 384.
76 Baev, 'Putin's Counter-Terrorism', p. 10.
77 Baev, 'Putin's Counter-Terrorism', p. 5.
78 C. Moore and P. Tumelty, 'Assessing Unholy Alliances in Chechnya: From Communism and Nationalism to Islamism and Salafism', *The Journal of Communist Studies and Transition Politics*, 25:1 (2009), pp. 73–94.
79 For more details on the evolution, transformation and radicalization of the anti-Russian insurgency in the North Caucasus see C. Moore, *Contemporary Violence: Post-Modern War in Kosovo and Chechnya* (Manchester: MUP, 2010).

10 Fixing the elusive

India and the foreignness of terror

Ted Svensson

The Indian response to the altered parameters of the dominant conceptualization of the threat of terrorism after September 2001 seems to represent both a widening and a contraction of the term. The widening consisted of a process whereby the Indian experience of violence defined as terrorism was made integral to a chain of equivalences infused with global connotations, whereas the contraction assumed the contours of an identifying of specific communities as perpetrators, and potential perpetrators, of conduct constituting 'acts of terror'. These were acts that, since they were conceived and represented as being performed within the frame of 'global' events, lacked a precise localized and bounded dimension. 'Terrorism', conversely, became synonymous with the borderless and vagrant, the ubiquitous and incessantly imminent. It thus signified a partial break with past portrayals of terror and the terrorist – such as in the case of the militancies in the Punjab and Kashmir – wherein situated and local factors appeared to be effortlessly deducible. In the fall of 2001, these notions were, due to global rearrangements, however, inexorably imbued with a less apparent, yet more disquieting, meaning. The initiation of the War on Terror by the United States meant that Indian attempts to delineate the meaning of terrorism simultaneously had to make existing fault-lines and antagonisms part of the concept, and closely entwine it with a discourse associating terrorist activities with extremism emanating from within the Islamist fold. It was a discursive transmutation that was afforded substance and a degree of solidity through two instances of 'terror' in the wake of the destruction in New York, namely the suicide mission against the state assembly of Jammu and Kashmir on 1 October 2001, in which 26 persons perished,[1] and the attempt to forcibly enter the Parliament on 13 December later the same year, in which seven lost their lives.[2]

What needs to be considered – while analyzing the fluctuation and stability of the signification of terror in the Indian context – is how the conceptual inflation and narrowing, articulated in and through the commencement of the War on Terror relate to, on the one hand, the seemingly author-less cycle of bomb blasts that has plagued India for a number years and, on the other hand, the stupefying attack in Mumbai in 2008, which appears to have been carried out by an unambiguously distinguishable agent. To what extent has the most recent decisive juncture eroded or strengthened sedimented interpretations and portrayals of the terrorist and the threat s/he represents? Does the ease with which institutional reforms, policy adjustments and legal amendments have been agreed upon signal a convergence of attitudes across the political spectrum regarding the apposite representation and containment of terrorism? A rigid delimiting of the insignia and texture of terrorism has been actualized in the interval between September 2001 and November 2008 whereby acts of terror have been closely associated with Islam, Muslims and activities originating from neighboring states.[3] It is a demarcation and representation that, however, fails to exhaust the array of grave security threats that exists in India. Two such security concerns that do not typically find an inclusion in the categories of 'terror' and 'terrorism' are the violence carried out by Maoist organizations, or so-called Naxalites, and by secessionist movements in the north-east.[4] Although the former has been rendered by the Indian Prime Minister Manmohan Singh as 'the biggest threat to the country'[5] it is rarely described as terrorism in state idiom. The same observation is applicable to the last-mentioned, which is also often reduced to secondary importance. One example being how the attention surrounding a series of explosions in the state of Assam on 30 October, which resulted in the death of 86 people, was demoted after the Mumbai attack.

Two moments of conceptual closure

In order to mark out the hegemonic representation of and response to terrorism in India, the analysis traverses and oscillates between two particularly significant moments in the generation and reproduction of the concept, namely the Parliament attack in December 2001 – which seemed to validate that India was victim of the same global terrorist conglomerate as the United States,[6] and that it suffered analogous expressions of orchestrated enmity – and India's 'own 9/11' in Mumbai in late November 2008. The two events amount to crucial junctures in the ascription of meaning to the concept of terror, as well as in the formation of attempts to prevent and counter it. Both contained an ostensible element of 'infiltration'[7] of non-citizens, and both appeared to have been devised entirely abroad. They, further, had come to in part mirror each other, since some of the developments initiated at the time of the Parliament attack finally acquired a totalizing and less-fluid character via the widely disseminated and protracted carnage in Mumbai. The arguments and sanctioned narrative propounded by the state in 2001 found their seeming confirmation in the Mumbai attack.

The last-mentioned is, however, somewhat surprising since the two events, discursively as well as symbolically, markedly diverge. Although four persons were charged for the alleged involvement, the particulars of the former incident are, for example, still vague; the names and identities of the 'terrorists' involved in the actual attack remain undisclosed, the possible backdrop to it has not been thoroughly explored, and India instantly embarked upon a pompous and perilous show of military potency that overwrote questions related to that very incident. In the instance of Mumbai in November 2008, the Pakistani state has not been portrayed as directly involved, the chronology and display of violence amounted to an unremitting media spectacle, which – similarly to 9/11 – had a transfixing effect on the audience, and it set an austere, yet dynamic, dialogue between India and Pakistan in motion. Rather than resulting in the expected and conventional altercation, the case of Mumbai has even revealed signs of an increase in interlocution and a renewed commitment to the Joint Anti-Terror Mechanism that was established in November 2006.[8]

The most manifest and potentially disastrous corollary of the failed attempt by five gunmen to force an entry into the Parliament in December 2001 was the decision by the Indian government to initiate an extensive mobilization of the armed forces along the Indo-Pakistan border. The impending hostilities in the end of 2001 meant that the United States, only a few months after the commencement of its War on Terror, had to attend to the circumvention of a full-scale conflict between two of its allies, both with nuclear capability, in the disputed undertaking.[9] Samina Yasmeen's remark on the possible unfolding of what appeared as an imminent confrontation asserts that the Indian administration, then dominated by the Hindu nationalist Bharatiya Janata Party (BJP), contemplated the option of 'launching pre-emptive strikes against selected targets in Pakistan' since these would constitute 'an appropriate response to Pakistani support for anti-Indian terrorist activities'.[10] At the same time, India had to take into consideration that its policy as regards the use of nuclear weapons was and remains principally informed by 'an acceptance of the logic of deterrence'.[11] Yasmeen's claim contains three key elements, namely the deliberation to utilize pre-emptive strikes, an explicit linking of the Pakistani state and terrorism, and the centrality of and alertness to the existence of nuclear weapons. These were all near to absent from the sanctioned and superseding response in 2008, which through diplomatic measures articulated the expectation that Pakistan would assist India in punishing the responsible and in preventing similar occurrences in the future.

Apart from being rhetorical and symbolic, the discursive reorientation in 2001 was coeval with the Indian Parliament's more material approval of a new anti-terror legislation. Ujjwal Kumar Singh has noted that the endorsement of the Prevention of Terrorism Ordinance on 24 October 2001, which later evolved into the Prevention of Terrorism Act (POTA) at the end of March 2002, has to be viewed in the light of international trends in the definition of terrorism and the prevalent tendency to pass extraordinary laws in the wake of 9/11.[12] Even though POTA was discarded in 2004, the abandonment merely translated into the inclusion of the extraordinary into the ordinary and 'permanent' via the concomitant amendments to the Unlawful Activities Prevention Act (UAPA).[13] The latter became consolidated when the Indian Parliament in December 2008 – in response to the atrocious events in Mumbai – once more amended the UAPA in a manner that further harmonized it with previously retracted anti-terror legislation. The revisions that were made in 2004 and borrowed from POTA included 'definition, punishment and enhanced penalties for "terrorist activities"' as well as 'the banning of "terrorist organisations" and interception of telephone and electronic communications'.[14] The amendments in 2008, among other changes, imparted the Act with a new and highly flexible definition of a terrorist act, a 180-day pre-charge detention period and comprehensive power to 'freeze' and 'seize' financial resources.[15]

In India, 34 organizations are designated as terrorist and, accordingly, banned under the UAPA. The list of proscribed groups span organizations seeking autonomy in parts of the north-east, militant groups in the Punjab, radical left-wing organizations, Tamil liberation movements and extremist outfits amalgamating opposition to the Indian state with an aspiration to establish an Islamic state. While employing the term 'terrorism', it is, however, the final type that has come to occupy the center-stage since 2001. One reason is to be found in the frequent and engrossing bomb blasts that have taken place.[16] In divergence with the limited amount of actualized 'acts of terror' in the United States and in Europe, India has witnessed a secession of events that have consumed numerous lives and injured an even larger number. Bombs have repeatedly exploded in busy public spaces, such as in markets, in public transport and at religious sites – including Hindu temples, mosques and a Sufi shrine. According to a compilation put together by the *South Asia Terrorism Portal*, India experienced 20 bomb blasts and other violent acts branded as 'Islamist terrorism' outside the territory of Jammu and Kashmir and the country's north-eastern parts between September 2001 and November 2008.[17] If we include the events in September 2001 and November 2008, the total number of civilians killed, according to the information collated by the portal, amount to 889 and the total number of injured – with no distinction made between civilians and security personnel – is 2,650. The groups named as responsible for one or many of these gruesome deeds include the Lashkar-e-Toiba (LeT), Students Islamic Movement of India (SIMI), Jaish-e-Mohammed (JeM), Harkat-ul-Jihadi-al-Islam (HuJI) and Indian Mujahideen (IM).

The generally accepted chronology and details of the Mumbai attack were articulated by the Minister of Home Affairs, P. Chidambaram, as early as 11 December 2008 in a debate in the Lok Sabha (House of the People). According to the repeatedly recounted and authoritative narrative, ten Pakistani members of the outlawed LeT – a group which has been frequently attributed responsibility for the planning and implementing of terrorist acts on Indian territory – entered Mumbai via the sea route on the evening of 26 November. They had departed from Karachi three days earlier and had en route seized control of a boat operated by Indian fishermen. Once in Mumbai, they divided into four groups; each group embarked on a calamitous mission that included meticulously premeditated, yet palpably arbitrary, attacks at several sites in the south part of the city. The loci of violence included one of the city's main train stations, the Chatrapati Shivaji Terminus, two five-star hotels, a hospital, a restaurant frequented by locals and foreign tourists alike and a Jewish community center. The episode lasted three days and, in the words of P. Chidambaram, consisted of 'indiscriminate firing, throwing of grenades and bomb blasts at 13 locations'.[18] Eventually, all but one of the assailants were killed. The trial against the lone surviving perpetrator, Mohammad Ajmal Amir Iman – often referred to as Ajmal Kasab – and two local accomplices, Fahim Ansari and Sabahuddin Ahmed, began on 17 April 2009. In addition, 35 Pakistani citizens have been indicted for their alleged involvement.

Reflecting on the description of the attack in November 2008 as 'India's 9/11', Srinath Raghavan has claimed that even though it is in many respects a flawed description, there is an overlap in the media representation of it and the original 9/11: both were televised live without interruption and caught the attention of the viewers in an exceptional manner.[19] We, in other words, witness another palpable divergence between the Parliament attack and the acts at the end of 2008. Whereas the latter were enacted in front of a vigilant and concurrently construing media, the attempt to enter the Parliament premises above all became engulfed in opaqueness – both with regard to the individual identity of the perpetrators and the finer intricacies of the event. While, as Raghavan stresses, the behavior of an insomnious media resulted in the diffusion of images of terrorism to an unprecedented extent,[20] the actual Parliament attack was not captured live.

According to Rajesh M. Basrur, India's postures during the pending confrontation in 2001–2002 ought to be regarded as a significant strategic reorientation.[21] The stance in 2008 seems to embody an additional revision. Is the variance in reaction principally a sign of altered parameters on the global level and, hence, an indication of a context more conducive to military build-up in 2001? Or, ought we to accentuate circumstances particular to the region, e.g. the precarious conditions in Pakistan after the murder of Benazir Bhutto and the restoration of democracy, the gradual discursive dissociation of states and 'terrorist outfits' in official idiom and perhaps the impact of ideational differences between the two parties respectively in power? The BJP was the main constituent of the governing National Democratic Alliance in 2001; seven years later, the Congress was the dominant part of the ruling United Progressive Alliance.

Subsequent to the Mumbai attack, two changes occurred that constituted direct responses to it. First, the UAPA was, as mentioned above (pp. 00–00), further amended and, second, it was decided that a National Investigation Agency ought to be inaugurated. According to the formulation of the National Investigation Agency Act, the objective is to establish a unit with a national reach, which will

> investigate and prosecute offences affecting the sovereignty, security and integrity of India, security of State, friendly relations with foreign States and offences under Acts enacted to implement international treaties, agreements, conventions and resolutions of the United Nations, its agencies and other international organisations and for matters connected therewith or incidental thereto.

The main novelty appears to be that the agency will fill the function of 'a police force created and administered by the central government, which would endow all personnel above the rank of sub-inspector with powers throughout Indian territory'.[22] It is, hence, a direct attempt to avert the malfunctions in the areas of communication, coordination and administration that were exposed in November 2008.

The external enemy within

Taken together, the above events constitute two decisive moments wherein certain notions of terror and the figure of the terrorist have come to permeate the dominant narrative on the resilience and fragility of the Indian state. In addition, they indicate the (baseless) origin and end of a vagueness and obliqueness regarding where the terrorist threat – necessitating measures of prevention – stemmed from during the interim years. Whereas the antecedent juncture failed to discursively elevate and totalize the singularity and centrality of the 'exterior' as the principal site for the planning and coordination of 'acts of terror' – a failure which facilitated a double bind between ambivalence and certainty in the naming of the responsible – the more recent moment made any acknowledgment of plasticity and the need for introspection impossible. In a manner reminiscent of the hasty unfolding of an explicit identifying of foreign militants as guilty in the aftermath of bomb blasts, Prime Minister Manmohan Singh chose, while the violence in Mumbai was still unrestrained, to state that the attack in all probability had 'external linkages'.[23] The Mumbai attack forcefully reified the meaning of terror according to a schema wherein the Indian state was merely accountable for the neglect to institute a dependable and efficient security structure.

As alluded to above, the incident in 2001 collapsed the distinction between the national and the global, and made the representation of the terrorist synonymous with an imagery of 'Islamic fundamentalism'.[24] The disintegrating of a clear distinction between the domestic, regional and international was also discernible in the aftermath of the Mumbai attacks;[25] an editorial in the *Economic and Political Weekly*, for example, chose to describe the event as 'a global phenomenon' since 'it took the lives of people of so many nationalities and seemed to herald a new and deadly form of terrorism that could visit other countries'.[26] Notions of a shared suffering and of the uniqueness of the attack have been recurrently articulated.

A constancy in the Indian state's conceptualizing of terror since 2001 has been the propensity to place all blame upon the neighboring states and upon the undesired porosity of borders in the region. The latter is not only valid in the case of the Indo-Pakistan border; the pervious quality of the Indo-Bangladesh border[27] has also received much attention and the Indo-Nepali border has been referred to as 'no-man's land'. It is noteworthy, as pointed out by Sujata Ramachandran, that immigration of Bangladeshis and, hence, overwhelmingly of Muslims, often has been represented through the employment of an imagery of 'infiltration' across a 'porous' boundary.[28] It is, however, interesting that when India in September 1992 tried to expel 132 'Muslim "infiltrators"' with their domicile in New Delhi, Bangladesh did not recognize them as Bangladeshi citizens.[29] The fixation with borders and their permeability is, although entwined with and spawned by an anxiety constituted in the present, no novel facet of India's self-depiction and self-delimiting. Since the very formation of India and Pakistan in 1947, the narrative on the elasticity and vulnerability of borders has been influential. The persistence of it becomes particularly visible if placed next to the Indian state's discourse on the first 'raiders' in the Kashmir conflict and the long-standing fear of unrestrained migration from East Pakistan to the north-eastern states. Both remain crucial parts of present-day portrayals of movement across these borders, of the presence of Pakistanis and Bangladeshis in India, and of the normality of the construction of fences and floodlights.

In an attempt to pin down the 'identity' of 'terrorists' in the Indian context, Rakesh Gupta accentuates that they are not persons who necessarily belong to the categories of the disadvantaged and dispossessed.[30] Conversely, they regularly have a background that might be described as 'middle class', 'semi-urban' and 'rural'.[31] Gupta's attempt to unearth the most common identity marker is, however, a problematizing that is not part of the hegemonic representation of terrorism in Indian media as well as in state-initiated discourse. As indicated above, a strong tendency since 2001 has been to identify the source of violence and of the motives behind attacks as external to Indian society and polity. The dominant tendency might be illustrated with an assertion articulated by Manmohan Singh at the Chief Ministers' Conference on Internal Security on 9 January 2009. The Prime Minister said that '[d]uring the past year, we faced a severe challenge from terrorist groups operating from outside our country. Many of them act in association with hostile Intelligence Agencies in these countries'.[32] Any recognition of the participation of Indians in acts of terror involves a reference to their connections with groups based in neighboring countries and it is regularly attached with an allusion to the phenomena of infiltration or illegal immigration. The terrorist in India has, in other words, become a person that is simultaneously familiar and distant. Apart from engendering a situation in which the 'real' motive or 'inner' self of the terrorist cannot be fully grasped, it frees the Indian state from full responsibility.

A core element of the discourse on an estranged, yet intimate, adversary is the emphasis laid upon madrasas as a source of extremism. As Jamal Malik notes:

> much of the current talk on madrasas has been associated with the emerging geo-political order which has sought to link these institutions to global terrorism. More often than not, the assertion has been that they have become something like a factory for global *jihad* and a breeding ground for terrorism; it is being increasingly argued that madrasa pedagogy produces fanaticism and intolerance, which are detrimental to pluralism and multicultural reality. [...] In India it has come under attack from Hindu nationalists who charge them of producing and harboring 'terrorists'.[33]

It is a depiction that Arshad Alam, amongst others, has contested. Alam writes that, far from the conception of madrasas as principally centered on erecting lines between 'Muslims' and 'others', 'madrasas are solely concerned with what is the correct interpretation of Islam'.[34] As a consequence, 'they create an "other" within rather than outside the community'.[35] It is, however, noteworthy that such a contestation merely confirms the claim, often articulated by advocates of Hindu nationalism, that parts of the Muslim community has gone through a radicalization.

Let us momentarily address one of the more paradoxical aspects of the Indian state's conception of 'security', and of its reliance on the image of an entwinement of terrorism, the exterior and the purely destructive, namely, violence by Maoist groups. As the repeated attacks committed by Maoists during the 2009 elections and the disturbances in the Lalgarh district of West Bengal in June of the same year have shown, the Maoist insurgency is a force to be reckoned with. It is a subversive element with more expanse and sway than that which is regularly held up as the main threat. Similarly to the conventional scholarly account of the reasons behind any expression of sympathy with acts of violence displayed by Indian Muslims, i.e. their socio-economic and political marginalization,[36] it is telling that the support of the Maoist movement is strongest among those marginalized in areas dominated by *adivasis* (tribals). It has an extensive presence in areas virtually abandoned by the Indian state. These areas have not experienced the economic success that is often part of depictions of contemporary India as economically thriving; or, as Sumit Ganguly describes it:

> [i]n strictly aggregate terms, India's economic performance remained quite robust [in 2008]. Yet, a more nuanced analysis reveals that this growth is regionally quite uneven [...]. For example, economic conditions in many eastern states – notably Orissa, Jharkhand, Bihar, and West Bengal – remain depressed.[37]

The challenge from Maoist outfits has become particularly pressing in three of these. At the same time as the Indian state is trying to eject the phenomenon of terrorism by affiliating it with regional and global currents, it has encountered an antagonism that is undeniably domestic.

The failure of success

The seemingly relentless series of bomb blasts, the reflexive linking of terrorism with Pakistan, Islam and cross-border elements, the key importance ascribed to the securitization of borders and of alien populations in the region, the complexity in designating instances of violence committed by Hindus as well as by irrefutably domestic groups as terrorism, the disquieting episode of Gujarat in 2002 – in which appendages of the state colluded in an organized instance of extensive violence against Muslims[38] – and the silent re-inscription of the provisions of anti-terror laws have all found their place in the attempt to lay down a fixed and cogent construal of terrorist activity in the Indian context. It is, hence, notable that, although P. Chidambaram in the abovementioned speech (pp. 00–00) enunciated the stipulation that 'given the nature of the threat, we cannot go back to "business as usual"',[39] the aftermath of the Mumbai attack represented just that. Apropos the alteration of the UAPA in December 2008, Ravi Nair has argued that the Act in its amended version 'merely borrow[s] provisions from the previous anti-terror laws, rather than offering a new approach, in spite of the past failures of stringent anti-rights laws to curb terrorist attacks'.[40] Nair, similarly to Singh before, stresses that we, in the wake of the abandoning of POTA and with the latest modification of the UAPA, witness a development that not only incorporates 'unjust draconian laws from the past, in some cases word for word, but also make[s] them a permanent feature of the criminal justice system'.[41] The trend seems to corroborate the here-postulated argument that the second moment confirmed and deepened already existing currents.

The two demarcating events outlined above do not merely indicate the outer boundary of the conceptualization of terror and, thus, the preferred mode of anticipation and preclusion. They also offer a depiction of divergent ways to respond to already-executed acts of terror. Whereas India in 2001 mobilized along the Pakistani border and the assailants were not mentioned by name, it – in sharp contrast – opted to rely on diplomatic pressure on its western neighbor and to deny the culpable anonymity after the Mumbai attack. Considerable parts of the evidence that India shared with Pakistan in January 2009 were also circulated to the Indian media. The 'dossier of evidence' includes a list of the nine 'terrorists' killed, in which they are described by name, age and residence.[42]

While pondering the issue of terrorism and its possible outcomes in South Asia, one genuine cause for anxiety is both states' possession of nuclear arms. It is a concern enhanced by the seeming linkage between crises – often engendered by 'acts of terror' – and an ensuing tendency to mobilize the nuclear repositories. Scott D. Sagan and Kenneth N. Waltz have noted that, both at the time of the Kargil conflict in 1999[43] and during the extensive assembling of troops along the Indo-Pakistan border in the winter of 2001–2002, Pakistan put its nuclear arsenal in a state of preparedness.[44] It is a deportment that might be compared with India's adopted stance, which appeared to, on the one hand, have to relate to the aforementioned 'logic of deterrence' and, on the other hand, found itself restricted by the ownership per se; or, as Rajagopalan has contended, '[t]he central problem that India faces [due to nuclearization] is that nuclear weapons have reduced India's conventional military options, especially in dealing with Pakistan'.[45] It has resulted in a situation where 'the fear of escalation does appear to be one of the self-imposed restraints on the use of conventional military force'.[46] It seems apt to assume that the experience in 2001–2002, when Pakistan demonstrated an inclination to include nuclear weapons in the preparations for war, combined with India's intrinsically constrained disposition, informed and became part of the mitigation of the official reaction to the Mumbai attack in 2008.

Christine C. Fair's observation that, regardless of the long-term acquaintance with and experience of 'urban conflict within the Indian army and India's various paramilitary and police organizations' these agencies have failed to 'absorb and disseminate the various lessons learned' still seems valid.[47] The latest episode wherein the inadequacies were on display, namely in Mumbai in November 2008, corroborates the assertion that 'there are few, if any, *joint* mechanisms to ensure that all of India's security apparatus can draw from accumulated operational knowledge'.[48] A general sense of system failure transpired in the aftermath of the Mumbai attacks, ranging from a critique of the local police's inability to respond to the level of violence unleashed by the perpetrators, the delayed response by politicians as well as the National Security Guard – which arrived in Mumbai first after 11 hours – the incapacity of the 'routine emergency services' and a lack of centralized information.[49]

Two additional issues that merit consideration, while discussing internal boundary drawing effected by a particular portrayal of the origin of terror and the traits of the terrorist, is the application of existing extraordinary legal instruments against particular communities and the disinclination of state agencies, prior to the fall 2008, to recognize the possibility of 'Hindu terrorism'. The former has, as Singh accentuates, been primarily utilized against certain sections of Indian society.[50] In a document drafted for the United Nation's Commission on Human Rights, Human Rights Watch highlighted that the inequitable deployment of POTA had resulted in an imbalanced persecution of religious minorities and of the political rivals of those in power.[51] Gautam Navlakha has similarly drawn attention to how, whereas Hindus involved in the violence in the state of Gujarat in 2002 were all released on bail, 86 Muslims accused of partaking in the incident that provided the spark and detained under POTA still await to be granted bail, although the Act was annulled in 2004.[52] Navlakha continues:

> [i]n other words, we cannot be blind to the fact that, in India, draconian laws, such as the Unlawful Activities Prevention Act (UAPA), POTA, Terrorist and Disruptive Activities (Prevention) Act (TADA) or Chapter VI of the Indian Penal Code (IPC) on offences against the State, have been used selectively and deliberately, to target ethnic communities and the underclass.[53]

A persistent element of the debate on terrorism in India is the accounts regarding young Muslim men disappearing in the wake of acts of terror and the recurrent use of that which has become known as 'encounter killings'. It has, for example, transpired that the police in Andhra Pradesh arrested roughly 100 Muslim men in the aftermath of two instances of explosions in Hyderabad during 2007; out of these, it has been established that 21 were subjected to torture and they have received economic compensation from the state.[54] The 2006–2007 annual report of the National Commission for Human Rights contains numerous references to illegal detentions and the use of torture by the Indian police.[55]

In combination with the persistent return of brutal acts of terror, the impression of an inconsistent and negligent utilization of extra-ordinary mechanisms has severely undermined the image of the Indian state as capable of managing the tasks of preventing and combating the threat of terror in a democratic manner. A related deficiency is the apparent inadequacy of the legal system. Apart from the unfortunate time it takes to process court cases, there has been a widespread tendency amongst lawyers to refuse to represent terror suspects.[56] The latter has been portrayed by A.G. Noorani as a development whereby 'mob justice replaces justice according to the law'.[57] 'The mob' he refers to is made up of lawyers or 'men who earn their bread by the law and are pledged to uphold it'.[58]

The above constitutes an essential part of a wider framework of rationalities wherein the Indian police has near to automatically assumed that Hindus are not involved in acts of terror. Although it seems misplaced to speak of success or the level of success in an analysis of 'terrorism', it appears to be uncontroversial to suggest that the Indian police has failed to always pursue its tasks in a manner reflecting a will to arrest the culpable. It has, at times, not investigated the evident. Navlakha, for example, draws attention to the seeming incongruity in the handling of the explosion on board the Samjhauta Express heading for Pakistan in February 2007.[59] The overwhelming majority of those who perished were Pakistani citizens. Seven years earlier, the issue of a train connection between India and Pakistan had transpired as the object of a controversy in which Hindu extremists articulated an intention to disrupt the service. The Indian police, however, routinely assumed that the perpetrators were to be found in Pakistan. As Navlakha contends, '[a]fter an initial flurry of activity and leaks about the leads, the trail turned cold'.[60] We might add that the same appears to be true in most cases where the blasts might be interpreted as having Muslims as the likely victims. In October 2008, it emerged that a number of bomb blasts that had taken place in the state of Maharashtra – and previously thought of as components of a scheme wherein militant Muslims with the support of organizations based outside of India had carried out a whole string of bomb blasts – with all probability had been executed by Hindu extremists.[61] There have also been media reports about the police being involved in planting evidence on or in connection with arrested suspects.[62]

Conclusion

Although the events in and after November 2008 initially seemed to reverse, or at least considerably alter, the framing of the responsibility articulated in the aftermath of acts of terror since 2001, it swiftly transpired that they merely corroborated ongoing trends, i.e. the transformation of the local and regional into the global, the absolving of the Indian state from genuine liability, and the more subtle forms of violence whereby certain sections of Indian society have been placed on the discursive outside of notions of belonging, loyalty and assumed innocence. The linking of Muslim identity in India with a proclivity to support the actions and ideational underpinnings of extremist Islamists based abroad has become thoroughly ingrained into the popular comprehension of terrorist activities and their breeding ground. Another sign to the continuity is the above-mentioned slow, yet profound, shift in legal thresholds that was once again endorsed in December 2008. It is particularly noteworthy that the experience of the Mumbai attacks entirely silenced an emerging narrative on 'Hindu terrorism'. What first seemed to represent an opportunity for a significant rupture in the representation of terrorism and, thus, in the boundary drawing between religious communities – a chance to allow for introspection and reconfiguration – merely evolved into a re-inscription of an existing blueprint. All references to motives with a material base have, accordingly, been expunged, which the omission of allusions to Kashmir in the prosecution of Ajmal Kasab indicates.[63]

Once again, as in the case of the Mumbai train blasts in July 2006, the Indian Prime Minister chose to isolate the drive behind terrorist acts as stemming from an urge 'to destabilize our secular polity, create communal discord and undermine our country's economic and social progress'.[64] Pranab Mukherjee, then Minister of External Affairs, analogously articulated the conception that the instances of terrorism during 2008 jointly coalesced into an objective to undermine the Indian economy; in his own words, 'I find a design to which is hurt India's economy. Our enemies are jealous of the progress that India has made.'[65] One consequence of the strong linking of terrorism and progress is, of course, that it becomes difficult to disentangle these terms in a critique of the extent and depth of the latter. In addition, India has, as P. Chidambaram propounded, with the region as a whole, found itself in 'the eye of the storm of terror' – a storm that L.K. Advani, leader of the opposition, chose to depict as having its 'epicentre' in Pakistan. The latter was a remark to which Pranab Mukherjee found it appropriate to add that it was evident 'that the epicentre of this attack and not only this one, but also series of attacks prior to this attack, is located in a neighbouring country'.[66] The prevalent logic of the Indian state's partial exemption from responsibility, and the connectedness and symmetry of the separate cases was, thus, reiterated. The elusive acts of terror in the intervening years seemed to, at last, have found an absolute and unequivocal interpretation.

Notes

1 S. Ganguly and R. Harrison Wagner, 'India and Pakistan: Bargaining in the Shadow of Nuclear War', *Journal of Strategic Studies*, 27:3 (2004), p. 493.
2 P.S. Tripathi, 'Terror in Parliament House', *Frontline*, 18:26 (2001/2002).
3 For a detailed account, see T. Svensson, 'Frontiers of Blame: India's "War on Terror"', *Critical Studies on Terrorism*, 2:1 (2009), pp. 27–44.
4 For a scrutiny of the separatist movements in the north-east and the Indian state's response to these challenges, see B. Lacina, 'Does Counterinsurgency Theory Apply in Northeast India?', *India Review*, 6:3 (2007), pp. 165–183.
5 V. Ramakrishnan, 'Maoist Connection', *Frontline*, 24:25 (2007/2008).
6 S. Ganguly has in a number of articles explored the augmented cooperation of India and the United States in the areas of foreign policy and military activities. See S. Ganguly, 'The Start of a Beautiful Relationship? The United States and India', *World Policy Journal*, 20:1 (2003), pp. 25–30; S. Ganguly, 'India's Foreign Policy Grows Up', *World Policy Journal*, 20:4 (2003/2004), pp. 41–47; S. Ganguly and A. Scobell, 'India and United States: Forging a Security Partnership', *World Policy Journal*, 22:2 (2005), pp. 37–43. Other scholars have noted India's increasingly close partnership with Israel in matters of 'trade and military agreements'. See R. Oza, 'Contrapuntal Geographies of Threat and Security: The United States, India, and Israel', *Environment and Planning D: Society and Space*, 25 (2007), pp. 9–32. See also P.R. Kumaraswamy, 'India and Israel: Emerging Partnership', *Journal of Strategic Studies*, 25:4 (2002), pp. 192–206.

7   Figures published in the 2006–2007 annual report of the Ministry of Home Affairs states that 'infiltration' across the Pakistani border – the so-called Line of Control (LoC) – in Jammu and Kashmir declined from 2,417 in 2001 to 573 in 2006. Ministry of Home Affairs, *Annual Report 2006–07: Departments of Internal Security, States, Home, Jammu & Kashmir Affairs and Border Management* (New Delhi: Ministry of Home Affairs, Government of India, 2007), p. 145. India has, according to a document titled *Fencing and Flood Lights of Borders* and published by the Ministry of Home Affairs in 2008, finalized the building of a fence and the erection of flood lights on large parts of the Indo-Pakistan border, whereas major schemes to carry out similar work are underway on the border with Bangladesh. In July 2009, approximately 1,800 kilometers of fencing had been completed along the Indo-Bangladesh border in a venture that is planned to be finished in 2010. 'Review of Border Security', *Press Information Bureau*, 7 July 2009. In March 2009, Myanmar began to fence its border with Bangladesh, thus creating a situation where Bangladesh is becoming enclosed by the adjacent states. S. Dutta, 'At 38, Bangladesh Finds Itself in a Cage', *Telegraph*, 27 March 2007.

8   N. Subramanian, 'Krishna's Statement Affirms Our Stand: Pakistan', *The Hindu*, 29 May 2009.

9   A.R. Swamy and J. Gershman, 'Managing Internal Conflicts: Dominance of the State', in M. Alagappa (ed.), *Asian Security Order: Instrumental and Normative Features* (Stanford: Stanford University Press, 2003), p. 497.

10   S. Yasmeen, 'India and Pakistan', in Mary Buckley and Robert Singh (eds.), *The Bush Doctrine and the War on Terrorism: Global Responses, Global Consequences* (London: Routledge, 2006), p. 94.

11   Ibid.

12   U.K. Singh, *The State, Democracy and Anti-Terror Laws in India* (New Delhi: Sage Publications, 2007), p. 22.

13   Ibid., pp. 302–310.

14   Ibid., p. 307.

15   See R. Nair, 'The Unlawful Activities (Prevention) Amendment Act 2008: Repeating Past Mistakes', *Economic and Political Weekly*, 44:4 (2009), pp. 10–14. In addition to the UAPA, which is applicable on the national level, a number of extraordinary laws with regional ambit exist, namely the Armed Forces Special Powers Act, the Disturbed Areas Act and the Maharashtra Control of Organised Crimes Act.

16   In India, a certain stoicism and preparedness for bomb blasts and attacks in crowds and in urban areas has developed as a result of numerous pernicious explosions in public places. An acceptance by the state of the relentlessness and unruliness of terror finds a manifestation in the existence, since 1 April 2008, of a Central Scheme for the Assistance to Victims of Terrorist and Communal Violence (Ministry of Home Affairs, 2008).

17   South Asia Terrorism Portal, 'Major Islamist Terrorist Attacks Outside Jammu and Kashmir and Northeast since 2000', http://satp.org/satporgtp/countries/india/database/OR_9–11_majorterroristattacks.htm.

18   *Lok Sabha Debates*, 11 December 2008.

19   S. Raghavan, 'Terror, Force and Diplomacy', *Economic and Political Weekly*, 43:49 (2008), p. 10.

20   Ibid.

21   R.M. Basrur, 'Kargil, Terrorism, and India's Strategic Shift', *India Review*, 1:4 (2002), p. 39. However, as Basrur subsequently argues (p. 40), the Kargil conflict in 1999 represented an earlier juncture that informed India's response in 2001; the experience of the Kargil confrontation led India to seriously attend to

the need for a high degree of vigilance on the India–Pakistan border, the critical importance of intelligence in pre-empting crises and conflicts of the Kargil type, the need to equip the armed forces with appropriate weapons and accessories for mountain combat, and the necessity of developing an integrated infrastructure for strategic planning.

22 'Laws Without Accountability', *Economic and Political Weekly*, 43:51 (2008), pp. 5–6.
23 'Text of the PM's Address to the Nation', *The Hindu*, 27 November 2008.
24 Singh, *The State, Democracy and Anti-Terror Laws in India*, p. 58.
25 One manifestation is available in the assertion of E. Ahamed, then Minister of State for External Affairs, that all signs indicated that the attack in Mumbai had been carried out by a '*global* terrorist organisation', namely Lashkar-e-Toiba. Sandeep Dikshit, 'Break State-Terror Outfit Nexus: Ahamed', *The Hindu*, 11 December 2008 (italics added).
26 'A Call for Sanity', *Economic and Political Weekly*, 43:49 (2008), pp. 5–6.
27 Increasing consideration has been devoted to an allegedly emerging nexus between secessionist groups in the north-east, radical Bangladeshi Islamists and the Pakistani Inter-Services' Intelligence (ISI). For example, see J. Saikia, *Terror Sans Frontiers: Islamist Militancy in North East India* (New Delhi: Vision Books, 2004). For an account of the modalities and characteristics of the ISI, see S. Gregory, 'The ISI and the War on Terrorism', *Studies in Conflict & Terrorism*, 30:12 (2007), pp. 1013–1031. The reading by Saikia and others links the presence of illegal Muslim immigrants in India's north-east, the easily penetrable border and the coinciding of interests nurtured by secular as well as religious extremists. R. Egreteau, however, pertinently reminds us that, although '[r]elations between the ISI and Northeastern militants are not just opportunistic, but very realistic', it needs to be taken into account that 'as far as the Northeast is concerned, despite the growing tentacles of Islamic militancy, it is totally false to think that the ISI and other Islamic-oriented agencies control the Northeastern groups or even dictate their policy, attitude and actions.' R. Egreteau, *Instability at the Gate: India's Troubled Northeast and its External Connections* (New Delhi: Centre de Sciences Humaines, 2006), p. 110.
28 S. Ramachandran, 'Of Boundaries and Border Crossings: Undocumented Bangladeshi "Infiltrators" and the Hegemony of Hindu Nationalism in India', *Interventions*, 1:2 (1999), p. 236.
29 Ibid., p. 237.
30 R. Gupta, 'Changing Conceptions of Terrorism', *Strategic Analysis*, 25:9 (2001), p. 1008.
31 Ibid.
32 M. Singh, 'PM Inaugurates Chief Ministers' Conference on Internal Security', 6 January 2009, http://pmindia.nic.in/speeches.htm.
33 J. Malik, 'Introduction', in J. Malik (ed.), *Madrasas in South Asia: Teaching Terror?* (London: Routledge, 2008), p. 2.
34 A. Alam, 'Making Muslims: Identity and Difference in Indian Madrasas', in I. Malik (ed.), *Madrasas in South Asia: Teaching Terror?* (London: Routledge, 2008), p. 59.
35 Ibid.
36 Ganguly has accordingly claimed that

> [t]he growth of indigenous Muslim radicalism in India can be traced to two important sources. At one level, it has its origins in the discrimination the vast majority of Muslims have faced in public life in the country. At another, its sudden emergence can be attributed to the increased political awareness of young, lower-middle class Muslims about their status within India. Political developments in other parts of the Islamic world – especially in the aftermath of the terrorist attacks of September 11, 2001 – undoubtedly have also influenced their political consciousness.
>
> (S. Ganguly, 'India in 2008: Domestic Turmoil and External Hopes',
> *Asian Survey*, XLIX:1 (2009), p. 43)

37 Ibid., p. 40.
38 For an elucidation, see D. Anand, 'The Violence of Security: Hindu Nationalism and the Politics of Representing "the Muslim" as a Danger', *The Round Table*, 94:379 (2005), pp. 210–212.
39 See note 19 above.
40 Nair, 'The Unlawful Activities (Prevention) Amendment Act 2008', p. 10.
41 Ibid., p. 12.
42 'Mumbai Terror Attacks: Dossier of Evidence', *The Hindu*, 2009, www.hindu.com/nic/dossier.htm.
43 R. Samaddar referred to the 'undeclared war' and a conflict that 'put the final seal on the conversion of the Kashmir problem from a political one into a security one'. R. Samaddar, *The Politics of Dialogue: Living Under the Geopolitical Histories of War and Peace* (Aldershot: Ashgate, 2004), p. 90. It is notable, however, that – even though it might aptly be denominated an 'undeclared war' – Max-Jean Zins's observation that it marked a transition in the treatment of the deceased soldiers is equally valid. In the ceremonies surrounding the dead bodies and their transportation to their families, an 'imagery of patriotic death' and of 'patriotic funerals' evolved. Max-Jean Zins, 'Public Rites and Patriotic Funerals: The Heroes and the Martyrs of the 1999 Indo-Pakistan Kargil War', *India Review*, 6:1 (2007), p. 40. We, thus, witness a contradictory synthesis of the negated and the commemorated.
44 S. Sagan and K. Waltz, *The Spread of Nuclear Weapons: A Debate Renewed, With New Sections on India and Pakistan, Terrorism, and Missile Defense* (New York: W.W. Norton & Company, 2003), p. 103.
45 R. Rajagopalan, 'India: The Logic of Assured Retaliation', in M. Alagappa (ed.), *The Long Shadow: Nuclear Weapons and Security in 21st Century Asia* (Stanford: Stanford University Press, 2008), p. 204.
46 Ibid.
47 C.C. Fair, 'Military Operations in Urban Areas: The Indian Experience', *India Review*, 2:1 (2003), 49–76.
48 Ibid., p. 51.
49 K. Sharma, 'Governance Failures and the Anti-Political Fallout', *Economic and Political Weekly*, 43:49 (2008), p. 13.
50 Singh, *The State, Democracy and Anti-Terror Laws in India*, pp. 58–63.
51 Human Rights Watch, *In the Name of Counter-Terrorism: Human Rights Abuses Worldwide* (2003), p. 15, www.hrw.org/sites/default/files/reports/counter-terrorism-bck_0.pdf.
52 G. Navlakha, 'Lessons from the Mumbai Attack', *Economic and Political Weekly*, 44:11 (2009), pp. 13–16.
53 Ibid., p. 15.
54 Human Rights Watch, 'India: Hold Torturers Accountable', 17 November 2008, www.hrw.org/sites/default/files/reports/counter-terrorism-bck_0.pdf.
55 National Human Rights Commission, *Annual Report 2006–2007* (New Delhi: National Human Rights Commission, 2007).
56 For example, see M. Sahu, 'UP Lawyer Takes up Cases of Terror Accused, Becomes Colleagues' Target', *Indian Express*, 4 May 2008.
57 A.G. Noorani, 'Lawless Lawyers', *Economic and Political Weekly*, 43, 40 (2008), p. 13.
58 Ibid.
59 Navlakha, 'Lessons from the Mumbai Attack', p. 15.
60 Ibid.
61 See P. Bidwai, 'Confronting the Reality of Hindutva Terrorism', *Economic and Political Weekly*, 43:47 (2008), pp. 10–13; A. Katakam, 'Of Saffron Variety', *Frontline*, 25:24 (2008).

62 S. Parashar, 'IB, Cops in Murky Frame-Up', *The Times of India*, 13 September 2007.
63 'Kashmir Not in 26/11 Final Charges', *The Hindu*, 21 May 2009.
64 Lok Sabha Debates, 11 December 2008.
65 'Enemies Jealous of Our Progress: Pranab', *The Hindu*, 18 January 2009.
66 Lok Sabha Debates, 11 December 2008.

11 Australian identity, interventionism and the War on Terror

Jack Holland and Matt McDonald[1]

This chapter examines Australia's participation in military intervention in the War on Terror and the role of the politics of identity. Like the Bush administration in the United States, the Australian government under conservative prime minister John Howard was consistently willing to suggest that the age of 'war' post-2001 necessitated new domestic ministries and agencies, new legislation (from police powers to periods of detention and ease of movement in and out of the country), and new forms of public participation in security governance. All of these were crucial components of Australia's War on Terror. In this chapter, however, we focus specifically on Australian interventionism in the War on Terror: the policy and practice of involvement in military incursions beyond the borders of the Australian state as a means of redressing the threat posed by fundamentalist Islamic terrorism. We examine the reasons given for Australian participation in Afghanistan and Iraq as part of this War on Terror, while also analyzing Australia's military interventionism in the immediate region, most prominently its mission in the Solomon Islands in 2003. We argue that understanding Australian military intervention in the War on Terror requires taking account of the important role of identity in underpinning the government's conception of security and providing a resource for the government to justify intervention to the Australian people.

Australian foreign and security policy under Howard

In many ways, Australia's active participation in military interventions in the War on Terror was eminently predictable. Indeed, the principles and commitments expressed by Prime Minister Howard in announcing his solidarity with and support for the United States after 11 September 2001, were an extension of principles and commitments elaborated consistently throughout Howard's tenure as prime minister. A complete survey of Australian foreign-policy imperatives and/or action prior to 2001 is not possible here, but two core dimensions of foreign policy are worth noting in this context: the centrality of a particular conception of the 'national interest', and the primacy attached to the US alliance in Australian thinking about security and its place in the region and the world. Both, we suggest, are intimately related to a particular conception of Australian national identity.

On coming to power in 1996, the Howard government was eager to distinguish its foreign policy style and approach from that of the previous Labor (ALP) government (1983–1996) and its foreign minister, Gareth Evans. Evans had embraced the idea of 'middle power diplomacy' and championed the notion of Australia as a 'good international citizen'.[2] For Evans, this meant a commitment not simply to participate in multilateral fora but to attempt to develop the normative basis of international society and provide some form of intellectual leadership in doing so. This style of diplomacy as a means of advancing Australian interests was particularly evident in Australia's role in the Uruguay Round of talks on the General Agreement on Tariffs and Trade (1986–1994), post-conflict intervention in Cambodia (1992–1995), and Australia's active role in the development of the UN Framework Convention on Climate Change in 1992. In security terms, the Labor government had again emphasized the importance of strengthening the international institutional framework (through international leadership on nuclear disarmament, for example) as a means for advancing Australian security. Moreover the government pointed to the need for constructive engagement with those regional neighbors (in particular Indonesia) who had traditionally been viewed as a source of threat.[3]

The commitment to the 'national interest' under the subsequent Howard government was beyond an attempt to demarcate foreign policy styles from that of the previous government. For the Howard government, the ALP had allowed its commitment to 'good international citizenship' to move suspiciously close to a cosmopolitanism that rejected the ultimate primacy that governments should give the rights and needs of their own citizens. Both Howard and Foreign Minister Downer were of the view that under the ALP, the US alliance had been allowed to drift dangerously relative to a naive emphasis on defense self-reliance, a dubious attempt to identify Australia as part of the Asian region, and a commitment to work through multilateral fora that had provided tangibly little for Australia. By contrast, in launching the government's second Department of Foreign Affairs and Trade White Paper – significantly titled *Advancing the National Interest* – Downer argued that:

> A foreign minister is chosen and paid to look after the interests of his country, and not to delegate for the human race. We are not about trumpeting our own international good citizenry simply for the sake of it. That is a trap for the ideologues and the naïve.[4]

The government's willingness to work outside the rules, norms and institutions of international society in defense of more narrowly defined Australian interests was all too evident in its approach to cooperation on global climate change; its approach to asylum-seekers and refugees; and ultimately in involvement in the War on Terror.[5]

The other key commitment in foreign policy terms under the Howard government – one, of course, central to the content given to the 'national interest' – was the commitment to the US alliance, particularly in security terms. On coming to power in 1996 the Howard government immediately moved to reinvigorate the US alliance, hosting ministerial talks in Sydney that concluded with the so-called 'Sydney Statement'. While accompanied by much fanfare, the statement amounted to little more than a reaffirmation of the central principles of the 1951 ANZUS (Australia–New Zealand–United States) Treaty combined with new agreements on training exercises and an upgrade of US intelligence bases.[6] Even before 9/11, Foreign Minister Downer argued that the US alliance was crucial in providing for Australian security; cementing the US into the Asia-Pacific region; and giving Australia more weight in both world affairs broadly and American foreign policy calculations specifically.[7] For the government, then, Australia could become a more powerful international player by tying itself closely to American foreign policy interests. Controversially, after leading a successful peacekeeping mission in East Timor, Prime Minister Howard enunciated the so-called 'Howard Doctrine', suggesting that Australia could become the US's 'deputy sheriff' in the region.[8] Although Howard subsequently backtracked from these comments – which were roundly criticized within the region – Australian interventionism in the Pacific after 2001 and representations of its regional 'responsibilities' suggested that the government continued to view its role in this way.[9]

The commitment to the US alliance was of course most evident in security and foreign policy, underpinned by the conception that Australia's links to the US were 'fundamental for our security'.[10] Aside from the obvious cases under discussion here – cooperation in military intervention in Afghanistan and especially Iraq – it is worth noting that the 1999 intervention in East Timor proceeded only after receiving backing from Washington, while in 2003 Australia committed itself to active participation in the US's plans for regional missile defense. Both of these developments are significant to note given the negative effect they had on relations with some of the largest countries in the Asian region, most notably Indonesia and China. Moreover, some argue that the commitment to the maintenance of the alliance for Australian security even encouraged the government to grant concessions to the United States in other areas of policy. This was a common suggestion regarding the 2004 Australia–US Free Trade Agreement (AUSFTA), which critics argued overwhelmingly favored American economic interests.[11]

It was the extent of Australia's commitment to the US alliance – one founded upon a fundamental sense of anxiety about Australian security and a narrowly defined conception of Australian values and the national interest – that saw Australian troops lining up alongside other members of the 'coalition of the willing' in Afghanistan and Iraq. The Howard government would deny that its conception of 'maintaining' the alliance equated to blind support for all elements of US foreign policy, but the notion of an umbilical conception of the alliance under the Howard government was certainly a prominent criticism from a range of analysts of Australian foreign policy, especially after 2001.[12] The Foreign Minister's admission in 2004 that Australia could not afford to risk the alliance (and Australian security) by not participating in intervention in Iraq did little to undermine these accounts of Australian obsequiousness.[13] While based on a narrow, realist conception of the national interest (in which Australia needed military protection in an anarchic world and dangerous regional environment), this support was also based on a narrow conception of Australian national identity.

11 September 2001 and Afghanistan

By coincidence, John Howard was in Washington, DC, on a state visit on 11 September 2001. From his hotel, he could see the smoke rising from the Pentagon, which he had visited the previous day. Although contested, a range of analysts suggest that Howard's presence in the US capital profoundly impacted upon his view of 9/11,[14] a point later acknowledged by Howard himself.[15] In the days that followed, the meaning the Howard government ascribed to the events and their relationship to Australia centered on three themes: the extraordinary nature of the attacks, which ushered in a 'new world'; the need to recognize the events as an attack on the values shared by Australia and the United States; and the need for Australia to show solidarity with the United States.

The suggestion that the 11 September 2001 attacks were extraordinary or exceptional was certainly not limited to the Australian Prime Minister, but his suggestion that the attacks ushered in a new era is significant to note. For Howard, 9/11 marked the end of a post-Cold War innocence and the dawn of a new world: one that was 'new and very dangerous'.[16] This claim of exceptionality permeated subsequent government justifications for a range of policy and practices in the context of the War on Terror, and was certainly employed in justifying military intervention. The same also applies to the suggestion that 9/11 constituted an attack on the shared values of Australians and Americans. While a range of voices in democratic states expressed similar sentiments and offered their solidarity with the people of the US,[17] Howard and the Australian government suggested that these shared values underpinned cooperation in military intervention and, indeed, Australia's broader foreign and security policy considerations. Howard argued that 9/11 was 'an attack on a way of life that we in Australia share in common with the Americans'.[18] He tied this to the idea that 9/11 suggested Australian vulnerability, arguing pointedly the following day that 'Australia is not immune' from terrorist attacks.[19] This expression of concern – whether genuine or invoked for political reasons – about the potential terror threat to Australia was a central feature of the Howard government's approach to the War on Terror and security.

Arguably the most striking theme of Howard's initial response to 9/11 was the emotion and sadness he conveyed. While again not unusual among a range of leaders, what was striking here was the linkage established from sorrow to emotional and then practical solidarity.[20] Again the day after the attacks, Howard noted that

> I think it is important that countries like Australia play a role in identifying ourselves with the Americans. I mean, just because you are big and strong doesn't mean that you can't feel lonely and you can't feel that your heart

has been ripped out. And I think that is [sic] very important, therefore, that Americans know that they have got some really good, reliable friends.[21]

He subsequently made the remarkable promise of Australian assistance to aid America 'in anything they might properly do to respond'.[22]

The promise of support from Howard was confirmed two days later. On 14 September, the Australian government unilaterally invoked the central treaty of the Australia–US alliance: the ANZUS treaty. This was a surprising move, not least as it was the first time since its inception in 1951 that ANZUS had been invoked, and that the original terms of the treaty quite clearly applied to defense issues in the Pacific Ocean. For Howard, this invocation was necessary to demonstrate the extent of Australian solidarity – a 'determination on our part to identify with the Americans' – and to reaffirm the belief that the 9/11 attacks constituted acts of war, which (under ANZUS) were manifestations of a common threat.[23]

The determination to assist the United States in this 'war' did not waver as attention turned to the Taliban regime in Afghanistan. While the Bush administration made the case that a military operation to remove the Taliban was legal and legitimate as an act of self-defense, the Australian government prepared its military for action. In late November and early December 2001, the government deployed 122 troops to Afghanistan, sending 1,550 military personnel by the end of major combat operations. In terms of its commitment to the overall invasion (Operation Enduring Freedom) and occupation (International Security Assistance Force) effort, such a military presence was relatively limited. This suggests that Australia's central contribution was ultimately toward perceptions of the intervention's credibility or legitimacy, an argument even more applicable to the later intervention in, and occupation of, Iraq.[24]

For the Australian government, the 'intellectual case'[25] for Australian participation in Afghanistan was the necessity of a strong international response to the threat posed by a state leadership (the Taliban) willing to sponsor the parties responsible for 9/11: al-Qaeda led by Osama bin Laden. Howard was eager to establish that military means were necessary tools for redressing this threat. Citing the lessons of historical appeasement learnt from the failure at Munich (which he would do again in justifying military action against Iraq), Howard asserted that 'passive indifference in the face of evil achieves absolutely nothing'.[26] More significantly, however, Howard defined the need for Australian participation in Afghanistan as 'an expression of Australia's strong commitment and strong desire to share with the American people a common defence of things we treasure together'.[27] In defining the 9/11 attacks as an attack on the values Australians shared with Americans, Howard suggested that Australia was compelled to participate in Afghanistan because Australians are 'a people prepared to fight our own fights'.[28] By participating in US-led intervention in Afghanistan, Australia would 'be seen to have played its part' in responding to 9/11 and defending the shared core values that were attacked that day.[29] Over the coming years, Howard consistently suggested that these values were under threat in a new age of terror, even on Australia's 'doorstep'.

Regional 'deputy sheriff'

Intervention in Afghanistan and Iraq were certainly the core War on Terror interventions in which the Australian government participated; but it is also important to note a series of smaller-scale regional interventions after 2001, particularly in the Solomon Islands in 2003. These interventions were under-pinned by the language (if not the concerns) of failed states providing a fertile ground for terrorist activity. And this new 'interventionism' was enabled by the elaboration and enactment of similar principles by the United States and the broader international climate of the War on Terror. Although Howard had cer-tainly indicated earlier a willingness to intervene in the immediate region – evident in the suggestion that Australia could act as the US' 'regional deputy' – the context of the War on Terror provided particular opportunities for acting in this way.

Successive Australian governments have broadly accepted the position of regional leader in the South Pacific, although have long experienced difficulty reconciling a sense of obligation to island states in the region with accusations of acting as a hegemon in dealings with its smaller neighbors. Foreign Minister Downer consistently acknowledged this tension, noting that: 'Australia has a strong commitment and devotes substantial resources to the South Pacific region. It is not, however, the region's policeman.'[30]

While this view continued to be elaborated until mid-2003, a precedent for a shift in policy was established with the 1999 intervention in East Timor. This intervention was in response to Indonesian-government-supported militias' attacks on the people and towns of East Timor after their 1999 referendum on self-determination. The success of the peace-keeping intervention under Austral-ian leadership was viewed as something of a vindication for the Howard govern-ment's willingness to take on a more prominent and forceful regional role. The intervention – backed by a United Nations Security Council resolution, the United States and ultimately (if under coercion) invited by Indonesia – was widely hailed as a success despite its damage to regional relations.[31] As noted, intervention was followed by the Howard government's attempt to define its regional role as that of the US's 'deputy sheriff'.

After 2001, the Howard government built on growing concerns about the need to ensure stability and strong governance in the Pacific by linking the threat of terrorism to that of 'failed states'.[32] The idea of failed states – characterized by a lack of control by central government over its people and territory – as a haven for terrorist activities became a prominent theme in the War on Terror dis-course generally. The 2003 DFAT White Paper noted that 'South Pacific nations, particularly those weakened by internal division and poor governance, are vulnerable to the activities of terrorists and so are an important target of the Gov-ernment's assistance programs'.[33]

This language was especially prominent in 2003 and particularly applied to the Solomon Islands, which had been suffering from internal conflict and ele-ments of lawlessness since 1998 that had escalated significantly in the first half of 2003. The Australian Strategic Policy Institute (ASPI) – a policy-oriented think tank – was commissioned by the government to complete a report on the Solomon Islands in the same year, which concluded that states such as the Solomons risked becoming 'a Petri dish in which transnational and non-state security threats can develop and breed'.[34] Although the government initially ruled out intervention (involved as they were in preparation for intervention in Iraq), Howard became convinced of the merits of leading an intervening force and hastily put one together in June–July.

The intervention in the Solomon Islands – Operation Helpem Fren, or the Regional Assistance Mission to the Solomon Islands (RAMSI) – was invited by Solomons Prime Minister Allan Kamekaza and its goal was to protect the government, establish law and order, and disarm militia groups. Commencing in July 2003, the multinational force led by Australia was again relatively small: initially involving 300 police supported by 1,700 military personnel. After this initial, ultimately successful, phase the emphasis shifted to broader reconstruction and nation-building. But the significance of Australia's Solomons intervention for our purposes is that it can be understood less as an attempt to address instability, violence and its relationship to deprivation for its own sake than as a tool for advancing Australian security and stability in the context of the War on Terror. Greg Fry notes that the government consistently invoked concerns about Australian security – tied to the danger of failed states and terrorism – in justifying the need for military intervention.[35]

The commitment to action to preserve security on 'our patch' was evident in smaller post-2001 interventions in Papua New Guinea and Nauru, and in the government's relatively belligerent position on regional security through the Pacific Islands Forum.[36] It was also evident in Howard's post-Bali declaration that Australia would be willing to launch a pre-emptive strike against terrorists in nearby states if there was evidence they were preparing an attack. This suggestion (interpreted by neighbors in Southeast Asia as a veiled threat) would have been all but unthinkable before the elaboration of the parallel 'Bush Doctrine' in 2002.

The War on Terror created a context in which Australia was able to pursue a more robust, militaristic approach to regional relations, conducted largely according to the government's own concerns about national security. Even the multinational nature of intervention in the Solomons belies what Michael O'Keefe has described as a form of 'hegemonic multilateralism' in Australia's own 'coalition of the willing'.[37] And, as O'Keefe goes on to suggest, Australia's approach to regional intervention was underpinned by a conception of identity that encouraged a view of the region – and ultimately of cultural and ethnic difference – as a potential source of threat. For Howard, such threats vindicated a commitment to military action where necessary, and in particular a commitment to support for US foreign policy initiatives in a new and dangerous world. Of course, nowhere was the extent of this support more evident than with the Australian decision to participate in intervention in Iraq.

Iraq

In his January 2002 State of the Union Address, President Bush infamously asserted that Iraq, Iran and North Korea formed an international 'axis of evil'. While some reports suggest an early determination in elements of the administration to link 9/11 directly to the Saddam Hussein regime, ultimately Iraq was excluded from the initial response.[38] Nevertheless, with the overthrow of the Taliban regime in Afghanistan receiving almost unprecedented international support, the United States saw an opportunity to pursue regime change in Iraq, eventually defining the 2003 intervention as a central part of the War on Terror.

Throughout 2002 and in early 2003, Prime Minister Howard continued to express solidarity with the United States and noted Australia's willingness to actively support the US in the War on Terror, a position that did not change as the administration increasingly defined Iraq as part of that 'war'. While not formally committing Australia to participation in the Iraq War until the eve of the conflict, a number of accounts suggest that Howard had come to a private agreement with President Bush some time in mid-2002 that Australian troops would participate in a future intervention.[39] Certainly, from an early stage the government echoed the core elements of the American case for intervention. The initial emphasis in John Howard's argument for strong action against Iraq was similar to that of other (eventual) participant states: Saddam Hussein's failure to meet disarmament obligations (established under UN Security Council Resolution 687 in 1991 and reiterated through Resolution 1441 of November 2002). This was evident in Foreign Minister Downer's suggestion (on the eve of intervention) that 'the disarmament of Iraq' constituted the 'unfinished business of the 1991 Gulf War'.[40] Prior to March 2003, however, the Australian government suggested that responsibility for a strong response to the threat to international security posed by Iraq rested with the United Nations. For Howard, it was clear that Iraq was in 'possession of agents of warfare, both biological and chemical, and also [had] an aspiration to develop a nuclear capacity'.[41] In this context, the UN was compelled to adopt a strong stance regarding Iraq in the interests of preserving international peace and stability. Increasingly, the Australian government defined this threat in the context of the broader War on Terror.

In October 2002, 202 people, including 88 Australians, were killed in the bombing of an Indonesian nightclub on the island of Bali. Denouncing the bombing, and ultimately suggesting that Australian tourists were a target, Howard reaffirmed Australian commitment to the War on Terror and the values that underpinned it:

> We reaffirm again our commitment to … an Australian community bound together by common values of openness, individual liberty and individual freedom. We fight terrorism because we love freedom; we fight terrorism because we want to preserve the way of life that this country has; we fight terrorism because we share the values of other countries that are in the war against terrorism; and we fight terrorism because it is intrinsically evil.[42]

Through notions of shared values under attack, Howard drew stark distinctions between the 'indescribable savagery' of the bombing and 'the civilized world'. The world leaders he chose to speak of when making this distinction were telling: George W. Bush, British Prime Minister Tony Blair, New Zealand Prime Minister Helen Clark and Her Majesty the Queen. Clearly, for Howard, the new times that 9/11 heralded were thrown into even starker relief after Bali. However, these new times and the new threats they posed were to be faced alongside Australia's traditional allies.

The following month, asserting that the Bali bombing strengthened Australia's commitment to fight and defeat terrorism, Howard addressed the question, 'Why Iraq?' In answering, he drew upon two themes that would be used repeatedly in the run up to intervention. First, Howard stressed, 'Iraq has form'.[43] This 'form' comprised of Iraq's history of using WMD and supporting terrorist groups. Second, Howard outlined a key tenet of the post-9/11 mindset and the doctrine of pre-emption: the nightmare scenario of WMD developed by rogue states falling into the hands of terrorist groups. Although only a powerful additional reason for intervention in late 2002, this possibility would become increasingly central to folding Iraq into the War on Terror, and featured prominently in the 2003 DFAT White Paper.[44]

In early 2003, while the Howard government was still suggesting it had not developed a position on involvement in intervention, the international debate surrounding Iraq intensified. Hans Blix reported on Iraqi weapons inspections to the UN Security Council in late January, citing a lack of cooperation but no 'smoking gun'. Howard asserted that the report was damning, with the few concessions that had been made achieved only because of pre-positioned forces, which Australia had contributed to.[45]

From January to March, breach of UNSC resolutions remained central to the Australian government's position on the need for strong action against Iraq. Representing the interchangeable 'world community', the 'community of nations' or 'international community', Howard like Blair pushed strongly to secure an eighteenth resolution from the Security Council specifically enabling intervention. As the chances of achieving the resolution waned, Howard began to suggest that the UN had lost some degree of legitimacy and credibility, and denigrated those within the UNSC (especially France) blocking the way of this resolution. He argued that disarmament of Iraq could not occur 'if we continue to have spoiling tactics from, say, the French, who appear intent on saying no to everything irrespective of its merit'.[46]

Replacing the specific breach of UNSC resolutions, the second and third strands of Howard's argument came to the fore. Increasingly, intervention in Iraq was presented as both part of the War on Terror and necessary for humanitarian reasons. The latter, although remaining supplementary in the run-up to intervention, would become increasingly significant in the war's aftermath as it became apparent no WMD would be found. Howard listed numerous examples of human rights atrocities in Iraq to argue that human rights considerations required the pursuit of regime change.[47]

In the lead up to intervention, integrating Iraq into the War on Terror was a more central and difficult task than justifying intervention with recourse to humanitarian concerns. At its most explicit and succinct, Howard represented a nightmare scenario that linked Iraq as a rogue state to WMD proliferation and terrorism:

> If a country like Iraq is allowed to keep chemical and biological weapons, inevitably other rogue states will want to do the same thing. And as the number of rogue states possessing those weapons increases, the possibility of them falling into the hands of terrorist organizations multiplies.[48]

The determination to link Iraq with the War on Terror was also evident in Howard's controversial attempt to link the 2002 Bali bombings to intervention in Iraq: 'We lost 88 Australians in Bali because of a willful act of international terrorism ... and I will, amongst other things, be asking Australians to bear those circumstances in mind if we become involved in military conflict with Iraq.'[49]

In the more dangerous post-9/11 and post-Bali world, the Australian government suggested that military intervention in Iraq was necessary so as to 'make it less likely that a devastating terrorist attack will be carried out against Australia'.[50] In this sense, Howard argued that Australia was a target for terrorists because it 'is a Western country with Western values'.[51] On the eve of war, intervention in Iraq was justified to secure Australia and protect the (Western) values of Australians as part of the War on Terror. In mid-March 2003, Australia committed 2000 Defence Force personnel to 'Operation Iraqi Freedom'. While again a relatively small component of the intervening force, this commitment was important in adding credibility or legitimacy to the conflict itself, and in the face of domestic and international opposition, tells us much about the Howard government's conception of Australian identity and security.

Identity and intervention: Howard's Australia

As the preceding analysis suggests, representations of Australia's history, beliefs and 'core values' were central to the processes through which military intervention became thinkable, and to the processes through which these interventions were sold.[52] Security itself can be seen as the definition of a group's core values, the threats to those values and the means available to protect or advance them. This section outlines the Howard government's conception of Australian identity in broad terms before turning to the question of how specific narratives of Australian history, culture and identity were employed in the context of justifying military intervention as part of the War on Terror.

Howard's Australia

Much has been written about John Howard's attempt to redefine Australian identity while Prime Minister, much of it beginning with the observation that Howard had come to power suggesting that there was little need for Australia to grapple with its identity at all.[53] What soon became clear was that Howard was rejecting the need for *debate* about Australian identity, suggesting instead that there was an essence of Australianness (defined in terms of 'mateship' and founded upon sacrifice in war) of which all genuine Australians were intuitively aware.[54] In the process, Howard not only advanced his own particular (narrow) conception of Australian identity, but also claimed 'the last word' on the composition of that identity, limiting scope for debate about the nature of Australian values and their relationship to practices carried out in the name of 'Australia'.[55]

John Howard's conception of Australian identity can be defined in broad terms as traditional, conservative and individualistic, one founded on cultural and historical ties to the Anglosphere (particularly Britain and the United States) and participation (and sacrifice) in the two world wars. The latter were central to justifications for intervention in the War on Terror, with Howard emphasizing the importance of being part of a Western community of nations and invoking the blood spilt by Australian soldiers in the world wars. Howard used the idea of membership of this Western community – with natural cultural ties to the UK and US – both as a lens through which to view the nature of threats in world politics and as a basis for foreign and security policy action. As noted, he asserted that terrorism was 'an enemy of Australia because of who we are, not what we have done',[56] a claim reiterated by Foreign Minister Downer in launching Australia's White Paper on the nature of the transnational terrorism threat.[57] In broader terms, the emphasis in security policy on cultural ties to 'great and powerful friends' – and more specifically the security protection required by Australia and provided by the US – was linked to an increasing tendency to view the immediate region as a source of threat.[58] This visceral anxiety about the region was in part founded upon a particular set of (realist) assumptions about world politics, but also suggests a tendency to locate threat in ethnic and cultural difference both within and outside Australia.[59] This stood in contrast to the previous government's attempts to define Australia as a multi-cultural state that was part of the Asian region.

Defining Australia ultimately as a 'Western nation' enabled Howard to explain the nature of threat to Australia and to justify traditionalist foreign policy as the best means to ensure Australian security.[60] Although elaborated more frequently and forcefully in the period after 2001, the tendency to view foreign and security policy in terms of values shared with 'great and powerful friends' had been a core dimension of Australian foreign policy since 1996.[61] Critics of the centrality of a narrowing 'cultural identity' to foreign policy have noted linkages to Australia's xenophobic past. For Camilleri:

> Howard's international conception in part reflects a deeper sense of White Australia's cultural and racial identity.... Howard's conception of the world mirrors his image of Australia. When he speaks of Australia's 'national character', of its 'distinct and enduring values', and of 'an Australian way', he is using code language to refer to key aspects of the white Anglo-Australian heritage.[62]

The narrowing and exclusion at the heart of John Howard's conception of Australian identity was therefore significantly tied to an interpretation of identity that emphasized Australia's white, Anglo-heritage. This was given its key historical expression, for Howard, in the deaths of 8,000 Australian soldiers at Gallipoli in Turkey in 1915 on what became known and celebrated annually as 'ANZAC Day'. For Howard, ANZAC Day commemorated the birth of Australia as a nation, while the specific battle against overwhelming odds illustrated the principles of 'mateship' that would come to provide the foundation for Howard's view of Australianness.[63] A range of critics have argued that under Howard the overwhelming primacy given to the ANZAC myth (the foundation of the Australian nation through brave sacrifice in blood) has dangerously narrowed Australian national identity and the scope to debate Australian history or identity.[64] Indeed, Mark McKenna argues that, in this context

> We are witnessing the narrowing of our national mythology to one key legend that encapsulates our values, defines the moment of our nation's birth and gives rise to a military tradition within which those values and ideals are given their most profound expression.[65]

We would argue that Howard particularly emphasized this conception of Australian identity and history in the context of the War on Terror, employing it to justify military intervention.

Narratives of identity and interventionism

Domestic support for – or at least acquiescence to – Australian interventions in the War on Terror was enabled through the recurrent narratives of identity and history that the Australian government drew upon. Howard in particular drew upon a series of narratives of Australian history, culture and identity specifically in the context of justifying intervention. The notion of 'mateship' was deployed to suggest a commitment to standing shoulder-to-shoulder with core allies, especially in battle; the idea of Australia's membership in the West and shared values with the US and UK served a similar purpose, while also suggesting the need for intervention as a form of 'self defense' of those values; while the ANZAC myth was particularly deployed to suggest the need for Australians to show courage and make the difficult decision to fight for the cause of good. These mutually reinforcing narratives – derived from a broader traditionalist conception of Australian identity – were central to the process through which intervention was justified.

'Mateship'

In a mid-2002 address on the War on Terror to a joint session of US Congress, John Howard emphasized the importance in the Australian character of 'mateship', a concept he unsuccessfully attempted to incorporate into the preamble of the Australian constitution. For Howard, 'mateship' in the context of the War on Terror meant standing shoulder-to-shoulder with friends, particularly in times of need. And 9/11 constituted a moment in which 'mates' needed to come forward to offer their support. Having fought 'side by side in every major conflict of the twentieth century' with the US, after 9/11 'Australia was immediately there to help'.[66] Howard suggested that Australia and the US were 'able to count on each other when it has mattered most',[67] while Bush obliged in turn by indicating that he was 'proud to call [Howard] my friend'.[68]

As Gleeson has noted, *emotional* solidarity in the context of 9/11 shifted to (or was conflated with) a notion of *practical* solidarity in the context of the War on Terror.[69] The Australian government built upon genuine sympathy for Americans with the tragedy of 9/11 to make a case for Australian participation in military intervention, using the language of 'mateship' in justifying this cooperation. In the immediate response to 9/11, Howard argued that this was 'an occasion where we should stand shoulder-to-shoulder with the Americans'.[70] By the time the Taliban was overthrown and the case was being made for intervention in Iraq, this representation was one unambiguously tied to a need to participate in military intervention to fight terrorism. As Howard argued, 'you can't fight something like this without standing together with the Americans'.[71] And even in the context of intervention in the South Pacific, the much-maligned suggestion that Australia could act as the US's regional deputy in the region implied a level of solidarity with the broader fight the US was leading. This was also, of course, tied to the shared values being protected or advanced.

Shared values

As noted, Howard and the Australian government consistently represented the 9/11 attacks as an attack on the 'shared values' of Australians and Americans, and described the War on Terror battle itself as one between civilization and barbarism. Here, Howard invoked a particular Western, Anglo-centric narrative of Australian identity to make a case for participation in military intervention in the War on Terror. Addressing US Congress in 2002, Howard argued that: 'Our pioneer past, so similar to your own, has produced a spirit that can overcome adversity and pursue great dreams. We've pursued a society of opportunity, fairness and hope.'[72]

As the case for intervention in Iraq was building, Howard also drew the United Kingdom more directly into representations of shared values:

> I'm a great believer that you should have close relations with the countries whose way of life is closest to your own. And there's not much doubt that when you look around the world it is countries like the United States and the United Kingdom ... where we identify in terms of our values far more readily.[73]

Even in the case of the Solomons, Howard's suggestion that 'the rest of the world expects Australia to shoulder a lot of the burden' positioned its role as that of taking 'responsibility to manage the security threat on behalf of the West'.[74]

As noted, the definition of security and national interests in terms of values and identity was a feature of the 2003 DFAT White Paper, released in the weeks preceding intervention in Iraq. Such representations certainly reinforce the idea that Australia should cooperate closely with the US (and the UK), including in intervention, but also in the process suggests limits to levels of cooperation with those who do not share these values, and even the possibility of viewing those 'outside' as threats. It is certainly possible to suggest that the continued attempt to identify Anglo, Western states as those with whom Australia identified rendered military intervention in culturally and ethnically different societies (such as those of the South Pacific or Middle East) more politically palatable. Importantly, the legitimization of forms of racism in Australian public life since the arrival of Pauline Hanson in the mid-1990s ensured that this vision of 'self' and 'other' in the War on Terror found some resonance in the broader Australian population.

ANZAC

If 'mateship' and shared values with Anglo-Western states were central to the Howard government's vision of Australia and its place in the world, the ANZAC myth provided the central historical reference point for the foundation of those values. While drawing together core elements of both the other narratives, particularly important here is the notion of Australia standing up to protect core values. Given the power of the ANZAC legend – even its status under Howard as a hegemonic myth of Australian identity – the definition of War on Terror intervention as an extension or manifestation of the ANZAC legend was a particularly powerful representational strategy.[75]

The idea of reluctant but brave participation in conflict – central to the representation of the ANZAC myth – was prominent in justifications for intervention in Afghanistan, the Solomon Islands and Iraq. On the day after 9/11, Howard suggested that 'This is an occasion where everybody's got to stand up and be counted and everybody who cares about the sort of life we like to take for granted and perhaps never should in our own country'.[76]

In the case of the Solomon Islands, Howard noted the need for Australia 'to do our fair share of the heavy lifting' in leading the intervening force.[77] And in the case of Iraq, he suggested that '[no] Australian wants unnecessary military conflict but … we have to take a stand'.[78] As the attempt to justify intervention in Iraq gained pace, Howard reiterated the claim central to the ANZAC myth: that the Australian nation was itself established through sacrifice in war. He suggested that 'We are fighting now for the same values the ANZACs fought for in 1915: courage, valor, mateship, decency [and] a willingness as a nation to do the right thing, whatever the cost'.[79]

While the ANZAC legend was central to justifications for intervention, Howard's commitment to this legend as the core of the Australian nation was evident a year later in addressing troops in Iraq on ANZAC Day in 2004:

> You are seeking to bring to the people of Iraq, who have suffered so much for so long, the hope of liberty and the hope of freedom, and your example, your behavior, your values, belong to that great and long tradition that was forged on the beaches of Gallipoli in 1915.[80]

These narratives – 'mateship', shared values with Western states and the ANZAC myth – were of course mutually reinforcing, based on a broader traditionalist conception of Australian identity. In justifying intervention in Afghanistan, the South Pacific and Iraq, Australia's commitment to 'mateship' meant standing shoulder-to-shoulder with those who shared Australian values, as Australians had done reluctantly but bravely in the face of evil in the previous century. This particular construction of Australian identity served to justify interventionism in the War on Terror and helped achieve the support or at least acquiescence required from the Australian people.[81] However, although certainly dominant and underpinning the most important foreign and security policy action on behalf of 'Australia', such a narrative and its linkage to the present did not go unchallenged.

The war of position

If foreign and security policy is, as we would argue, a site of competing articulations of a group's core values, threats to those values and the means of preserving or advancing them, then the government's articulation of Australian identity regarding intervention is only part of the story. What also needs to be understood is how such a narrative came to 'win out' over alternatives. Of course the position and mandate of Prime Minister Howard and his government is central in this regard, but so too is the capacity to marginalize and silence alternative accounts of Australian identity and of its relationship to contemporary practices (such as military intervention). A range of political parties, non-governmental organizations, journalists and academics directly contested different dimensions of the Australian government's involvement in the War on Terror, articulating in the process different narratives of Australian history, culture and identity.[82] But these accounts ultimately failed in the short-term to resonate sufficiently with the Australian population to precipitate major policy change or the loss of the government's legitimacy, notwithstanding majority public opposition to intervention in Iraq at the point of invasion.[83] This failure was related to the government's successful framing of opponents as unpatriotic or unconcerned about Australian security; to the power of a broader discourse of post-2001 fear and insecurity; and to support for the government's position by important actors and constituencies both domestically and internationally.

The willingness of the Howard government to narrow the scope of public debate has already been noted in the context of Howard's own views on public dialogue about the composition of Australian identity.[84] In the War on Terror context, the government was willing and able to position opponents of various interventions as unpatriotic and even 'un-Australian'. In the case of the former, those opposing intervention in Iraq, for example, were at times likened to appeasers of Hitler in World War II: unwilling to 'stand up' for values and key freedoms at stake, and prepared to allow a dictator's brutal regime to remain in power.[85] The emphasis on core and shared values generally in justifying intervention also arguably created a situation in which critics were less able to demur from the government without questioning those values themselves. This is suggested in Mark McKenna's analysis of the ways in which the ANZAC myth was employed to justify military intervention.[86] And the suggestion of the need to 'support our troops' also invoked memories of Vietnam, when public anger with Australian participation in that conflict in 1970s saw protesters target returning personnel. Here, outspoken opposition was positioned as disloyal to those risking their lives in theaters of war. At all of these levels, the government's representations of the need for intervention also involved narrowing the space for debate about intervention or the values being protected or advanced.

The fear and anxiety that permeated the government's discourse of security generally – and the War on Terror specifically – also mitigated against strong opposition to intervention. The government's continued reference to imminent terrorist threats to Australia posed by fundamentalist Islamic terrorists (from failed states, rogue states, inattentive regional neighbors and even insufficient public concern) suggested the need for a 'militarized vigilance' in the face of the dangers of terrorism. This fear was arguably furthered through public information campaigns asking Australians to play their role in monitoring each other and readying themselves for a terrorist apocalypse;[87] in constant references to the new and dangerous time and international context in which Australia found itself; and in the suggestion that Australia's best hope for long-term survival as a nation was to align itself closely to its 'great and powerful friend' – the United States. Control of access to official intelligence is important in this regard, especially given arguably disproportionate representations of the threat posed by 'failing states' and the selective use of intelligence regarding Iraq's WMD program in justifying intervention in Iraq.[88]

Finally, the position of the government's conception of security and identity was also strengthened by the reiteration and/or support of its central claims by other key actors. Most directly, in the month after 9/11 the leader of the opposition, Kim Beazley, echoed key governmental representations of the attacks and the nature of Australia's obligations in the War on Terror:

> September the 11th has changed the way we nations now think about security and what we have to do to defend ourselves. We have to stand shoulder to shoulder with George Bush and Tony Blair to root out and destroy international terrorism.[89]

Here, core features of the Howard government's justification for military intervention in the War on Terror (membership in the West, the need to stand 'shoulder to shoulder' with these allies, the new and threatening post-9/11 world, and the need for a robust response) were reiterated by the key political alternative to the conservative coalition in Australia. And when the Australian Labor Party later attempted to dissociate its approach with that of the government, in arguing for the withdrawal of all troops in Iraq in the lead-up to the 2004 Australian election, the American Ambassador to Australia joined President Bush in criticizing this policy. The Howard government seized on these comments to suggest that a change of government would jeopardize the alliance, arguing that the ALP's foreign policy reflected a 'visceral, irrational anti-Americanism'.[90]

Domestically, Howard's broader identity and security project built upon the right-wing, nationalist and xenophobic politics of independent Member of Parliament Pauline Hanson, who had come to prominence in the Australian political scene in the mid-1990s, claiming that Australia risked being 'swamped by Asians'. Indeed, the conception of security and identity so central to the Howard government's hard-line on asylum-seekers and its conception of the region as a source of threat built in important ways on the political agenda articulated by Hanson. These voices provided crucial ballast to the Australian government's conception of security and identity, allowing the government to strengthen its policy position and (further) marginalize critics.

Conclusion

Australia's participation in intervention in the War on Terror cannot be understood without attention to the role of identity. For all of the Howard government's initial attempts to suggest that Australian foreign policy would thenceforth operate on the basis of a hard-headed pursuit of the national interest, it has been consistently and abundantly clear that a particular conception of Australian identity has provided the lens through which the Howard government has approached the world, and crucially a reservoir of resources which it has used to justify military intervention in the War on Terror.[91] Howard's conception of Australia as a white, Western country (ultimately in an alien regional environment) underpinned the commitment to the US alliance that was to take Australia from Afghanistan to Iraq and give Howard the confidence to pursue an interventionist foreign policy in the South Pacific (one based paradoxically on anxiety about the region as a source of threat). Perhaps the most telling single government statement in understanding Australia's participation in intervention in Iraq (albeit after one avenue for justification – the presence of a WMD program – had become unsustainable) was Foreign Minister Downer's indication in 2004 that

> It wasn't a time in our history to have a great and historic breach with the United States. If we were to walk away from the American alliance it would leave us as a country very vulnerable and very open, particularly given the environment we have with terrorism in South-East Asia, [and] the North Korean issue.[92]

The world, and in particular Australia's region, were dangerous; Australia needed its 'great and powerful friend' to protect it; and participation in the war in Iraq was the 'insurance' premium required for ensuring this protection.[93]

The point we would make here is that there is nothing inevitable about this interpretation of the world, the region, Australian values or the nature of the US alliance. A range of analyses have consistently suggested that the extent of the threat posed by terrorism has been overstated, while others (including key bodies within government) have concluded that Australia's military interventions in the War on Terror actually makes it more likely that Australia will be targeted.[94] Even if the idea that the region constitutes a source of threat is accepted, it does not follow necessarily that the use or threat of military intervention serves to mitigate against this threat. And it is certainly not clear that the US alliance – again, even if accepted as necessary for Australian security – can only be maintained through active diplomatic and military support for all US foreign and security policy initiatives.

Finally, Howard's interpretation of Australian values and invocation of them to justify intervention must be recognized as just that: an interpretation. There is no core, timeless essence of Australian identity, even while some myths (ANZAC, for example) are particularly sedimented and resonant in the national imagination. At different points in time (including under the current Labor government), dominant narratives of Australian identity have emphasized multiculturalism and egalitarianism as key values of the Australian self, applied to reconciliation with indigenous populations, a more humane immigration and asylum policy, and the expansion of the welfare state. In foreign policy terms, different governments (again, including the current Labor government) have articulated the need to consider foreign policy interests from outside the straightjacket of the US alliance, and have suggested that Australian interests and security can best be advanced through constructive regional engagement and the pursuit of 'middle power' diplomacy in an international society of states. And, of course, even sedimented narratives of identity (e.g. the ANZAC sacrifice as the birth of the Australian nation) can be applied in different ways to contemporary events, to point to the need to avoid the bloodshed of war wherever possible, or the dangers of foreign policy tied to the interests of 'great and powerful friends'.[95] John Howard has not had the 'last word' on Australian identity, but coming to terms with his conception of Australian identity is crucial to making sense of the government's approach to Australian security and the processes through which intervention in the War on Terror became possible for Australia.

Notes

1 This chapter draws upon research undertaken for an ESRC-funded project (RES-000–22–2126) involving Matt McDonald and Richard Jackson, led from the University of Warwick. This broader project explores justifications for intervention in Afghanistan and Iraq by the leaders of the US, UK and Australia. We are grateful to Matt Merefield for his excellent research work as part of this project and for his

comments on this chapter. Jack Holland would like to acknowledge and thank the John W. Kluge Center at the Library of Congress, Washington, DC, for providing an excellent environment in which to conduct this research.

2 See G. Evans and B. Grant, *Australia's Foreign Relations in the World of the 1990s* (2nd ed.) (Melbourne: Melbourne University Press, 1995); and A. Linklater, 'What is a Good International Citizen?', in P. Keal (ed.), *Ethics and Foreign Policy* (Sydney: Allen and Unwin, 1992).

3 See S. Philpott, S, 'Fear of the Dark: Indonesia and the Australian National Imagination', *Australian Journal of International Affairs*, 55:3 (2001), pp. 371–388; and A. Burke, *Fear of Security: Australia's Invasion Anxiety* (Melbourne: Cambridge University Press, 2008), pp. 150–168.

4 A. Downer, 'Advancing the National Interest', Speech to the National Press Club, 7 May 2002.

5 M. McDonald, 'Constructing Insecurity: Australian Security Discourse and Policy Post-2001', *International Relations*, 19:3 (2005), pp. 297–320.

6 AUSMIN, 'Sydney Statement. Australia–US: A Strategic Partnership for the 21st Century', Joint Security Declaration (1996), www.dfat.gov.au/geo/us/ausmin/sydney_statement.html.

7 A. Downer, 'Australia's Alliance with the United States: Maintaining the "Fabric of Peace"', speech to the Australia–United States Alliance and East Asian Security Conference, Sydney, 29 June 2001.

8 See R. Leaver, 'The Meanings, Origins and Implications of the Howard Doctrine', *The Pacific Review*, 14:1 (2001), pp. 15–34.

9 See G. Fry and T. Kabutaulaka (eds.), *Intervention and State-Building in the Pacific* (Manchester: Manchester University Press, 2008).

10 DFAT, *Advancing the National Interest: Australia's Foreign and Trade Policy White Paper* (Canberra: Commonwealth of Australia, 2003), p. xvi.

11 L. Weiss, E. Thurbon and J. Matthews, *How to Kill a Country: Australia's Devastating Trade Deal with the United States* (Sydney: Allen and Unwin, 2004); A. Capling, *All the Way with the USA: Australia, United States and Free Trade* (Sydney: University of New South Wales Press, 2005).

12 For example, M. Beeson, 'Australia's Relationship with the United States: The Case for Greater Independence', *Australian Journal of Political Science*, 38:3 (2003), pp. 387–405; Burke, *Fear of Security*; J. George, 'Will the Chickenhawks Come Home to Roost?', *Australian Journal of International Affairs*, 57:2 (2003), pp. 235–242; K. Lee Koo, 'Terror Australis: Security, Australia and the "War on Terror" Discourse', *Borderlands* E-journal, 4:1 (2005), www.borderlands.net.au/vol.4no1_2005/leekoo_terror.htm.

13 T. Allard, 'Going to War Secured US Alliance, Says Downer', *Sydney Morning Herald*, 3 March 2004.

14 For example, D. Debats, T. McDonald and M. Williams, 'Mr. Howard Goes to Washington: September 11, the Australian–American Relationship and Attributes of Leadership', *Australian Journal of Political Science*, 42:2 (2007), pp. 231–251; R. Garran, *True Believer: John Howard, George Bush and the American Alliance* (Sydney: Allen and Unwin, 2004); K. Gleeson, 'Australia and the Construction of the War on Terror'. Paper presented at International Studies Association Conference, San Francisco, 26–29 March 2008.

15 J. Howard, *Address to the National Press Club*, 11 September 2002.

16 J. Howard, Television Interview with Ray Martin, *60 Minutes*, Channel 9, 16 September 2001.

17 See E. Guittet, 'European Political Identity and Democratic Solidarity After 9/11', *Alternatives*, 29:4 (2004), pp. 441–464.

18 J. Howard, Interview with Mike Munro, *A Current Affair*, Network Nine, 12 September 2001.

19 J. Howard, Press Conference, Ambassadors' Residence, Washington, DC, 12 September 2001.
20 Gleeson, 'Australia and the Construction of the War on Terror'.
21 J. Howard, Press Conference, Ambassadors' Residence, Washington, DC, 12 September 2001.
22 J. Howard, Interview with John Laws, Radio 2UE, 12 September 2001.
23 J. Howard, Joint Press Conference with the Deputy Prime Minister and the Minister for Foreign Affairs, Parliament House, Canberra, 14 September 2001.
24 See J. Verrier, 'Australia's Self-Image as a Regional and International Security Actor: Some Implications of the Iraq War', *Australian Journal of International Affairs*, 57:3 (2003), p. 461; R. Bell, 'Extreme Allies: Australia and the USA', in J. Cotton and J. Ravenhill (eds.), *Trading on Alliance Security: Australia in World Affairs, 2001–5* (Oxford: Oxford University Press, 2007), p. 28.
25 Howard argued that there was an 'intellectual case for a commitment as well as the strong conceptual and emotional case for involvement'. J. Howard, Press Conference Prior to the Deployment of SAS Troops, Sheridan Hotel, Perth, 22 October 2001.
26 J. Howard, Speech to the Australian Defence Association, Melbourne, 25 October 2001.
27 J. Howard, Press Conference, Melbourne, 17 October 2001.
28 J. Howard, Speech to the Australian Defence Association, Melbourne, 25 October 2001.
29 Ibid.
30 Cited in A. Regan and R. May, 'Reassessing Australia's Role in Papua New Guinea and the Island Pacific', in J. Cotton and J. Ravenhill (eds.), *The National Interest in a Global Era* (Oxford: Oxford University Press, 2001), pp. 150–151.
31 Space precludes a discussion of the context and development of intervention in East Timor. On Australian foreign policy regarding East Timor and Indonesia, and on the crisis itself, see C. Fernandes, *Reluctant Saviour: Australia, Indonesia and the Independence of East Timor* (Melbourne: Scribe, 2004); and Burke, *Fear of Security*, chapters 4 and 5.
32 On the former, see Regan and May, 'Reassessing Australia's Role in Papua New Guinea and the Island Pacific'; on the latter, see B. Greener-Barcham and M. Barcham, 'Terrorism in the South Pacific? Thinking Critically About Approaches to Security in the Region', *Australian Journal of International Affairs*, 60:1 (2006), pp. 67–82; and M. O'Keefe, 'Australia and Fragile States in the Pacific', in J. Cotton and J. Ravenhill (eds.), *Trading on Alliance Security: Australia in World Affairs, 2001–5* (Oxford: Oxford University Press, 2007).
33 DFAT, *Advancing the National Interest: Australia's Foreign and Trade Policy White Paper* (Canberra: Commonwealth of Australia, 2003), p. 38.
34 Cited in Fry, Greg, '"Our Patch": The War on Terror and the New Interventionism', in G. Fry and T. Kabutaulaka (eds.), *Intervention and State-Building in the Pacific* (Manchester: Manchester University Press, 2008).
35 Ibid., see also O'Keefe, 'Australia and Fragile States in the Pacific', pp. 146–147.
36 Fry, 'Our Patch'; O'Keefe, 'Australia and Fragile States in the Pacific'.
37 O'Keefe, 'Australia and Fragile States in the Pacific', p. 145.
38 See B. Woodward, *Bush at War* (New York: Simon and Schuster, 2002).
39 For example, T. Kevin, 'Australia's Secret Pre-Emptive War Against Iraq', *Australian Journal of International Affairs*, 58:3 (2004), pp. 318–336.
40 Cited in B. O'Connor, 'Perspectives on Australian Foreign Policy, 2003', *Australian Journal of International Affairs*, 58:2 (2004), p. 209.
41 J. Howard, Address to the National Press Club, 11 September 2002.
42 J. Howard, Address to the Parliament: Bombings in Bali, 14 October 2002.
43 J. Howard, Address to the Committee for Economic Development of Australia, 'Strategic Leadership for Australia Policy Directions in a Complex World', Four Seasons Hotel, Sydney, 20 November 2002.

44 DFAT, *Advancing the National Interest*, pp. xi–xii; 41–44.
45 J. Howard, Press Conference, Parliament House, Canberra, 28 January 2003.
46 Cited in D. Shanahan, 'Howard Joins the Attack on Paris', *The Australian*, 15 March 2003, p. 1.
47 J. Howard, Address at the Launch of the SA Division's Enterprise Forum, Adelaide Festival Centre, Adelaide, 14 March 2003.
48 Ibid.
49 Cited in M. Riley *et al.*, 'PM Unrepentant on Bali Link', *Sydney Morning Herald*, 11 March 2003, p. 9.
50 J. Howard, Address at the Launch of the SA Division's Enterprise Forum, Adelaide Festival Centre, Adelaide, 14 March 2003.
51 Ibid.
52 This point builds on work in critical constructivist approaches to international relations, which are concerned primarily with these 'how possible?' questions. Here, the mutually constitutive relationship between agents and structures encourages a focus on the processes through which security policy and practices are intersubjectively negotiated. See, for example, R. Doty, 'Foreign Policy as Social Construction', *International Studies Quarterly*, 37:3 (1993), pp. 297–320; J. Weldes, 'Constructing National Interests', *European Journal of International Relations*, 2:3 (1996), pp. 275–318. For discussion of the research questions 'how possible?', 'how thinkable?' and 'how sold?', see J. Holland, 'Coalition Foreign Policy in the "War on Terror": A Framework for Analyzing Foreign Policy as Culturally Embedded Discourse', presented at International Studies Association Annual Conference, San Francisco, 25–29 March 2008.
53 J. Curran, *The Power of Speech: Australian Prime Ministers Defining the National Image* (Melbourne: Melbourne University Press, 2004); G. Hage, *Against Paranoid Nationalism: Searching for Hope in a Shrinking Society* (Sydney: Pluto, 2003); J. Warhurst (ed.), *The Howard Decade in Australian Government and Politics*, Special Issue of *Australian Journal of Political Science*, 42:2 (2007), pp. 189–381; J. Brett, 'Relaxed and Comfortable: The Liberal Party's Australia', *Quarterly Essay*, 19 (2005).
54 Hage, *Against Paranoid Nationalism*, chapter 5.
55 Curran, *The Power of Speech*, chapter 6.
56 J. Howard, Address to the Institute of Public Affairs at The Australian Club, Melbourne, 20 May 2004.
57 A. Downer, 'Transnational Terrorism: the Threat to Australia', speech to the National Press Club, 15 July 2004.
58 See Burke, *Fear of Security*, pp. 207–229.
59 See A. Burke, 'Australia Paranoid: Security Politics and Identity Policy', in Burke and McDonald (eds.), *Critical Security in the Asia-Pacific* (Manchester: Manchester University Press, 2007); and Burke, *Fear of Security*.
60 See M. Wesley and T. Warren, 'Wild Colonial Ploys: Currents of Thought in Australian Foreign Policy Making', *Australian Journal of Political Science*, 35:1 (2000), pp. 9–26; O. Harries, 'Punching Above Our Weight?', *Boyer Lectures*, ABC Radio National, 21 December 2003, www.abc.net.au/rn/boyerlectures/stories/2003/987633.htm.
61 R. Lyon and W. Tow, 'The Future of the Australian–US Security Relationship', paper presented at Strategic Studies Institute, December (2003), www.strategicstudiesinstitute.army.mil/pdffiles/00047.pdf; J. Fitzpatrick, 'European Settler Colonialism and National Security Ideologies in Australian History', in R. Leaver and D. Cox (eds.), *Middling, Meddling, Muddling: Issues in Australian Foreign Policy* (St Leonards: Allen and Unwin, 1997).
62 J. Camilleri, 'A Leap into the Past – in the Name of the National Interest', *Australian Journal of International Affairs*, 57:3 (2003), pp. 448–449.

63 See G. Seal, *Inventing ANZAC: The Digger and National Mythology* (Brisbane: UQ Press, 2004).

64 For example, M. McKenna, 'Patriot Act', *The Australian*, 6 June 2007, www.theaustralian.news.com.au/story/0,20867,21813244–25132,00.html; T. Smith, 'Conscripting the ANZAC Myth to Silence Dissent', *Australian Review of Public Affairs Digest*, 11 September 2006.

65 McKenna, 'Patriot Act'.

66 J. Howard, Address to Joint Meeting of the US Congress, 12 June 2002.

67 Ibid.

68 Cited in B. O'Connor, 'Perspectives on Australian Foreign Policy, 2003', *Australian Journal of International Affairs*, 58:2 (2004), p. 208.

69 Gleeson, 'Australia and the Construction of the War on Terror'.

70 J. Howard, Press Conference, Ambassadors' Residence, Washington, DC, 12 September 2001.

71 J. Howard, Television Interview with Ray Martin, *60 Minutes*, Channel 9, 16 September 2001.

72 J. Howard, Address to Joint Meeting of the US Congress, 12 June 2002.

73 J. Howard, Interview with Ray Hadley, Radio 2GB, 2 October 2002.

74 Fry, 'Our Patch'.

75 McKenna, 'Patriot Act'.

76 J. Howard, Interview with John Laws, Radio 2UE, 12 September 2001.

77 Cited in Fry, 'Our Patch'.

78 J. Howard, Interview with Neil Cavuto, Fox 9 News Channel, 7 March 2003.

79 Cited in McKenna, 'Patriot Act'.

80 J. Howard, Address to the Australian Troops, Baghdad, Iraq, 25 April 2004.

81 See R. Jackson, *Writing the War on Terrorism: Language, Politics and Counter-Terrorism* (Manchester: Manchester University Press, 2005) for discussion of the need for popular acquiescence in democratic states within the 'coalition of the willing'.

82 See M. McDonald, 'Constructing Insecurity'; and M. McDonald and R. Jackson, 'Selling War: The Coalition of the Willing and the "War on Terror"', paper presented at International Studies Association Conference, San Francisco, 26–29 March 2008.

83 See M. Goot, 'Neither Entirely Comfortable Nor Wholly Relaxed: Public Opinion, Electoral Politics, and Foreign Policy', in J. Cotton and J. Ravenhill (eds.), *Trading on Alliance Security: Australia in World Affairs, 2001–5* (Oxford: Oxford University Press, 2007), pp. 268–275.

84 On the ways in which the Howard government attempted to circumscribe public debate and marginalize critics generally, see C. Hamilton and S. Maddison, *Silencing Dissent: How the Australian Government is Controlling Public Opinion and Stifling Debate* (Sydney: Allen & Unwin, 2007).

85 A range of analyses of debates in the United States have made similar points about the processes through which critics were marginalized or indeed rhetorically coerced into support for the government's position. See, for example, J. Cramer, 'Militarized Patriotism: Why the U.S. Marketplace of Ideas Failed Before the Iraq War', *Security Studies*, 16:3 (2007), pp. 489–524; and R. Krebs and J. Lobasz, 'Fixing the Meaning of 9/11: Hegemony, Coercion, and the Road to War in Iraq', *Security Studies*, 16:3 (2007), pp. 409–451.

86 McKenna, 'Patriot Act'.

87 M. McDonald, 'Be Alarmed? Australia's Anti-Terrorism Kit and the Politics of Security', *Global Change, Peace and Security*, 17:2 (2005), pp. 171–189.

88 Greener-Barcham and Barcham, 'Terrorism in the South Pacific?'; Australian Broadcasting Corporation (ABC), 'Government Partly "Selective" on Iraq Intelligence', *The 7.30 Report*, 1 March 2004, www.abc.net.au/7.30/content/2004/s1056607.htm.

89 Cited in Gleeson, 'Australia and the Construction of the War on Terror'.

90 A. Downer, 'Question Without Notice: Foreign Affairs: United States of America', *House of Representatives Hansard*, 3 August 2004.
91 DFAT, *Advancing the National Interest*.
92 Cited in T. Allard, 'Going to War Secured US Alliance, Says Downer'.
93 Camilleri, 'A Leap into the Past – in the Name of the National Interest'.
94 See McDonald, 'Constructing Insecurity'.
95 See McKenna, 'Patriot Act'.

12 Counter-terrorism in Southeast Asia post-9/11

Andrew T.H. Tan

Following the seminal terrorist attacks on 11 September 2001 in the United States, Southeast Asia, especially the Malay Archipelago, came into prominence as the so-called 'Second Front' in the US-led war against global terrorism. This was not surprising, as the Malay Archipelago has the world's largest population of Muslims. With its heavily-jungled terrain, in the context of a crisis of governance in Indonesia in the post-Suharto era, and the presence of long-standing Muslim insurgencies in places such as Aceh, Patani and Mindanao, it was feared that al-Qaeda-linked terrorists fleeing worldwide counter-terrorist action would easily find refuge in the region.

This chapter explains the challenge of terrorism in Southeast Asia and how this is a complex, historical phenomenon that predated al-Qaeda and the events of 9/11. It examines the difference in perceptions underlying regional responses to the events of 9/11 compared to those of the USA. It then examines the response from the region as a whole through initiatives undertaken by multilateral bodies such as the Association of Southeast Asian Nations (ASEAN), bilateral and multilateral cooperation, and efforts by individual states. It evaluates the successes and failures in regional counter-terrorism since 9/11, and concludes with an assessment of the problems and prospects for counter-terrorism in the region. This chapter argues that, because the challenge of terrorism in this strategic region is complex and historical, states in the region have adopted holistic and comprehensive counter-terrorism strategies, in contrast to the purely hard security measures hitherto favored by the previous Bush administration as conceptualized in its global War on Terror.

The threat of radical Islamist terrorism in Southeast Asia[1]

Events after 9/11 appeared to lend support to fears that global terrorism would emerge as a threat in the region. In early 2002, the regional al-Qaeda-linked Islamist network, the Jemaah Islamiah (JI), was exposed following the recovery of surveillance videotapes in Afghanistan by US forces during Operation Enduring Freedom. The JI had planned a major series of coordinated terrorist attacks in Singapore targeting Western embassies, several key US companies, US ships and military personnel, and local military facilities. Subsequently, 15 members of the hitherto secret network were arrested.[2] Had the attacks taken place, it would have been the largest terrorist attack after 11 September 2001.

The threat from al-Qaeda has been real, as the first major terrorist attack after 9/11 did take place in Southeast Asia. This was the deadly Bali attack in Indonesia, which took place in October 2002. Suicide bomb attacks killed a total of 202 people, of whom 164 were foreign nationals, the majority Australians.[3] The JI was also subsequently responsible for other attacks in the region, such as the Marriott Hotel attack in Jakarta in 2003, the bomb attack on the Australian High Commission in Jakarta in 2004, and the second Bali attack in October 2005.[4]

The objective of the JI is to establish a pan-Islamic caliphate in Southeast Asia that would cover the Malay Archipelago. According to research by the International Crisis Group, the JI can in fact be traced to the abortive Darul Islam (DI) rebellion in the 1950s, which aimed to establish an Islamic state in Indonesia.[5] The Darul Islam was eventually defeated at a cost of 25,000 lives. However, its ideal of an Islamic state survived in underground circles. The founders of the JI, Abu Bakar Bashir and Abdullah Sungkar, consider themselves to be the ideological successors of the Darul Islam. In the 1970s, they established a boarding school in Java from which many JI members were educated. After fleeing to Malaysia after attracting the attention of the authorities, they established the JI network there which has been dated to the early 1990s. The network built links throughout the region through ex-Afghan mujahideen volunteers from Southeast Asia who had returned after fighting the Soviets in Afghanistan in the 1980s. Through the Afghanistan link, the JI network developed close ties with al-Qaeda, receiving both funding and ideological training from it. The JI replicated al-Qaeda in the region, establishing a regional network of autonomous cells united by radical ideology. However, the JI operated independently of al-Qaeda and usually makes its operational decisions locally.[6] JI members also sometimes possess dual memberships in local militant groups.[7] After the fall of the Suharto regime in 1998, Abu Bakar Bashir was able to return to Indonesia in 1999. In mid-2000, he established the Majelis Mujiheddin of Indonesia (MMI) as an umbrella organization bringing together various militant Muslim organizations, as part of efforts to spread the ideology of radical Islam.[8]

The JI has also been involved in local Christian–Muslim sectarian violence in the Indonesian islands of Maluku and Sulawesi, which resulted in the deaths of over 10,000 people between 1999 up to the Malino peace accord in 2002. The conflict was initially local in orientation, the root cause being economic competition and conflict between local Christians and Javanese Muslim migrants in the context of the financial and economic crises then engulfing Indonesia.[9] While these grievances are political, economic and social in nature, the religious divide provided the opportunity for Javanese-based radical groups to become involved. These included the Laskar Jihad (later disbanded in 2002), elements of the old Darul Islam, the Mujahideen KOMPAK (the military wing of a Muslim charity), and a Makassar-based Muslim militia, the al-Qaeda-linked Laskar Jundullah. The JI proselytized in the region and became actively involved in what it considered to be a fertile region for the spread of its radical ideology. Thus, low-level attacks continued despite the peace accord reached between the Christian and Muslim communities in 2002, as the JI as well as other radical elements have continued to wage jihad.[10]

Another radical terrorist challenge has emanated from the Abu Sayaff Group (ASG) which operates mostly in the southern Philippines. The ASG was founded in the early 1990s by Abdulrajak Janjalani, who had brought back with him enthusiastic mujahideen volunteers in the Afghan conflict against the Soviets. The name Abu Sayaff is a tribute to Osama bin Laden's ally Rasool Sayyaf, with whom Janjalani fought during the Afghan conflict.[11] Al-Qaeda provided funding through Osama bin Laden's brother-in-law, Mohammad Jamal Khalifa, who had married a Filipina and lived in Manila, where he ran a Muslim charity.[12] Al-Qaeda also provided training, including sending Ramzi Yousef (responsible for the World Trade Center bombing in New York in 1993) to train ASG members in the use of sophisticated explosives. A fire in his flat in Manila in 1995 led the authorities to recover his laptop, which revealed a plot to kill the visiting Pope as well as the audacious Operation Bojinka (named after a town in Bosnia), in which the JI and al-Qaeda planned to simultaneously destroy 11 US airliners in the Asia-Pacific using liquid explosives.[13] The same liquid bomb plot was later attempted in Britain, in 2006.[14]

The ASG has carried out a number of terrorist and criminal activities, such as bombings, assassinations, extortion and kidnapping for ransom. It has been responsible for many terrorist attacks throughout the Philippines. The ASG carried out the daring raid on the Malaysian island resort of Sipadan Island in April 2000, where it kidnapped 21 hostages, including 12 Western tourists.[15] It also carried out a daring bomb attack at the Philippine Embassy in Jakarta in 2000, severely injuring the Philippine ambassador.[16] More seriously, the ASG and the JI were responsible for a joint operation in February 2004, when a ferry in Manila Bay was bombed, killing 116 people.[17] The Super Ferry bombing was the worst terrorist attack in Southeast Asia since the Bali bombing in October 2002.

The events of 9/11 also triggered growing anxieties over maritime security in the region. This is due to the fact that the world's most strategic waterway and chokepoint, the Straits of Malacca, is located within the Malay Archipelago. The Straits of Malacca is very narrow (being only 800 meters wide at its narrowest point) and is extremely crowded, as one-quarter of the world's trade, half the world's oil and two-thirds of its natural gas trade pass through its waters. Any disruption through a major terrorist attack would have devastating consequences, as the waterway is the economic lifeline for the booming economies of Northeast Asia. However, the high rates of piracy around Indonesian waters (until recently, the highest in the world), the presence of radical Islamist groups in the vicinity and the crisis of governance in Indonesia following the fall of the Suharto regime in 1998 led to fears of terrorists linking up with pirates who possess deep knowledge of the local seas to launch a devastating maritime version of 9/11. A scenario that has been suggested is the hijack of a chemical tanker and its use as a floating bomb to devastate a major container hub such as

Singapore.[18] Given the global economy's dependence on seaborne trade and just-in-time manufacturing processes, such an attack would have a massive economic and psychological impact. Such scenarios have been taken seriously because of al-Qaeda attacks at sea, such as the attack on the USS *Cole* in 2000 and the French oil tanker, the *Lindberg*, in 2002, both in Yemen. The JI had also planned to attack US naval vessels in late 2001 as part of its failed bomb plots in Singapore.[19] A senior al-Qaeda operative captured by the US in 2002 also revealed that the masterminds of the USS *Cole* attack had planned to attack another US ship visiting Malaysia.[20] The fear of maritime terrorism in the Malay Archipelago was such that in June 2005, Lloyd's Market Association's Joint War Committee classified the Straits of Malacca as an area in danger of wars and related perils, on the grounds that the modus operandi of pirates operating there are now similar to modern-day terrorists.[21] This raised insurance premiums and made maritime security an important challenge and priority for littoral and major user states.

The US global War on Terror

The terrorist attacks in the USA on 9/11 were unprecedented as it was by far the deadliest act of terrorism in modern times. Until 9/11, the most serious terrorist act was the Abadan theater fire in Iran in 1978 that killed 400 people.[22] 9/11 led to a forceful response from the United States. President George Bush declared a War on Terror after the attack, vowing 'a broad and sustained campaign to secure our country and eradicate the evil of terrorism'.[23]

Shocked by the high number of casualties and the fact that citizens of some 80 nations had been amongst the victims, the international community swiftly condemned the attacks. The US was thus able to successfully mobilize international support against al-Qaeda and other groups linked to al-Qaeda. The United Nations thus called for 'international cooperation to bring to justice the perpetrators, organizers, and sponsors of the outrages of 11 September 2001'.[24] On 28 September 2001, the UN Security Council adopted Resolution 1373, which called on states to criminalize assistance for terrorist activities, deny financial support and safe haven to terrorists, and share information about groups planning terrorist attacks. The resolution also urged states to become parties to all international conventions and protocols relating to terrorism.[25] These resolutions were accompanied by worldwide security action, as governments in Europe, Southeast Asia, the Indian sub-continent and the Middle East arrested and detained members of al-Qaeda as well as radical Islamists linked to it.

The unprecedented terrorist attack also appeared to validate the claims of the advocates of the 'new' terrorism, such as Bruce Hoffman, who argued that new terrorist groups have emerged to join more traditional ethno-political types. These new groups have less comprehensible nationalistic or ideological motivations, and embrace much more amorphous religious and millenarian aims. They are less cohesive in their organization, with a more diffused cell-like structure and membership. They are potentially far more lethal given their attempts at mass casualty terrorist acts, using both conventional explosives or weapons of mass destruction, as the sarin nerve gas attack on the Tokyo subway by the Aum Supreme Truth demonstrated in 1995. Increasingly, such groups do not bother to explain or justify their attacks, as their aim is to punish and destroy. Thus, such groups see violence as an end in itself, not just a means to an end.[26] The internationalization of terrorism has also become more pronounced in a borderless global economy, making such groups difficult to track since they are much more mobile and much less dependent on state support. Such new terrorist groups have also been able to use modern communications and the Internet to reach out to a much wider base of support than was possible in the past.[27] The improved prospects for terrorism have thus made possible new transnational actors with new weapons and the ability to inflict massive impacts through their capacity for mass casualty terrorist acts.

The Bush administration's response to the strategic threat posed by the new terrorism was broadly outlined in the National Security Strategy in September 2002. The strategy noted the threat of mass casualty terrorism, but also affirmed that the US had enormous power and should therefore strive to use it in the pursuit of goals such as defeating global terrorism, defusing regional conflicts, preventing the proliferation of weapons of mass destruction and spreading democracy.[28] In February 2003, the US launched the National Strategy for Combating Terrorism, which adopted the assumptions of the advocates of the 'new' terrorism. The new strategy described how globalization has facilitated the rise of new, transnational terrorist networks such as al-Qaeda, which operate transnationally and are less dependent on state sponsors. The 'new' terrorist threat is thus 'a flexible, transnational network structure, enabled by modern technology and characterized by loose interconnectivity both within and between groups'.[29] The new strategy also advocated a pre-emptive approach aimed at identifying and defusing terrorist threats before they reached US borders.[30]

The Bush administration's solution to the threat to global terrorism as epitomized by al-Qaeda's attack on 9/11 has been to declare a global War on Terror that has emphasized the kinetic application of the USA's enormous military power. It adopted a uni-dimensional strategy emphasizing a 'kill or capture' approach based on hard security measures, instead of utilizing the full range of diplomatic, political, economic and social instruments in addition to military security measures that would comprehensively address the root causes of terrorism and thus contain its challenge. The failures of the Bush administration's strategy against global terrorism is not within the scope of this chapter, suffice to note its failure to adopt a comprehensive approach to counter-terrorism that would have been more effective and stood a better chance of success.[31]

Regional perceptions

The response of governments in Southeast Asia to the events of 9/11 was to rally in support of the United States and to condemn the attacks. Singapore, a key US ally in the region, held a memorial at the National Stadium on 23 September

2001 that was attended by 15,000 people. At the rally, Prime Minister Goh Chok Tong stated that 'Singapore would stand with the US in the fight against terrorism, even *though it has to manage both regional and domestic sensitivities in doing so*'.[32] Goh thus alluded to local and regional Muslim sensitivities to the US reaction to 9/11, anticipating that Muslim societies in the region would not be providing wholehearted support for the global War on Terror.

Malaysia's Prime Minister Mahathir also condemned the attacks on 9/11.[33] He was able, in its aftermath, to justify tough security measures, including the use of draconian preventive detention laws, against Muslim fundamentalists who had been putting pressure on his government. In January 2002, he stated that 'we have taken action without having been called upon by others to do so ... so far, no one has accused Malaysia of providing a safe haven for terrorists'.[34] This was, however, not an accurate statement, as there has been circumstantial evidence that Malaysia had been the launching pad for a number of al-Qaeda-linked terrorist plots or attacks, such as the abortive Operation Bojinka in 1995, the attack on the USS *Cole* in Yemen in 2000, the abortive Singapore bomb plots of 2002 and the 9/11 attacks.[35] Moreover, the opposition fundamentalist Partai Islam, reflecting anti-US sentiments on the ground, appeared to support Osama bin Laden in his pronouncements.[36]

Indonesia's President Megawati was the first head of state to visit the US after 9/11, a strong symbolic gesture as Indonesia is the world's largest Muslim country. Megawati condemned the attack and made a pledge to support the war against terrorism. But, at the same time, the reaction in Indonesia was anti-US. Large anti-US demonstrations in Indonesia culminated with calls to 'sweep' and expel US citizens.[37] Even mainstream parties joined in the anti-US mood, amidst calls for jihad or holy war in many mosques in the country. The Indonesian government's subsequent reaction to the US-led Operation Enduring Freedom in Afghanistan demonstrated its desire for a balancing act given the domestic reality of strong anti-US sentiments. The Indonesian government stated its 'deep concern' over US military action, but at the same time called on the Indonesian people not to overreact in expressing their concern and sympathy for the suffering of the Afghan people, nor to engage in 'activities that violate the laws and [that] may disturb security and public order'.[38] President Megawati also criticized the US, stating that 'no individual, group or government has the right to try to catch terrorist perpetrators by attacking the territory of another country'.[39] In September 2003, Vice-President Hamzah Haz ridiculed suggestions that the country had a serious terrorist threat, and accused the US of being the 'king of terrorists'.[40]

These initial reservations underwent a gradual change following the deadly Bali bombing in October 2002 which killed 202 people. The revelations that the attack was carried out by the JI was initially met with widespread denial as most Indonesians chose to believe that it was a CIA-backed plot aimed at discrediting Islam.[41] Australia provided forensic assistance as many of the victims were Australian, and gradually the full story of the JI plot emerged. The subsequent arrest of the Bali bombers, their lack of remorse in their advocacy of jihad in court, as well as other deadly terrorist attacks in Indonesia, soon changed domestic perceptions regarding the radical Islamist terrorist threat. The Bali attack was followed by the bombing of the Marriott Hotel in Jakarta in August 2003, which killed 12 people, mostly Indonesians. The bomb attack on the Australian High Commission in Jakarta in 2004 also led to the deaths of 11 people, all Indonesians. Finally, the second Bali attack in October 2005 that killed 23 people devastated the local tourist economy.[42]

However, there remains widespread skepticism in the region to the notion of a 'new' terrorism. The reasons are not difficult to ascertain. The Bali attack and other subsequent terrorist attacks demonstrated that al-Qaeda's training and funding have had a significant impact on local militant groups, improving their operational effectiveness and organization, and raising the lethality of terrorist attacks to a new level previously unseen in the region. Suicide terrorism, for instance, has been a very recent phenomenon in the region, and can be attributed to al-Qaeda's influence. But the JI is not in fact a 'new' terrorist group, as it traces its roots to the Darul Islam movement in the 1950s. It thus predates both al-Qaeda and 9/11. In fact, Muslim alienation and rebellion has been a longstanding security challenge to the region's governments. Muslim separatist insurgencies in Aceh in Indonesia, Mindanao in the southern Philippines and Patani in southern Thailand have been ongoing for years, long predating al-Qaeda and 9/11. Analysts have attributed their persistence and severity to the failure of state legitimacy following decolonization. As Sukhumbhand Paribatra and Chai-anan Samudavanija have observed:

> in post-colonial SE Asia, it has been conveniently forgotten by central governments that the constructing of what is more accurately a state-nation merely means that external or western imperialism had been replaced by an internalized one, which is potentially more brutal and enduring.'[43]

Detailed studies of these three Muslim separatist insurgencies indicate that while al-Qaeda had attempted to penetrate and build links with these local rebel groups, it has met with mixed results, as it has had to battle the pre-existing nationalist imperative that has so far remained stronger.[44] Indeed, the Muslim separatist insurgencies in the Malay Archipelago share many common characteristics, such as a strong historical sense of local identity, which has been sustained by deep adherence to Islam and its use as a focal rallying point in opposing the central government. More significantly, there are also fundamental grievances, such as the presence of migrant communities, discrimination, mismanagement, corruption, and insensitive policies pursued by the central governments involved.

Al-Qaeda has thus not surprisingly attempted to profit from these local Muslim grievances. However, it has met with very mixed results. The main separatist group in Mindanao, the Moro Islamic Liberation Front (MILF), did in fact establish ties with Osama bin Laden, who provided funding and training prior to 9/11. But the events of 9/11 led to the MILF leadership abandoning those linkages. Instead, under the leadership of its present leader, Murad Ibrahim, the MILF has strongly emphasized its nationalist credentials, declaring it to be a 'legitimate liberation organization', that 'counts on committed popular member-ships who are not fanatical about their religion', and that would not link up with 'terrorism or any extremist groups using religious faith as a tool for terroristic activities'.[45] The MILF has proven to be a serious partner in peace negotiations with the Philippine government. Under pressure from the Philippines, the US has therefore not designated the MILF as a terrorist organization, although the Abu Sayaff Group has been. In Aceh, in Indonesia, the main rebel group, the Gerakan Aceh Merdeka (GAM) has consistently emphasized its nationalist credentials and rebuffed al-Qaeda when its deputy chief, Al-Zawahiri, visited the province in 2000. Following the events of 9/11, GAM sent a message of condolence to the US Ambassador in Jakarta.[46] GAM has since signed a comprehensive peace accord, laid down its arms and is participating in the democratic political process.

In Thailand, the Thaksin government that came to power in 2002 took the US lead in the global War on Terror, emphasizing a tough military approach to the insurgency. This resulted in the over-reaction by security forces, which led to the deaths of 108 Muslims in April 2004, and 85 unarmed Muslim protesters at Tak Bai in October 2004.[47] Indeed, the increase in the level and organization of sepa-ratist violence from 2001, with the use of more sophisticated techniques hitherto seen only in Iraq, such as remote-controlled Improvised Explosive Devices (IEDs), reflected enhanced linkages with global jihadist elements.[48] Yet, despite claims by the Thai authorities that the insurgents had deep links with al-Qaeda, Western tourists and interests have not been targeted and the insurgency has remained local and nationalist in orientation. According to key al-Qaeda–JI com-mander Hambali, now in US custody, the insurgents had rebuffed al-Qaeda when approached for assistance to carry out bombings in Thailand.[49]

There are clearly much more complex variables at work in Southeast Asia, and the war against terrorism in the region cannot therefore be reduced to the simplistic and general assumption of the US-led War on Terror that Muslim rebels in the region are all somehow linked to al-Qaeda and its radical ideology. The presence of historical, fundamental grievances that long predated the events of 9/11 point to the need to understand the complexities of Muslim alienation and rebellion, in order to devise appropriate and effective counter-terrorism strat-egies that would also prevent disaffected locals from signing up to al-Qaeda's global jihad.

Thus, because of doubts over the accuracy of the 'new' terrorism paradigm in describing the terrorism phenomenon in the region, and also because of long-standing practices in dealing with Muslim rebellion, the regional response and strategy against terrorism has differed from US prescriptions. To varying degrees of competence, regional governments tend to employ comprehensive approaches to counter-terrorism, which goes beyond purely military-security approaches and includes diplomacy, political negotiations, economic development, social meas-ures, psychological warfare and the rehabilitation of captured militants.

Regional responses

Responses at the level of ASEAN

The ASEAN states joined in the condemnation of the 11 September attacks and supported the UN Security Council Resolutions 1368 and 1373. On 5 November 2001, ASEAN also issued a joint declaration condemning terrorism and agreed to cooperate to combat it following the events of 11 September.[50] It also agreed on common measures in an action plan against terrorism, such as strengthening national mechanisms, enhancing intelligence exchange and supporting the UN in playing a bigger role in combating it.[51] ASEAN intelligence chiefs met in January 2002 and discussed the threat to the region posed by militant Islamic groups.[52] The ASEAN Regional Forum (ARF) meeting in July 2002 also produced a ground-breaking statement on a set of financial measures to cut off terrorist funding. The document commits member states to freeze assets of terrorist groups and exchange intelligence information to destroy their finances. ARF ministers also agreed to hold regular meetings of senior officials to monitor compliance to commitments.[53]

In the aftermath of the deadly Bali attack, APEC leaders in October 2002 also agreed to a raft of measures to counter terrorism, such as enhancing security in trade, expanding the Container Security Initiative (involving pre-screening of cargo containers), choking off terrorist financing and promoting cyber-security.[54] The ASEAN Summit of October 2002 endorsed measures against money-laundering and terrorism financing, as well as the establishment of a Southeast Asian Regional Center for Counter-Terrorism (SEARCCT) in November 2002 in Kuala Lumpur.[55] Multilateral cooperation in intelligence sharing, establishing uniform laws and counter-terrorism was stepped up under an Action Plan adopted earlier by the ASEAN states in May 2002. Among the projects adopted under the Action Plan was training on anti-terror intelligence-gathering and psychological warfare to be provided by Malaysia, a workshop on combating international terrorism to be hosted by Indonesia, and logistical support for training in bomb detection, airport and document security by Singapore. It also agreed that each member-state would form a special anti-terrorist team to act as the contact point.[56] In July 2002, the US and ASEAN also signed a joint declaration to provide for 'greater cooperation in intelligence exchange and other joint action to deal with international terrorism'. However, while ASEAN made this commitment to fight terrorism, it also made clear that it was doing so for its own security, not on behalf of the US, and that terrorism cannot be defeated without addressing its root causes.[57]

In January 2007, ASEAN leaders signed a convention on counter-terrorism cooperation, which recognized the importance of a global legal framework to combat terrorism, agreed that terrorism offenses such as hijacking, hostage-taking or bombing were not political offenses, and that terrorists could not hide behind political justifications to evade justice. ASEAN member-states agreed to cooperate to prevent terrorist attacks, the financing of terrorism and terrorist movement across national borders, as well as to enhance intelligence cooperation.[58]

In sum, therefore, a number of regional initiatives have been undertaken in order to strengthen institutional mechanisms as well as to enhance regional cooperation in order to better combat transnational terrorism. However, the ASEAN states have taken a legal and cooperative approach to the problem of terrorism, and have been careful to delineate an approach that is different from that of the US prescriptions. Indeed, according to a document prepared by ASEAN for the UN Counter-Terrorism Committee, while ASEAN viewed terrorism as a profound threat to international peace and security, it is committed to combating it in accordance with the Charter of the United Nations, relevant UN resolutions, and international laws. In addition, 'cooperative efforts in this regard should consider joint practical counter-terrorism measures in line with specific circumstances in the region and in each member country'.[59]

Bilateral and multilateral cooperation

Bilateral and multilateral security cooperation have also occurred outside the ambit of ASEAN. In May 2002, for instance, Malaysia, Indonesia and the Philippines signed a counter-terrorism treaty that would strengthen border controls and allow the countries to share airline passenger lists, establish hotlines, share intelligence as well as standardize procedures for search and rescue.[60] External powers have also become involved. The USA, for instance, signed a Declaration on Cooperation to Combat International Terrorism with Malaysia in May 2002.[61] After the Bali bombing in 2002, Indonesia accepted Australian forensic assistance as well as aid in the establishment of a counter-terrorism center, the Jakarta Centre for Law Enforcement Cooperation, located in Semarang.[62] Australia and ASEAN also issued a Joint Declaration for Co-operation to Combat International Terrorism in 2004, in which both sides pledged to exchange intelligence, strengthen capacity-building, curb document and identity fraud, and terminate terrorism financing, among other measures.[63]

However, it has been in maritime security that cooperation has been somewhat more fruitful. Given heightened fears of terrorist attacks on vulnerable shipping in the region, the US took active steps to improve maritime security in the Straits of Malacca. This has taken many forms, such as improving bilateral cooperation with the littoral states, namely Malaysia, Indonesia and Singapore, the provision of indirect military support for counter-terrorism in the southern Philippines, and measures to improve maritime security.[64] However, because of popular anti-US sentiments in Indonesia and Malaysia, there have been deep domestic sensitivities that both governments have had to pay attention to. Thus, they opposed suggestions under the Regional Maritime Security Initiative (RMSI) floated by the US Pacific Command in March 2004 that the US might station forces in the vicinity of the Straits of Malacca to secure sea-lanes and carry out counter-terrorism operations.[65]

This prospect, however, had the effect of galvanizing cooperation amongst the littoral states. The three littoral states of the Straits of Malacca have since developed close maritime security cooperation. Since 2004, the three have carried out coordinated year-round patrols, linked by communications hotlines, as well as joint air patrols.[66] The Malacca Straits Patrols are multilateral in nature and have been deliberately restricted in scope to avoid sovereignty issues. Thus, the patrols are coordinated, not joint, with a handing-off procedure and without the right of hot pursuit. Both Singapore and Indonesia have also cooperated to establish a technical system under Project SURPIC, which is designed to share information between the two countries in order to achieve a common operating picture.[67] The 'Eye in the Sky' initiative consists of combined maritime air patrols by the three littoral states as well as Thailand. These aircraft can over-fly each state's territory. However, to allay any mutual suspicion, an officer of the country over which a patrol would fly would also be present on board.[68] Regional capacity has been boosted by Thailand joining the Malacca Straits Patrol in 2009.[69]

Since 9/11, the region has also received assistance from Japan, which is anxious to ensure the security of the Straits of Malacca and its environs, as the Straits is its vital economic lifeline. Moreover, al-Qaeda had threatened to attack Japan on account of its alliance with the US and its dispatch of troops to Iraq.[70] Japan has dispatched its Coast Guard to the region for anti-piracy and counter-terrorism training exercises with a number of states in the region. Given its constitutional constraints on the deployment of military forces in the region, it has emphasized capacity-building and governance. Japan's assistance has thus taken the form of the provision of training and equipment in the areas of immigration control, aviation security, customs cooperation, export control, law-enforcement cooperation and measures against terrorism financing.[71] It has also funded the installation and maintenance of navigational aides and buoy-tenders, provided technical assistance to upgrade marine safety data-management systems and conducted hydrographical surveys.[72]

Japan has also sponsored the Regional Cooperation Agreement on Combating Piracy and Armed Robbery Against Ships in Asia (ReCAAP), which was signed by 16 countries in 2004 and entered into force in September 2006. The ReCAAP Agreement sets up mechanisms for achieving international cooperation, sets out the obligations of member countries to prevent piracy and also takes up capacity building initiatives. ReCAAP is built around the pillars of information sharing, capacity building and cooperative arrangements, and has established an Information Sharing Centre in Singapore. Some 14 countries have ratified the ReCAAP Agreement, including Japan, Philippines and Singapore.[73] However, although Indonesia and Malaysia were parties to the Agreement in 2004, both have not ratified it, due primarily to sovereignty issues.

Indeed, the issue of sovereignty is clearly paramount for Malaysia and Indonesia. Thus, the foreign ministers of Malaysia, Indonesia and Singapore meeting in August 2005 in Batam, Indonesia, to discuss the safety of navigation, environmental protection and maritime security in the Straits of Malacca reiterated in their Joint Statement that the primary responsibility over the safety of navigation, environmental protection and maritime security in the Straits of Malacca and Singapore would lie with the littoral states.[74]

Individual state approaches to counter-terrorism

Individual states within the region have also undertaken steps to deal with the domestic terrorist threat. In Malaysia, the Sipadan hostage crisis and the daring Sauk arms heist by the militant Al Ma'unah, both in 2000, highlighted to the Malaysian leadership the security threat posed by militants. Thus, well before 9/11, Defence Minister Tun Najib identified Islamic militancy as Malaysia's greatest internal security threat, and warned that 'we must be on guard as any wrong teaching of Islam, or any inflammatory instigation by certain elements can wreak havoc on our internal stability'.[75] He also called on the armed forces to be able to deal with a full spectrum of threats, including low-intensity conflict and urban warfare, which could be mounted by militants.[76] Given the thousands of Malaysians who had studied in madrassahs in Pakistan, there were genuine fears that some might have fallen prey to extremist preaching. Intelligence was thus stepped up.[77] The government also made efforts to counter radical teachings, drafting in moderate scholars and academics in order to battle extremist views. The difficulty in Malaysia is the political competition between an unpopular ruling coalition widely seen as corrupt and out of touch, and an opposition that has taken the moral high ground. The main fundamentalist Muslim party, Partai Islam, has continued to maintain strong support amongst Malay Muslims and has posed a serious challenge to the authority and legitimacy of the ruling Barisan Nasional. The anti-US sentiments on the ground have also constrained the Malaysian government from being seen to be supportive of US initiatives in the global War on Terror. It must therefore steer an adroit line in countering the challenge of terrorism while assuaging the sensitivities of its domestic Muslim constituency.

Neighboring Singapore's response to terrorism has been by far the most vigorous and comprehensive of all the states in the region. As the abortive bomb plots of 2002 demonstrated, Singapore is a prime al-Qaeda target, on account of its pro-US orientation, ties with Israel and being home to thousands of Western multinationals. After 9/11, Singapore has strongly supported all US initiatives in the war against global terrorism, to the annoyance of its neighbors. Singapore shares the same perspective, though not the strategy, of the US. As Kishore Mahbuhani, Singapore's Ambassador to the UN, stated in October 2001, this is 'a fight between people who stand for civilized society, and those out to destroy it'.[78]

Soon after 9/11, Singapore promulgated a Homefront Security doctrine in November 2001, under which a new security architecture to counter the new global terrorism would be put into place.[79] To operationalize the new doctrine, Singapore opted for a network approach, consisting of a few inter-ministerial agencies to coordinate various aspects of policy, intelligence and operations. This contrasts with the US approach, which was to establish a super-agency, the Department of Homeland Security.

In typical Singapore fashion, the response has been focused and impressively thorough. It passed a Strategic Goods (Control) Bill in 2002 regulating items that could be used to make nuclear, biological or chemical weapons.[80] It strengthened civil-defense capabilities to deal with any attack involving weapons of mass destruction, including response teams, decontamination facilities in train subway stations, and the establishment of a Regional Emerging Diseases Intervention (REDI) Centre, a joint US–Singapore initiative, in 2003 to counter any pandemic or biological attack.[81] Similar to the Citizen Preparedness Program in the USA, Singapore also promulgated a National Security Awareness Program.[82] It enhanced airport security, deployed air marshals on board Singapore Airlines, and announced plans to develop countermeasures against portable surface-to-air missiles aimed at civilian airliners.[83] As one of the world's major ports, it also swiftly implemented the requirements of the International Ship and Port Security (ISPS) Code, and the amendments to the Safety of Life at Sea (SOLAS) Convention, which came into effect on 1 July 2004, and which require ships and ports to implement enhanced security measures.[84]

Singapore has supported all US initiatives aimed at countering terrorism and improving maritime security. Singapore, together with the Philippines, joined the US-led Proliferation Security Initiative (PSI), which Malaysia and Indonesia has avoided as it is seen as a unilateral measure, as well as being controversial since it involves unilateral security action in the high seas.[85] Singapore also became the first Asian port to join the US Customs-led Container Security Initiative (CSI) when it signed an agreement to do so in 2002 and launched a program in March 2003 to screen US-bound containers and inspect suspicious cargo.[86] In 2004, Singapore also joined the US Coast Guard-led International Port Security Program (IPSP), which will allow the US Coast Guard to inspect Singapore's port facilities and verify their implementation of the IPSP code. Singapore also welcomed the US Pacific Command's Regional Maritime Security Initiative (RMSI), which was floated in March 2004. As the plan suggested pre-emptive security action by US forces in the Straits of Malacca, it was met with strong objections by Malaysia and Indonesia, as it would violate their sovereignties.[87] The scope and depth of US–Singapore bilateral security cooperation has, however, led to perceptions in Indonesia and Malaysia that Singapore has become America's stalking horse in the region.

Singapore's comprehensive approach to counter-terrorism is encapsulated in its National Security Strategy unveiled in August 2004, entitled 'The Fight Against Terror'. The strategy emphasized interagency cooperation, regional and international cooperation, strengthening of national resilience as well as the ability to detect, prevent and mitigate against terrorist attacks. The underlying reason for the comprehensive response to radical Islamist terrorism is revealed in the document, as the new transnational terrorism is acknowledged, in the context of a multiracial Singapore, 'to pit different communities against each other, weakening the multi-racial, multi-religious character of Singapore that is vital to our success'.[88]

What is interesting is that the approach to counter-terrorism by Malaysia and Singapore has been tampered by their historical experience with communist insurgency in the Malayan Emergency in the 1950s. The British success in counter-insurgency has been much studied as a template for countering insurgencies and terrorism elsewhere, and its legacy can still be seen in the local counter-terrorism strategy. In brief, success in Malaya has been attributed to 'the abandonment of a coercion and enforcement approach in favor of a hearts and minds approach', which paved the way for a relatively peaceful and prosperous aftermath to the fighting.[89] This hearts-and-minds approach is part of a comprehensive strategy that uses a range of military, political, economic, social and psychological instruments, rather than merely the application of kinetic military power to defeat the adversary, which has been the US approach under Bush administration.

The Singapore government is much aware of the need for a hearts-and-minds approach, given the ideological nature of the radical Islamist threat. Indeed, the Minister of Home Affairs Wong Kan Seng noted that 'the greatest challenge is in the realm of the mind and the heart'.[90] Thus, following the indefinite preventive detention of alleged JI operatives under the draconian Internal Security Act, the Singapore government released a White Paper entitled 'The Jemaah Islamiyah Arrests and the Threat of Terrorism' in January 2003 in order to explain to its own skeptical Muslim population who had been arrested, what they were accused of and the threat that the JI posed.[91] The detainees also received correct treatment, their welfare vetted by visits by family and community representatives, to prevent any overt mistreatment or perception of mistreatment that could reverberate and increase the hostility and resentment of local Muslims, thereby worsening the threat of terrorism. Another objective is the rehabilitation of the detainees, following the successful 'turning' of communist insurgents during the Malayan Emergency. Detainees who recanted provided a valuable tool in countering radical propaganda and contributed to the winning of hearts and minds by demonstrating the sincerity of the government's approach, as well as bolstering its legitimacy. Thus, detainees have been provided with religious counseling in order to put them on the right path. Once detainees demonstrate sufficient remorse and are no longer considered a security threat, they would be released and reintegrated back into society.[92] This strategy is in marked contrast to the Bush administration's approach in the global War on Terror, with its renditions, use of torture, secret detention camps and the wall of secrecy regarding those detained.

Similarly, in Malaysia, security measures coupled with a soft hand is credited with ensuring that Malaysia has kept any militant violence well under control. The resolution of the Sauk arms heist in 2000 by members of the Al Ma'unah is instructive. Members of the militant group took over an armory in Sauk in the state of Perak, escaping with a cache of weapons, and were eventually cornered by army commandoes. The militants executed two non-Muslim hostages they had captured and the whole siege could have ended badly. Instead, the military blasted the militants through loudspeakers with songs sung by P. Ramli, a popular singer. Suitably softened, unarmed commandoes then went over to talk to the group, succeeding in disarming them.[93] Of the over 100 alleged militants belonging to several militant groups such as the Al Ma'unah, the Kampulan

Militan Malaysia (KMM) and the JI detained under indefinite preventive detention under the Internal Security Act, some have been deemed to have been successfully rehabilitated and have been released and reintegrated into society. Indeed, former KMM and JI leader Wan Min Wan Mat was released in 2005, whereupon he urged fellow JI leaders Azahari Husin and Noordin Mohammed Top to renounce violence.[94] Thus, Zachary Abuza noted that the governments of Singapore, Malaysia and Indonesia have released almost 40 percent of their JI detainees, the three governments being acutely aware of the ideological nature of the struggle, thus recognizing the need to create a counter-narrative to JI's radical ideology.[95]

The Philippines has welcomed military assistance from the US in combating the Moro rebellions in the southern provinces. This has included transport aircraft, helicopters, patrol craft, armored personnel carriers, assault rifles and anti-terrorism training.[96] In January 2002, US troops arrived to provide training and technical assistance to the Philippine Armed Forces against the Abu Sayaff.[97] The US has also, through USAID, provided development aid to Mindanao and Sulu, focusing on reintegrating former separatists, and improving local governance and infrastructure.[98] Australia too has provided assistance in the form of 28 patrol boats and an annual grant of A$4 million in training assistance, which has helped to improve naval patrol capabilities.[99] Somewhat belatedly, the Philippine government replaced its previous military-oriented 14-Point plan to counter terrorism with a new 16-Point Counter-Terrorism Program in 2005. It also promulgated the Human Security Act of 2007. The two documents together provide the Philippines with a coherent counter-terrorism strategy, one which focuses on a comprehensive approach comprising political, diplomatic, economic, military and legal means. The new strategy includes conflict management, post-conflict peace-building, economic development and addressing the root causes of conflict. An Anti-Terrorism Council has been established to coordinate the new strategic approach, which involves institutions such as the armed forces, intelligence, police, civil defense, immigration and other agencies.[100] This comprehensive approach mirrors that taken by other states in the region, such as Singapore.

In Indonesia, the initial reaction to the War on Terror was tepid, even hostile, as Indonesians reacted with cynicism to US claims of a radical Islamist terror threat. But the Bali attack in 2002, and other subsequent terrorist attacks carried out by the JI, changed perceptions. Mainstream political parties, such as the Nahdatul Ulama and Muhammadiyah, also began to launch counter-moves to recapture the political ground from fundamentalist parties that had been gaining ground. In 2002, the government also announced a Bill on Eradicating Terrorism, although this was in reality aimed more at separatist insurgents in Aceh and Irian Jaya.[101]

Indonesia's commitment to countering the radical Islamist terror threat was strongly boosted by the election of Susilo Bambang Yudhoyono in 2004, who is remembered for his moving eulogy to the victims of Bali at its anniversary in 2003, where he denounced the 'terrorists who wanted to make a senseless demonstration of their hatred for others'.[102] Indonesia has since developed a very professional counter-terrorism force, Densus 88 (or Detachment 88), which is well funded, trained and equipped, and which has been responsible for many counter-terrorism successes against JI operatives in recent years. As observed by Abuza, the Indonesian government has not focused on hard military measures but on police and intelligence responses, as well as the rehabilitation of captured militants. Indeed, Indonesia has been able to turn senior JI members, who are now leading the rehabilitation efforts for lower-level cadres. The Indonesian government is well aware of the ideological nature of the struggle and has thus been keen to create a counter-narrative to JI's radical ideology.[103] The general approach thus deviates from the US prescription based on a 'kill or capture' policy under Bush's War on Terror, and is similar to the hearts-and-minds approach adopted by Singapore and Malaysia.

Evaluating regional counter-terrorism

Improved regional and international cooperation, and efforts at the national level, have resulted in an improved security environment in 2009. Due largely to preventive measures, often involving the use of draconian preventive detention provisions of their respective Internal Security Acts, both Singapore and Malaysia succeeded in disrupting radical Islamist groups and cells, thus containing the terrorist threat. Unlike in Indonesia, no major mass-casualty terrorist act has taken place.

In Indonesia, with the political resolution of the sectarian conflict in Maluku and Sulawesi, and the peace accord in Aceh, the level of civil violence has abated substantially since 2004–2005. With strong political direction against terrorism provided by President Yudhoyono, Indonesia's security services have scored notable successes against JI. In November 2005, for instance, Azahari Husin, a JI leader and key bomb-maker, was killed in a counter-terrorism raid.[104] In January 2007, police raids in Poso in Sulawesi island after three schoolgirls were beheaded by militants resulted in the deaths of 17 and the arrest of more than 20 JI members.[105] This led to the further arrests of JI operatives in Java who had been responsible for the violence in Poso, as well as the seizure of explosives and weapons. Security forces also recovered JI documents which revealed plans to assassinate police officers, prosecutors and judges. In June 2007, another key JI leader, Yusron Mahbudi (Abu Dujana), was arrested. The successes in 2007 have dealt a major blow to JI's overall operational capabilities.[106]

As a result of major efforts by regional states, the international community and external powers, maritime security has also improved. In the whole of 2007, there were in fact no recorded cases of pirate attacks in the Straits of Malacca.[107] Thus, overall, the various measures undertaken to prevent any possible maritime terrorist attack seem to have had positive results.

The threat from radical Islamist terrorism, however, has not been extinguished. Key JI figures such as Mohamed Noordin Top, who leads a militant wing of the JI known as 'al-Qaeda in the Malay Archipelago', and Dulmatin, another key bomb-maker, remain at large. Another wanted man is Mas Selamat

Kasturi, the JI leader who headed its Singapore cell. Mas Selamat sensationally escaped from detention in Singapore in early 2008, sparking a worldwide Interpol alert as he had previously planned major terrorist operations.[108] The presence of ex-mujahideen from Afghanistan, new recruits from local conflict areas such as in Sulawesi and Maluku, and a solid core estimated to total more than 900, mean that there continues to be a significant terrorist threat from the JI. This was demonstrated when a JI plot to bomb a café in Sumatra, in Indonesia, was thwarted with the arrest of ten militants led by a Singaporean and the recovery of bombs in July 2008.[109] The long-awaited execution of the three Bali bombers, Imam Samudra, Amrozi Nurhasyim and Ali Ghufron, in November 2008 also led to fears that their martyrdom could inspire further terrorist attacks.[110]

Apart from the JI, there remain fears of violence from disaffected Muslims throughout the Malay Archipelago. In Aceh, despite the Helsinki Peace Accord in 2005 that led to the disarming of GAM and its participation in the political process, the continued presence of underlying economic and political grievances, as well as the failure to deliver economic development, could lead to disaffected youth turning to radical Islamist ideology, leading to a resumption of violence. In the Philippines, the declaration by the Supreme Court in 2008 that the comprehensive peace accord signed by the government with the MILF is unconstitutional, coupled with opposition to the peace accord by Catholic groups in the south as well as by the armed forces, have led to a resumption of fighting and the displacement of 400,000 people.[111] The prospects of a lasting peace in the south are poor. Not only do the Catholics oppose concessions to the Muslims, but the presence of extremists on the Muslim side in the form of the ASG ensures that violence would have continued in any case.

In Thailand, political instability in the wake of the military coup against the Thaksin government in September 2006 has seriously affected efforts in counter-terrorism. The election of a new civilian government in Thailand in December 2007 did not contribute to better prospects for peace, as the victorious People's Power Party was closely connected to the deposed Thaksin government that had pursued a tough military–security approach to the insurgency, with disastrous results. The subsequent political infighting between the populist pro-Thaksin forces and the royalist–military camp resulted in civil disturbances in 2008 which led to the closure of Bangkok airport.[112] The lack of central political leadership has resulted in a lack of coherence in strategy toward the southern provinces. More seriously, the continued emphasis on the use of force, and the failure to address the fundamental grievances of the Malay Muslims, provide opportunities for radical Islamists to gain new recruits to their cause. Should this happen, southern Thailand could become transformed into the region's Chechnya.

Conclusion

Despite the flurry of ASEAN regional initiatives, the reality is that regional cooperation in countering terrorism has been not been well coordinated, due to the declaratory nature of ASEAN pronouncements, the constraints of conflicting national interests, domestic politics, mutual suspicions and abiding concerns over sovereignty. Domestic political sensitivities, stemming from anti-US sentiments by local Muslims, mean that countries in the region need to steer an adroit path between counter-terrorism measures and appearing to be bowing to US pressure to participate in its global War on Terror, which many local Muslims perceive to be a war on Islam.

Although regional intelligence and police cooperation have been excellent, bilateral tensions and mutual suspicions have been a significant barrier in furthering security cooperation. The Malacca Straits Patrols and 'Eye in the Sky' initiatives in improving maritime security have, for instance, been carefully designed to avoid both sovereignty issues and to allay mutual suspicions. Malaysia–Singapore relations, for instance, continue to be stymied by a range of bilateral issues which stem from their historical relationship following Singapore's expulsion from Malaysia in 1965, which have led to security cooperation being tainted with mutual suspicions.[113] In 2002, relations between Malaysia on one hand, and Indonesia and the Philippines on the other, also deteriorated over Malaysia's tough action against illegal migrants and workers from the two countries.[114]

At the broader regional level, the ASEAN states have also been reluctant to compromise on the principle of non-interference in internal affairs, fearing that this will open a Pandora's box into foreign intervention into their internal affairs. Malaysia and Indonesia have also been particularly concerned over sovereignty issues, especially in granting counter-terrorism roles to external powers in territory or waters considered to be under their jurisdiction.

Despite the problems, there are reasonably positive prospects, if one is realistic, because the region has, to varying levels of competence, adopted comprehensive counter-terrorism strategies that have been proven to be more appropriate to local circumstances. Because of doubts over the accuracy of the 'new' terrorism paradigm in describing the terrorism phenomenon in the region, and also because of long-standing practices in dealing with Muslim rebellion, the regional response and strategy against terrorism has differed from US prescriptions based on a uni-dimensional 'kill or capture' approach under the Bush administration's global War on Terror.

Instead, regional governments have tended to employ comprehensive approaches to counter-terrorism, which go beyond purely military–security approaches and includes diplomacy, political negotiations, economic development, social measures, psychological warfare and the rehabilitation of captured militants. This is due to historical regional experiences in dealing with terrorism, such as the Malayan Emergency in the 1950s, which was successfully dealt with using a comprehensive strategy designed to win hearts and minds. Indeed, governments in the region are generally sensitive in avoiding overt mistreatment or perception of mistreatment that could reverberate and increase the hostility and resentment of local Muslims, thereby worsening the threat of terrorism. The rehabilitation of militants is considered an important tool in the propaganda war against the radical Islamists, as rehabilitated militants could in turn lead in the counter-narrative that could reduce militant recruitment. The comprehensive approach is best encapsulated in the 16-Point Counter-Terrorism Program and Human Security Act in the Philippines, which pays attention to economic development and the resolution of fundamental grievances, as well as taking a true inter-agency approach, although in the Philippine case, the problem is its effective implementation.

Above all, however, the states in the region are fully aware of the long-term ideological hearts-and-minds nature of the battle with the radical Islamists. They do not, therefore, speak of achieving 'victory' as the Bush administration had sought as an objective. Aware of the deep complexities and presence of fundamental grievances underlying what has been a historical problem in the region, states in the region take a long-term perspective and aim to use every instrument at their disposal to win the battle for the soul of their Muslim communities. The varied nature of Muslim grievances, and the difficulties that have been encountered in meeting the challenges posed by radical Islamism, mean that the war against terrorism in Southeast Asia will be long-drawn out. Containment, not victory, will be the most realistic outcome.

Notes

1 The term 'Islamist' used here refers only to those who adhere to violent, radical ideology. It is not a reference to the overwhelming majority of Muslims or the religion of Islam.

2 A.T.H. Tan, *A Political and Economic Dictionary of Southeast Asia* (London: Europa/Routledge, 2004), pp. 136–137; 'US Brands Indonesian Group Terrorist', CNN.com, 23 October 2003, http://edition.cnn.com/2002/WORLD/asiapcf/southeast/10/23/indonesia.terror/.

3 'Bali Death Toll Set at 202', BBC News, 19 February 2003, http://news.bbc.co.uk/2/hi/asia-pacific/2778923.stm.

4 A.T.H. Tan (ed.), *The Politics of Terrorism* (London: Routledge, 2006), p. 165.

5 See *Al Qaeda in Southeast Asia: The Case of the Ngruki Network in Indonesia*, Asia Briefing No. 20, 8 August 2002, International Crisis Group, www.crisisgroup.org.

6 *Jemaah Islamiyah in Southeast Asia: Damaged But Dangerous*, Asia Briefing No. 63, 26 August 2003, International Crisis Group, Executive Summary, www.crisisgroup.org.

7 See *Indonesia Backgrounder: Jihad in Central Sulawesi*, Asia Report No. 74, 3 February 2004, International Crisis Group, www.crisisgroup.org.

8 Z. Abuza, *Tentacles of Terror: Al Qaeda's Southeast Asian Network*, paper for the APCSS Biennial Conference: Enhancing Regional Security Cooperation, 16–18 July 2002, Honolulu, Hawaii, p. 19.

9 'Spite Islands', *Far Eastern Economic Review*, 20 January 2000, p. 18.

10 *Indonesia: Tackling Radicalism in Poso*, Asia Briefing No. 75, 22 January 2008, International Crisis Group, pp. 1–2, www.crisisgroup.org.

11 P.L. Bergen, *Holy War: Inside the Secret World of Osama bin Laden Inc.* (London: Orion, 2001), pp. 237–238.

12 S. Reeve, *The New Jackals: Ramzi Yousef, Osama bin Laden and the Future of Terrorism* (London: Andre Deutsch, 1999), pp. 72–73.

13 R. Frank and J. Hookway, 'Abu Sayyaf: The Long Tentacles of Terror', *Wall Street Journal*, 25 September 2001, p. A12.

14 'Airline Terror Plot Disrupted', BBC News, 10 August 2006, http://news.bbc. co.uk/2/hi/uk_news/4778575.stm.
15 *Straits Times*, 27 April 2000, p. 20.
16 *Straits Times*, 2 August 2000, p. 35.
17 'Bomb Caused Philippine Ferry Fire', BBC News, 11 October 2004, http://news. bbc.co.uk/2/hi/uk_news/4778575.stm.
18 See, for instance, G.G. Ong, 'Pre-Empting Maritime Terrorism in Southeast Asia', *ISEAS Viewpoints* (Singapore: Institute of Southeast Asian Studies), 29 November 2002.
19 *Straits Times*, 12 January 2002.
20 Yun Yun Teo, 'Target Malacca Straits: Maritime Terrorism in Southeast Asia', *Studies in Conflict and Terrorism*, 30 (2007), p. 547.
21 C.Z. Raymond, 'The Threat of Maritime Terrorism in the Malacca Straits', *Terrorism Monitor*, 4:3 (9 February 2006), p. 8, www.jamestown.org/terrorism/news/ uploads/TM_004_003.pdf.
22 'After the Abadan Fire', *Time*, 4 September 1978, www.time.com/time/magazine/ article/0,9171,912118–1,00.html.
23 Radio Address of the President to the Nation, 15 September 2001, www.american-rhetoric.com/speeches/gwbush911radioaddress.htm.
24 Condemnation of Terrorist Attacks in the United States, United Nations General Assembly, 12 September 2001, www.un.org/documents/ga/docs/56/agresolution. htm.
25 United Nations Security Council Resolution 1373, 28 September 2001, www.un.org/ Docs/scres/2001/sc2001.htm.
26 Bruce Hoffman, 'The Congruence of International and Domestic Trends in Terrorism', *Terrorism and Political Violence*, 9:2 (Summer 1997), pp. 8–9. The new terrorism is described more fully in Hoffman's seminal work, *Inside Terrorism* (New York: Columbia University Press, 2006). A more succinct description of the new terrorism also appears in Bruce Hoffman, 'The New Terrorism', in Andrew Tan and Kumar Ramakrishna (eds.), *The New Terrorism: Anatomy, Trends and Counter-Strategies* (Singapore: Times Academic/Eastern Universities Press, 2003).
27 *Straits Times*, 3 May 2000.
28 The National Security Strategy of the United States of America, September 2002, www.lib.umich.edu/govdocs/pdf/nss02.pdf.
29 National Strategy for Combating Terrorism, February 2003, www.globalsecurity. org/security/library/policy/national/counter_terrorism_strategy.pdf, pp. 7–8.
30 National Strategy for Combating Terrorism, February 2003, pp. 10, 12, 15–28.
31 For an assessment of the failures of the Bush administration's strategy against global terrorism, see Andrew T.H. Tan, *US Strategy Against Global Terrorism: How it Failed and Where it is Headed* (New York: Palgrave Macmillan, 2009).
32 *Straits Times*, 24 September 2001. Emphasis mine.
33 See, for instance, his speech at the ISIS conference on terrorism in Kuala Lumpur on 16 November 2001.
34 *Straits Times*, 26 January 2002, p. A23.
35 Rohan Gunaratna, *Inside Al Qaeda: Global Network of Terror* (London: Hurst, 2002), pp. 93–94.
36 Joseph Loow, *Deconstructing Political Islam in Malaysia: UMNO's Response to PAS's Religio-Political Dialectic*, Working Paper No. 45, Institute of Defence and Strategic Studies, Nanyang Technological University, Singapore, March 2003, p. 15.
37 Hadi Soesastro, 'Southeast Asia and Global Terrorism: Implications on State and Human Security', *Indonesian Quarterly*, 30:1 (2002), p. 32.
38 Bantarto Bandoro, 'Global Coalition Against Terrorism: Security Perspective and ASEAN's Role', *Indonesian Quarterly*, 30:1 (2002), p. 55.
39 Bantarto Bandoro, 'Global Coalition Against Terrorism', pp. 47–48.

40 'Indonesian Deputy's Attack on US Raises Fears of Split', *Sydney Morning Herald*, 5 September 2003, www.smh.com.au/articles/2003/09/04/1062548965995.html.
41 'Threats and Responses: South Asia; More Attacks On Westerners Are Expected in Indonesia', *New York Times*, 25 November 2002, http://query.nytimes.com/gst/fullpage.html?res=9C0CE2D71139F936A15752C1A9649C8B63&sec=&spon=&page wanted=all.
42 Andrew T.H. Tan (ed.), *The Politics of Terrorism*, p. 165.
43 Sukhumbhand Paribatra and Chai-Anan Samudavanija, Chai-Anan, quoted in Lim Joo Jock and S. Vani (eds.), *Armed Separatism in Southeast Asia* (Singapore: Institute of Southeast Asian Studies), p. 32.
44 See Paul A. Rodell, 'Separatist Insurgency in the Southern Philippines', Kamarulzaman Askandar, 'The Aceh Conflict: Phases of Conflict and Hope for Peace', and Thitinan Pongsudhirak, 'The Malay–Muslim Insurgency in Southern Thailand', in Andrew T.H. Tan (ed.), *A Handbook of Terrorism and Insurgency in Southeast Asia* (Cheltenham: Edward Elgar, 2007).
45 *Mindanao Times Interactive News*, mindanaotimes.com.p/news, 2 March 2002.
46 Andrew T.H. Tan, *Security Perspectives of the Malay Archipelago* (Cheltenham: Edward Elgar, 2004), pp. 178–179.
47 'Who Was Behind Thai Attacks?', BBC News, 30 April 2004; 'Grieving Begins in Thailand's South', BBC News, 29 April 2004, http://news.bbc.co.uk/2/hi/asia-pacific/3669353.stm; and 'Deadly Demo Puts Thais on Tightrope', *The Age*, 30 October 2004, www.theage.com.au/articles/2004/10/29/1099028209065.html?from=storylhs.
48 'Terror Suspect Hambali Quizzed', BBC News, 15 August 2003, http://news.bbc.co.uk/2/hi/asia-pacific/3152755.stm.
49 'Targeting Thailand', *Time*, 19 January 2003.
50 *Straits Times*, 4 November 2001.
51 *Straits Times*, 6 November 2001.
52 *Straits Times*, 30 January 2002.
53 'War Against Terrorism Breathes New Life into ASEAN Forum', *Straits Times*, 2 August 2002.
54 APEC Leaders' Statement on Fighting Terrorism and Promoting Growth, Los Cabos, Mexico, 26 October 2002, www.apec.org.sg.
55 Declaration on Terrorism by the Eighth ASEAN Summit, www.aseansec.org.
56 *Straits Times*, 18 May 2002.
57 *Straits Times*, 30 July 2002.
58 ASEAN Convention on Counter-Terrorism, www.aseansec.org/19250.htm.
59 ASEAN Efforts to Counter Terrorism, www.aseansec.org/14396.htm.
60 *The Star*, 8 May 2002.
61 Elina Noor, 'Terrorism in Malaysia: Situation and Response', in Rohan Gunaratna (ed.), *Terrorism in the Asia-Pacific: Threat and Response* (Singapore: Times/Eastern Universities Press, 2003), pp. 168–169.
62 Jakarta Centre for Law Enforcement Cooperation, www.jclec.com/index.php?option=com_content&task=view&id=14&Itemid=28.
63 ASEAN–Australia Joint Declaration for Cooperation to Combat International Terrorism, www.aseansec.org/16205.htm.
64 See Andrew T.H. Tan, 'Singapore's Cooperation with the Trilateral Security Dialogue Partners in the War Against Global Terrorism', *Defence Studies*, 7:2 (June 2007), pp. 197–198.
65 'US Plan to Secure Key Shipping Lane Upsets SE Asia', CNSNews.com, 6 April 2004, www.cnsnews.com/ForeignBureaus/Archive/200404/FOR20040406a.html.
66 'Malacca Straits Anti-Piracy Patrols Start Next Week', *MIMA News Flash*, July 2004, www.mima.gov.my/mima/htmls/mimarc/news/newsflash_files/news-cut/july04.htm, accessed 19 August 2007, and 'Joint air patrols over Malacca Strait to start next week: Indonesia', *AFP*, 8 September 2005.

67 'Closer Bonds with Project SURPIC', *Cyberpioneer* (Ministry of Defence, Singapore), 27 May 2005, www.mindef.gov.sg/imindef/publications/cyberpioneer/news/2005/may/27may05_news2.html.

68 Willard Payne, 'Crossfire War: Malacca Strait – Joint Air Patrols Instituted by Four Nations', *News Blaze*, http://newsblaze.com/story/20050916092021nnnn.nb/top-story.html.

69 'Maritime Security New Frontier for Thailand', *The Nation*, 6 October 2008.

70 'Al Qaeda Threatens Japan, Poland, Bulgaria Over Iraq', *The Namibian*, 22 July 2004, www.namibian.com.na/2004/July/world/0456659A85.html.

71 'Japan's Counter-Terrorism Assistance', Ministry of Foreign Affairs, www.mofa.go.jp/policy/terrorism/assist0306.html, accessed 9 January 2006.

72 David Rosenberg, 'Dire Straits: Competing Security Priorities in the South China Sea', *Japan Focus*, April 2005, http://japanfocus.org/article.asp?id=254.

73 ReCAAP Information Sharing Centre, www.recaap.org/index_home.html.

74 *The Batam Joint Statement of the 4th Tripartite Ministerial Meeting of the Littoral States on the Straits of Malacca and Singapore*, Media Resource Center, Ministry of Foreign Affairs, Singapore, 2 August 2005, http://app.mfa.gov.sg/2006/press/view_press.asp?post_id=1406.

75 'Muslim Militants: Military Must be on Guard', *Straits Times*, 11 November 2000, p. A29.

76 Mohamad Najib Abdul Razak, *Defending Malaysia: Facing the Twenty-First Century* (London: ASEAN Academic, 2001), pp. 83–85, 97.

77 'Malaysians Studying in Pakistan Worry Government', *Straits Times*, 26 January 2002, p. A23.

78 Statement by Ambassador Kishore Mahbubani on 1 October 2001 to the UN General Assembly, www.unis.unvienna.org/unis/pressrels/2001/ga9921.html.

79 *Straits Times Interactive*, straitstimes.asia1.com, 5 November 2001.

80 Strategic Goods (Control) Bill, www.parliament.gov.sg/Legislation/Htdocs/Bills/020044.pdf.

81 'Singapore Builds Up Capability Against Biological and Chemical Attacks', *Straits Times*, 17 January 2003. See also 'Chemical Attack? Clean Up at N-E Line', *Straits Times*, 14 February 2003, and *Fact Sheet on US–Singapore Regional Emerging Disease (REDI) Center*, www.globalhealth.gov/Singapore_REDI_MOU.shtml.

82 'Government to Launch Security Awareness Programme to Raise Vigilance', *Straits Times*, 17 January 2003, and 'First ISD Mobile Exhibit Educates Heartlanders on Security Threats', *Straits Times*, 20 July 2003.

83 'Singapore to Deploy Air Marshals on SIA, Silkair Flights', *Channel New Asia*, 20 January 2003, and 'Singapore Lays Out Plans to Beat Airline Terrorists', *Straits Times*, 5 January 2004.

84 'IMO Adopts Comprehensive Maritime Security Measures', Conference of Contracting Governments to the International Convention for the Safety of Life at Sea, 1974: 9–13 December 2002, www.imo.org/Newsroom/mainframe.asp?topic_id=583&doc_id=2689.

85 'Singapore Participates in US-led Security Exercise in Arabian Sea', *Channel News Asia*, 11 January 2004 and *Proliferation Security Initiative*, www.state.gov/t/np/c10390.htm.

86 'Singapore Begins Screening US-Bound Containers', *Straits Times*, 17 March 2003.

87 'US Plan to Secure Key Shipping Lane Upsets SE Asia', CNSNews.com, 6 April 2004, www.cnsnews.com/ForeignBureaus/Archive/200404/FOR20040406a.html.

88 *The Fight Against Terror* (Singapore: Ministry of Home Affairs, 2004), p. 59.

89 Richard Stubbs, *Hearts and Minds in Guerilla Warfare: The Malayan Emergency 1948–1960* (Singapore: Oxford University Press, 1989), p. 264.

90 *Straits Times*, 21 February 2004.

91 *The Jemaah Islamiyah Arrests and the Threat of Terrorism* (Singapore: Ministry of Home Affairs, 2003).
92 'JI Detainee's Long Road to Reform: From Bomb Makers to Peace Lovers?', *Straits Times*, 3 February 2007, pp. 8–9.
93 The account regarding P. Ramli is based on the author's interviews in Malaysia. For a full account of Al Ma'unah, see Elina Noor, 'Al Ma'unah and the KMM in Malaysia', in Andrew T.H. Tan (ed.), *A Handbook of Terrorism and Insurgency in Southeast Asia*, pp. 167–193.
94 Elina Noor, 'Al Ma'unah and KMM in Malaysia', p. 183.
95 Zachary Abuza, 'The State of Jemaah Islamiyah: Terrorism and Insurgency in Southeast Asia Five Years After Bali', *The Jebsen Center for Counter-Terrorism Studies, Research Briefing Series*, 2:1 (November 2007), p. 6.
96 *Far Eastern Economic Review*, 6 December 2001, pp. 24–25; *Time*, 28 January 2002.
97 'Next Stop Mindanao', *Time*, 28 January 2002, pp. 20–21.
98 'Widening the War in the Southern Philippines', *Asia Times*, 18 May 2007, www.atimes.com/atimes/Southeast_Asia/IE18Ae01.html.
99 'Australia Gives RP 28 Boats, A$4 Million Grant', *Philippines Today*, 5 March 2009, www.philippinestoday.net/index.php?module=article&view=361.
100 Arturo C. Lomibao, 'Achievements and Challenges in Counter-Terrorism in the Philippines Seven Years After 9/11', *Philippine Institute for Political Violence and Terrorism Research Paper series*, November 2008, pp. 4–7.
101 Hadi Soesastro, 'Southeast Asia and Global Terrorism', pp. 32, 37.
102 Speech given by Susilo Bambang Yudhoyono, Indonesian Security Minister at the Bali Memorial Service on 12 October 2003, www.saxton.com.au/default.asp?idocid=367&sc8=196&nc8=150.
103 Zachary Abuza, 'The State of Jemaah Islamiyah: Terrorism and Insurgency in Southeast Asia Five Years After Bali', p. 6.
104 'Azahari Was Shot Dead', *Sydney Morning Herald*, 10 November 2005.
105 *Jihadism in Indonesia: Poso on the Edge*, Asia Report No. 127, 24 January 2007, International Crisis Group, p. 1, www.crisisgroup.org.
106 *Indonesia: Jemaah Islamiyah's Current Status*, Asia Briefing No. 63, 3 May 2007, International Crisis Group, p. 2, www.crisisgroup.org.
107 'Malacca Straits Pirate-Free Last Year Due to Joint Patrols', *AFP*, 13 April 2008.
108 'Interpol Alert Follows Suspect Escape', *Associated Press*, 29 February 2008, www.wtopnews.com/?nid=105&sid=1353308.
109 'Indonesia Police Smash JI Plot to Bomb Café', News.com.au, 3 July 2008, www.news.com.au/story/0,23599,23963544–401,00.html.
110 'Indonesia Executes Bali Bombers', BBC News, 9 November 2008, http://news.bbc.co.uk/2/hi/asia-pacific/7717819.stm.
111 'Philippines: Thousands Suffering the Impact of Shattered Mindanao Peace Talks', Amnesty International, 28 October 2008, www.amnesty.org/en/for-media/press-releases/philippines-thousands-suffering-impact-shattered-mindanao-peace-talks-20.
112 'How Did Thai Protesters Manage it?', BBC News, 3 December 2008, http://news.bbc.co.uk/2/hi/asia-pacific/7762806.stm.
113 For a detailed account, see Andrew Tan, *Malaysia–Singapore Relations: Troubled Past and Uncertain Future?* (Hull: University of Hull, 2000).
114 *Straits Times*, 27 August 2002, p. 3.

Index